RECONCEPTUALISING EUROPEAN EQUALITY LAW

This important new book seeks to widen the understanding of the principle of equality within European law. It deconstructs the European Court of Justice's adjudication of cases in the field and explores how the Member States' courts decide on the question of equality. This detailed rigorous research allows the author to argue for a reconceptualised equality doctrine. Such an adaptation, she argues, will provide judges, practitioners and academics with the tools to balance institutional considerations against substantive interpretation. Theoretically ambitious, while grounded in practical application, this is a significant restatement of one of the key principles of European law: the equality doctrine.

Volume 69 in the series Modern Studies in European Law

Modern Studies in European Law
Recent titles in this series:

What Form of Government for the European Union and the Eurozone?
Federico Fabbrini, Ernst Hirsch Ballin and Han Somsen

The UK and European Human Rights: A Strained Relationship?
Edited by Katja S Ziegler, Elizabeth Wicks and Loveday Hodson

The European Union in International Organisations and Global Governance: Recent Developments
Edited by Christine Kaddous

Nudge and the Law: What Can EU Law Learn From Behavioural Sciences?
Edited by Alberto Alemanno and Anne-Lise Sibony

Fundamental Rights in EU Internal Market Legislation
Vasiliki Kosta

Uniformity of Customs Administration in the European Union
Kathrin Limbach

The Impact of Union Citizenship on the EU's Market Freedoms
Alina Tryfonidou

Equal Citizenship and Its Limits in EU Law
Päivi Johanna Neuvonen

European Law on Unfair Commercial Practices and Contract Law
Mateja Durovic

The European Union's External Action in Times of Crisis
Edited by Piet Eeckhout and Manual Lopez-Escudero

The Legitimacy of Family Rights in Strasbourg Case Law: Living Instrument or Extinguished Sovereignty?
Carmen Draghici

Strengthening the Rule of Law in Europe: From a Common Concept to Mechanisms of Implementation
Edited by Werner Schroeder

The Pluralist Character of the European Economic Constitution
Clemens Kaupa

Exceptions from EU Free Movement Law
Edited by Panos Koutrakos, Niamh Nic Shuibhne and Phil Syrpis

For the complete list of titles in this series, see 'Modern Studies in European Law' link at www.hartpub.co.uk/books/series.asp

Reconceptualising European Equality Law

A Comparative Institutional Analysis

Johanna Croon-Gestefeld

·HART·
PUBLISHING
OXFORD AND PORTLAND, OREGON
2017

Hart Publishing
An imprint of Bloomsbury Publishing Plc

Hart Publishing Ltd
Kemp House
Chawley Park
Cumnor Hill
Oxford OX2 9PH
UK

Bloomsbury Publishing Plc
50 Bedford Square
London
WC1B 3DP
UK

www.hartpub.co.uk
www.bloomsbury.com

Published in North America (US and Canada) by
Hart Publishing
c/o International Specialized Book Services
920 NE 58th Avenue, Suite 300
Portland, OR 97213-3786
USA

www.isbs.com

First published 2017

British Library Cataloguing-in-Publication Data
A catalogue record for this book is available from the British Library.

ISBN: HB: 978-1-50990-966-7
ePDF: 978-1-50990-969-8
ePub: 978-1-50990-968-1

Library of Congress Cataloging-in-Publication Data

Names: Croon-Gestefeld, Johanna, author.

Title: Reconceptualising European equality law : a comparative institutional analysis / Johanna Croon-Gestefeld.

Description: Oxford [UK] ; Portland, Oregon : Hart Publishing, 2017. | Series: Modern studies in European law ; volume 69 | Includes bibliographical references and index.

Identifiers: LCCN 2016045794 (print) | LCCN 2016046241 (ebook) | ISBN 9781509909667 (hardback : alk. paper) | ISBN 9781509909681 (Epub)

Subjects: LCSH: Equality before the law—European Union countries. | Sex discrimination against women—Law and legislation—European Union countries. | Civil rights—European Union countries.

Classification: LCC KJE5142 .C76 2017 (print) | LCC KJE5142 (ebook) | DDC 342.2408/5—dc23

LC record available at https://lccn.loc.gov/2016045794

Typeset by Compuscript Ltd, Shannon
Printed and bound in Great Britain by Lightning Source UK Ltd

To find out more about our authors and books visit www.hartpublishing.co.uk. Here you will find extracts, author information, details of forthcoming events and the option to sign up for our newsletters.

Foreword

Johanna Croon-Gestefeld's book truly makes sense of equal protection law. This is a subject matter where often the elegancy of judicial language is only matched by the apparent incoherence and inconsistency of judicial decisions. *Reconceptualising European Equality Law* challenges the usual language and conceptual apparatus of equality law in order to make sense of those judicial decisions. It does so by looking at the institutional variables that often determine those decisions but are not made explicit on them.

By doing so Johanna Croon-Gestefeld actually presents a more accurate (and useful) description of equality law while, at the same time, starting a debate on what really shapes (and ought to shape) that body of the law.

It takes courage to confront orthodoxy. It takes intelligence and persistence to master a different and unfamiliar analytical approach. It takes intellectual creativity and thoroughness to apply that analytical approach to an important area of law never before explored in that way. Johanna Croon-Gestefeld has done all this and done it well. She has assembled and assessed European Union and German law on an important and challenging subject, equal protection law. Using comparative institutional analysis, she deconstructs the rationales employed in judicial opinions and reconstructs a more viable analysis on both the positive (descriptive) and normative (prescriptive) levels. We are strong believers in the power of comparative institutional analysis, but even we must admit that it is a challenging approach to employ well. Johanna Croon-Gestefeld has met this challenge. We may not agree with all she has written (although we agree with most). But those differences are to be expected and indeed welcomed in the context of such an ambitious endeavor. The combination of breadth and careful consideration of detail provides a significant addition to legal analysis in general and in the comparative institutional approach to legal analysis in particular.

What is remarkable about this book is not only how it attempts (and largely succeeds) to reconstruct and make sense of substantial parts of European equality law, including some of its more discussed and controversial subjects such as reverse discrimination (in the context of purely internal situations) or affirmative action, it is equally remarkable how she tries to do it. Johanna Croon-Gestefeld uses comparative institutional analysis to question the traditional concepts of equality law but tries to do that while remaining sensitive to the need to work within the parameters of an existing legal community. She is not interested in deconstructing European equality law. She is genuinely interested in making sense of it. Johanna Croon-Gestefeld is as committed to challenge the traditional approach to equality law as she is to remain engaged in a constructive relationship with that approach. It is for this reason that this book should be of equal interest to academics and practitioners alike. You need to read it if you really want to understand or reform European equality law.

Neil Komesar and Miguel Maduro

Acknowledgements

The book is an extended version of my PhD Thesis. Writing such a work is often considered a lonely exercise. For me, it was just the opposite. I met some of the most inspiring, wonderful people along the way and could always count on their support as well as on that of my family. Without their help, I would not have been able to produce this book.

I would especially like to thank Miguel Maduro for his academic advice, his never-ending encouragement to pursue my ideas and his invaluable support. Moreover, I owe many thanks to my second supervisor Neil Komesar for giving me the inspiration to write this book. I would also like to thank Mattias Kumm and Christoph Möllers, who have given me further helpful advice as members of my PhD defence panel, as well as Anne Röthel for granting me the time and support in the correction process. Furthermore, I want to thank the EUI Department of Law for providing me with an 'intellectual home' and their help on the thesis, namely Loïc Azoulai, Marlies Becker, Marise Cremona, Siobhan Gallagher, Angelika Lanfranchi, Rosanna Lewis, Hans Micklitz, Dennis Patterson, Ernst-Ulrich Petersmann and Bruno de Witte. Furthermore, I owe many thanks to Ciaran Burke and Stephen Coutts for the language corrections.

The research leading to this book has been funded by the EUI Department of Law and the German Academic Exchange Service DAAD, whom I would like to thank very much for their financial support. Parts of an earlier version of chapter 3 have been published in the *European Law Journal* 2013, Volume 19, 153–73; chapter 4 has been included after the defence of the PhD thesis.

The book is dedicated to Jan, who has stood by my side throughout the entire project.

Johanna Croon-Gestefeld
Hamburg, July 2016

Contents

Case List

I. EUROPEAN CASES

A. European Court of Justice

B. Court of First Instance

C. European Court of Human Rights

II. NATIONAL CASES

A. Federal Constitutional Court

B. United States Supreme Court

C. United Kingdom Courts

List of Abbreviations

AG	Advocate General
A no	Application Number
Art	Article
Arts	Articles
BGBl	*Bundesgesetzblatt*
bk	Book
BT-Drs	*Bundestagsdrucksache*
BVerfGE	*Bundesverfassungsgerichtsentscheidung*
CFEU	Charter of Fundamental Rights of the European Union
ch	Chapter
CML Rev	Common Market Law Review
COM	Communication
Dir	Directive
EC	European Community
ECJ	European Court of Justice
ECR	European Court Reports
ECSC	European Coal and Steel Community
ECHR	European Convention on Human Rights
ECtHR	European Court of Human Rights
ed	Editor
edn	Edition
eds	Editors
EEC	European Economic Community
eg	for example
EL Rev	European Law Review
et al	and others
EU	European Union
f	following (1 more page)
ff	following (2 or more following pages)

fn	footnote (reference to a footnote outside the chapter)
GV NW	*Gesetz-und Verordnungsblatt für das Land Nordrhein-Westfalen*
ibid	ibidem
ie	that is
ML Rev	Modern Law Review
n	footnote (reference within the chapter)
no	number
OJ	Official Journal of the European Union
p	page
para	paragraph
paras	paragraphs
Reg	Regulation
s	section
TEEC	Treaty Establishing the European Economic Community
TEU	Treaty on European Union
TFEU	Treaty on the Functioning of the European Union
trans	translator
UK	United Kingdom
US	United States
vol	volume

1

Introduction

> The Union is founded on the values of respect for human dignity, freedom, democracy, **equality**, the rule of law and respect for human rights, including the rights of persons belonging to minorities. These values are common to the Member States in a society in which pluralism, **non-discrimination**, tolerance, justice, solidarity and **equality between women and men** prevail.
>
> Article 2 TEU[1]

> [A]nti-discrimination law is normatively deficient.
>
> The neoliberal predicament exposes the truth about anti-discrimination law. As a medium of social policy, it is powerless.
>
> A Somek, *Engineering Equality*[2]

THE CONCEPT OF equality appears front and centre in accounts of European law. One would consider any textbook on Union law that aims at providing a comprehensive depiction of the field insufficient, in the event that it fails to engage with the topic of eradicating discrimination. Its relevance is highlighted throughout both primary and secondary law: there is the principle of non-discrimination in the area of free movement, the provision on equal pay for men and women in Article 157 of the Treaty on the Functioning of the European Union (TFEU)[3] and the series of directives passed in the context of the equality agenda of the Union. Moreover, the Treaty on European Union (TEU) mentions equality as one of the fundamental values upon which the Union is built. The significance of the concept for EU law finds its most recent expression in the fact that the Charter of Fundamental Rights of the European Union (CFEU)[4] dedicates an entire chapter to 'equality'. Given these multiple references, it is safe to assume that the framers of the Treaties as well as other actors involved in European law-making have in the past, up to and including the present, attached great importance to the concept of equality.

[1] Art 2 Consolidated Version of the Treaty on the European Union [2012] OJ C326/13 (emphasis added).

[2] A Somek, *Engineering Equality. An Essay on European Anti-Discrimination Law* (Oxford, Oxford University Press, 2011) 12 and 177.

[3] Art 157 Consolidated Version of the Treaty on the Functioning of the European Union [2012] OJ C326/47.

[4] Charter of Fundamental Rights of the European Union [2000] OJ C364/1.

Yet, the simple fact that we may agree that equality takes up a prominent place in European law tells us little about its functioning or how we should evaluate its application. Neither can we infer from it what kind of equality—a formal or a more material reading—is pursued within the European legal system. As the quote by Somek shows, the approach taken by European actors to anti-discrimination law is deeply disputed. He maintains the opinion that EU equality law is applied in such a way as to favour persons who already perform well in a competitive market place environment. Under the fig-leaf of equality law, sympathy for the weaker parts of society and mutual consideration are being replaced by a neoliberal paradigm.[5] On the other side of the spectrum, certain commentators consider EU equality law as going too far, as transgressing the boundaries of individual responsibility and leading to forced conformity.[6] In addition, European equality law is commonly criticised for its incoherence and perceived unpredictability.[7] The argument goes that EU equality law is difficult to comprehend due to its diversification. Many themes in EU law are dealt with under the catchphrase of equality, from import quotas[8] through the prohibition of discrimination on grounds of nationality[9] to the treatment of pregnant women at the workplace.[10] In this context, it has become a rather tedious exercise to reconcile the different strands of case law by the European Court of Justice.

I. EQUALITY: A FUNDAMENTAL PRINCIPLE BASED ON NOT SO STABLE FUNDAMENTS

Considering that the three elements highlighted above—the fundamental status given to equality, the ideological dispute surrounding it and its (at least assumed)

[5] Somek (n 2) 15.

[6] This view is especially prominent with regard to the equality directives; see the discussion on the implementation of the equality directives in German law, eg E Picker, 'Antidiskriminierungsgesetz—Der Anfang vom Ende der Privatautonomie?' (2002) 57 *Juristische Zeitung* 880.

[7] See S Besson, 'Gender Discrimination under EU and ECHR Law: *Never Shall the Twain Meet?*' (2008) 8 *Human Rights Law Review* 647, 657; T Kingreen, 'Gleichheitsgrundrechte und soziale Rechte' in D Ehlers (ed), *Europäische Grundrechte und Grundfreiheiten* 2nd edn (Berlin, De Gruyter, 2005) § 18 marginal no 14; U Kischel, 'Zur Dogmatik des Gleichheitssatzes in der Europäischen Union' (1997) 24 *Europäische Grundrechtezeitschrift* 1; K Odendahl, 'Gleichheit vor dem Gesetz' in S Heselhaus and C Nowak (eds), *Handbuch der europäischen Grundrechte* (Munich, Beck, 2006) § 43 marginal nos 26, 30–32; A Sattler, 'Allgemeiner Gleichheitssatz und spezielle Gleichheitssätze in der Rechtsprechung des Europäischen Gerichtshofes' in J Ipsen and E Schmidt-Jortzig (eds), *Recht—Staat—Gemeinwohl: Festschrift für Dietrich Rauschning* (Cologne, Carl Heymanns, 2001) 251, 267; H-J Schütz, T Bruha and D König, *Casebook Europarecht* (Munich, Beck, 2004) 839; similar H Jarass, *EU-Grundrechte* (Munich, Beck, 2005) 290 f. Less critically, D Schiek points out in 'From European Union Non-discrimination Law Towards Multidimensional Equality Law for Europe' in D Schiek and V Chege (eds), *European Union Non-Discrimination Law: Comparative Perspectives on Multidimensional Equality Law* (Abingdon, Routledge-Cavendish, 2009) 3, 5 that European non-discrimination law is very fragmented.

[8] eg Case 245/81 *Edeka Zentrale AG v Federal Republic of Germany* [1982] ECR 2745.

[9] eg Case C-148/02 *Carlos Garcia Avello v Belgian State* [2003] ECR I-11613.

[10] eg Case C-179/88 *Handels- og Kontorfunktionærernes Forbund i Danmark v Dansk Arbejdsgiverforening* [1990] ECR I-3979; Case C-394/96 *Mary Brown v Rentokil Ltd* [1998] ECR I-4185;

incoherence—overlap, we encounter difficulties when trying to provide a single coherent explanation for the concept. Drawing a clearer picture of how the general principle of equality functions in EU law is the purpose of this book.

A starting point for approaching the issue is to look at the reasons for the fundamental status of equality. We attach such importance to the principle of equality, because we consider it to be one of the fundamental values people throughout Europe can agree upon. Not only do Member States' national constitutions stipulate guarantees of equal treatment, but a longstanding tradition of egalitarian discourse can be found on the old continent. The first evidence of 'equality' appearing on the philosophical and political agenda can be found in writings originating in the Greek city-states.[11] In the modern age, the French Revolution with its battle cry for *'liberté, égalité et fraternité'*, moved the demand for equal treatment to the forefront of the European conscience.[12] Moreover, already the Rome Treaty of 1957,[13] otherwise very reserved in its treatment of fundamental rights and principles, included equality provisions. Its free movement provisions prohibited discrimination against goods on grounds of their origin and against economically active persons on the basis of their nationality. Further, Article 119 of the Treaty establishing the European Economic Community entrenched the principle of equal pay for men and women in European primary law.[14] In this sense, the general principle of equality and its fundamental status within Union law contains an attractive integrative power. People throughout Europe share the sentiment that the European Union safeguards equality. Such an understanding, experienced as a consensus, furthers the general feeling of being able to relate to each other. As a consequence, European equality law opens up a space in which European citizens feel included in the broader integration project.

Case C-191/03 *North Western Health Board v Margaret McKenna* [2005] ECR I-7631; Case C-460/06 *Nadine Paquay v Société d'architectes Hoet + Minne SPRL* [2007] ECR I-8511 and Case C-232/09 *Dita Danosa v LKB Līzings SA* [2010] ECR I-11405.

[11] H Haller, *Die Verrechnung von Vor- und Nachteilen im Rahmen von Art 3 Abs 1 GG Eine Untersuchung zur Kompensation von Grundrechtseingriffen* (Berlin, Duncker und Humblot, 2007) 181, with reference to O Dann, 'Gleichheit' in O Brunner, W Conze and R Koselleck (eds), *Geschichtliche Grundbegriffe. Historisches Lexikon zur politisch-sozialen Sprache in Deutschland*, vol 2 (Stuttgart, Klett-Cotta, 1975) 997, 1000.

[12] See Haller (n 11) 190 ff.

[13] Treaty Establishing the European Economic Community (EEC).

[14] Art 119 EEC reads:

> Each Member State shall during the first stage ensure and subsequently maintain the application of the principle that men and women should receive equal pay for equal work.
>
> For the purpose of this Article, 'pay' means the ordinary basic or minimum wage or salary and any other consideration, whether in cash or in kind, which the worker receives, directly or indirectly, in respect of his employment from his employer.
>
> Equal pay without discrimination based on sex means:
>
> (a) that pay for the same work at piece rates shall be calculated on the basis of the same unit of measurement;
> (b) that pay for work at time rates shall be the same for the same job.

However the fundamental status that is commonly attached to the principle of equality in EU law is not built on stable ground. Only at a superficial level can we agree on the importance of equality and what to associate with it. It seems as if our agreement on its fundamental status rests on an 'incompletely theorised agreement'.[15] Three points reveal this incompleteness: first, just because national constitutions evoke the same principles does not mean that they share the same conception. Depending on the constitutional culture from which they emanate, they are filled with differing content.[16] Second, one should not forget that the first discourses on equality in the history of Europe were found in societies characterised by extreme exclusion. When Aristotle was framing his principle of equality,[17] it certainly did not include equal treatment of those so unfortunate to be born as women, slaves or denizens. Third and with reference to the equality provisions introduced in the European Treaties, a correct account ought to point out that they had an instrumental function. While today we conceive of the principle of equality within EU law as a fundamental value and like to think that this has been the case since the creation of the Community, such a depiction would distort the facts. Equal treatment of nationals and non-nationals coming from other Member States acted as a tool to bring about economic harmonisation.[18]

The main reason for designing the fundamental freedoms as norms of non-discrimination was to create a common market. In other words, considerations as to their human rights implications were remote. The TFEU's article on equal pay for men and women is an even more striking example of this instrumentalist rationale. It was because French national legislation required equal pay for the sexes that this principle made its way into the text of its early predecessor, the Treaty establishing the European Economic Community. Fearing competitive distortion and the movement of labour to countries in which women worked for lower salaries,[19] the French government insisted that equal pay be a requirement that other Member States would also have to implement. The introduction into the Treaty of the principle of gender equality was therefore not based on the idea of women's emancipation at a scale that cut across national boundaries. Instead, its genesis was owed to an economic mind-set aimed at the creation of an economic community for economic purposes.

[15] See generally C Sunstein, 'Incompletely Theorized Agreements' (1995) 108 *Harvard Law Review* 1733, who cites the principle of equality as proof of his argument.

[16] eg P Häberle, *Europäische Verfassungslehre* (Baden-Baden, Nomos, 2011) 10.

[17] For a more thorough presentation, see ch 2 s II.A.

[18] See generally (for other grounds of differentiation) Besson (n 7) 656; C O'Brien, 'Equality's False Summits: New Varieties of Disability Discrimination, "Excessive" Equal Treatment and Economically Constricted Horizons' (2011) 36 *EL Rev* 26, 28.

[19] eg A Arnull, *The European Union and its Court of Justice* 2nd edn (Oxford, Oxford University Press, 2006) 535; E Ellis and P Watson, *EU Anti-Discrimination Law* 2nd edn (Oxford, Oxford University Press, 2012) 23; E Sharpston, 'The Shock Troops Arrive in Force: Horizontal Direct Effect of a Treaty Provision and Temporal Limitation of Judgments Join the Armoury of EC Law' in M Maduro and L Azoulai (eds), *The Past and Future of EU Law. The Classics of EU Law Revisited on the 50th Anniversary of the Rome Treaty* (Oxford, Hart Publishing, 2010) 251, 256.

However, the economic origins of the fundamental principle of equality in EU law no longer appear first and foremost in its accounts. Rather, the EU principle of equality has evolved into a more comprehensive concept. We may not be entirely sure about its roots, but now it is there. For one, a fair number of secondary legislative acts are dedicated to promoting equality, lending support to the idea that it is of particular significance to EU law.[20] Additionally, we should recognise that the 'spill-over' effect placed alongside the functionalist approach represents an integral part of the tool kit of European law and helps explain the importance attached to equality in Union law. The non-discrimination provisions in the area of free movement and on equal pay have developed into rules that derive their justification independent of the economic reasons for which they were once implemented, and at this stage they have an impact on areas of law that go beyond purely economic regulation. Moreover, they are considered to give expression to the ideal of equality, without having to make the detour of functionalist reasoning. It is fair to say that judicial activists contributed to this development.[21] Scholars, lawyers and national judges working with the European Treaties realised the potential of the texts to foster the ideal of equal treatment. Although the provisions were not designed to promote the value of equality, social action shaped them into their present form through discourse.[22] Another part of the explanation can be found in the wider transformation of Europe and European law. The transition from a purely economic community to a community of values and rights has led to an increase in the significance of the principle of equality. Advancements such as the introduction of equality as a founding principle of the Union or the insertion of the chapter on equality in the Charter are more than mere lip-service to egalitarian ideals.

This evolution of the general principle of equality in EU law leaves us with the following picture: on the one hand, equality has become a concept in its own right

[20] eg Council Directive 76/207/EEC of 9 February 1976 on the implementation of the principle of equal treatment for men and women as regards access to employment, vocational training and promotion, and working conditions [1976] OJ L39/40, Council Directive 2000/43/EC of 29 June 2000 implementing the principle of equal treatment between persons irrespective of racial or ethnic origin [2000] OJ L180/22; Directive 2002/73/EC of the European Parliament and of the Council of 23 September 2002 amending Council Directive 76/207/EEC on the implementation of the principle of equal treatment for men and women as regards access to employment, vocational training and promotion, and working conditions [2002] OJ L269/15; Council Directive 2004/113/EC of 13 December 2004 implementing the principle of equal treatment between men and women in the access to and supply of goods and services [2004] OJ L373/37 and Directive 2006/54/EC of the European Parliament and of the Council of 5 July 2006 on the implementation of the principle of equal opportunities and equal treatment of men and women in matters of employment and occupation [2006] OJ L204/23.

[21] See generally on the influence of law activists on the evolution of EU gender equality law, C Kilpatrick, 'Gender Equality: A Fundamental Dialogue' in S Sciarra (ed), *Labour Law in the Courts. National Judges and the European Court of Justice* (Oxford, Hart Publishing, 2001) 31, especially 50 ff.

[22] As AP van der Mei points out, European equality law 'has both functional and foundational or existential value' in 'The Outer Limits of the Prohibition of Discrimination on Grounds of Nationality: A Look Through the Lens of Union Citizenship' (2011) 18 in *Maastricht Journal* 62, 63.

and is applicable in a multitude of areas.[23] On the other hand and as the preceding paragraphs tried to depict, the principle has not been informed by a single coherent theory and suffers from this incomplete theorisation. Consequently, a lack of comprehensibility has come to haunt EU equality law. What can justify Member States' differential treatment of their own nationals and EU citizens coming from other countries? Can we argue for a quota for women in the workplace even if the guarantee of equality strictly prohibits discrimination on grounds of sex? Can a practice of reverse discrimination[24] be reconciled with the idea of a Union of equal citizens? And how can answers to such diverse questions be reconciled in a single concept?

II. THE NEED FOR RECONCEPTUALISING EQUALITY LAW OR THE RATIONALIST HUMAN RIGHTS PARADIGM

As if these questions were not challenging enough the problems surrounding the general principle of equality in EU law ought to be considered in the broader context of European human rights adjudication. Some readers may have noticed that the discussion has so far been phrased in terms of 'traditional legalism', meaning that fundamental rights need only be interpreted to find the correct meaning of constitutional texts.[25] However, given that many actors at different levels are involved in the creation and implementation of European law, I am of the opinion that it is insufficient to focus exclusively on an interpretive account in order to analyse European equality law.[26] We may be well advised to not only look at the written legal argumentation, but also at the actors making the decisions and the reasoning behind the grounds of their decisions. Consequently, this analysis needs to address the broader issue of how far a purely interpretive framework is capable or adequate to offer coherent accounts of fundamental principles, particularly in the context of the European Union, and by which conceptual frameworks it ought to be complemented.

In his seminal piece *The Transformation of Europe*,[27] Weiler argued that developments in Union law cannot be adequately understood without examining

[23] Besson (n 7) 656 ('principle of non-discrimination [as] a social and even a human right'); S Prechal, 'Equality of Treatment, Non-Discrimination and Social Policy: Achievements in Three Themes' (2004) 41 *CML Rev* 533, 534 ('concept of non-discrimination [as] a fundamental principle of social policy with constitutional aspirations').

[24] Reverse discrimination describes situations in which people, whose situation is not governed by EU law, are treated less favourably than persons able to establish a connecting factor to EU law. In greater detail, see ch 5.

[25] In this sense, see M Kumm, '*Internationale Handelsgesellschaft, Nold* and the New Human Rights Paradigm' in M Maduro and L Azoulai (eds), *The Past and Future of EU Law. The Classics of EU Law Revisited on the 50th Anniversary of the Rome Treaty* (Oxford, Hart Publishing, 2010) 106.

[26] Similar P Caro de Sousa, *The European Fundamental Freedoms: A Contextual Approach* (Oxford, Oxford University Press, 2015) 4, 34 ff.

[27] JHH Weiler, 'The Transformation of Europe' (1991) 100 *Yale Law Journal* 2403.

developments in its overall legal system in unison with the developments of the Union's and the Member States' political processes. Describing the methodology underlying the article, he stated:

> It is perhaps ironic, but my synthesis and analysis are truly in the tradition of the 'pure theory of law' with the riders that 'law' encompasses a discourse that is much wider than doctrine and norms and that the very dichotomy of law and politics is questionable.[28]

In other words, Weiler dismissed as too limited a point of view that looks upon law as simply a set of norms subject to interpretation according to legal doctrine. Instead, he argued that law needs to be looked at along with the powers that create and shape it.

Regarding the field of European fundamental rights more specifically, the explanatory strength of 'traditional legalism' can further be called into question for the following reason: fundamental rights protection in the European Union is characterised by its broadly defined 'scope of interests protected as a right'.[29] Instead of having a narrowly tailored set of rights that enjoy almost unlimited protection, one opted for a framework that safeguards the most diverse (and at times banal) individual interests in such a way that they constantly have to be reconciled with each other. Due to the wide scope of European fundamental rights protection, its central theme is no longer deciding which interests deserve a priori protection, but the process of balancing the competing interests.[30] Consequently, if balancing is an essential element of rights protection, the actors performing balancing are of particular importance. In so doing, another feature of European fundamental rights law becomes significant: within the European framework many diverse actors are responsible for ensuring rights protection. Not only are there safeguards at the Union as well as at the Member State level,[31] but at both levels different actors, such as courts and legislators, are involved. In other words, decision making power is distributed amongst different institutions on a horizontal and a vertical level.

[28] ibid, 2409.

[29] M Kumm, 'Institutionalising Socratic Contestation: The Rationalist Human Rights Paradigm, Legitimate Authority and the Point of Judicial Review' (2007) 1 *European Journal of Legal Studies* 153, 162.

[30] Kumm (n 25) 108 (with reference to Case 11/70 *Internationale Handelsgesellschaft mbH v Einfuhr- und Vorratsstelle für Getreide und Futtermittel* [1970] ECR 1161 and Case 4/73 *J Nold, Kohlen- und Baustoffgroßhandlung v Commission of the European Communities* [1974] ECR 491) and 110.

[31] It should not be left unmentioned that the European Court of Human Rights also exists as an additional actor in the area of fundamental rights protection in Europe. On the current relationship between the European Court of Human Rights and the European Union see Case *Bosphorus Hava Yollari Turizm v Ireland* A no 45036/98 (2006) 42 EHRR 1. As far as the plans for accession of the European Union to the European Convention on Human Rights are concerned, it appears that after the European Court of Justice's Opinion 2/13, ECLI:EU:2014:2454 the chances of their realisation in the near future have significantly decreased. On this, see S Douglas-Scott, 'Opinion 2/13 on EU accession to the ECHR: a Christmas bombshell from the European Court of Justice', www.verfassungsblog.de/opinion-213-eu-accession-echr-christmas-bombshell-european-court-justice/#.VQAgGMkXksw.

Focusing on the aspects of '[a]n expansive scope of rights'[32] and balancing,[33] Kumm argues that '[t]he traditional legalist paradigm of human and constitutional rights is effectively replaced by a rationalist human rights paradigm'.[34] He states that one will not be able to give an adequate depiction of how the law functions or understand its workings by only looking at legal texts. On the contrary, the interplay of these two factors leads to a situation, in which fundamental rights texts are of little guidance in deciding cases and that 'a closer analysis of what courts are actually doing in many jurisdictions is likely to reveal that constitutional texts are less important than is conventionally believed'.[35] Kumm infers from this that fundamental rights balancing, especially in the form of proportionality analysis needs to be performed in ways that legitimises its outcomes. Courts can only be equipped with legitimate authority to review political decisions, if their judicial reasoning is conceivable as a '*collective judgment of reason* about what justice and good policy requires'.[36]

My analysis builds on these findings, but modifies Kumm's method of conceptualising European fundamental rights law under a new paradigm. I argue that the move to justificatory balancing as the focal point of rights protection in conjunction with the variety of actors performing such balancing requires an approach that focuses on the institutions involved. Under these circumstances, the question deserving greater attention is who gets to decide on the protection. So if we want to understand why a case was decided in a certain manner, we need to concentrate more on the institution making the decision, instead of attempting to explain a given outcome with the help of legal texts only. Therefore, I suggest thinking about the topic of European fundamental rights protection—and for the purposes of this study in particular about European equal rights protection—from an institutional choice perspective. In this sense, I argue for an institutionally enriched version of rationalist equality analysis[37] anchored in the tradition of comparative institutional analysis.[38]

III. EU LAW AS THE LABORATORY OF CONSTITUTIONAL THEORY

The selection of the general principle of equality in European law remains to be explained. After all, national constitutions also usually provide for vaguely paraphrased equality guarantees with different actors, namely constitutional courts and national parliaments, competing for the prerogative of interpretation. Yet, an

32 Kumm (n 25) 110.
33 ibid, 110.
34 ibid, 106.
35 ibid, 114.
36 Kumm (n 29) 175 (emphasis added).
37 Thanks to M Kumm for expressing it in these concise terms.
38 For this, see ch 3.

examination of the European principle of equality under an institutional paradigm is particularly interesting for two reasons.

First, within the European Union, the vertical component is added to the distribution of decision making power. Institutions both at the national and the supranational level are potentially in a position to rule on a measure's fairness, so that the demarcation of who gets to define the meaning of equality in a given situation is a central theme. One may object to this argument by saying that there are established rules, according to which competences are distributed amongst the European Union and the Member States. In response to this, I maintain that even defined rules are subject to ongoing interpretation and development. For example and as will be explained in detail in the following, if the European Court of Justice perceives an increased risk of misrepresentation of a particular interest in Member State decision making processes, it is more likely to step in to scrutinise national law pursuant to European standards.[39] Further, the relation between national and European law is in continuous flux. As for instance the discussion of the *Ruiz Zambrano* judgment[40] in chapter 5 will show, even rules which are thought to be firmly established in European law, such as the purely internal rule, can be subject to change.

Second, examining the principle of equality in its European environment has particular appeal because Union law serves as a laboratory for prevailing issues of constitutional theory. Constitutional topics, which have been subject to longstanding discourses in national liberal democracies, resurface in new clothes. They now need to be dealt with in a novel theoretical framework; a framework that is informed by diverse constitutional cultures and traditions shaped over a long period of time throughout the continent. As a consequence, settled understandings of the law and conventional perceptions of constitutional principles are called into question. Finding convincing explanations of the functioning of European Union law and how its principles should duly be interpreted is not a mere repetition of constitutional discussions at the national stage. Instead, it requires further development and deepening of our analyses. In this sense, European law serves as a catalyst for us to think anew about (ostensibly) accepted truths of constitutional law. I would like to just mention two examples, where European Union law has already forced us to reconsider our understanding of constitutional law: the notion of federalism and the role of the proportionality analysis.

Starting with federalism, Schütze draws attention to the fact that different movements have given differing definitions of the concept, some of which have fallen into disuse over the course of time. He suggests that the evolution of the European Union challenges us to go back to these neglected conceptions in order to explain the existing structure.[41] He writes that 'three federal traditions emerge[d]

[39] See M Maduro, *We, the Court* (Oxford, Hart Publishing, 1998). His theory is presented in detail in ch 4.

[40] Case C-34/09 *Gerardo Ruiz Zambrano v Office national de l'emploi (ONEm)* [2011] ECR I-1177.

[41] R Schütze, *From Dual to Cooperative Federalism. The Changing Structure of European Law* (Oxford, Oxford University Press, 2009).

in the modern era'[42] (roughly commencing in the eighteenth century). Whereas the first perceived federal entities as international (con)federations agreed upon by sovereign states,[43] the second came into being through the second American Union and saw federalism as a form of governance somewhere 'in between ... an international and a national structure'.[44] According to this second tradition, a federal Union derives its legitimacy 'from the supreme authority in each State, the authority of the people themselves'.[45] Third, a tradition was born in continental Europe, which linked the idea of federalism inherently to the concept of the nation state.[46] 'Within this European tradition, federalism came to refer to the *constitutional* devolution of power within a sovereign nation'.[47] This third way of defining federalism became the prevalent account under which European integration was analysed and created a discourse that understood divisibility of sovereignty as an aberration instead of an integral part of federalism.[48] By tracing the origins as well as the history of these three diverse traditions, Schütze highlights that one can understand the concept of federalism to be completely in line, instead of in tension, with a system of governance whereby sovereignty is distributed amongst different levels and power cooperatively exercised. Therefore, developments in European Union law served as a catalyst for rethinking federalism and gave rise to a disquisition on the reinterpretation of a (supposedly) familiar concept. Since the common account of federalism could not explain the new European modes of governance, Schütze explored alternative conceptions and applied them to the changed conditions.

We can detect a similar procedure in the case of proportionality analysis. Proportionality analysis has its roots in German administrative law[49] where it was originally developed to review the necessity and appropriateness of policing measures 'in relation to the objective being pursued'.[50] In a series of early rulings by the Federal Constitutional Court,[51] it found its way into German constitutional law.

[42] ibid, 15.

[43] ibid, 16 ff.

[44] ibid, 23.

[45] J Madison, 'Federalist Paper No 39' in A Hamilton, J Madison and J Jay, *Die Federalist Papers*, Barbara Zehnpfennig tr (Darmstadt, Wissenschaftliche Buchgesellschaft, 1993) 244, 247.

[46] Schütze (n 41) 30.

[47] ibid, 31, with reference to D Elazar, *Constitutionalizing Globalization. The Postmodern Revival of Confederal Arrangements* (Oxford, Rowman and Littlefield, 1998) 39.

[48] Schütze (n 41) 31 f.

[49] P Craig, *EU Administrative Law* 2nd edn (Oxford, Oxford University Press, 2006) 591; T von Danwitz, 'Der Grundsatz der Verhältnismäßigkeit im Gemeinschaftsrecht' (2003) 14 *Europäisches Wirtschafts- und Steuerrecht* 393 with further references.

[50] Craig, ibid 591; See also J Schwarze, *EU Administrative Law* revised 1st edn (London, Sweet and Maxwell, 2006) 685 ff.

[51] First mention of it is in *BVerfGE* 3, 383. Further early rulings *BVerfGE* 7, 377; 8, 71; 10, 354 and 13, 97. On the origins of proportionality analysis in German constitutional law, see E Grabitz, 'Der Grundsatz der Verhältnismäßigkeit in der Rechtsprechung des Bundesverfassungsgerichts' (1973) 98 *Archiv des öffentlichen Rechts* 568, 569 f or L Hirschberg, *Der Grundsatz der Verhältnismässigkeit* (Göttingen, Otto Schwartz und Co, 1981) 1 and 16 ff.

The analysis' application in the constitutional setting was followed by a broader debate on its capacity to rationalise, as well as systematise human rights discourse.[52] However, by now, these initially fiercely led debates on the effects of balancing competing rights on the substance of those rights and the analysis' legitimacy have given way to widespread accepted consensus amongst German constitutional scholars that proportionality analysis is an integral part of fundamental rights control.[53] Only in the wake of the introduction of proportionality analysis in the case law of the European Court of Justice has the debate on its adequateness experienced a revival.[54] Questions, such as how procedure affects substance in fundamental rights law, are back on the table.[55] In the peculiar context of European law, old issues are not only reconsidered, but also complemented by new ones. For example, the debate on proportionality analysis in EU law has taken on the theme of demonstrating understanding for differing national values.[56] In addition, investigations now examine the role of national courts in preliminary reference procedures that comprise an element of proportionality analysis.[57] Even more, the insights gained through those examinations feed back on our comprehension of the judiciary's role in purely national proportionality analyses.

Yet, the power of Union law to challenge settled understandings does not stop at formal or methodological concepts. It makes us question substantive notions as well. One of these notions—the one I am particularly interested in—is the general principle of equality. Here, European law markedly displays its ability to work as a catalyst for rethinking common conceptions and the elements of European

[52] See eg Hirschberg (n 51); P Lerche, *Übermass und Verfassungsrecht* (Cologne, Carl Heymanns, 1961). For an exchange on the rationality versus irrationality of fundamental rights balancing, see R Alexy, *Theorie der Grundrechte* (Baden-Baden, Suhrkamp, 1994) 143 ff (the argument essentialised in ibid, 'The Construction of Constitutional Rights' (2010) 4 *Law & Ethics of Human Rights* 20) and J Habermas, *Between Facts and Norms. Contributions to a Discourse Theory of Law and Democracy* (Cambridge, Massachusetts Institute of Technology Press, 1996); B Schlink, 'Der Grundsatz der Verhältnismäßigkeit' in P Badura and H Dreier (eds), *Festschrift 50 Jahre Bundesverfassungsgericht* 2nd vol (Tübingen, Mohr Siebeck, 2001) 445.

[53] In this sense, see von Danwitz (n 49) 393, although the author is also critical of some of the excess of judicial control according to proportionality standards by German courts, see ibid, 402. For example, A Heusch, *Der Grundsatz der Verhältnismäßigkeit im Staatsorganisationsrecht* (Berlin, Duncker und Humblot, 2003).

[54] See amongst others Craig (n 49) 590; N Hõs, 'The Principle of Proportionality in the *Viking* and *Laval* Cases: An Appropriate Standard of Review?' (2009) EUI Working Paper, 2009/06, http://cadmus.eui.eu//handle/1814/11259. See generally T-I Harbo, 'The Function of Proportionality Analysis in European Law' (DPhil thesis, European University Institute 2006) 136 ff.

[55] On the point Harbo (n 54) 270 writes:

> If ... PA [proportionality analysis] is not of a substantial but merely of a procedural or methodological nature—a way in which courts structure their reasoning—one could assume that it is prima facia value neutral in this regard. However, although PA may be free of substance in the meaning that is does not advance or limit fundamental rights, PA may nevertheless be value infected since a particular way of structuring legal reasoning may also have substantial implications.

[56] See Craig (n 49) 633 f.

[57] ibid, 636 ff.

equality law characterising the field contribute to this. But let me explain this thought in greater detail. As was previously pointed out, the beginnings of EU equality law show an interlinkage between equality guarantees and economic considerations. Therefore, the question arises as to whether equal treatment is an end in itself or whether other aims should be pursued with its help. Furthermore, the concept of indirect discrimination found its way into Union law long before most of its Member States adopted it in the context of their national jurisdictions. In this sense, Union law showed new ways to conceptualise a notion with a long history and with this move contributed to an extension of equality protection in Europe. Finally, Europe challenges our perceptions of the 'proper' scope of equality provisions. If most legal philosophers worked on the assumption that such guarantees are only valid within a discrete society, now we are faced with establishing how far our obligation to equal treatment actually extends in a supranational setting.[58]

These deliberations converge in the same question: which notion of equality do we want to espouse? Or, since this thesis is not so much concerned with legal philosophy but with legal practice, to reframe the question in terms of the rationalist human rights paradigm: who should decide on the 'right' notion of equality in European law?

IV. THE INSTITUTIONAL CHOICE APPROACH TO EU EQUALITY LAW

This thesis develops the argument that comparative institutional analysis[59] is an advantageous tool to examine the functioning of the general principle of equality in European law. It argues that the European Court of Justice as well as national constitutional courts are often guided by more or less hidden institutional considerations when deciding equality cases.

Looking at European equality law from an interpretive point of view the subject matter admittedly conveys a picture of such diversity that it borders on inconsistency. Yet, as the following chapters will depict, it is the limitations of the traditional interpretive paradigm that make us place an emphasis on incoherence in this area of law. Instead of remaining at the level of critiquing the case law within the interpretive framework—an exercise which is no doubt of great importance for assessing legal outcomes—I suggest that it is beneficial to widen our viewpoint. If one is willing to approach EU equality law from a different perspective, more particularly that of comparative institutional choice, the subject loses much of

[58] Further A Sangivoanni, 'Solidarity in the European Union' (2013) *Oxford Journal of Legal Studies* 1; particularly on EU citizenship D Thym, 'The Elusive Limits of Solidarity: Residence Rights of and Social Benefits for Economically Inactive Union Citizens' (2015) 52 *CML Rev* 17. One could, of course, approach this subject also from a different angle and ask for the proper definition of a society in the European context.

[59] As developed by N Komesar in *Imperfect Alternatives: Choosing Institutions in Law, Economics, and Public Policy* (Chicago, University of Chicago Press, 1994) and ibid, *Law's Limits* (Cambridge, Cambridge University Press, 2001).

its incoherence. Instead, patterns of reasoning become evident that often help to explain why the European Court of Justice decided cases in the way it did.

Given that the concrete conception of equality is such a disputed topic, those institutions called upon to interpret 'equality' ask themselves whether they are the most competent actors regarding the variables of interest representation, numbers and complexity to decide.[60] As a deconstruction of case law by the European Court of Justice will show, such comparative institutional assessment informs the Court's reasoning. Moreover, it has done so in such a pervasive manner that it has shaped interpretive discourse and standards of testing in equality law.

After explaining the philosophical origins of the concept of equality, the examination shows through four 'case studies' how institutional choice guides judges in their equality decisions: application of different standards of testing, assessment of Member States' preferential treatment of their own nationals compared to persons coming from other Member States, the treatment of reverse discrimination and the case of affirmative action for women in the EU. Building upon these findings, the thesis concludes that we would be well-advised to acknowledge the impact of institutional choice considerations on EU equality law and to make use of the institutional choice framework in our analyses of this field of law. As a consequence, the last chapter argues that equality jurisprudence should be adapted so as to offer room for directly addressing institutional considerations ancillary to interpretive deliberations. With this in mind, an alternative model of equality *Dogmatik* is presented that squares institutional and interpretive analyses.

Before I give a more detailed overview of the thesis' chapters, one caveat must be mentioned: the general principle of equality in European law is an extensive topic. It seems impossible to provide an analysis that encompasses the case law in its entirety. For this reason, the thesis follows the heuristic method, meaning that individual (often leading) cases are examined in order to verify or disprove more general points. Furthermore, the analysis deals only with the general principle of equality in the relationship between the 'state', namely the European Union or its Member States, and the individual. It only concerns its vertical application. The horizontal application of the principle of equality between private parties, which has been given expression through the set of equality directives passed since 2000,[61] lies beyond the scope of this project. However, reference to the directives will occasionally be made and the aim is to develop an account of European equality adjudication, which can also be applied to the principle's horizontal dimension.

The remainder of this introduction will provide a more detailed overview of the thesis, which is structured as follows.

[60] Komesar, *Law's Limits*, ibid especially 3–34.

[61] Starting with Council Dir 2000/78/EC of 27 November 2000 establishing a general framework for equal treatment in employment and occupation [2002] OJ L303/16. On this subject, see M Bell, *Anti-Discrimination Law and the European Union* (Oxford, Oxford University Press, 2002). For a depiction of the setting up of domestic equality institutions in wake of the directives scheme, see B de Witte, 'National Equality Institutions and the Domestication of EU Non-Discrimination Law' (2011) 11 *Maastricht Journal* 157.

Chapter 2 recounts the philosophical origins of the concept of equality and of non-discrimination law. As I will develop more thoroughly, although equality is generally considered a valid and socially important concept, agreement on its details cannot be reached. A result of this conceptual indeterminacy is that constitutional guarantees of non-discrimination can be interpreted in many—and more importantly very different—ways. A conclusion is reached that the essential characteristic of equality as a legal concept is its ability to depict the *relational* side of fundamental rights. In other words, the concept is of great value, as it helps us to assess how a person is treated in relation to others. In its pure form, it calls for comparison and stipulates that differential treatment shall only take place if differences amongst two compared groups justify the differential treatment. In addition to giving an overview on the concept's theoretical groundings, the chapter inquires as to whether there is a difference between the principle of non-discrimination and the principle of equality in EU law.

Chapter 3 explores the subject of different testing standards employed by the European Court of Justice in its equality adjudication. It argues that similar to the case law of the German Federal Constitutional Court three distinct testing standards are at play. As will be shown, the Luxembourg Court at times confines itself to a reasonableness test, at times engages in strict comparative review and at times performs means-ends balancing in a non-discrimination context. Following up on this depiction, the chapter introduces the framework of comparative institutional analysis and states that the specific mechanism of review in a given case should depend on the judges' assessment of their comparative aptitude to make a decision. Depending on how well or imperfectly the political process functions in an area of law under equality review, the European Court of Justice should (and often does) examine cases with different intensity.

Chapter 4 is dedicated to a study of the European Court of Justice's case law on the principle of discrimination on grounds of nationality. The chapter explicates that although the principle of non-discrimination states that no EU citizen may be discriminated against due to his or her nationality, this prohibition comes with inbuilt limitations. It looks more closely at the compatibility of national electoral laws as well as social benefit laws, which are reserved to a country's own citizens, with EU law. Though the differentiating lines of these laws run between a country's nationals and EU foreigners, they are nevertheless generally reckoned to be in accordance with EU law. Again, comparative institutional analysis is employed to explain that considerations about the relative ability of potential decision makers—in particular the national political processes versus the European judiciary—should influence the European Court of Justice's handling of such cases.

Chapter 5 turns to 'reverse discrimination', the phenomenon by which individuals able to rely on European norms enjoy greater freedoms than those in situations governed by national law only.[62] It looks at the issue from a European law

[62] See A Balthasar, '"Inländerdiskriminierung" in der EU nach dem EG-Vertrag und aus österreichischer Sicht' (1998) 53 *Zeitschrift für öffentliches Recht* 143, 146; S O'Leary, 'The Past, Present and

perspective and examines the European Court of Justice's approach on the topic.[63] Although the Court phrases its decisions touching upon reverse discrimination in terms of the applicability of Union law, there is a strong egalitarian element to the subject. At its core is the question whether the non-discrimination principle in EU law goes as far as to prohibit differential treatment of European citizens in purely internal situations and those in situations with a connection to Union law.[64] This thesis argues that the judges are guided by institutional considerations when delimiting the scope of application of EU law—the more they consider the national political processes to have malfunctioned in a case of reverse discrimination, the likelier they are to attend to the matter.

Chapter 6 examines the case law by the European Court of Justice on affirmative action for women, specifically on women's quotas. This field of European law has been criticised both for doing too much[65] and for doing too little[66] to facilitate equal treatment of the sexes. Given that this critique is connected to recognition that non-discrimination law can be used as a tool for social transformation, the thesis argues that comparative institutional analysis can help us also understand European affirmative action law. It establishes that the European Court of Justice is guided by the parameters of interest representation, scale and competence when deciding whether to substitute national quota schemes for its own conceptions of equal treatment. In this exercise, I draw on findings of the debate on the constitutionality of affirmative action in the United States to depict that comparative institutional analysis offers a framework to conceptualise not only the United States Supreme Court's, but also the European Court of Justice's, affirmative action adjudication. On this, I would like to add one further explicatory note: in the discussion of the American jurisprudence, the thesis also addresses the discrimination experienced by Blacks in the United States. Following works from the discipline of Critical Race Theory, I decided to use the term Black with an uppercase 'B' to denote the group of people, who are American citizens from African descent.[67] As Möschel explains in this context, the reason behind this choice in terminology is 'the idea that "Black" or "Blacks" does not simply denote the skin colour but

Future of the Purely Internal Rule in EU Law' in M Dougan, N Nic Shuibhne and E Spaventa (eds), *Empowerment and Disempowerment of the European Citizen* (Oxford, Hart Publishing, 2012) 37, 38; C Ritter, 'Purely Internal Situations, Reverse Discrimination, Guimont, Dzodzi and Article 234' (2006) 31 *EL Rev* 690, 691.

[63] For a discussion of reverse discrimination by national courts, especially German and Austrian courts, see J Croon-Gestefeld, 'Umgekehrte Diskriminierungen nach dem Unionsrecht—Unterschiedliche Konzepte im Umgang mit einem gemeinsamen Problem' (2016) 51 *Europarecht* 56.

[64] See *Ruiz Zambrano* (n 40) Opinion of AG Sharpston, para 123.

[65] See B Schubert, *Affirmative Action und Reverse Discrimination* (Baden-Baden, Nomos, 2003) 102 with reference to eg M Sachs, 'Anmerkungen zu *Marschall*' (1998) *Deutsches Verwaltungsblatt* 183, 185.

[66] eg S Fredman, 'After *Kalanke* and *Marschall*: Affirming Affirmative Action' (1998) 1 *Cambridge Yearbook of European Legal Studies* 199.

[67] See also M Möschel, *Law, Lawyers and Race: Critical Race Theory from the US to Europe* (New York, Routledge, 2014) 6.

constitutes a specific heritage, history, experience, and personal identity and as such requires the use of a noun'.[68]

For my inquiry into the functioning of the general principle of equality in European law, I chose the four themes of (a) different testing standards, (b) discrimination on the basis of nationality, (c) reverse discrimination and (d) affirmative action as subjects of a more detailed analysis for the following reasons. As regards the topic of differing tests in equality review, it serves as the base for showing that European equality adjudication is diverse and follows different patterns depending on the specific context. Building on this insight, the examination turns to three of the issues I consider as belonging to the most controversial of European equality law. Discrimination on grounds of nationality is examined as the prohibition thereof is undoubtedly one of the central provisions in EU law. What this work explores specifically is under which conditions the European Court of Justice considers differential treatment on grounds of nationality to be nonetheless justified. Reverse discrimination is of specific interest to my work, because it features the odd facet of being labelled 'discriminatory' but is rarely discussed in terms of equality. Moreover, the subject is located at the border of European Union law and therefore also at the border of European Union equality law. Since problems with conceptual frameworks are often revealed in borderline cases, I believe that it is an interesting area for testing the explanatory strength of comparative institutional analysis. With respect to the examination of affirmative action adjudication, the topic was chosen as it touches upon many of the prevailing equality themes in a condensed manner, boiling down to the paradoxical question whether one shall discriminate against individuals for the sake of equality. This analysis seeks to show that the alternative framework of institutional choice can help to explain the European Court of Justice's dealing with the topic.

Coming back to the overall structure of the thesis, chapter 7 summarises the findings of the preceding chapters. It suggests that the *Dogmatik* of equality testing should be adapted so as to openly address those institutional considerations which already guide judges in their assessment, but usually do not surface in written decisions. Bridging the divide between first order interpretive and second order institutional questions, it argues that equality testing can be modified in such a way as to connect relative human rights assessment to the assessment of institutions' relative decision making powers.

[68] ibid.

2

The Notion of Equality

I. WHY EQUALITY?

EQUALITY—WHAT A SONOROUS word and compelling ideal. Has it not been invoked time and again as one of the most potent of human values, as a guiding principle for politics and private life alike?[1] Yet, as soon as one tries to clarify what makes the notion of equality so captivating, the issue becomes more complex. After all, the sentence that 'all men are equal' already contains some ready obstacles, it being either a tautological or a fallacious statement.[2] It could be tautological in the sense that it implies a common humanity shared by mankind. But this could also be expressed by the statement that 'all men are men', without equality bringing any additional meaning to the argument. Or it could amount to a fallacious proclamation, if it was supposed to say that all men are equal in the sense of being the same. Assuming agreement on the fact that each person is a unique individual, with particular talents and characteristic features, and should be treated as such, the statement must be considered outright wrong. Looking at this puzzle, why should we then care about equality?

This chapter intends to provide an attempt to answer this fundamental question. It seeks to reflect upon the content of the value under review. What ideal is it that one is striving for when one invokes equality? Since the research is legal in nature, it will neither be devoted to the subject of distributive justice, nor extensively deal with the 'equality of what?' debate, which figures prominently within philosophical discussions.[3] Further, the remarks on the rationale of equality are not intended to substantively contribute to the discussion of 'why equality', but rather to depict the state of the art and clarify the point of view taken in the analysis.

[1] See F Oppenheim, 'Egalitarianism as a Descriptive Concept' in L Pojman and R Westmoreland (eds), *Equality. Selected Readings* (Oxford, Oxford University Press, 1997) 55; J Schaar, 'Equality of Opportunity, and Beyond' in Pojman and Westmoreland, ibid 137 and L Temkin, 'Inequality' in Pojman and Westmoreland, ibid 75.

[2] J Lucas, 'Against Equality' in Pojman and Westmoreland, ibid 104, 105 f. Similar W Sadurski, *Equality and Legitimacy* (Oxford, Oxford University Press, 2008) 102 f.

[3] For an overview on some of the most prominent writings in the field, see A Sen for equality of capabilities in *Inequality Reexamined* (Oxford, Oxford University Press, 1995) and R Dworkin for equality of resources in *Sovereign Virtue. The Theory and Practice of Equality* (Cambridge, Harvard University Press, 2000), as well as an introduction into the concept of equality of welfare in ibid, 'What Is Equality? Part I: Equality of Welfare' (1981) 10 *Philosophy & Public Affairs* 185. Further L Alexander and M Schwarzschild, 'Liberalism, Neutrality, and Equality of Welfare vs Equality of Resources' (1987) 16 *Philosophy & Public Affairs* 85.

The chapter's central claim is that equality, as one value among others, matters. Equality is an important concept, as it brings the relational side of fundamental rights to the fore. It enables us to evaluate an individual's demand for respect and just treatment in comparison to that of other members of society.

In order to develop this point, the following chapter is structured as follows: as a first step, the general discourse on equality will be introduced. That is to say, the topic will be presented as dealt with in political philosophy. In a second step, the examination will be narrowed down to a discussion on the reasons for the principle of equality as a legal concept. The last part of the chapter is dedicated to an examination of a question that appears repeatedly in egalitarian discourse: the question on the relationship between equality and non-discrimination. I will argue that in the context of European law these two terms can be understood as interchangeable notions reflecting the same egalitarian principle.

A. Reasons for Having the Concept of Equality

i. Interpersonal Explanations

So why equality? In order to approach the topic, one may well start with the cake example.[4] A mother has baked a cake and distributes two of its pieces among her children, Phil and Joe. Both sons receive slices big enough to satisfy their hunger and desire for cake, but Phil gets a much bigger slice than his brother. This fact causes Joe to complain. His complaint is neither directed against himself getting a slice too small to satisfy his needs, nor against his brother getting a big slice, but against getting a *smaller* slice than his brother. He objects to the different treatment. To be more explicit, his protest is not so much aimed against his brother receiving *better* treatment than himself, but against being treated *worse*. His criticism conveys that he holds his worse treatment to be unjustified. Joe cannot phrase this complaint in absolute terms, for example by stating that his brother's favourable treatment amounts to a limitation of his individual freedom.[5] Instead, he makes a *comparative*, a *relative* claim.[6]

Every person has at one time or another experienced the innate feeling of being treated unjustifiably worse, of being treated *unfairly*. One may interpret this

[4] Among others, used by Sen in his Tanner Lecture on Human Values; see A Sen, 'Equality of What?', The Tanner Lecture on Human Values, delivered at Stanford University, 22 May 1979, 195 (198 ff), www.tannerlectures.utah.edu/_documents/a-to-z/s/sen80.pdf; similar D Rae, *Equalities* (Cambridge, Harvard University Press, 1981) 21 (with further reference).

[5] For this reason, Krebs describes this phraseology of equality terminology as its intrinsic or strict usage. A Krebs, 'Gleichheit oder Gerechtigkeit. Die Kritik am Egalitarismus' in C Nimtz (ed), *GAP Proceedings 4* (Paderborn, Mentis, 2001) 563, 565.

[6] eg N Smith, 'Why Do We Speak Of Equality?' (2005) 11 *Otago Law Review* 53, 62 ('equality is a *relational* concept').

sentiment as a weak argument for egalitarianism,[7] or as its strongest basis. Certain critics lean towards the former understanding and argue that people, asserting unfair treatment, are actually only expressing a feeling of envy.[8] They claim that a negative feeling like envy should not be accommodated, or at least not be the origin of a principle supposed to govern human relations. So when Joe complains about his brother receiving a bigger share of the treat, he is seen as nothing but a green-eyed monster. In response, one may assert that other fundamental values can also easily be reduced to human vices when taken to such an abstract level of argument. In the end, liberty could be considered as nothing else but the fulfilment of egoism. Alternatively, one can perceive this feeling—the repulsion against unfair treatment—as a 'properly basic belief'[9] in the value of equality. Even if it is not possible to trace it back to a more definite explanation, people deeply feel that equality matters. Yet, on a more theoretical level, this raises the criticism that basic pre-analytical conceptions should not be the foundation of philosophical deliberations. Some develop philosophical concepts fairly detached from beliefs held by the common man, whereas others attempt greater reconciliation of their theories with prephilosophical judgments. Thus, the objection originates from a more general disagreement as to the 'analytic-synthetic distinction, and therefore about the status of philosophy itself'.[10] But if one is willing to accept the view that philosophical investigation may be guided by individual judgements,[11] then the egalitarian ideal can be perceived as a generalisation of the feeling that no one should be treated worse than any other person without proper justification.[12] Difference in treatment without legitimate justification just does not feel fair.

GA Cohen, a distinguished defender of egalitarian theory, builds upon this initial sentiment for his explanation of the rationale behind equality and transforms it into an argument of political theory. According to him, policy arguments have to pass what he calls the interpersonal test before they can be considered good arguments.[13] More explicitly the test seeks to examine whether an argument can serve as a justification of a policy, independent of which member in a society utters it to whom. Accordingly, the factor of who is presenting the argument is not taken into account. This way, people who might benefit from a specific policy are forced to take a point of view different from the one they are accustomed to

[7] The definition of egalitarian, as employed in this work, is meant to describe a person who believes in the value of equality and considers it to be of considerable importance. As Raz correctly points out, all egalitarians are necessarily value pluralists, because equality needs a referential value filling the principle with content. J Raz, 'On the Value of Distributional Equality' (2008) Paper No 41/2008 Legal Research Paper Series, University of Oxford, 6, papers.ssrn.com/sol3/papers.cfm?abstract_id=1288545.

[8] See Lucas (n 2) 109, who expresses that the envy factor at least changes the character of the equality argument to the negative.

[9] L Pojman, 'On Equal Human Worth: A Critique of Contemporary Egalitarianism' in Pojman and Westmoreland (n 1) 282, 284, who cites Alvin Planting as a source of this expression.

[10] GA Cohen, *Rescuing Justice and Equality* (Cambridge, Harvard University Press, 2008) 3 f.

[11] A view taken by Cohen; ibid, 4.

[12] K Nielson, 'Equality and Liberty: A Defense of Radical Egalitarianism' in Pojman and Westmoreland (n 1) 204, 206.

[13] Cohen (n 10) 42.

and are required to disregard their normally held incentives. The test of interpersonal presentation objectifies the examination of policy arguments. In GA Cohen's words, it 'makes vivid that the justification of policy characteristically depends on circumstances that are not exogenous with respect to human agency'.[14] Applying the test to the cake example, the policy that Joe shall receive a smaller piece than his brother is good policy, if the mother, were she in the position of her son Joe, could still offer valid justifications for her choice in distribution. Conversely, the argument will fail, if she, were she in the shoes of her son, cannot explain her distributory practice convincingly. Hence, the interpersonal test succeeds in one important aspect: it raises awareness of the fact that individuals stand in relation to each other and that they define their own situation in comparative terms to that of others. It therefore brings to the fore the relative element of human behaviour within a community.[15]

ii. Social Contract Basis

Through its communitarised feature, GA Cohen's view comes close to the theories in the social contract tradition, as proposed by Rousseau and Rawls.[16] Rousseau argues in his *Discourse on the Origins of Inequality* that members of the human kind had been equal in the initial state of nature, and that only societal developments, such as the evolution of the right to property, brought about differences amongst men.[17] One may not share Rousseau's view about the state of nature as an ideal condition but his historical argument, that social association has created new inequalities (for example between the governing and the governed or between various professions) or aggravated existing ones, is not impaired by this reservation. Rousseau seeks to overcome these discrepancies by the establishment of a social contract, which shall be guided by the general will. In turn, the opinion of each citizen is supposed to influence the formation of the general will with equal weight and consequently, the notion of equality forms one of the key elements in Rousseau's contractarian theory. Rawls takes up the idea of equality being an essential element in the social contract and transposes it into contemporary legal philosophy. His book, *A Theory of Justice*, has been identified as 'the long awaited successor to Rousseau's social contract ... the Rock on which the

[14] ibid, 42 f.

[15] See ibid 43, 46 ff.

[16] Cohen's view might not be so easily reconciled with the social contract theories, as put forward by Hobbes and Kant. Equality does not feature prominently in Hobbes' social contract theory. His conviction that authoritative power within a state should be assigned to an absolute sovereign especially lacks egalitarian connotations. His social contract focuses on the idea that a state may offer security to its inhabitants from the warlike state of nature, not on the idea of equal concern or entitlement. Thus, he bases his argument for the social contract on its individual benefit for each party (see Stanford Encyclopedia of Philosophy, plato.stanford.edu/entries/kant-social-political/).

[17] J-J Rousseau, *Discourse on the Origins of Inequality (Second Discourse), Polemics, and Political Economy*, vol 3, Judith Bush, Roger Masters and Christopher Kelly trs (Hanover, University Press of New England, 1992) 41 ff.

Church of Equality can properly be founded in our time'.[18] Two aspects of Rawls's work are of vital importance in understanding the relation of his theory with the notion of equality. These are regularly discussed and even more often quoted, but shall nevertheless quickly be recalled at this point. First, the author creates a modified version of the social contract with the help of a hypothetical. According to it, parties to the social contract find themselves in the 'original position' and are prevented by 'the veil of ignorance' from knowing their own position in the society that is about to be created. So when they set out to form the social contract, their position of ignorance forces them to act impartially. As they cannot know whether they are more privileged in talent or wealth than others they are said to strive for a fair contract.[19] Second, Rawls thinks that when the parties in the 'original position' are asked to set out the principles that will be applied to value what counts among them as just or unjust, they will choose the following: (1) everyone will have an equal right to the most extensive basic liberties compatible with similar liberty for others. (2) Social and economic inequalities must satisfy two conditions: (a) they are to the greatest benefit of the least advantaged (the difference principle) and (b) they are attached to positions open to all under conditions of fair equality of opportunity.[20]

These propositions show what Parfit calls 'an objection to natural inequality'[21] as one of the foundations of Rawls's theory. He continues by stating that 'Rawls himself claims that, in an account of justice, equal division is the natural first step and provides the benchmark by reference to which we can defend our final principles'.[22] For the purposes of our analysis, this means that Rawls acknowledges the fact that greater natural capacity does not merit a more favourable starting place in society.[23] Moreover, it shows that he values the ideal of equality as a significant foundational principle of a societal structure. The fact that Rawls personally stresses the egalitarian notion in his work by regularly referring to his theory of justice as 'Justice as Fairness'[24] seems to prove the point that he himself would agree with such a reading of his œuvre.

[18] R Nisbet, 'The Pursuit of Equality' (1974) 33 *The Public Interest* 103, cited in L Pojman, 'Are Human Rights based on Equal Human Worth?' (1992) 52 *Philosophy and Phenomenological Research* 605, 618.

[19] J Rawls, *A Theory of Justice* (Cambridge, Belknap Press of Harvard University Press, 1999) starting at 103.

[20] ibid, 53.

[21] D Parfit, *Equality or Priority? Lindley Lecture* (Lawrence, University of Kansas Press, 1995) 39.

[22] ibid, 39.

[23] Yet Rawls refuses to draw the conclusion that one should ignore or eliminate these distinctions. Instead he proposes that these contingencies work for the good of the least fortunate (Rawls (n 19) 87). The question of whether the difference principle can be reconciled with Rawls's first principle of justice does not need to be resolved in order to claim that Rawls was an egalitarian in the sense that he valued equality as a principle among others. For a discussion of the tension between the Rawlsian case for the difference principle, namely the accommodation of differences among people, and its inegalitarian content, see Cohen (n 10) 151 ff.

[24] eg 'Justice as Fairness' forms the title of his first ch in *A Theory of Justice.*

iii. Right to Treatment as an Equal

The advancement of the egalitarian idea in social contract theory is mirrored by an extensive discussion of the subject within moral philosophy. While being careful not to oversimplify, one may argue that the notion of equality as an essential part of ethics has informed the writings of many philosophers, among them Kant's groundwork of the metaphysic of morals as well as Dworkin's works. Kant's statement that 'human beings qua rational have an inherent dignity and so ought to treat each other as ends and never merely as means'[25] can be understood in strictly egalitarian terms. The doctrine conveys the idea that each man deserves to be respected as a rational agent and that equal respect is owed to all, because all men are equally rational agents.[26] In other words, all men are entitled to be treated with equal respect. This argument has been referred to as the touchstone of most egalitarians.[27] Though representatives of egalitarianism still widely cite this basic expression as one of their sources of inspiration, Kant's perception of equality is nowadays commonly seen in a slightly different light. His metaphysical perspective, calling for a high level of abstraction, is especially no longer generally viewed as convincing.[28] His doctrine becomes coherent through the claim that all men share the characteristic of being rational agents. But with the notion of 'rational agent', Kant introduces a transcendental element in his theory, which is detached from findings in the 'real world'. The move makes it difficult to reconcile his theory with the overt fact that human nature is diverse.

For these reasons, Dworkin, in *Taking Rights Seriously*, sets out to create a political theory that is 'metaphysically unambitious' but grounded on the principle of equality.[29] In order to do so, he presumes that everyone will accept the postulate that the government must treat people with equal concern and respect.[30] He then argues that the ultimate question of political theory is identifying which kinds of inequalities amongst people shall be permitted. According to Dworkin, a convincing answer may only be reached if one draws a distinction between the right to *equal treatment* and the right to *treatment as an equal*. The former denotes the right to an equal distribution of some opportunity, resource or burden; the latter describes the right to be treated with the same concern and respect as anyone else. Whereas the right to treatment as an equal is said to be fundamental, the right to

[25] I Kant, *Groundwork of the Metaphysics of Morals. A German-English Edition*, M Gregor and J Timmermann trs (Cambridge, Cambridge University Press, 2011) (BA 66/7), IV 429.5; in a free translation by Pojman (n 9) 282. His theory on the social contract is more difficult, though possible, to square with egalitarian ideas. For current purposes, the analysis confines itself to describing the egalitarian implications in his moral philosophy.

[26] B Williams, 'The Idea of Equality' in Pojman and Westmoreland (n 1) 91, 94.

[27] Pojman (n 9) 282.

[28] ibid, 282 f; Williams (n 26) 94.

[29] R Dworkin, 'The Original Position' (1973) 40 *University of Chicago Law Review* 532.

[30] See R Dworkin, *Taking Rights Seriously* (London, Duckworth, 1978) starting at 223 and ibid, *Sovereign Virtue. The Theory and Practice of Equality* (Cambridge, Harvard University Press, 2000) 1.

equal treatment is derivative and more restricted. It only comes into operation if it advances the realisation of the right to treatment as an equal. As an example Dworkin analyses the right of 'one person, one vote'. Even assuming that differently weighed votes will produce greater social benefit for all, he argues that all votes should be counted with equal weight, as every other mechanism would fail to observe a person's right to treatment as an equal. Furthermore, he proclaims that individual liberties 'must be recognised only when the fundamental right to treatment as an equal can be shown to acquire these rights'.[31] So to answer the question as to which inequalities should be deemed permissible, policies that create discrepancies are allowed, if all individuals' interests are equally taken into account.[32] But the question whether all interests have been fairly contemplated is not the same as asking 'why equality matters', or—to phrase it in Dworkin's terminology—why the right to treatment as an equal shall be regarded as fundamental. The author offers a hint to his beliefs about the reasons for equality, when he gives the example of a mother having two children, one dying of a disease that is making the other uncomfortable. The mother possesses an only limited dose of a drug that can cure the disease. Her stock of the medicine is not sufficient to make both children get healthy. So how shall she decide on the distribution of the medicine? Dworkin argues that the mother would not be showing equal concern if she flipped a coin to decide who shall receive the drug (and how much of it).[33] Instead, she needs to consider both her children's situation with equal respect and compare their needs. One could dismiss this example as an irrelevant answer and maintain that Dworkin at no point in his theory explains the reasons that make him believe in the importance of equality; thereby replacing Kant's metaphysical assumption with a pure presumption.[34] Instead, one could link the drug example to the one about fair distribution of a cake given at the beginning of the chapter. Not only from the child's perspective, but also in an abstract sense, there is a 'properly basic belief'[35] that is neither subject to nor requiring further explanation that persons matter equally.[36]

iv. Libertarianist Critique

The opinion, that equality as a concept has a distinct value, is subject to two forms of criticism. There is the assertion that liberty and equality are in tension with each other[37] and that in this ongoing battle, priority should be granted to liberty

[31] ibid, *Taking Rights Seriously*, 274.

[32] ibid, 247 and 274.

[33] ibid, 227. For a discussion, see D Sabbagh, *Equality and Transparency. A Strategic Perspective on Affirmative Action in American Law* (New York, Palgrave Macmillan, 2007) 52.

[34] See for this analysis: Pojman (n 9) 284.

[35] See n 9.

[36] Pojman (n 9) 284.

[37] See for example P Westen, 'The Empty Idea of Equality' (1982) 95 *Harvard Law Review* 537, 539, with further references in fn 5.

(*in dubio pro libertate*).[38] Further, critics dispute that the concept of equality is able to express anything that cannot also be expressed in non-egalitarian terms. According to their view, egalitarians are, like universalists, interested in providing everyone with fundamental rights protection and basic needs satisfaction. Thus, they are nothing but universalists in disguise who have simply not yet become aware of their position.[39]

Turning to the first criticism, libertarians such as Hayek argue that freedom and equality stand in opposition to each other and that preference should be given to liberty. Though Hayek claims not to object to equality as such,[40] he asserts that liberty is bound to produce inequality in many respects[41] and welcomes this circumstance. Once people are given the tools to self-actualise, some will be more successful than others in the enterprise. To give an example, if two bars are opened by different people, one will most likely become more popular than the other, be it because its drinks are better mixed or its proprietor is a better host. Hayek maintains that every attempt to achieve strict equality will lead to a uniformity that limits individual freedom. To reach this conclusion, he works on the two following propositions: first, no person is capable of determining conclusively the potentialities of other human beings. A system designed to establish equality will only be possible at the cost of extensive control.[42] Second, greater capacities by some members of society must always be regarded as a gain for the community. In other words, the fact that some persons are more successful than others is positive, as it produces a net gain.[43]

One may refute his analysis on two grounds. To begin with, it seems to be based on the assumption that the capacities of different people are determined by individual choice or are simply given and thus acceptable. The fact that people can influence their talents and traits of character only to a very limited extent disproves the first part of the argument. One will never become an excellent piano player, no matter how hard one tries, if one is not musically talented. Concerning the second part, on what grounds does Hayek argue that the 'given' differences between members of society are 'acceptable'? After all, people are born with differing talents, raised in different families and come from divergent backgrounds without having any influence on the natural lottery of birth.[44] In addition, Hayek's

[38] U Klug, 'Autonomie, Anarchie und Kontrolle—Rechtsphilosophische und rechtsdogmatische Probleme' in A Kaufmann, E-J Mestmäcker and H Zacher (eds), *Rechtsstaat und Menschenwürde. Festschrift für Werner Maihofer zum 70. Geburtstag* (Frankfurt, Vittorio Klostermann, 1988) 234, 251, with reference to P Schneider, 'In dubio pro libertate' in E von Caemmerer (ed), *Hundert Jahre deutsches Rechtsleben. Festschrift zum hundertjährigen Bestehen des Deutschen Juristentages*, vol 2 (Karlsruhe, CF Müller, 1960) 263 ff.

[39] H Frankfurt, 'Equality as a Moral Idea' (1987) 98 *Ethics* 21, 32 ff.

[40] F Hayek, *The Constitution of Liberty*, 2006 printing (London, Routledge Classics, 1960) 77.

[41] ibid, 75.

[42] ibid, 85 and 88.

[43] ibid, 78.

[44] Hayek is aware of this point and limits his critique in an important way. He writes that 'the acquisition...of additional capacities...must always be regarded as a gain for that community...provided... that others are not thereby deprived of the opportunity of acquiring the same or other abilities' (ibid, 78).

view is so individualised that it fails to take into account that the exercise of personal freedom takes place within a community. With minor exceptions, personal success depends on other people's working power and commitment. Without their support of our actions, we would not be able to materialise our own capacities.

More fundamentally, just as one might state that achieving equality in various ways creates limitations on freedom, one can say that liberties create limitations on equality.[45] Total equality will lead to uniformity, but in turn, 'total liberty of wolves is death to lambs'.[46] The fact that the two principles are in tension with each other does not make it necessary to renounce equality for the sake of liberty or vice versa.[47] Rather, one should strive to find the proper balance, with the scales leaning in some instances more to the side of liberty and in other instances more towards equality. Nothing more, but also nothing less, is the demand of egalitarians, who think that equality matters as one concept among others. Alternatively, one may dissolve the alleged tension between equality and liberty by reconciling the two notions in one cogent concept. One strand within egalitarian theory proclaims that liberty guarantees are nothing else than concretisations of the overarching right to be treated as an equal.[48] Adherents to this view hold for example that the right to freedom of speech is an expression of the basic ideal that everyone should have an equal say or that no one's opinion should a priori be higher estimated than any other's.

This inclusive approach brings us to the second criticism, namely that egalitarians are not so much interested in equality, but rather desire every human being to have as much of the good things as possible. For instance, Frankfurt in his essay *Equality as a Moral Idea* writes that the actual intention of egalitarians is not so much to abolish quantitative discrepancies, but to ameliorate qualitative conditions. He claims that they are concerned about the fact that certain people have too little, not about these people having less than others.[49] Therefore, Frankfurt uncouples his interpretation of egalitarian ideas from comparative conceptions. The distribution of goods (including fundamental rights protection) and burdens is important not in relative, but only in absolute terms. This approach is in line with his perception that the pursuit of equality makes people focus on the wrong factors. He argues that they, instead of looking at the particular features of their life, constantly compare their situation to those of other members within

[45] Similar in reasoning K Hesse, 'Der Gleichheitsgrundsatz im Staatsrecht' (1951/52) 77 *Archiv des öffentlichen Rechts* 167, 203.

[46] S Fredman, *Discrimination Law* (Oxford, Oxford University Press, 2002) 23.

[47] eg P Kirchhof, 'Der allgemeine Gleichheitssatz' in J Isensee and P Kirchhof (eds), *Handbuch des Staatsrechts der Bundesrepublik Deutschland*, vol 5, 2nd edn (Heidelberg, CF Müller, 2000) § 124 marginal nos 103 ff, especially 104.

[48] Dworkin's remarks in *Taking Rights Seriously* (London, Duckworth, 1978) 227 serve as a prime example of this reasoning.

[49] Frankfurt (n 39) 32.

a society.[50] Yet, Frankfurt's argument disregards the elements of *scarcity* and *community*. So long as goods are scarce, their distribution amongst individuals matters. This can be easily seen by looking at the drug example, where the mother has to choose whom of her children to administer the last dose. Were there sufficient medicine for both of the children, there would be no need to discuss the question of the fairest distribution. Both children would get the doses necessary for them to become well again. But even in the case of sufficient goods to satisfy everyone's basic needs, the question on their fair distribution will not cease. It is fallacy to believe that men will stop comparing themselves with others as soon as they have reached a level of adequate living. The cake example, given at the beginning of the chapter, deals with this second consideration. Joe will not stop asking why his brother has received a bigger slice, just because he has gotten one himself. He wants to assess in abstract terms whether he considers the distribution a fair one. Given the fact that we do not live like hermits, but in a community, it is unavoidable that we compare our situation to that of others.

v. *Résumé*

The preceding paragraphs intended to address the overarching question of 'why equality matters'. Their purpose was to explain that one should value equality as a philosophical concept, because it enables us to ascertain the relative dimension of human relationships when making moral judgements. It gives us the tools to argue that individuals are entitled not just to treatment with respect, but to treatment with the *same* respect as other members of society. Suffice to say that some critics will disagree with the explanation offered; but this is the case with all fundamental questions of life and ethics.[51] However, even people remaining unconvinced that equality is a morally meaningful concept will accept the statement that many persons have chosen it as a point of guidance. It is a basic structural principle within democratic societies. In addition, not just in the public, but also in the private realm, a large majority of people have chosen to act according to the standard of equal respect. This indicates that a simple reason for upholding the ideal of equality can be detracted not by looking at its almost untraceable origins, but by examining its outcomes: the belief in equality helps us form a better, *fairer* society[52] and ensure societal peace.

[50] ibid, 22.

[51] R Posner quotes in *How Judges Think* (Cambridge, Harvard University Press, 2008) 100 a passage of the Savoy opera *Iolanthe* by A Sullivan and GS Gilbert that is on the point:

> I often think it's comical ...
> How Nature always does contrive ...
> That every boy and every gal
> That's born into the world alive
> Is either a little Liberal
> Or else a little Conservative!

[52] See E Chemerinsky, 'In defense of Equality: a Reply to Professor Westen' (1983) 81 *Michigan Law Review* 575, 599.

B. Reasons for Equality as a Legal Concept

Yet, this cursory reply to the bigger question of 'what are the reasons for equality as a moral concept?' has not answered why equality matters as a legal concept. The obvious answer seems to be that the legal concept aims at realising the moral concept within its sphere and with the tools particular to the legal domain. Laws shall be drafted in a manner respectful of equality, courts and administration shall apply them fairly, and private contracts shall not exploit any given imbalance of power between the parties. These approaches then ensure that each individual is treated with equal respect.

Besides this explanation, the debate as to the validity of equality as a moral notion is paralleled by a separate, independent discussion on its value as a legal notion. Westen initiated one of the more prominent and influential rounds in the ongoing discourse with his article *The Empty Idea of Equality*.[53] The exchange of arguments that followed his publication is characteristic of the debate on the legal general principle of equality. Westen's hypothesis is that equality—a term which is for him captured in the expression that 'people who are alike should be treated alike'[54]—cannot add anything valuable to legal discourse and is therefore an empty idea. To his mind, statements of equality logically entail simpler statements of freedom rights and the transformation of freedom rights arguments into equality statements creates conceptual confusion.[55] He bases his assessment on two arguments: first, in order to find out which people are alike, one needs to define a point of reference. This definition implies moral judgement, therefore 'alike people' are such who shall be treated alike according to our moral estimations. Therefore, he argues, we have successfully replaced 'people who are alike' with 'people who shall be treated alike' and arrive at the tautological statement that 'people who … should be treated alike should … be treated alike'.[56] As Greenawalt summarises the argument: 'Given the presence of a standard indicating how various people are to be treated, the idea of equality adds nothing to the determination of proper treatment and is therefore superfluous'.[57]

Westen's second criticism concerns not so much the inner logic of the principle, but rather challenges the assumption that equality has an impact on the application of rules. He writes that equality is usually referred to when one wants

[53] Westen (n 37) 537. For more recent contributions to the debate, see, eg S Moreau, 'In Defense of a Liberty-based Account of Discrimination' in D Hellman and S Moreau (eds), *Philosophical Foundations of Discrimination Law* (Oxford, Oxford University Press, 2013) 71 and D Hellman, 'Equality and Unconstitutional Discrimination' in D Hellman and S Moreau (eds), *Philosophical Foundations of Discrimination Law* (Oxford, Oxford University Press, 2013) 51.

[54] Westen (n 37) 539.

[55] ibid, 542.

[56] ibid, 547.

[57] K Greenawalt, 'How Empty is the Idea of Equality?' (1983) 83 *Columbia Law Review* 1167, making reference to Westen (n 37) 547.

to state that laws should be applied in a consistent manner; that is to say that a rule should be applied each time in accordance with its own terms.[58] He then concludes that to state that 'likes shall be treated alike' amounts to nothing more than saying that 'every person should be given his due'.[59] Hence, the clarification of what one can consider as 'due' becomes the essential issue. To his mind, the interest of legal academics as well as practitioners should lie with the furtherance of coherent freedom rights adjudication that dispenses with the concept of equality.

But does Westen's thesis hold true that legal equality is nothing but a shallow concept that distracts us from examining the 'real' questions about freedom rights protection? His fundamental critique, which admittedly has an appeal at first sight, has been followed by multiple essays defending equality as a valuable legal principle.[60] A first defence analyses the claim that the statement 'likes shall be treated alike' is a circular concept. To recall, Westen claims that 'the answer to the question "who are 'like' people" is "those who should be treated alike;"'[61] and that the formula is therefore tautological. Chemerinsky argues that Westen might have been successful in establishing that the answer to the question 'who are "like" people' can be formulated as 'those who should be treated alike'.[62] But he continues by stating the sentence would only be tautological, if one answered the question 'who shall be treated alike?' with the words 'like people'. According to Chemerinsky, his colleague would not answer to 'who should be treated alike?' with the words 'like people'. 'Instead, one is referred to a set of values which society uses to decide which people we want to treat the same and which differently'.[63] Thus Westen's criticism of the concept of equality may be reduced to the declaration that it is contingent upon other moral estimations.[64]

In connection, critiques argue in a second defence to Westen's theory that it rests on an error in reasoning, when it asserts that equality is a superfluous concept. *The empty idea of equality* points to the fact that equality is insufficient to answer legal challenges. But to therefore derive 'that because equality is insufficient it is also unnecessary is to commit a basic logical fallacy'.[65] Westen has skilfully demonstrated that equality alone will not do to decide cases, but he has not shown that we can do without it.

[58] Westen (n 37) 551.

[59] ibid, 557.

[60] To list some of the most prominent replies: A D'Amato, 'Is Equality a Totally Empty Idea?' (1983) 81 *Michigan Law Review* 600; Chemerinsky (n 52) 575; Greenawalt (n 57) 1167; K Simons, 'Equality as a Comparative Right' (1985) 65 *Boston University Law Review* 387.

[61] Chemerinsky (n 52) 578. Further on the discussion A Somek, *Rationalität und Diskriminierung. Zur Bindung der Gesetzgebung an das Gleichheitsrecht* (Vienna, Springer, 2001) 599 f.

[62] Chemerinsky (n 52) 578.

[63] ibid.

[64] For the fully developed argument, see ibid, 578 f.

[65] ibid, 576.

Nevertheless, these two objections cannot invalidate Westen's theory in its entirety, because the argument is more complex. The author suggests that each claim, phrased in equality rights terms, can be articulated in freedom rights terms. He assumes that freedom rights can perform the task now commonly believed to be assigned to equality. For this reason, he introduces the notion of 'comparative conditional rights' that call for 'quantitatively identical treatment'.[66] For example, he argues that one should understand the American privileges and immunities clause ('The Citizens of each State shall be entitled to all Privileges and Immunities of Citizens in the several States')[67] not as a concretisation of the principle of equality, but rather as a liberal guarantee. In his opinion, the clause is framed in the form of a 'comparative right', that provides for the 'quantitatively identical treatment' of persons.[68] However, the effects of this shift in assessment away from equality towards freedom rights amount to nothing more than a change in labelling.[69] Even under his proposal, the judge has to ask how to provide for the same, equal, quantitatively identical treatment of people in a like situation when interpreting the clause; the terms same, equal and quantitatively identical being wholly interchangeable in this exercise. Further, the introduction of such abstract subcategories within freedom rights stands in contrast to the aim of Westen's theory, namely to simplify fundamental rights theory.

In addition it cannot explain certain legal practices. If one recalls a range of recent equality decisions by national constitutional courts or the European Court of Justice and asks whether they could have been decided strictly in terms of freedom rights, one will answer in the affirmative in some instances. The reasoning would potentially be more burdensome, but nevertheless possible. For example, instead of asking why one group of persons were not addressees of a beneficiary measure whilst others were, one could ask whether it was legal to exclude a certain group of persons from receiving the benefits, given the measure's impact on their fundamental rights. In other instances, this exercise is doomed to fail exactly because freedom rights are not designed to address relative elements.

Even if Westen's critique is ultimately refuted, his work is of distinctive value, because it exposes the weaknesses in the theory of legal equality.[70] It highlights that the concept is so undefined and that so many views are held with regard to its content, that legal argumentation with egalitarian components can be quite confusing and therefore unsatisfactory. In order to clarify and to obtain a better understanding of the general principle of equality, the next section will explain its prevailing conceptions and set them in relation to each other.

[66] Westen (n 37) 554 ff.
[67] Art IV, s 2, cl 1 US Constitution.
[68] Westen (n 37) 554 ff.
[69] See Chemerinsky (n 52) 597; Greenawalt (n 57) 1179.
[70] Chemerinsky (n 52) 599.

II. WHAT KIND OF EQUALITY?

A. From Formal to Substantive Equality

The oldest notion of equality is formal equality. In its most elementary form, it holds that 'likes shall be treated alike'. To recall, this statement is the one Westen relies on in his critique of equality and has been alluded to in the preceding passages. For the purpose of this analysis, it may nevertheless be useful to portray the conception in greater detail. The prime assumption of formal equality is that the general principle of equality sets forth that a law shall be applied *equally* to all persons who meet its legal requirements. Under this reading, equality ought to be understood as 'equality before the law'.

Its proponents would consider the following statement as a proper depiction of the principle of equality at work:

Instead of arguing that

> *A, B, and C, who have all lost their job, shall receive unemployment benefits (1),*

one may express their entitlement in these terms:

> *A, B, and C shall be treated alike with respect to the benefits, as they are all unemployed (2).*[71]

In the opinion of supporters of a formal equality reading, statement (2) is a proper postulation of the principle that 'likes shall be treated alike'. However, such an interpretation bestows upon the equality guarantee a merely derivative and descriptive character. The significance of the equality guarantee is limited to the statement that A, B and C shall be treated alike, because all meet the prerequisite of unemployment that was established in statement (1). In other words, statement (2) only expresses the consequences of the application of statement (1) and puts forward that A, B, and C are *equally* entitled to unemployment benefits. But if one limits the meaning of equality in such a way, the word *equally* in the last sentence will serve no purpose. Statement (2) then merely conveys that laws should be applied when their conditions are met.[72] To summarise, according to its formal notion, the principle of equality only postulates that the requirements of a norm need to be adhered to in every case. For this reason, one may call it the *derivative* or *lexical* reading of equality,[73] though it is more widely known under the name 'Aristotelian principle'.

It was given its name because Aristotle addressed the subject in the fifth book of his *Nicomachean Ethics*.[74] But in fact, the formula bearing his name is only

[71] Simons devises this logical deduction albeit without this specific example in his essay, see Simons (n 60) 393 ff.

[72] ibid.

[73] ibid, 394.

[74] Aristotle, *The Nicomachean Ethics*, H Rackham tr, 9th edn (Cambridge, Harvard University Press, 1975) V.3. 1131a10–b15. Further explanations on his understanding of the concept may be found in

a curtailed version of the philosopher's remarks. Aristotle asserted that equality meant that 'likes shall be treated alike and unalikes be treated accordingly',[75] and thus proposed a proportionality model for equality. In his view, people had different merit, be it because of their free or unfree birth, their wealth or their virtue. This conviction made him argue for a distribution of assets amongst people in proportion to their differing individual merit. As a result, he thought that every allocation of assets that deviated from such ideal proportional distribution violated the principle of equality. Therefore, Aristotle's postulation of strictly proportional equality means not so much that alike persons shall be treated alike, but rather that people may only be treated alike, if they feature an *exactly equal degree* of some characteristic.[76]

How this proposal can be applied in reality is subject to contestation. On the one side, it is argued that such demand for strict proportional equality is absurd, if one considers that two persons are never the same, but unique. Even if one limits one's examination to a specific, decisive characteristic, one may find people with similar, but rarely with the same attributes (in quantity and quality).[77] On the other side, the European Court of Justice has decided to apply the 'real'

Politics, III.9.1280 a8-15, III. 12. 1282b 18–23. Furthermore, it shall be pointed out that Aristotle relied for his findings on Plato's works, Plato had developed a distinction between equality based on measure, weight and numbers and a proportional equality, due to which the stronger is allocated a greater share than the weaker. Plato, *Gesetze Buch I–VI* in G Eigler (ed), É Chambry and F Schleiermacher trs, vol 8/1, 2nd edn (Darmstadt, Wissenschaftliche Buchgesellschaft, 2001) VI 757; ibid, *Der Staat* in G Eigler (ed), É Chambry and F Schleiermacher trs, vol 4, 2nd edn (Darmstadt, Wissenschaftliche Buchgesellschaft, 2001) VIII 557 ff. See O Dann, *Gleichheit und Gleichberechtigung. Das Gleichheitspostulat in der alteuropäischen Tradition und in Deutschland bis zum ausgehenden 19. Jahrhundert* (Berlin, Duncker und Humblot, 1980) 40; H Haller, *Die Verrechnung von Vor-und Nachteilen im Rahmen von Art. 3 Abs 1 GG* (Berlin, Duncker und Humblot, 2007) 183; Kirchhof (n 47) § 124 marginal no 47.

[75] Aristotle's conception of equality is part of a more complex theory of justice. According to him, there is a type of justice in the general sense (*iustitia generalis*). He believes this justice to be virtue in relation to others because it is the practice of laws that are themselves the expression of perfect virtue. In other words, it is the sum of lawful conduct. This justice in the general sense can be distinguished from justice in the particular sense (*iustitia particularis*). The latter is specifically concerned with the fairness of treatment, as it establishes that no person shall take more than his share. Yet, the two notions are related, as every unfair act is an unlawful act, but not every unlawful act is also unfair. Therefore, justice in the particular sense forms a subcategory of justice in the general sense. Again, justice in the general sense is divided into corrective justice (*iustitia commutativa*) and distributive justice (*iustitia distributiva*). Corrective justice operates in private transactions and aims to express that payment and reward shall be in adequate, 'arithmetical' proportion. Distributive justice, on the other hand, is at work at the apportioning of assets within a community and takes a closer look at the relation between the individual and the community. The principle governing this form of justice stipulates that a community shall distribute its assets among its members in proportion to the individuals' merit (*axia*). So the two shares of a communal asset (c, d) are in a proportional relation to the different merit of the two individuals receiving them (a, b), (a:c = b:d). See W Veith, 'Gerechtigkeit' in M Heimbach-Steins (ed), *Christliche Sozialethik. Ein Lehrbuch* (Regensburg, Pustet, 2004) 315, 317 ff.

[76] J Waldron, 'Basic Equality' (2008) New York University Public Law and Legal Theory Working Paper Series, papers.ssrn.com/sol3/papers.cfm?abstract_id=1311816. See also Smith (n 6) 64.

[77] See S Huster, *Rechte und Ziele. Zzur Dogmatik des allgemeinen Gleichheitssatzes* (Berlin, Duncker und Humblot, 1993) 41.

version of the Aristotelian principle in its adjudication. It is settled case law that the European principle of equality stipulates that 'comparable situations must not be treated differently and different situations must not be treated in the same way (unless such treatment is objectively justified)'.[78]

But even according to this amplified interpretation, formal equality that argues only for equal application of the law may not be able to explain all that there is to the principle. It encounters difficulties when it tries to explain the above given example in a slightly modified version.

Consider the following statements:

> *A, who has lost his job, shall receive unemployment benefits (1*).*
> *If A gets to receive unemployment benefits, B and C, who have also lost their jobs, shall receive unemployment benefits as well (2*).*[79]

Merely interpreting sentence (1*) will not be sufficient to argue that B and C shall receive financial support, too. An *equal* application of the rule set forth in sentence (1*) states nothing with regard to the treatment of B and C. The reasoning, applied in the second version of the example, has changed in comparison to the one explained above: whereas statement (2) only describes the consequences of a correct application of statement (1); sentence (2*) adds a substantive element to the consideration, as it asks what should be inferred from A's position in sentence (1*) for the situation of B and C. Now, one holds B and C to be entitled to receive the support because it has been promised to another person, namely A. Though B and C were, unlike A, initially not in a situation that gave them a free standing right to the benefit, their position towards A makes them eligible to receive the grant. Consequently, a relative component is introduced into the consideration, which results in, as Simons argues, B's and C's claim 'embod[ying] an equality right in an essential way'.[80] To underline the peculiar nature of this reading of equality, it is referred to as the *prescriptive* or *substantive* notion of equality.[81]

But which notion of equality, formal or substantive, should one prefer? More importantly, does one have to choose between these conceptions? Three points speak in favour of substantive equality; the third one being decisive.

[78] Inter alia Case 106/83 *Sermide SpA v Cassa Conguaglio Zucchero and others* [1984] ECR 4209, para 28; Case 203/86 *Spain v Council* [1988] ECR 4563, para 25; Case C-311/90 *Josef Hierl v Hauptzollamt Regensburg* [1992] ECR I-2061, para 18; Joined Cases C-133/93 C-300/93 and C-362/93 *Antonio Crispoltoni v Fattoria Autonoma Tabacchi and Giuseppe Natale and Antonio Pontillo v Donatab Srl* [1994] ECR I-4863, para 50; Case C-44/94 *The Queen v Minister of Agriculture, Fisheries and Food, ex parte National Federation of Fishermen's Organisations and others and Federation of Highlands and Islands Fishermen and others* [1995] ECR I-3115, para 46; Case C-304/01 *Spain v Commission* [2004] ECR I-7655, para 31; Case C-141/05 *Spain v Council* [2007] ECR I-9485, para 40; Case C-442/04 *Spain v Council* [2008] ECR I-3517, para 35; and Case C-59/11 *Association Kokopelli v Graines Baumaux SAS* [2012] ECLI:EU:C:2012:447, para 70.

[79] The example seeks to illustrate the argument by Simons (n 60) 393 ff. See also Somek (n 61) 600.

[80] Simons (n 60) 394.

[81] ibid.

The first argument goes against formal equality and holds that such reading of equality contributes to preserving the status quo. Its very character is the focus on an appraisal of the facts as they are found in reality. Formal equality neither has the aim to pursue nor the potential to achieve social change. Instead, it serves as a means to ensure the equal application of the law. Interestingly, proponents of formal equality attached importance to the concept as a tool to secure the differences between castes within society.[82] This latter finding stands in stark contrast to one of the contemporary understandings of equality law, which sees it as a progressive tool for social change.[83] However, adherents to formal equality can defend their point of view by saying that they value such prospect differently. Consequently, the argument does not disprove the validity of formal equality. Depending on an interpreter's approval or disapproval of change through law, he or she will lean more towards substantive or formal equality.

A second justification for preferring the legal conception of substantive equality is that it fits with the philosophical deliberations on 'why we should care about equality'. As established above, key to understanding the concept of equality is the critical acclaim of its relational aspect. Equality has its place within law and morals, because it draws attention to the fact that people live in communities and assess their condition not only in absolute terms, but also in comparison to others. The formal notion has difficulties in conveying this feature. The substantive notion, on the other hand, can better include the relational aspect in its theory. Yet, again, this argument may be dismissed by proponents of formal equality on the grounds that they disagree with the assessment of the reasons for equality in the first place.

What tips the scale in favour of the substantive conception is the third point: formal equality fails to explain that laws can be tested according to egalitarian standards, whereas substantive equality is capable of doing so. Since it is nowadays common to test a norm's compatibility with the general principle of equality and since formal equality cannot account for this fact, substantive equality is the proper interpretation. To elaborate further on the point, many constitutional texts stipulate that the legislature shall be bound by an equality guarantee. As for Germany, the binding force of the principle is stipulated in Article 1(3) Basic Law.[84] Regarding the European Union, Article 6 TEU sets forth that Commission,

[82] Haller (n 74) 183 with reference to Aristotle (n 74) V 5 (1130b–1131a); V 7 (1131b). One should also keep in mind that the group of 'beneficiaries' of equality that Aristotle had in mind was very limited. Only men with full citizen status had a right to equal treatment. Oppressed groups, such as women and slaves, did not even feature in his theory of equality. For a critical analysis of Aristotle's beliefs on gender (in)equality, see E Spelman, *Inessential Woman. Problems of Exclusion in Feminist Thought* (Boston, Beacon Press, 1988) 37 ff.

[83] A point, which I will turn to in great detail in ch 6.

[84] Art 1(3) Basic Law: 'Die nachfolgenden Grundrechte binden Gesetzgebung, vollziehende Gewalt und Rechtsprechung als unmittelbar geltendes Recht'. In English: 'The following basic rights shall bind the legislature, the executive, and the judiciary as directly applicable law'.

Council and Parliament are, when drafting laws, bound by fundamental rights, as stipulated in the Charter and common to the traditions of the Member States. Looking at these provisions, the questions with regard to equality become: has the legislature devised a fair law? Has it drawn correctly the boundaries between people falling within its scope of application and those remaining outside of it?[85] The assessment turns to the inner soundness of the norms. A formal interpretation of equality is unable to give an answer to these questions. The statement that a law shall apply equally to each person falling within its ambit does not resolve the issue of the norm's internal legitimacy. It simply rests on the assumption that the law is in accordance with the Constitution;[86] a supposition that does not square with the legislature's obligation to respect constitutional equality guarantees. The substantive conception, on the other hand, is more easily reconcilable with the legislature's commitment to fundamental rights, because it leaves room for considerations with respect to a law's fairness, not just to the fairness of a law's application.

Yet, two qualifications are in order: even though this thesis argues that substantive equality is the preferable reading of the principle, formal equality still has many followers and is employed by courts throughout Europe as the valid conception of equality. Second, the move from formal to substantive equality creates its own difficulties. The sentence 'likes shall be treated alike' has lost all of its supposedly apparent simplicity. Instead, value assessments and moral convictions come to the fore. The question as to 'who shall be treated alike?' is to a great extent replaced by the question 'what is to be considered alike?'. The legal theorist (and later judge at the German Federal Constitutional Court) Leibholz pointed to this newly arisen dilemma when he said that equality as a legal concept is not to be confused with an *égalité mathématique*.[87] It might be easy to assess whether two numbers are equal; but to argue that two persons or two situations deserve equivalent treatment in law and morals is a different exercise.

B. The Diversity of Substantive Equality

Which values shall be taken into account? With regard to which criteria shall people be treated equally? These are the very basic, yet complex questions on the nature of substantive equality. Unsurprisingly, people disagree regarding the correct design of the conception in detail. Their ongoing discussion can be divided into a debate that focuses on the legal notions of substantive equality and a philosophical debate taking place under the heading 'equality of what?'. As this analysis is concerned with the general principle of equality in jurisprudence, the following sub-chapter

[85] Greenawalt (n 57) 1177.

[86] See for example Chemerinsky (n 52) 583 f.

[87] G Leibholz, *Die Gleichheit vor dem Gesetz. Eine Studie auf rechtsvergleichender und rechtsphilosophischer Grundlage* (Berlin, Otto Liebmann, 1925) 38; see also Haller (n 74) 207 f. Westen uses a similar expression, see Westen (n 37) 583.

seeks to concentrate on the most prominent views held in the legal debate. Where suitable, their assessments will be linked to the 'equality of what?' debate within political philosophy.

A first definition given is the one of *equality of result*.[88] According to this reading, substantive equality is concerned with achieving a fair distribution of burdens and goods. These shall be allocated in such a manner, that the result be equal.[89] To put it differently, the *effects* of measures on individuals are the relevant criteria for equal treatment. One may illustrate this thought with the help of the example of women's quota—a theme I will turn to in greater detail in chapter 6. A society has realised that its private companies employ few women in leading positions and finds this fact dissatisfying. To counter the underrepresentation of women in the work force, the state authorities decide to introduce a quota for women in executive positions. Until representation of women on executive boards matches the percentage of women within society, measures will be applied that call for their preferential treatment. The state thus aims at a—according to its belief—fair distribution of the good 'participation in economic resolution taking'. In order to achieve this goal, it is willing to introduce far reaching measures.

Within the philosophic debate, there has been the suggestion of 'equality of welfare' as an interpretation of substantive equality that approximates to 'equality of result'.[90] It resembles the claim for 'equality of results' in so far as it demands an equal level of welfare for all individuals within a society; welfare being defined as personal preference satisfaction. In the end, each person shall receive the support necessary to reach a level of individual welfare that is equal to the level of all other members of society.

As these short explanatory remarks show, 'equality of result' is a far reaching conception. It calls for the privileging of certain groups, until an equal outcome has been achieved. This point of view is problematic in that it may intervene significantly in people's lives. As Hayek pointed out in his aforementioned critique, it takes thorough inquiries to make the assessment of whether the result of equal distribution has been achieved.[91] Even more, if one wants to achieve equality in result, one's decision will almost inevitably be based on broad generalisations. The prescribed harmonisation measures run the risk of not paying attention to the prime underlying egalitarian theme, namely that each individual is entitled to equal respect. A further point of criticism is that 'equality of result' does not take

[88] For an alternative account of the core conceptions of equality see C McCrudden, 'Equality and Non-Discrimination' in D Feldman (ed), *English Public Law* (Oxford, Oxford University Press, 2011) 581, 582 ff. The author perceives the principle of equality to contain the notions equality as rationality, equality as protective of prized public goods, equality as preventing status-harm and equality as a positive duty.

[89] Fredman (n 46) 11.

[90] For a good introduction into the discussion, see Alexander and Schwarzschild (n 3) 85 and Dworkin (n 3) 185.

[91] Similar Hayek (n 40) 75 ff, especially 77. This concern also underlies his work. *The Road to Serfdom* 50th anniversary edn (Chicago, University of Chicago Press, 1994).

personal responsibility, that is to say the belief that each person is responsible for his decisions and actions, sufficiently into account.[92] Whether members of society exert themselves to reach a certain result has no impact on the outcome to which the 'equality of result' aims. If people are willing to contribute to the realisation of a goal, their efforts will not be recognised. Conversely, individuals that show no interest in contributing to the cause will receive greater support to reach the stated aim.

For these reasons, the alternative '*equality of opportunity*' has been suggested. It rests on the belief that opportunities in advancement, as well as in benefits and resource distribution should be freely available to all members of a society.[93] How they use these opportunities then falls within their responsibility.[94] Therefore, it is in conformity with the approach of 'equality of result' in so far as it seeks to abolish adverse circumstances, on which individuals have no influence. Yet, it also differs from it, as it attaches greater importance to personal responsibility.[95] Concerning the question on the proper criteria for equal treatment, 'equality of opportunity' suggests that people's opportunities to reach certain goals in life are the appropriate points of reference. The definition of these goals then depends on the context. Turning back to the example of quotas for women, a society following the notion of 'equality of opportunity' would also name 'representation of women in the workforce' as a desired goal. Yet, it would only ensure that women are not barred from access to high ranking positions due to their gender and would provide for equal education and training opportunities for men and women. As the illustration shows, the conception calls less strictly than 'equality of result' for equalisation measures. At the same time, the approach goes beyond the demands of formal equality, because it includes considerations looking beyond the given status quo

[92] Against 'equality of welfare', a further objection has been raised. The conception calls for an equal level of satisfaction in life for all members of society, but people have different preferences in life. Some are satisfied with very little, while others develop expensive tastes. So, some might be satisfied with drinking water, while others reach the same level of satisfaction only through the enjoyment of a glass of champagne. 'Equality of welfare' is criticised for allocating a greater part of a good to persons that have developed a more expensive taste. See for the critique: Dworkin (n 3) 48 ff.

[93] For further introductory reading on the topic, R Arneson, 'Equality and Equal Opportunity for Welfare' in Pojman and Westmoreland (n 1) starting at 137, respectively 229 and Sadurski (n 2) 81 ff. Roemer offers a slightly different definition of equality of opportunity, J Roemer, *Equality of Opportunity* (Cambridge, Harvard University Press, 1998) 1. In his mind, 'two conceptions of equality of opportunity are prevalent today in Western democracies'. One is concerned with the establishment of a level playing field, so that all will eventually have the same potential in competing for a position. The other conception claims that all individuals who possess the attributes relevant for a position, should have the same chances of running for it. The second can be regarded as the classic formulation which holds that careers should be open to talents and is referred to as formal equality of opportunity. See further Stanford Encyclopaedia of Philosophy, plato.stanford.edu/entries/equal-opportunity/#1 and D Strauss, 'The Illusory Distinction between Equality of Opportunity and Equality of Result' (1992) 34 *William and Mary Law Review* 171, 173.

[94] Strauss (n 93) 171.

[95] Similarly, Somek has identified 'equality of opportunity' as a 'combination of competitiveness and solidarity', see A Somek, *Engineering Equality. An Essay on European Anti-Discrimination Law* (Oxford, Oxford University Press, 2011) 83.

in its notion of equality. This constellation makes Fredman argue that 'equality of opportunity' 'steers a middle ground between formal equality and equality of results'.[96]

If one wanted to link legal 'equality of opportunity' to the debate within political philosophy, the notion of 'equality of resources' would come close. Dworkin, as one of its fiercest proponents, argues that the real difficulty of egalitarian reasoning lies in reconciling personal responsibility for one's actions with the collective responsibility of showing equal concern to all. His theory attempts such reconciliation by proposing to compensate for all disadvantages that the natural lottery has imposed upon individuals, but not for such disadvantages that have been created through an individual's choice.[97] Notwithstanding the similarities, his theory of 'equality of resources' is said to depart from the commonly held view on 'equality of opportunity' as it also demands for compensation of unequal innate gifts.

These observations reveal the challenge of substantive equality theory: it is an intricate exercise to draw the line between those factors that shall entitle an individual to compensation and those that shall not. In connection, it becomes difficult to explain the precise differences between equality of opportunity and equality of results. Strauss examined this subject matter in the article *The Illusory Distinction Between Equality of Opportunity and Equality of Result.*[98] In line with Dworkin's approach, he asserts that the underlying assumption of 'equality of opportunity' is 'that a person's fortunes should not be determined by factors over which he or she has not control'.[99] In a second step, he also agrees with Dworkin that people should thus be compensated for a lack of talents and abilities, upon which they have no influence.[100] Further, he acknowledges that such compensation is difficult to achieve. The innovative part of his research is the conclusion he draws from the findings: society will at times have to put so much effort into the achievement of 'equality of opportunity', that the outcome will resemble 'equality of result'.[101] Therefore, the distinction between the two kinds of substantive equality is rendered useless. The sole question becomes: how much equality of opportunity do we want?[102] Apart from the fact that the term 'substantive equality' has been replaced with 'equality of opportunity', we are back to the initial question on the content of the concept.

In order to evade these obstacles, Fredman argues in favour of a *holistic* approach to the issue.[103] In her view, the comparative strategy in equality assessment—neutral

[96] Fredman (n 46) 14.

[97] To recall, equality of result is subject to criticism, as it demands that people's expensive tastes shall be accommodated just as much as the more humble persons' preferences. Since Dworkin refuses to offer remedies for differences that are the result of individual choice, his theory can rebut the expensive tastes argument.

[98] Strauss (n 93) 171.

[99] ibid, 175.

[100] ibid.

[101] ibid 178.

[102] ibid 179.

[103] Fredman (n 46) 16.

on its face—needs to be replaced with one driven by values. She suggests that her approach shall be informed by the following standards: personal dignity, remedies for past discriminations, distributive justice and participatory democracy. Fredman proposes that the consideration of these virtues will change the character of equality reasoning in such a way, that it progresses from an 'imposition of the dominant culture'[104] to a guarantee of respect for diversity. Her interpretation is in line with an understanding of equality that wants the concept to be conceived in broader terms than the approaches presented so far. To name just the most prominent assenters, the 'Critical Race Theory' movement in the United States shares this broad conception of equality.[105] While being careful not to oversimplify, Critical Race Theory argues that racism and therefore discrimination is deeply engrained in the legal context. According to the theory, the law—including non-discrimination law—is often employed in ways that entrench existing privileges. It further states that these differentiations or discriminations can only be overcome if one embraces a much broader understanding of equality than those offered by the prevailing equality conceptions. In order to develop such understanding, Critical Race Theory draws upon studies from the fields of sociology, political science, history, etc and also employs the technique of storytelling to convey its findings.

Although the approach deserves praise, since it is able to depict the context of discrimination in an encompassing manner, it will not be further pursued in this book.[106] The reason for this is that the approach is predominantly descriptive in nature.[107] Further, the broad interpretation that Fredman or scholars of Critical Race Theory give to the notion of equality entails certain difficulties when deployed in the legal field. In this respect, I want to address two aspects that merit closer attention. First Fredman's depiction seems to assume that the existing notions of equality are not guided by values, at least not to a sufficient extent. As can be seen from the analysis on the grounds for equality, as well as from the discussion on substantive equality, egalitarian reasoning is far from being free of moral judgements. To the contrary, equality has been criticised as an ambiguous concept due to its dependence on other values. Second, in the previous section it has been argued that the comparative element is the defining character of equality. Fredman proposes to replace the comparative approach in equality reasoning with a non-comparative assessment, which is guided by the above mentioned standards. Consequently, the factor, which has in this disquisition been identified

[104] ibid.

[105] For an introduction into Critical Race Theory, see, eg D Bell, *Race, Racism and American Law* 6th edn (New York, Aspen, 2008); K Crenshaw, N Gotanda, G Peller and K Thomas (eds), *Critical Race Theory. The Key Writings that Formed the Movement* (New York, The New Press, 1996) and A Harris, 'Critical Race Theory (2012) www.works.bepress.com/cgi/viewcontent.cgi?article=1030&context=angela_harris.

[106] For an application of Critical Race Theory in Europe, see M Möschel, 'Color Blindness Or Total Blindness? The Absence of Critical Race Theory in Europe' (2007/2008) 9 *Rutgers Law Review* 57.

[107] For a reasoned critique of Critical Race theory, see J Pyle, 'Race, Equality and the Rule of Law: Critical Race Theory's Attack on the Promises of Liberalism' (1999) 40 *Boston College Law Review* 787.

as unique to the principle of equality, features in her thesis merely as one element amongst others.[108]

Despite these criticisms, Fredman's work must be appreciated not only because it contributes an additional explanation to the discussion on substantive equality, but also because it highlights another ambiguity within equality reasoning, namely whether the notion shall be understood in individual or in group terms. There are two options for scrutinising equality cases: either, one assesses the particular situation of a person, or one looks at the situation of the group, respectively class, that the individual belongs to. As this thesis will later show with reference to the American affirmative action debate, equality adjudication can result in very different outcomes, depending on whether one conceptualises equality as an individual or a group based right.[109] Fredman argues in favour of a group focused perspective.

Judging from the multiplicity of views held on the subject, the participants to the debate may come to one understanding: they agree to disagree. In effect, Rae established that there are 108 notions of equality (if not more) employed in egalitarian discussions.[110] To name just a few: Result, Welfare, Opportunity, Resources, Holistic, Individual, Collective[111]—there are various conceptions on substantive equality. What is more, the content of these conceptions needs to be defined with reference to other abstract conceptions, as well. Again, as practice shows, these assessments are performed differently depending on the precise context.[112] Taking these findings together, a fragmented picture of equality analysis emerges. The fact that one cannot settle for one definition of substantive equality within legal theory promotes not only the diversity in reasoning and decisions, but also their imprecision.

C. Extension and Dilution

Looking at the state of affairs, one may recapitulate: a move from formal to substantive equality has taken place. From a procedural perspective, this transition conveys the idea that legislative acts are subject to judicial review, too. Equality

[108] See also N Bamforth, 'Conceptions of Anti-Discrimination Law' (2004) 24 *Oxford Journal of Legal Studies* 693, 704.

[109] See especially O Fiss, 'Groups and the Equal Protection Clause' (1976) 5 *Philosophy and Public Affairs* 107.

[110] Rae (n 4) 133.

[111] Not to forget additional categories, such as: equality of opportunity of welfare, equality of fair opportunity, etc.

[112] Commenting on the practice of the Federal Constitutional Court in equality review, Osterloh and Nußberger note: 'Overall, application of the general principle of equality in the adjudication of both senates of the Federal Constitutional Court proves to be a problem of balancing specific to different regulatory contexts' (L Osterloh and A Nußberger, 'Artikel 3' in M Sachs (ed), *Grundgesetz Kommentar* 7th edn (Munich, Beck, 2014) marginal no 7).

no longer means only equality *before* the law, but also equality *of* the law. Yet, as simple as it is to establish whether a law has been applied uniformly, as difficult it is to assess whether a law is fair in substance. For this reason, an alteration in the content of the principle goes along with its broadening in scope. So, looking from a material perspective, the meaning of 'likes shall be treated alike' has changed. As the preceding section tried to establish, it has become a value laden concept. Since one cannot agree as to its exact content, the formation of substantive equality has led to a dilution of its standards.

What can one infer from these findings? The preceding paragraphs established that laws are subject to equality review and that a precise definition of substantive equality remains missing. In addition, the chapter's first sub-section on the grounds for equality showed that equality has conceptual eligibility, because it enables judges, lawyers and lawmakers alike to define the relational side of fundamental rights. In the end we are sure that equality matters but we are not so sure what we actually understand by equality.

III. THE RELATIONSHIP OF EQUALITY AND NON-DISCRIMINATION

Neither are we certain about an additional topic that commonly appears in debates on the principle of equality: the relationship between equality and non-discrimination. Looking at European Union law in particular, the connection between the two is an unresolved issue. This can for example be inferred from the comments by Advocate General Kokott in her opinion on *Test Achats.*[113] She remarks: 'As there is no fundamental difference *for the purposes of the present case* between the concepts "principle of equal treatment", "principle of non-discrimination" and "prohibition of discrimination", I will use them as synonyms'.[114] But can one *generally* assume that there is no fundamental difference between equality and non-discrimination? In other words, are they two distinct concepts or not?

On a very theoretical level, Holmes investigated in her disquisition *Anti-Discrimination Rights Without Equality*[115] the relation between the principle of equality and the principle of non-discrimination. As the title already reveals, she holds the belief that the two are not only distinct, but also independent from each other. Her main argument is 'that, as a conceptual matter, anti-discrimination rights are not equal treatment norms: they do not require that all people (perhaps in a certain category) are treated the same'.[116] In her analysis, Holmes attempts to prove her claim by classifying egalitarian and anti-discrimination principles according to different categories. In this exercise, she uses the distinctions between

[113] Case C-236/09 *Association Belge des Consommateurs Test-Achats ASBL and others* [2011] ECR I-773.

[114] ibid, Opinion AG Kokott, para 29 at the end, emphasis added.

[115] E Holmes, 'Anti-Discrimination Rights Without Equality' (2005) 68 *MLR* 175.

[116] ibid.

deontological and teleological, as well as between action and non-action regarding principles.[117] A principle is deontological in nature, if it seeks to honour a value per se, irrespective of its facilitation of further goals; whereas a principle is teleological, if it seeks to promote a certain aim.[118] As far as action regarding principles are concerned, they set out to achieve 'a state of affairs constituted by human action'.[119] In contrast, non-action regarding principles are able to define their pursued goal without reference to human action.[120] What is more, Holmes holds that, if one looks at the relation between these principles, one recognises that '[n]on-action-regarding principles can only be telic ... The only way to honour the value they mention (eg utility) is by promoting it'.[121] Differently put, she argues that principles, which do not call for specific human action, only make sense in so far as they aim for a state of affairs (*telos*), which is closer to a perfect realisation of the value underlying the respective non-action-principle.

With these preliminary distinctions in mind, Holmes proceeds by examining the principle of equality in a grid of possible constellations of deontological/teleological and action/non-action regarding principles.[122] She argues that equality can be understood as an action-regarding principle, pursuant to which institutions need to treat all people in a group equally so as to honour the value of equality per se (deontological) or pursuant to which institutions are required to act in a certain manner so as to treat people in a given group equally (teleological). Further, she writes that one may also perceive equality as a non-action regarding principle, according to which one shall take every action that facilitates an end

[117] ibid, 176.
[118] ibid, with further references.
[119] ibid.
[120] ibid. Holmes gives utility as an example for a non-action regarding principle. Utility can be achieved by a variety of means and the principle of utility does not require us to follow one explicitly given course of action so as to enhance it.
[121] ibid, 177.
[122] ibid, 177–82. The most refined and relevant grid for our analysis is at 180, table 4 (strictly egalitarian principle):

	Deontic	Telic
Action-regarding	All As should be treated as some As are treated in respect of x (Substantive example: Give all children the same pocket money you give to some children)	Do that action by which all As will be treated as some As are treated in respect of x (Substantive example: Do what it takes for all children to be given the same pocket money that some children are given)
Non-action-regarding	No deontic version	Do that action by which all As will end up situated as some As are situated in respect of x (Substantive example: Do what it takes for all children to end up with the savings that some children have)

situation in which people 'end up equally situated'.[123] Via the means of this classification scheme, she illustrates the distinction between formal and substantive notions of equality, since the former seeks to promote equal treatment, whereas the latter aims to achieve equality of results.

The same compartmentalisation is then performed with respect to the principle of anti-discrimination.[124] As regards the action-regarding side of anti-discrimination principles, Holmes develops an examination that largely corresponds with the investigation on the principle of equality. She states that the action-regarding variant of the anti-discrimination principle comes in a deontological and a teleological version. On the one hand, the principle of anti-discrimination may stipulate that institutions must not discriminate on a specific ground. On the other hand, it may require institutions' actions so that certain individuals are not discriminated against. However, as far as the non-action-regarding facet of the principle is concerned, the author argues that the results of the examination of the principle of equality and non-discrimination significantly deviate from each other. According to Holmes, '[d]iscrimination names an action, a form of treatment … So discrimination is always treatment'.[125] Building upon the premise that discrimination necessarily entails action, she claims that non-action-regarding variants of anti-discrimination principles are unthinkable. Therefore, she arrives at the conclusion that equality and anti-discrimination are of an entirely different character, because the principle of anti-discrimination, in contrast to the principle of equality, does not allow for a teleological, non-action-regarding understanding, pursuant to which individuals belonging to a defined group end up situated in the same state of non-discrimination as other members of that group.

Baines summarised this rather complex account in the following way: according to Holmes' examination, comparison is used in different ways in the assessment of a violation of the principle of equality or in the assessment of the principle of non-discrimination.[126] Whereas comparison is constitutive to equality analysis, it is considered instrumental to non-discrimination analysis.[127] The crucial question is thus 'instrumental as to the pursuit of *what*?' From the fact that Holmes writes on

[123] ibid, 178.

[124] ibid 182, table 5 (Types of anti-discrimination principle):

	Deontic	Telic
Action-regarding	Do not discriminate among As on ground *R* in respect of x	Do that action by which As will not be discriminated against on ground *R* in respect of x
Non-action-regarding	No non-action-regarding version	No non-action-regarding version

[125] ibid, 183.

[126] B Baines, 'Equality, Comparison, Discrimination, Status' in F Faraday, M Denike and MK Stephenson (eds), *Making Equality Rights Real. Securing Substantive Equality under the Charter* (Toronto, Irwin Law, 2006) 73.

[127] ibid, 74.

non-discrimination that '[i]t is not the inequality that is at issue, but the *grounds* for making distinctions',[128] one must infer that she considers non-discrimination not to be confined to the pursuit of equality. She makes this point even clearer when she states '[a]nti-discrimination laws can … be justified by equality, or any other value at which they are instrumentally aimed'.[129]

Although I appreciate Holmes' approach as the most sincere attempt in legal theory (that I am aware of) to explain the relation between equality and non-discrimination, the following reflections make me believe that her conceptual differentiation does not stand up to scrutiny. First, the principle of non-discrimination is said to differ from the principle of equality due to the fact that it cannot feature a non-action-regarding version; that 'discrimination is always treatment'.[130] This statement seems to amount to no more than an assumption—an assumption that is moreover not widely shared. It appears that proof of voluntary malign treatment is needed, in order for something to be labelled discriminatory. However and with reference to European Union law, this does not match with the interpretation of anti-discrimination law according to which objective (unjustified) disadvantage is sufficient for the establishment of discrimination.[131] Furthermore, the account that discrimination is *necessarily* a form of treatment does not match with the existence of structural discrimination. According to this notion, discrimination must be understood in a broader sense as disprivilege that affects people in the entirety of their living circumstances through social, communal and economic disadvantages.[132] The question therefore is whether one can formulate a non-action regarding version of the anti-discrimination principle. Employing the terminology used by Holmes, the variant could be captured in the sentence 'Do that action by which As will end up situated in a state of affairs in which they are not discriminated against on ground *R* in respect of x'. That this statement is a reasonable alternative account of the non-discrimination principle is proven by affirmative action campaigns to take one example. There, supporting measures are introduced so that in the end, women are not discriminated on grounds of their sex (*R*) in respect of representation at the workplace (x). The second criticism on Holmes' account turns to her claim that anti-discrimination laws need not aim at greater equality. She argues that non-discrimination is not preoccupied with equality, but with 'the *grounds* for making distinctions'.[133] This sentence is

[128] Holmes (n 115) 191.

[129] ibid, 193.

[130] ibid, 183.

[131] Bieber, Epiney and Haag speak of 'material discrimination' (R Bieber, A Epiney and M Haag, *Die Europäische Union. Europarecht und Politik* 11th edn (Baden-Baden, Nomos, 2015) § 10 marginal no 6 (on Art 18 TFEU) and § 11 marginal no 36 (on Art 34 TFEU)).

[132] See E Benda, *Notwendigkeit und Möglichkeit positiver Aktionen zugunsten von Frauen im öffentlichen Dienst. Rechtsgutachten erstattet im Auftrag der Senatskanzlei—Leitstelle Gleichstellung der Frau—der Freien und Hansestadt Hamburg* (Hamburg, Leitstelle zur Gleichstellung der Frau, 1986) 7 f, with reference to employment. Further H Pfarr, 'Die Frauenquote' (1995) 12 *Neue Zeitschrift für Arbeitsrecht* 809, 811.

[133] Holmes (n 115) 191.

puzzling in its emphasis on the *grounds*, because the grounds by themselves do not contain any negative (or positive) judgement. Whether it is sex, gender, race or age—these criteria only acquire their negative connotations through the differentiations that rely on them and bring about disadvantageous effects on certain individuals. So in the end, anti-discrimination law also circles around the question 'is it justified to treat some people different than others?'.

Besides Holmes' hypothesis, there are other propositions that seek to structure the relationship between equality and non-discrimination. To begin with, one frequently encounters the view that equality and discrimination are in a state of super- and suborder. Pursuant to the presumption of equality, persons should be treated equally unless there are reasons for treating them differently.[134] Equal treatment is thus seen as the starting position. If a decision making entity then wants to differentiate, it will have to give reasonable grounds for doing so. Therefore, the burden of proof lies with the institution that intends to treat two persons or situations differently, not with the one that pursues equal treatment. Though the presumption aims to conceptualise the relation between equal and discriminatory, in the sense of differential treatment, it cannot explain why one sometimes speaks of the principle of equality and at other times of the principle of *non*-discrimination. On a less theoretical level, it is argued that the principle of equality is an overarching, general concept, whereas non-discrimination principles are more specific in nature.[135] For example, certain authors hold that non-discrimination enters the discussion when differentiations connected to special criteria are examined. If judges must decide on the legality of differentiations that can be linked to certain suspect criteria (for example race, gender, nationality), they will use the language of anti-discrimination. On the other hand, in the event that they review distinctions, which are not linked to certain tainted criteria (for example production sector, size of public procurement), they will base their assessment on the compatibility of a measure with the general principle of equality.[136] An alternative account is developed by Robin-Olivier when she argues that, at least as far as European Union law is concerned, the principle of equality is a general concept that has to be distinguished from its more specific derivatives, which constitute non-discrimination provisions.[137]

[134] See eg DE Browne, 'The Presumption of Equality' (1975) 53 *Australasian Journal of Philosophy* 46; Greenawalt mentions an additional consequence of the presumption of equality, ie 'when reasons exist both for and against equal treatment, equal treatment should be given preference unless the reasons for unequal treatment are stronger'; Greenawalt (n 57) 1175.

[135] See eg S Besson, 'Gender Discrimination under EU and ECHR Law: *Never Shall the Twain Meet?*' (2008) 8 *Human Rights Law Review* 647, 653. Seeing non-discrimination as 'another form of equality' Rae (n 4) 78.

[136] Holmes touches upon this connection when she states that anti-discrimination norms in contrast to equality provisions feature a 'forbidden ground of discrimination'; Holmes (n 115) 183.

[137] S Robin-Olivier, *Le Principe d'Egalité en Droit Communautaire* (Aix-Marseille, Presses Universitaires d'Aix-Marseille, 1999) 218 ff. Also embracing this view, G Rutherglen, 'Concrete or Abstract Conceptions of Discrimination?' in D Hellman and S Moreau (eds), *Philosophical Foundations of Discrimination Law* (Oxford, Oxford University Press, 2013) 115, 116 f.

Conversely, one can conceptualise non-discrimination to be the more comprehensive principle when compared to equality.[138] The underlying argument is that discrimination encompasses harassment, that is to say any 'conduct ... with the purpose or effect of violating the dignity of a person and of creating an intimidating, hostile, degrading, humiliating or offensive environment,'[139] whereas equality is only inadequately capable of depicting the aspect of making someone feel less worthy for who she is.

A further expression on the relation between equality and non-discrimination sees the principles 'as two faces of the same coin'.[140] Whereas non-discrimination focuses on a right to equal treatment and prohibits unjustified discriminations,[141] equality epitomises a 'positive' obligation 'on the part of the state and the transition towards status-based equality'.[142] Or, as Schiek sees the interconnection: 'It seems more adequate to view equality and discrimination as two different ways to approach the subject: equality mirrors the positive state of affairs one wishes to achieve by (*inter alia*) prohibiting discrimination'.[143] According to this interpretation, non-discrimination is thus either seen as an aiding principle contributing to the realisation of equality, or as the negative formulation of the principle of equality.

Given that there exists reasonable disagreement on the relationship between the two concepts and since 'constitutional *theory* must always be about constitutional *practice*,'[144] the important question to ask is how the European Court of Justice, as the institution primarily under inspection, perceives the relationship. Looking at its case law, a picture emerges that the Court considers equality and non-discrimination to be interchangeable.[145] Differently put, when the Court

[138] In this direction L Waddington and M Bell, 'More Equal Than Others: Distinguishing European Union Equality Directives' (2001) 38 *CML Rev* 587, 595 f.

[139] Art 2(3) of Council Dir 2000/43/EC of 29 June 2000 implementing the principle of equal treatment between persons irrespective of racial or ethnic origin [2000] OJ L180/22 or Art 2(3) of Council Dir 2000/78/EC of 27 November 2000 establishing a general framework for equal treatment in employment and occupation [2002] OJ L303/16.

[140] Besson (n 135) 653. Lenaerts calls them 'expressions réciproque', see K Lenaerts, 'L'Égalité de Traitement en Droit Communautaire—Un Principe Unique aux Apparences Multiples' (1991) 27 *Cahiers de Droit Européen* 3, 38.

[141] T Tridimas, *The General Principles of EU Law* 2nd edn (Oxford, Oxford University Press, 2007) 64.

[142] ibid.

[143] H Collins, 'Discrimination, Equality and Social Inclusion' (2003) 66 *MLR* 16; D Schiek, 'From European Union Non-discrimination Law Towards Multidimensional Equality Law for Europe' in D Schiek and V Chege (eds), *European Union Non-Discrimination Law. Comparative Perspectives on Multidimensional Equality Law* (Abingdon, Routledge Cavendish, 2009) 3, 10.

[144] R Schütze, *From Dual to Cooperative Federalism* (Oxford, Oxford University Press, 2009) viii.

[145] eg *Association Kokopelli* (n 78) para 70; G Barrett, 'Re-examining the Concept and Principle of Equality in EC Law' (2003) 27 *Yearbook of European Law* 117, 130; J Englisch, 'Zur Bedeutung des gemeinschaftsrechtlichen Gleichheitssatzes im Recht der Gemeinschaftsbeihilfen' (2009) 44 *Europarecht* 488, 493; Lenaerts (n 140) 38; Tridimas (n 141) 64. Considering this interchangeability problematic S Prechal, 'Equality of Treatment, Non-Discrimination and Social Policy: Achievements in Three Themes' (2004) 41 *CML Rev* 533, 543 ff.

decides on matters that concern equality and/or non-discrimination, it does not differentiate between the two concepts according to a set of established criteria. Rather, judges often seem to choose the wording, which has been employed in the relevant precedents, or which they are familiar with from their own legal background. In this context, it is important to recall that the bench at the European Court of Justice is composed of judges coming from 28 different Member States, with 28 different legal traditions. When they write decisions as rapporteurs, they employ 'equality' or 'non-discrimination' without having a particular motive for their choice of words. This trend, that the concept one is more familiar with is covered in greater detail, can also be discovered in the literature on European equality law. This is not to say that judges or commentators attach greater importance to their chosen principle, but that their legal background informs their perspective of looking at equality, that is to say non-discrimination norms. To give a brief example, German scholarship frequently stresses that the interpretation of EU equality, namely non-discrimination law, resembles the *Dogmatik* of the Basic Law's general principle of equality (*Gleichheitssatz*).[146]

To conclude, the following analysis of European equality law is informed by two insights, which may be deemed unsatisfactory by critical readers but are at least not in opposition to present theory and practice: first, legal scholarship has not yet been able to develop a commonly adhered-to distinction between equality and non-discrimination. Second, the European Court of Justice itself does not follow a coherent differentiation between the two notions. Therefore, the following chapters, which turn on the functioning of the general principle of equality in the case law of the European Court of Justice, will also employ the terms equality and non-discrimination interchangeably.

[146] See, eg Jürgen Schwarze, *EU Administrative Law*, revised 1st edn (London, Sweet and Maxwell, 2006) 545 ff.

3

Equality Testing: Different Kinds of Scrutiny

AS THE LAST chapter sought to depict, there is a variety of legitimately held views on the 'correct' interpretation of the concept of equality.[1] These differences of opinion are not confined to the level of political or legal theory, but radiate into the conceptions of the general principle of equality at the level of constitutional law. Given the absence of a homogenous understanding of equality, equality guarantees are potentially the most difficult norms to interpret in the respective constitutional rights catalogues.[2] Moreover, the difficulty of their interpretation is aggravated by the fact that equality provisions are frequently vague and general statements. The lapidary brevity of expressions, such as 'all men are equal before the law'[3] leave ample room for interpretations that are filled with pre-established convictions about the meaning of equality.

Taking these aspects together, one realises that judges are offered little guidance in their review of equality. It falls to them to assess cases according to a principle that appears in positive law in a rather undefined manner and the precise content of which is heavily disputed. The following examples taken from German constitutional case law highlight the difficulty of equality scrutiny:

> A law permits workers that have been employed in a formerly privatized clinic to switch back to employment in public service. The only ones not being granted the option are the cleaning personnel.[4]

[1] This incertitude is expressed in sentences such as 'the understanding of the principle of equality and the prohibition of discrimination are even more dependent upon historical and cultural circumstances than those of other fundamental rights' (J Kokott, 'Gleichheitssatz und Diskriminierungsverbote in der Rechtsprechung des Bundesverfassungsgerichts' in P Badura and H Dreier (eds), *Festschrift 50 Jahre Bundesverfassungsgericht*, vol 2 (Tübingen, Mohr Siebeck, 2001) 127). See also H Haller, *Die Verrechnung von Vor-und Nachteilen im Rahmen von Art 3 Abs 1 GG* (Berlin, Duncker und Humblot, 2007) 210 with further references; W Heun, 'Artikel 3' in H Dreier (ed) *Grundgesetz-Kommentar*, vol 1, 3rd edn (Tübingen, Mohr Siebeck, 2013) marginal no 1, where the author states that the historical and philosophical roots of the principle of equality shape the interpretation of Art 3(1) Basic Law.

[2] L Osterloh and A Nußberger, 'Artikel 3' in M Sachs (ed), *Grundgesetzkommentar* 7th edn (Munich, Beck, 2014) marginal no 1. In this respect, Sadurski speaks of the 'fundamental ambiguity' of the concept, W Sadurski, *Equality and Legitimacy* (Oxford, Oxford University Press, 2008) 99.

[3] Art 3(1) Basic Law ('Alle Menschen sind vor dem Gesetz gleich').

[4] *BVerfGE* 126, 29.

A norm designed to ban smoking in public areas allows restaurants to provide for closed smoking rooms. Operators of discothèques are required to enforce a strict non-smoking policy, with no exceptions granted.[5]

§ 18(1) number 18 of the German inheritance and beneficence tax exempts donations to political parties from the taxing requirement, whereas donations to voters' associations at the municipal level are fully assessed.[6]

A person who lives in a same-sex relationship and whose partner works for public service is not covered by the state's retirement pension scheme for dependants in the event of her partner's death.[7]

These four cases, ranging from matters of taxation to recognition of LGBT (lesbian, gay, bisexual and transgender) rights, have in common that they all were reviewed by the German constitutional court pursuant to the short but essential proclamation that 'all men are equal before the law'.

Given these universal challenges, it should not come as a surprise that the European Court of Justice is also confronted with the question on how to interpret the European Union's general principle of equality in a consistent manner. One can even say that its task is even more demanding than that of many of the Member State courts. Not only is it required to inform its interpretations of the general principles of European Union law through the constitutional traditions of different Member States (Article 6 TEU) but it also needs to perform non-discrimination assessments in the most diverse areas. The introduction to this book already mentioned that such review can range from assessing the compatibility of import quotas with the Union's principle of equality to questions of discrimination based on nationality or sex. As a consequence of these high demands, experts have difficulties in explaining the application of the concept by the European Court of Justice in words sufficiently clear and straight-forward that match the importance generally attributed to it. Instead, many commentators hold the view that the concept in its very general form is inconsistently applied and insufficiently supported by methodology.[8] This criticism comes primarily, though not

[5] *BVerfGE* 121, 317.

[6] *BVerfGE* 121, 108.

[7] *BVerfGE* 124, 199.

[8] See U Kischel, 'Zur Dogmatik des Gleichheitssatzes in der Europäischen Union' (1997) 23 *Europäische Grundrechtezeitschrift* 1; K Odendahl, 'Gleichheit vor dem Gesetz' in S Heselhaus and C Nowak (eds), *Handbuch der europäischen Grundrechte* (Munich, Beck, 2006) § 43 marginal nos 26, 30–32; A Sattler, 'Allgemeiner Gleichheitssatz und spezielle Gleichheitssätze in der Rechtsprechung des Europäischen Gerichtshofes' in J Ipsen and E Schmidt-Jortzig (eds), *Recht—Staat—Gemeinwohl: Festschrift für Dietrich Rauschning* (Cologne, Carl Heymanns, 2001) 251, 267; HJ Schütz, T Bruha and D König, *Casebook Europarecht* (Munich, Beck, 2004) 839; similar H Jarass, *EU-Grundrechte* (Munich, Beck, 2005) 290 f. C McCrudden and S Prechal speak of 'methodological confusion' in 'The Concepts of Equality and Non-Discrimination in Europe: A practical approach' in European Network of Legal Experts in the Field of Gender Equality, 1, www.ec.europa.eu/social/BlobServlet?docId=4553&langId=en. Less critically, D Schiek points out in 'From European Union non-discrimination law towards multidimensional equality law for Europe' in D Schiek and V Chege (eds), *European Union Non-Discrimination Law: Comparative Perspectives on Multidimensional Equality Law* (London, Routledge-Cavendish, 2009) 3, 5 that European non-discrimination law is very fragmented.

exclusively, from German scholarship with its emphasis on *Dogmatik*, namely the exercise of giving a logical coherent account of law's controlling values, justifications and problem solving mechanisms.[9]

In opposition to these appraisals, this analysis argues that there is more coherence and theoretical underpinning to be found in the Court's equality reasoning than one might recognise at first sight. But in order to understand the connections, we must change the perspective with which we are accustomed to look at the law and engage in a comparative institutional analysis. The chapter sets out to develop the claim in greater detail by first giving an overview of the testing standards applied by the European Court of Justice in its review pursuant to the general principle of equality. In this section, I explain that the Court tests equality cases at three different levels of intensity. Second, I present the tripartite technique by the Federal Constitutional Court in equality review to then examine how far the explanations developed in German legal doctrine can be applied to the European sphere in order to explain the diversity of testing standards. In this context, the traditional interpretive account of the European Court of Justice's workings will be presented and deconstructed. Finally, it shall be substituted with an alternative: comparative institutional analysis.

I. THREE STANDARDS OF SCRUTINY

A. EU Equality Law

Generally speaking, the European Court of Justice has developed a triad of testing mechanisms for checking whether a law is compatible with the Union's general equality clause. Its approaches range from low through heightened and then to strict scrutiny, and comprise of comparative evaluation as well as other forms of balancing. In this context, attention must be paid to three factors: first the caveat issued in the introduction needs to be briefly recalled. EU non-discrimination law is such a wide-ranging field that there has to be a delimitation of the scope of my examination. Accordingly, this chapter concerns itself with the testing standards by the European Court of Justice in regard to the general principle of equality in EU law. Only where it seems reasonable does it make reference to the directives established under Article 19 Treaty on the Functioning of the European Union (TFEU), as well as to Article 157 TFEU and the case law on women's quotas originating therein. Second, these different strands of equality testing are presented in a stylised manner in order to highlight their differences. This is not to say that the Court follows three strictly demarcated approaches, but rather, that they function

[9] B Rüthers, 'Rechtsdogmatik und Rechtspolitik unter dem Einfluss des Richterrechts' (2003) Rechtspolitisches Forum 10, www.uni-trier.de/fileadmin/fb5/inst/IRP/Rechtspolitisches_Forum/15_Ruethers_EBook_geschuetzt.pdf. Further C Bumke, 'Rechtsdogmatik' (2014) 69 *Juristenzeitung* 614.

in a continuum. Third, as regards the approaches' application, one must be aware that all three testing standards exist side by side.[10]

i. Low Scrutiny

Starting with the inquiry, the judgment in *Kind* may serve well as an example for the first standard of review.[11] In the case at hand, a German butcher claimed compensation for losses he incurred due to the enforcement of Council Regulations (EEC) No 1837/80[12] and 3191/80 on agriculture.[13] The regulations set out to achieve single reference prices for mutton and lamb within the Community and stipulated requirements for exporters to pay premiums when exporting from one Member State to another with higher mutton and lamb prices. The claimant argued that the legislation amounted to discrimination, as the regulations granted Member States discretion in choosing their specific methods of market intervention and this led to differences in the premium payment obligation depending on region. Examining the case, the judges at the European Court of Justice stated that 'different treatment may not … be regarded as discrimination … unless it appears to be *arbitrary*, or in other words, as stated in other judgments, devoid of adequate justification and not based on objective criteria'.[14] When the judges applied the formula to the case, they found the introduction of different payment obligations to be justified, as it was only temporary[15] and pursued the objective aim of a gradual achievement of a uniform agricultural market.[16]

The standard of review finds expression not only in the quoted formula, but also in similar remarks, such as: 'The principle requires that similar situations shall not be treated differently unless differentiation is objectively justified'.[17]

[10] Pointing towards this aspect Odendahl (n 8), § 43 marginal no 30.

[11] Case 106/81 *Julius Kind KG* v *EEC* [1982] ECR 2885.

[12] Council Regulation (EEC) No 1837/80 of 27 June 1980 on the common organization of the market in sheepmeat and goatmeat [1980] OJ L183/1.

[13] Commission Regulation (EEC) No 3191/80 of 9 December 1980 on transitional measures concerning non-recovery of the variable slaughter premium for sheepmeat and goatmeat products exported from the Community [1980] OJ L332/14.

[14] ibid, para 22, emphasis added. It shall be noted that 'criteria' is in this context to be best interpreted as 'grounds' or 'reasons' and not to be equated with 'criteria of differentiation'.

[15] ibid, para 9.

[16] ibid, para 24.

[17] Joined Cases 117/76 and 16/77 *Ruckdeschel and others v Hauptzollamt Hamburg-St Annen* [1977] ECR 1753, para 7. Slightly modified, the testing formula reads as follows: similar situations shall not be treated differently unless such treatment (eg see Case C-63/93 *Duff and others v Minister for Agriculture and Food, Ireland* [1996] ECR I-569, para 26; Joined Cases C-9/97 and C-118/97 *Raija-Liisa Jokela and Laura Pitkäranta* [1998] ECR I-06267, para 45; or in the context of Art 18 TFEU Case C-403/03 *Schempp v Finanzamt München V* [2005] ECR I-6421, para 28 and Case C-544/07 *Rüffler v Dyrektor Izby Skarbowej* [2009] ECR I-03389, para 59)/such a distinction (see Case C-344/03 *Commission v Portugal* [2005] ECR I-08911, para 24)/the difference (see eg Case C-313/02 *Wippel v Peek & Cloppenburg GmbH & Co. KG* [2004] ECR I-09483, para 56) is objectively justified. Further enunciations to be found in Joined Cases 424/85 and 425/85 *Frico and others v Voedselvoorzienings In- en Verkoopbureau* [1987] ECR 2755, paras 11 f; Case 167/88 *AGPB v ONIC* [1989] ECR 1653, paras 23 f; Joined

Via these statements, the European Court of Justice signifies that it will refrain from an in-depth examination of differences or commonalities of two compared situations and instead assess differential treatment only according to low scrutiny. If one interprets the approach, one sees that the judges limit themselves to checking whether there are 'reasonable grounds justifying the differentiation', or—to put it differently—whether the differentiation has to be considered 'arbitrary'. Schwarze's view is representative of this reading, in that he paraphrases the Court's case law as stating that 'the equality principle ultimately requires that there should be no arbitrary like or unlike treatment'.[18] As a matter of fact, whenever the European Court of Justice applies this low scrutiny standard in instances where it assumes two groups to be different and has been able to detect some reason for differentiation, it most commonly declares the differential treatment to be justified.

ii. Strict Scrutiny

According to a second testing standard, the Court engages in a review of strict scrutiny. The judges assess the legality of the differential treatment in light of the differences amongst two compared groups. More precisely, once they have established that they consider one group to be distinct from the other according to one specific criterion, they assess whether this 'otherness', that is to say that criterion of differentiation, justifies the groups differential treatment.[19] First, an adequate

Cases C-267/88 to C-285/88 *Wuidart and others v Laiterie coopérative eupenoise société coopérative and others* [1990] ECR I-435, paras 13 f; Case C-311/90 *Hierl v Hauptzollamt Regensburg* [1992] ECR I-2061, paras 18 and 19; Case C-56/94 *SCAC Srl v Associazione dei Produttori Ortofrutticoli* [1995] ECR I-1769, para 27.

[18] J Schwarze, *European Administrative Law* revised 1st edn (London, Sweet and Maxwell, 2006) 670; cited in G Barrett, 'Re-examining the Concept and Principle of Equality in EC Law' (2003) 22 *Yearbook of European Law* 117, 135.

The Court's intention to show its self-restrained side can also be seen by the fact that it sometimes underlines its equality reasoning with statements that emphasise on its respect for the discretion given to the legislature in the design of laws. See among others *Julius Kind* (n 11) para 24; Case 58/86 *Coopérative agricole d'approvisionnement des Avirons v Receveur des douanes de Saint-Denis and directeur régional des douanes, Réunion* [1987] ECR 1525, para 17; Case C-4/96 *NIFPO and Northern Ireland Fishermen's Federation v Department of Agriculture for Northern Ireland* [1998] ECR I-681, paras 58 ff; Case C-56/99 *Gascogne Limousin viandes SA v Office national interprofessionnel des viandes de l'élevage et de l'aviculture (Ofival)* [2000] ECR I-3079, para 38.

[19] As the description of the strict scrutiny test shows, it differs from the 'strict scrutiny' evaluation as it is known from the US constitutional context. In the US context, strict scrutiny denotes a test according to which a court has to determine (a) if the law under review serves a compelling state interest and (b) if 'the law is a narrowly tailored means of furthering' the interest or is 'the "least restrictive alternative" available to pursue' the end, A Winkler, 'Fatal in Theory and Strict in Fact: An Empirical Analysis of Strict Scrutiny in the Federal Courts' (2006) 59 *Vanderbilt Law Review* 793, 800. American constitutional scholars debate, if strict scrutiny review in their country contains or may contain elements of balancing, see R Fallon, 'Strict Judicial Scrutiny' (2007) 54 *UCLA Law Review* 1267, 1300 ff; J Mathews and A Stone Sweet, 'All Things in Proportion? American Rights Review and the Problem of Balancing' (2011) 60 *Emory Law Journal* 101, 116 f. As far as this study is concerned, strict scrutiny—unless specifically used in the US context (see ch 6)—describes a court's equality review taking place at the highest level of intensity and involves comparative assessment.

comparator—taking into account the aim of the measure—is chosen and then the differences between the selected groups are weighed against the disadvantageous effects on one of them in order to assess whether the differential treatment is justified. Thus, the judges at the European Court of Justice engage in a comparative review. In this line of reasoning, valid questions may be: if two engineers have received their education in different Member States, does it justify their differential treatment in one of those countries? Or can the criterion of age convincingly explain why older employees are treated differently from younger ones? As these examples show, when judges at the European Court of Justice perform this sort of testing, they engage in comparative review. The difference between low scrutiny and strict scrutiny equality testing is substantial: whereas pursuant to the above mentioned formula of low scrutiny, comparison between the differently affected groups is possible but not necessary, it becomes mandatory under an equality review of strict scrutiny in European law. Judges exercising strict scrutiny move beyond searching for an objective *reason* for the differentiation and towards scrutinising whether objective *differences* amongst the compared groups justify the differentiation.

This additional approach is enunciated in formulations, making reference to the leading case *Klöckner Werke*,[20] such as: 'it is settled case-law that discrimination consists in particular in treating like cases differently, involving a disadvantage for some operators in relation to others, without that difference in treatment being justified by the existence of substantial objective differences'.[21] The approach features widely in the Court's adjudication on the general principle of equality[22] and is employed regularly to test differentiations according to suspect categories'. This last heading covers measures that are connected to a history of past discrimination and distinguish according to immutable characteristics. Given that these characteristics, such as gender, race or sexual orientation, are impossible or extremely difficult to change and that people featuring them have been victims of longstanding discriminatory practices, courts usually engage in controlling such differentiations more thoroughly. Looking at the European Court of Justice's case law, one prominent example of strict review with reference to differences between groups is the Court's reasoning in cases on equal pay for men and women.[23]

[20] Joined Cases 17/61 and 20/61 *Klöckner-Werke and Hoesch v High Authority* [1962] ECR 325. It needs to be pointed out that the Court in *Klöckner-Werke* in the end did not perform strict scrutiny review, but a rather superficial assessment, see 325, 345.

[21] Case C-351/98 *Spain v Commission* [2002] ECR I-8031, para 57. See further Case 250/83 *Finsider v Commission* [1985] ECR 131, para 8; Case C-390/98 *HJ Banks & Co Ltd v The Coal Authority and Secretary of State for Trade and Industry* [2001] ECR I-6117, para 35; Case C-462/99 *Connect Austria Gesellschaft für Telekommunikation GmbH v Telekom-Control-Kommission, and Mobilkom Austria AG* [2003] ECR I-5197, para 115; Case T-217/02 *Ter Lembeek International NV v Commission of the European Communities* [2006] ECR II-4483, para 207.

[22] See for a short excerpt the previous footnote. Further Case 817/79 *Roger Buyl and others v Commission* [1982] ECR 245; Case 283/83 *Firma A Racke v Hauptzollamt Mainz* [1984] ECR 3791.

[23] As far as direct discrimination is concerned. Starting with Case 43/75 *Gabrielle Defrenne v Société anonyme belge de navigation aérienne Sabena* [1976] ECR 455; see further Case C-284/02 *Land Brandenburg v Ursula Sass* [2004] ECR I-11143; Case C-559/07 *Commission v Greece* [2009] ECR I-47.

In these instances the judges also seek to detect whether there are differences unrelated to the workers' gender that may justify differential treatment, such as the employees' length of service.[24]

iii. Intermediate Scrutiny

Between the low and the strict scrutiny assessment, there is a standard of intermediate review. Pursuant to it, the European Court of Justice engages in a review that is on the one hand more meticulous than mere testing for 'objective justifications' but that, on the other hand, does not weigh the differences between the compared groups with the negative effects on the disadvantaged group, as is symptomatic for the case law in the second category.

One can detect a typical example of this kind of reasoning in the European Court of Justice's ruling in the case *Arcelor*,[25] where the Court had to decide on the validity of a directive on the creation of a greenhouse gas emission trading scheme.[26] The directive stipulated that the trading scheme applies to installations in the steel sector, but excluded the aluminium and chemical industries from its scope. The applicants in the main proceedings were undertakings in the steel sector and complained that they were unfairly burdened by the measure, when seen in comparison to companies doing business in the aluminium and plastics sector. In the review of the case, the Court opted neither to weigh the differences between the producers with the effects of the measure on the disadvantaged group, nor to engage in an arbitrariness review. Instead, they engaged in a variation of proportionality analysis that enabled them to take into account aspects unrelated to the differences between the compared industries. More specifically, the Court examined whether there was a legitimate aim pursued by the differentiation and whether the differentiation was apt and necessary when seen in light of that goal.[27] It held that the establishment of a trading scheme was so novel and complex that it justified the legislature's step-by-step approach in initially regulating the steel sector (among others) before broadening the directive's scope to encompass aluminium or plastics producers. It argued that the inclusion of further sectors in the directive in question would 'have made the management of the allowance trading

[24] eg Case 109/88 *Handels- og Kontorfunktionærernes Forbund I Danmark v Dansk Arbejdsgiverforening* [1989] ECR 3199; Case C-17/05 *BF Cadman v Health & Safety Executive* [2006] ECR I-9583.

[25] Case C-127/07 *Société Arcelor Atlantique et Lorraine and Others v Premier Ministre and Others* [2008] ECR I-9895.

[26] Dir 2003/87/EC of the European Parliament and of the Council of 13 October 2003 establishing a scheme for greenhouse gas emission allowance trading within the Community and amending Council Directive 96/61/EC [2003] OJ L275/32.

[27] *Arcelor* (n 25) especially para 65. This method on reasoning strongly resembles proportionality analysis, as performed by courts when reviewing justifications for freedom rights infringements. For detailed information on proportionality analysis, see eg R Alexy, *Theorie der Grundrechte* (Frankfurt, Suhrkamp, 1994) 71 ff; A Barak 'Proportionality and Principled Balancing' (2010) 4 *Law & Ethics of Human Rights* 1; T-I Harbo 'The Function of the Proportionality Principle in EU Law' (2010) 16 *European Law Journal* 158.

scheme more difficult and increased the administrative burden, so that the possibility that the functioning of the scheme would have been disturbed ... cannot be excluded'.[28] Hence, the judges justified the differentiation on the ground that the legislature sought the smooth implementation of the scheme. The desired administrative ease cannot reasonably be expressed in terms of the differences between the compared sectors. After all, why was one industry burdened and not the other in exchange? Therefore, the judges assessed whether an aim, external to the groups' differences, justified the differential treatment.[29]

Similar reasoning can be detected in an analysis of the case law dealing with women's quotas[30] or the implementation of the Equality Directives.[31] Only briefly touching upon the subject, Article 157(4) TFEU[32] states that

> the principle of equal treatment shall not prevent any Member State from maintaining or adopting measures providing for specific advantages in order to make it easier for the underrepresented sex to pursue a vocational activity or to prevent or compensate for disadvantages in professional careers.

Preferential treatment of women in the workplace is permitted, even if it works to the disadvantage of individual male workers. When courts assess legislation or other measures made pursuant to the article, they do not compare the different capabilities and qualifications of applicants for a job, but balance the aim of achieving greater representation of women in the workforce against the negative effects of the quota on men's career developments. Likewise, Article 6(1) of Directive 2000/78 states that differential treatment on grounds of age may be justified, if legitimate employment policy, labour market and vocational training objectives are pursued. As a consequence, differentiations between younger and older employees may be justified along two lines of reasoning. First and just as depicted in the presentation of strict scrutiny testing, differences amongst the two groups may justify their differential treatment as long as they are not prejudicial or stereotypical in nature. Second, it is within the judge's discretion to discover justifications for differentiations, which are related to social policy

[28] *Arcelor* (n 25) para 65.

[29] S Huster, *Rechte und Ziele. Zur Dogmatik des allgemeinen Gleichheitssatzes* (Berlin, Duncker und Humblot, 1993) 213 ff, 468 and 469.

[30] Case C-450/93 *Eckhard Kalanke v Freie Hansestadt Bremen* [1995] ECR I-3051; Case C-409/95 *Hellmut Marschall v Land Nordrhein-Westfalen* [1997] ECR I-6363; Case C-158/97 *Badeck and others v Hessen* [2000] ECR I-1875; Case C-407/98 *Katarina Abrahamsson and Leif Anderson v Elisabet Fogelqvist* [2000] ECR I-5539.

[31] Council Dir 2000/43/EC of 29 June 2000 implementing the principle of equal treatment between persons irrespective of racial or ethnic origin [2000] OJ L180/22; Council Dir 2000/78/EC of 27 November 2000 establishing a general framework for equal treatment in employment and occupation [2002] OJ L303/16 and Dir 2006/54/EC of the European Parliament and of the Council of 5 July 2006 on the implementation of the principle of equal opportunities and equal treatment of men and women in matters of employment and occupation [2006] OJ L204/23.

[32] See further eg Recital 22, Dir 2006/54/EC of the European Parliament and of the Council of 5 July 2006 on the implementation of the principle of equal opportunities and equal treatment of men and women in matters of employment and occupation [2006] OJ L204/23.

objectives. Through this argumentation, they can assess whether legitimate aims for the structuring and development of labour markets are being pursued in a proportionate manner[33] and therefore take factors into account that are not related to the differences between the affected individuals.

This approach is distinguishable from the two previously presented. It differs from the low scrutiny account as it enables judges to go beyond a mere detection of objective grounds for differentiation and to balance competing interests in a thorough and systematised manner. It differs from the strict scrutiny standard because it is non-comparative in nature. In each of the mentioned instances—whether by its own choice or due to legal requirements—the Court replaces comparative equality evaluation for a proportionality analysis. As proportionality analysis equips the judges with tools that allow them to balance means with ends and to take a variety of factors into account that are otherwise barred from or difficult to incorporate in comparison, scrutiny at intermediate intensity takes place.

B. German Equality Law

This kind of equality review is not limited to European Union law but is also applied within German constitutional law at different levels of intensity. The next section aims to show that, similar to the European case law, the adjudication by the Federal Constitutional Court can be divided into three categories that are applied side by side: cases solved pursuant the arbitrariness review, legal disputes decided under the 'new' formula, and law suits ruled upon according to the proportionality formula. Building upon these findings, the subsequent passage seeks to then explore whether the doctrinal account developed for German equality jurisprudence can be utilised in order to explain the functioning of equality review at the European level.

i. The Arbitrariness Formula

An examination of German equality law reveals that the interpretation of Article 3(1) GG, the German equality guarantee, has undergone considerable evolution since the Basic Law's initial enactment. The first time the German Constitutional Court reviewed the legality of a norm regarding its compatibility with Article 3(1) GG was in its *Südweststaat* decision.[34] There the Court had to decide whether the differential treatment of different parts of the German

[33] eg Joined Cases C-159/10 and C-160/10 *Gerhard Fuchs and Peter Köhler v Land Hessen* [2011] ECR I-6919; Case C-447/09 *Reinhard Prigge and Others v Deutsche Lufthansa AG* [2011] ECR I-8003; Case C-286/12 *Commission v Hungary* [2012] ECLI:EU:C:2012:687.

[34] *BVerfGE* 1, 14. The facts of the case were the following: after the Second World War, the south-western territory of Germany was divided into three separate entities (Baden, Württemberg-Baden and Württemberg-Hohenzollern) which stood under French and American control. In order to reorganise the area, a law was created to regulate the formalities of a referendum on the issue, which stipulated

population in the course of the restructuring of the Länder after the establishment of the Federal Republic amounted to discrimination. Presented with the question, the judges took the opportunity to explicate their stance towards equality review. They held that

> the equality guarantee is violated when a reasonable ground, that is due to the nature of things or otherwise objectively plausible, cannot be found for the legal differentiation or equal treatment; in short, if the provision must be called arbitrary.[35]

This standard for review has come to be known under the name of 'arbitrariness formula' (*Willkürformel*) and requires a low level of scrutiny. Given the fact that the equality principle of the Basic Law with its general wording is imprecise, it was possible to concretise the guarantee by establishing that the demand for equality is another manifestation of the prohibition of arbitrary norm setting.[36] According to that rule, norms may only be deemed unfair and hence unconstitutional if they call for clearly unobjective differential treatment.[37] This led commentators to argue that the Federal Constitutional Court was willing to negate a violation of the equality guarantee whenever any argument, no matter how obscure, could be provided for in favour of the norm's compatibility with Article 3(1)GG.[38]

ii. The New Formula

The more frequent the 'arbitrariness formula' was applied and the more often judges rendered decisions finding laws to be in conformity with the equality guarantee, the louder critics objected to it. Essentially they argued that the

that the region was to be divided into four electoral districts and that approval in three of these districts sufficed to create a uniform Land. Questioning the legality of the law, the government of Baden challenged the norm before the Federal Constitutional Court, inter alia claiming its incompatibility with the equality guarantee. At a time when the parceling of the German territory into separate Länder was still a work in progress, it argued that the Basic Law generally demanded approval of a majority of each state's population in order to allow for reorganisation and only excluded the area of the *Südweststaat* from this requirement. The representatives of Baden considered this differential treatment as a discrimination of the Badenese people. (*BVerfGE* 1, 14 [52]).

[35] *BVerfGE* 1, 14 (52). In the original: 'Der Gleichheitssatz ist verletzt, wenn sich ein vernünftiger, sich aus der Natur der Sache ergebender oder sonstwie einleuchtender Grund für die gesetzliche Differenzierung oder Gleichbehandlung nicht finden läßt, kurzum, wenn die Bestimmung als willkürlich bezeichnet werden muss.'

[36] See Haller (n 1) 209, referring to G Leibholz, *Die Gleichheit vor dem Gesetz. Eine Studie auf rechtsvergleichender und rechtsphilosophischer Grundlage* (Berlin, Otto Liebmann, 1925) 72.

[37] Osterloh and Nußberger (n 2) marginal no 9, with reference to *BVerfGE* 12, 326 (333); 14, 142 (150); 19, 101 (115); 23, 135 (143); 52, 277 (281); 55, 72 (90); 89, 132 (142).

[38] See R Wendt, 'Der Gleichheitssatz' (1988) 7 *Neue Verwaltungszeitschrift* 778, 779 f, who argues with reference to *BVerfGE* 43, 108 that such reasons need not appear in the legal materials themselves. He states that pursuant to settled case law, the Constitutional Court holds that it suffices if reasonable grounds for differentiation exist, irrespective of the legislature's awareness of them when passing the law.

With regard to the law on the reorganisation of the south-western territory, the court in the end held that the particular treatment of the region was justified, because its fragmentation was more provisional than that of other regions and because there was a common belief that the current situation was untenable; *BVerfGE* 1, 14 (53).

imprecision of the formula deprived the testing standard of significant meaning.[39] To counter this criticism and as judges became more experienced with the interpretation of the new constitution, the desire arose to establish a more nuanced mode of equality review. Prodded by broad approval in Western German society and equipped with greater self-confidence, the Federal Constitutional Court decided to develop a testing standard that called for a higher level of scrutiny in its *Präklusion I* decision, a case that concerned the differential treatment of facts in civil proceedings.[40] In its reasoning, the judges stated:

> The general principle of equality demands that all men are to be treated equal before the law. Accordingly, this fundamental right is violated especially in the event that one group of norm addressees is treated differently in comparison to other norm addressees, although there are no differences of such kind and such extent that they could justify the differential treatment.[41]

Since with this dictum the court approved a standard of review it had disregarded before, constitutional lawyers labelled the testing standard the 'new formula' (*neue Formel*).[42] By contrast, the Court itself refrained from highlighting the statement as a development in its equality jurisprudence and introduced it as a formula that merely restated the existing testing standard.[43] Furthermore the new approach did not replace the existing one but enabled the judges to choose, depending on the context of the case, to either resort to the arbitrariness test or to employ the new formula. In fact, the novel approach was not used to solve the case before the court. Arguing on the premise that the equality clause specifically called for equal treatment of individuals, the judges reasoned that the norm in question did not differentiate between persons, but distinguished between two situations.[44]

[39] German scholarship referred to the characteristic of the 'arbitrariness formula' as 'leerformelhafte Ungenauigkeit'. See S Boysen, 'Artikel 3' in I von Münch and P Kunig (eds), *Grundgesetz Kommentar*, vol 1, 6th edn (Munich, Beck, 2012) marginal no 13; Heun (n 1) marginal no 21; R Maaß, 'Die neuere Rechtsprechung des BVerfG zum allgemeinen Gleichheitssatz—Ein Neuansatz?' (1988) 7 *Neue Verwaltungszeitschrift* 14, 20; F Schoch, 'Der Gleichheitssatz' (1988) 103 *Deutsches Verwaltungsblatt* 863, 875.

[40] *BVerfGE* 55, 72. More specifically the federal parliament had passed a law to simplify and expedite court procedures in 1976. The new provision stipulated that facts in civil law cases, which had not been presented in a timely manner in first instance, were barred from being pleaded in second instance. In the event that the facts had not at all been brought to the court's attention in first instance, their submission in second instances was however still permitted. Claimants and lower court judges perceived this differentiation to amount to discrimination and therefore referred the question of its compatibility to the Federal Constitutional Court.

[41] *BVerfGE* 55, 72 (88).

[42] Two of the first authors using the expression 'new formula' were Maaß (n 39) 14 and Wendt (n 38) 778.

[43] This course of action spurred a debate as to the observance of the standard of testing by the Court's two senates. Whereas the first senate has repeatedly cited the statement, the second senate has been more hesitant to introduce the formula, at least with regard to terminology; see Haller (n 1) 217 with reference to E Stein, 'Artikel 3 Abs. 1' in E Denninger, W Hoffmann-Riem, H-P Schneider and E Stein (eds), *Kommentar zum Grundgesetz für die Bundesrepublik Deutschland*, vol 1, 3rd edn (Neuwied, Luchterhand, 2001) marginal no 34.

[44] Namely the presentation of facts in an untimely fashion or no presentation of them whatsoever in first instance proceedings.

As a result, they applied the analysis based on arbitrariness and reached the conclusion that the norm was compatible with Article 3(1) GG.

Though irrelevant for the concrete decision, the introduction of the 'new formula' in *Präklusion I* marked the beginning of heightened scrutiny testing by the Federal Constitutional Court in equality cases. The new standard departed from the arbitrariness review in so far as it posed stricter requirements for a differentiation to be justified.

iii. Something in Between

Within German legal cycles, the two standards described above are acknowledged as integral parts of the Federal Constitutional Court's methodology for equality rights testing. Generally, they are held to exhaustively govern the mechanisms of egalitarian review.[45] Furthermore, the two expressions form part of the Court's settled case law on the general principle of equality.[46] Yet, some past cases of Germany's highest court sit uneasily with this depiction. The Federal Constitutional Court has also reviewed cases pursuant to an intermediate level of scrutiny, subjecting them to proportionality analysis known from its freedom rights testing.

The *Zweifamilienhaus* decision[47] serves as an example of this third approach towards equality testing. The case concerned a special provision in the German income tax code. It denied taxpayers, whose situation was governed under the earnings tax system for employed people, to offset certain losses. Had they not been subject to earnings tax, but instead to income tax for self-employed persons (and for recipients of other sources of capital), they would have had the chance of deduction. People that were subject to the heavier taxation scheme filed a constitutional complaint before the Federal Constitutional Court alleging that their right to equal treatment was violated. In the ruling, the following statements can be found:

> When regulating mass occurrences, as they exist especially in tax law and administration, the legislature needs not be concerned about the equal treatment of all imaginable individual cases. Rather, it is authorized to take a general point of view, which it has formed through its experiences. On this basis, it may use generalized and typified regulations,

[45] Authors relying on the dichotomy are C Brüning, 'Gleichheitsrechtliche Verhältnismäßigkeit' (2001) 56 *Juristenzeitung* 669; B-O Bryde and R Kleindiek, 'Der allgemeine Gleichheitssatz' (1999) 21 *Jura* 36; M Gubelt, 'Artikel 3' in I von Münch and P Kunig (eds), *Grundgesetz Kommentar*, vol 1, 5th edn (Munich, Beck, 2000) marginal nos 10 ff; C Gusy, 'Der Gleichheitssatz' (1988) 41 *Neue Juristische Wochenschrift* 2505; Kokott (n 1) 127; Maaß (n 39) 14; G Robbers, 'Der Gleichheitssatz' (1988) 41 *Die Öffentliche Verwaltung* 749; Schoch (n 39) 863; Wendt (n 38) 778. In contrast, authors and commentaries relying on a trichotomy of testing standards are Huster (n 29); M Kloepfer, *Gleichheit als Verfassungsfrage* (Berlin, Duncker und Humblot, 1980) and Haller (n 1) 264 ff (the last with tendency).

[46] To cite only a few judgments issued over a long period of time, employing the arbitrariness formula: *BVerfGE* 55, 114 (128); 90, 226 (239); 105, 73 (110); 123, 1 (19); 125, 1 (18). As far as the new formula is concerned, the judges refer to it as an integral part of the Federal Constitutional Court's jurisprudence, for another example see also *BVerfGE* 126, 29, citing as settled case law *BVerfGE* 55, 72 (88); 84, 197 (199); 100, 195 (205); 109, 96 (123); 110, 274 (291).

[47] *BVerfGE* 84, 348.

> without violating the equality guarantee due to the unavoidably connected hardship for certain cases. However, the typification requires that occurring hardship and unfairness *concerns only a relatively small number of persons* and that the *violation against the principle of equality is of only minor intensity*.[48]

> At last, administrative reasons cannot be invoked as arguments speaking in favour of ... [the measure]. In general, such aspects are apt to justify the differential treatment of comparable economic and social situations. But this presupposes that administrative problems of *considerable extent* would occur in the event of equal treatment, which could not be resolved by *a simpler, less affecting* regulation.[49]

> [T]he legislature is authorized to provide generalized and typifying solutions. But if this leads to considerable departures from the principle of equality that do not only *concern a relatively small number of people*, the measures are only in conformity with Article 3(1) GG, if a *less intrusive* solution, based on objective grounds, is impossible.[50]

Looking at these statements, one can first notice that the judges engaged in a thorough review in *Zweifamilienhaus*. They did not stop at assessing whether the 'provision must be called arbitrary';[51] instead, they engaged in a detailed evaluation of the effects of the norm and the practicability of its alternatives. Formulations such as 'hardship that concerns only a relatively small number', 'violation of

[48] *BVerfGE* 84, 348 (359 f), emphasis added. In the original:

> Bei der Ordnung von Massenerscheinungen, wie sie insbesondere auch im Steuerrecht und in der Steuerverwaltung auftreten, braucht der Gesetzgeber außerdem nicht um die Gleichbehandlung aller denkbaren Einzelfälle besorgt zu sein. Er ist hier vielmehr berechtigt, von einem Gesamtbild auszugehen, das sich aus den ihm vorliegenden Erfahrungen ergibt (vgl *BVerfGE* 11, 245 [254]; 78, 214 [227]). Auf dieser Grundlage darf er generalisierende, typisierende und pauschalierende Regelungen verwenden, ohne allein schon wegen der damit unvermeidlich verbundenen Härten gegen den allgemeinen Gleichheitssatz zu verstoßen (vgl *BVerfGE* 11, 245 [254]; 17, 1 [23]; 21, 12 [27]; 26, 265 [275 f]; 63, 119 [128]; 71, 146 [157]; st Rspr.). Die Typisierung setzt allerdings voraus, daß die durch sie eintretenden Härten und Ungerechtigkeiten nur eine verhältnismäßig kleine Zahl von Personen betreffen und der Verstoß gegen den Gleichheitssatz nicht sehr intensiv ist.

[49] *BVerfGE* 84, 348 (364), emphasis added. In the original:

> Für den Ausschluß der Absetzungen nach § 7 Abs. 5 EStG von der Eintragung auf der Lohnsteuerkarte können schließlich auch verwaltungstechnische Gründe nicht ins Feld geführt werden. Solche Gesichtspunkte sind zwar grundsätzlich geeignet, die Verschiedenbehandlung an sich vergleichbarer wirtschaftlicher und gesellschaftlicher Sachverhalte zu rechtfertigen (vgl zuletzt *BVerfGE* 81, 108 [117] mwN). Das setzt aber voraus, daß bei einer Gleichbehandlung erhebliche verwaltungstechnische Schwierigkeiten entstünden, die nicht durch einfachere, die Betroffenen weniger belastende Regelungen behoben werden könnten.

[50] *BVerfGE* 84, 348 (365), emphasis added. In the original:

> Zwar ist der Gesetzgeber auch hier zu generalisierenden, typisierenden und pauschalierenden Lösungen befugt. Entstehen dabei aber erhebliche Abweichungen vom Gleichheitssatz und betreffen sie nicht nur eine verhältnismäßig kleine Anzahl von Personen (vgl *BVerfGE* 63, 119 [128]), so ist Art 3 Abs 1 GG allenfalls dann nicht verletzt, wenn eine schonendere Zwischenlösung aus sachlichen Gründen nicht möglich ist.

[51] *BVerfGE* 1, 14 (52).

only minor intensity' or 'administrative problems of considerable extent' indicate that the Court took various factors into account and balanced them.

The second aspect to notice is that this balancing exercise differs from the one set out in the new formula. As has been stated before, the 'new formula' stipulates that the differences amongst the compared groups ought to be weighed against the effects of the differential treatment on the disfavoured group. In the *Zweifamilienhaus* decision, however, such assessment of the characteristic differences between the two groups of taxpayers does not take place. Instead, very practical concerns as to the administrative complexity of the measure or the number of persons affected by it are considered. Such assessments cannot be framed as a comparison, as demanded by the 'new formula', but constitute an additional approach pursuant to which it is asked whether there are aspects, other than the differences amongst the compared groups, that may justify differential treatment.

C. The Doctrinal Discourse on Equality

The evolvement of the Federal Constitutional Court's equality case law has been accompanied by critical scholarly debate on the topic.

i. Leibholz and Judicial Restraint

Leibholz developed a theory capable of explaining the courts' confinement to arbitrariness testing in equality testing, even before becoming judge at the Federal Constitutional Court and being significantly involved in shaping the Court's approach to equality review. Though a firm believer in the value of equality, he argued that the interplay between political freedom by the elected legislature and judicial checks on the exercise of this freedom called for a lenient review exercised by the Court. To summarise the author's main arguments, Leibholz established from the very beginning that two persons were never wholly alike and that the general principle of equality only intended to guarantee that individuals who were in some respect, that is to say relatively, alike had to be treated equally in that respect.[52] In other words, he believed that equality called for consideration of people's individual characteristics in a particular case.[53] Furthermore, he held the view that the decision as to who is to be considered 'relatively alike' was first and foremost within the realm of the law making process and that the judiciary was not apt to advance a coherent and accurate conception of equality.[54] For these reasons, he proposed that courts should limit themselves to checking whether the legislature had acted arbitrarily when designing a law; defining arbitrariness as the antagonism to the somehow reasonable, which could be properly followed and

[52] See G Leibholz, 'Die Gleichheit vor dem Gesetz und das Bonner Grundgesetz' (1951) 66 *Deutsches Verwaltungsblatt* 193, 195.

[53] Leibholz (n 36) 45.

[54] ibid, 74 and 78.

acted upon.[55] In his theory, he intended to employ the notion of 'arbitrariness' only to describe situations which epitomised a complete negation of equality.[56] With his comments, he not only deliberately refused to give a positive definition of equality that could have formed the basis of a testing standard but also set the stage for an extremely limited standard of review.

ii. Stein and Balancing

However as adjudication evolved towards an at times more thorough review of cases, German legal doctrine had to adapt in order to accommodate these changes. In this context, it should be mentioned that the doctrinal positioning of the 'new formula' is to this day disputed. The tendency is to consider it as an intensification of arbitrariness review, standing in continuum with the latter.[57] Expressions by the Federal Constitutional Court, such as the one that equality scrutiny, depending on the subject matter under review, 'ranges from mere arbitrariness review to stricter review according to proportionality criteria'[58] or its statement that differential treatment is only in accordance with Article 3(1) GG, if there are '*reasons* of such kind and such extent, that they justify the differential legal consequences'[59] are decisive for this reading.

The dispute centres on the problematic aspect that the new formula, originally stipulating an examination of *differences* between persons has been reformulated into a requirement for assessing the *reasons* for their differential treatment. The consequences of this argumentative shift are more far reaching than one might think at first sight. Whereas the first version is strictly comparative in nature, the second is not. Had the new formula originally been comparative and therefore much in line with the abstract conceptual understanding that equality is essentially about defining a person's human rights position relative to that of others, its later version has lost its comparative outlook and is therefore, just as the arbitrariness formula, detached from the principle's roots in legal theory.[60]

Working under the premise of this conceptual ambiguity, Stein developed in exemplary fashion a three-part testing standard to strict equality review.[61] According to his test, one (1) defines the adequate criterion of distinction and (2) establishes the aim of differentiation, (3) to then balance the two with each other.

[55] ibid, 72; see Haller (n 1) 209.

[56] Leibholz (n 36) 72. See also Huster (n 29) 48.

[57] H Jarass, 'Artikel 3' in H Jarass and B Pieroth (eds), *Grundgesetz für die Bundesrepublik Deutschland—Kommentar* 14th edn (Munich, Beck, 2016) marginal no 16.

[58] *BVerfGE* 88, 87 (96).

[59] *BVerfGE* 93, 99 (111) (emphasis added). Further, *BVerfGE* 58, 369 (374); 82, 126 (146).

[60] See A Somek, *Rationalität und Diskriminierung. Zur Bindung der Gesetzgebung an das Gleichheitsrecht* (Vienna, Springer, 2001) 342 and generally ibid, 39, 42 and 110.

[61] Stein (n 43) marginal nos 35 ff; E Stein and G Frank, *Staatsrecht* 21st edn (Tübingen, Mohr Siebeck, 2010) 405 and 412 ff. For further explanations eg A Epiney, *Umgekehrte Diskriminierungen* (Cologne, Karl Heymanns, 1995) 449 ff; Gubelt (n 45) marginal nos 17 ff; Gusy (n 45) 2507; Haller (n 1) 270; Kloepfer (n 45) 61; Schoch (n 39) 874.

Starting with the identification of an appropriate criterion of distinction,[62] the task is less formalistic than might appear. Choosing the correct (or incorrect) criterion for differentiation is the same as choosing the right (or wrong) comparator, an exercise which has been correctly labelled the most difficult and most problematic in equality review.[63] The reasons for its intricacy are twofold: although it sets the stage for the following steps of review, the equality principle does not offer any guidance for the choice. In light of the lack of guidance in positive law, the choice is largely defined by value-laden assessments and ideological predisposition.[64] Further, depending on how narrow or large one wants to define the group of comparators, it becomes more or less difficult to justify their differential treatment. In the case of narrow definition, both groups share many features making different treatment hard to justify. In the case of ample definition, the amount of similarities decreases making differential treatment seem more understandable.

Having found an adequate criterion, the aim of differentiation must be detected and held to be constitutional.[65] Approaching this question from an impartial point of view, one might consider that the aim of differentiation in a constitutional setting may be limited to the achievement of fair outcomes. So, if asked the question of the purpose of a distinction, one may answer that the line is always drawn between two cases because one believes this allocation of benefits or distribution of burden to be fair. From this perspective one may further rightly argue that the requirement is an unnecessary element in testing, as it only restates the most basic demand of the principle of equality, fair treatment.

However upon closer inspection, proponents use the phrase 'aim of differentiation' as a synonym for the 'aim of the norm itself'.[66] An example, which Kloepfer presents in his work on the testing standard, implies this understanding. The author tests a norm that grants scholarships only to persons with low income with regard to its compatibility with the equality clause. Focusing on the differentiating aspect of the law, he writes that the aim to grant scholarships only to those in financial need and not to the better off constitutes a legitimate goal.[67] Analysing the section that follows this statement, he arguably does not consider the preferential treatment of persons who could otherwise not afford higher education as the aim of differentiation. Instead, he asserts that the goal is the furtherance of scholarly opportunities.

[62] For an example of this reasoning, see Gubelt (n 45) marginal no 20.

[63] See S Fredman, *Discrimination Law* (Oxford, Oxford University Press, 2002) 98; further P Caro de Sousa, *The European Fundamental Freedoms: A Contextual Approach* (Oxford, Oxford University Press, 2015) 98.

[64] Gubelt (n 45) marginal no 17; HP Ipsen, 'Gleichheit' in F Neumann, HC Nipperdey and U Scheuner (eds), *Die Grundrechte*, vol 2 (Berlin, Duncker und Humblot, 1954) 111, 178; K Hesse, 'Der Gleichheitssatz in der neueren deutschen Verfassungsentwicklung' (1984) 109 *Archiv des öffentlichen Rechts* 174, 177.

[65] See Epiney (n 61) 451 ff; Gusy (n 45) 2507; Kloepfer (n 45) 61; Schoch (n 39) 874.

[66] Schoch (n 39) 874 only states that the aim of differentiation must be set by the law maker. Gusy (n 45) 2507 is more explicit when he argues that the law's purpose is the aim of differentiation. The latter interpretation was taken up by Gubelt (n 45) marginal no 21 and Epiney (n 61) 451.

[67] Kloepfer (n 45) 61.

According to the suggested approach, one must—as the third and last step—balance the criterion of differentiation against the aim of differentiation.[68] Judges are asked to decide whether the differentiation was apt, necessary and appropriate to achieve the law's goal.

As an analysis of the reasoning reveals, the approach is in accordance with the modified expression of the 'new formula' close to proportionality testing, as it is known from a freedom rights context:[69] the differentiating measure is assessed in light of the statutory purpose behind the law in question. Nevertheless, even if one works under the premise that the law's purpose is held to be the same, independent of scrutiny taking place in the freedom rights or equality rights context, there remains one difference in testing: whereas in freedom rights cases, the impact of a measure on personal liberties is balanced against the statutory aim, equality review calls for a weighing of the differences between compared groups and the statutory aim.[70]

iii. Huster and the Internal-External Aims Divide

However not all scholars were satisfied with this conceptualisation of German equality review. Mindful of the discrepancy, which exists between weighing differences between persons against aims of differentiation and balancing reasons for differentiation against aims pursued by them, Huster developed a third approach.[71] It is based on fundamental ideas of action theory, as established by Aristotle in the *Nicomachean Ethics*, and structures equality testing according to the premise that there are two kinds of activities: actions pursuing aims *external* to the action and actions pursuing aims *internal* to the action. The first category encompasses all actions a person undertakes in order to institute something novel; in order to create a change. Referring to Aristotle, he cites the example of a doctor, whose action is patients' treatment so as to achieve the aim of their recovery.[72] The doctor's action and his pursued aim can be formulated in a means-end-relationship: he works in order to re-establish his patients' health. Activities that set out to achieve internal aims, on the other hand, cannot adequately be described in terms of

[68] Stein (n 43) marginal nos 41 f; Stein and Frank (n 61) 413 f.

[69] For this assessment, see Hesse (n 64) 188 ff; Robbers (n 45) 751; Wendt (n 38) 784 ff. Showing the parallels, but also the ends to this similarity Bryde and Kleindiek (n 45) 38. For a critique, see Heun (n 1) marginal nos 27 f.

[70] See L Michael, 'Die drei Argumentationsstrukturen des Grundsatzes der Verhältnismäßigkeit—Zur Dogmatik des Über- und Untermaßverbotes und der Gleichheitssätze' (2001) 41 *Juristische Schulung* 148, 153. Contrary to this analysis, he seems to hold the view that this difference is of minor importance.

[71] Huster (n 29) especially 164 ff. The attribution of this progress in German equality dogmatics to Huster shall not leave unmentioned that the work by Kloepfer (n 45) built the fundament of his deliberations. Adopted, albeit also critiqued, for Austrian equality adjudication by Somek (n 60) 111, 115, 117, 138.

[72] Huster (n 29) 147 referring to Aristoteles, *Nikomachische Ethik* 10th edn, F Dirlmeier trans (Berlin, Akademie Verlag, 1999) 5; bk 1, 1094 a.

means and ends. Here the example of a warrior who fights in a life-threatening situation so as to be courageous is given.[73] Although one can easily detect that there is a relationship between the action (fighting) and the aim (courage), it is not causal as in the first category; instead action and aim are deeply entwined and connected with each other.[74] The relation might be most adequately expressed by formulations such as 'the warrior is courageous whilst fighting' or 'the warrior fights in a courageous way'.[75]

Huster's approach is novel and remarkable as he succeeds in transferring these fundamental ideas of action theory into the realm of equality reasoning. Making use of the distinction between different kinds of activities, he argues that differentiations may be justified on two types of grounds: either because *internal* differences amongst the groups justify differentiations or because *external* aims may be legitimately pursued through the differential treatment. With this extension, Huster is able to explain the complete case law of the Federal Constitutional Court on the principle of equality.

In a first step, the test developed by him obeys the logic of comparison and demands application of the 'new formula', as it was initially stated. It envisions that judges engaging in equality review should weigh differences between groups in comparison with the effects of differential treatment on the disadvantaged group.[76] If they come to the conclusion that the differences are valid enough to justify the differentiation, the norm is held to be in accordance with the equality guarantee. If they decide that the differential treatment cannot be justified because of differences between the groups, the norm is held to be an unjustified violation of Article 3(1) Basic Law. The author claims that this part of the balancing exercise is able to judge on the constitutionality of cases of differential treatment which pursue *internal* aims. That is to say, this analytical component provides a tool to check whether such differentiations are allowed under the general principle of equality, whose sole purpose is to achieve fair treatment. Due to the strong linkage in these cases between the internal aim of fair treatment and the differentiation, the examination is designed to answer the question whether or not *interpersonal* differences among the compared groups may justify the differentiation. Most cases undergoing equality review are solved at this testing level.

But what about cases such as the *Zweifamilienhaus* decision? The internal aim of differential taxation is fairness in the levy of taxes between such individuals who are financially well-off and those that have less money at their disposal. Yet, considerations with regard to the practicability of alternative regulation or administrative efficiency cannot reasonably be expressed in terms of differences between the compared groups. They are therefore not aims *internal* to the differentiation.

[73] Huster (n 29) 148 referring to Aristoteles (n 72) 60 ff; book 3, 1115 a–1117 b.
[74] See Huster (n 29) 149.
[75] ibid, 148.
[76] ibid, 195 ff and 468.

In these cases, the first part of the test reaches its limits.[77] For that reason, Huster sets out to establish a second stage of review. In the event that a justification due to internal factors fails, an infringement of the equality guarantee might nevertheless be justified due to *external* aims. These external aims shall be balanced against the effects of the differentiation, for example one considers whether the merits in administrative ease can outweigh the disadvantageous effects on the more heavily taxed group. For judicial practice, this means that judges shall assess whether the differentiation in questions was apt, necessary and proportional (*strictu sensu*) to achieve a certain goal.[78]

In sum, legal doctrine reveals that German equality adjudication is characterised by the coexistence of different standards of review, which are not only distinct from each other because of their dependence or independence from comparison but also because of their differentiating levels of scrutiny. With respect to these features, European Union and German equality law share common aspects.

II. TRADITIONAL INTERPRETIVE EXPLANATION

A. Transposing the Account of German Equality Adjudication

As stated from the outset, the purpose of this chapter is not merely to depict the different standards of review, but rather to examine why this segmentation exists and how it functions. Why are measures at times reviewed according to the low, at other times according to intermediate and sometimes even according to strict scrutiny? Starting with the research, I detected that there had been surprisingly little written on the *Dogmatik* of European equality review.[79] The appraisal that the European Court of Justice alternates between low and strict scrutiny appeared to have been deemed satisfactory.

In contrast, German legal scholarship, with its preference for systematised accounts of the law, has established a common narrative to explain the Federal Constitutional Court's reasons for at times engaging in low and at times engaging

[77] Huster mentions that typification in law making is a prime example of the insufficiency of traditional approaches to answer all questions emerging in the context of equality review. See Huster (n 29) 245 ff.

[78] ibid, 213 ff and 468 f. The example already points at the limits which are set to proportionality testing in equality matters. In typification cases, one can easily make the claim that the test's necessity requirement can never be met. Under the aspect of necessity, judges need to decide whether there were comparable, equally apt means which could have achieved the goal. It is conceivable that each time typifications are applied, the introduction of an exception for the specific case at hand would have led to the same measure of legal certainty without infringing upon the individual right to equality. To make such high demands on the necessity criterion leads the review of typifications at absurdum, as the proclaimed aim is to simplify and unitise.

[79] With the most notable exceptions of Barrett (n 18) 117; Kischel (n 8) 1; K Lenaerts, 'L'Egalité de Traitement en Droit Communautaire, un principe unique aux apparences multiples' (1991) 26 *Cahiers du Droit Européen* 3; S Plötscher, *Der Begriff der Diskriminierung im Europäischen Gemeinschaftsrecht* (Berlin, Duncker und Humblot, 2003); Schwarze (n 18).

in heightened scrutiny in equality matters. In light of the commonalities in types of review (described in the last number of paragraphs), the following passage analyses whether one can transpose some of the ideas developed in German legal scholarship to the European sphere in order to explain EU equality review.

Elaborating on their stance towards review under Article 3(1), the Basic Law's equality clause, the Federal Constitutional Court stated:

> Depending on the subject of regulation and the criteria for differentiation, different limits result from the general principle of equality for the legislature, which range from mere prohibition of arbitrary law-making to stricter scrutiny according to equivalence, viz proportionality, standards. The sliding scale of requirements follows from the wording and purpose of Article 3(1) Basic Law as well as from the context of other constitutional provisions.[80]

With this pronouncement, the German judges declared that they will heighten or lessen their scrutiny in non-discrimination cases, as they perceive it to be indicated by constitutional requirements. In search for more concrete parameters with regard to the choice of scrutiny, commentators argued that the Court is guided by three deliberations when deciding which test to apply. First, the judges engage in a more thorough review if the differential treatment of two persons impacts upon the affected groups' exercise of other fundamental rights guaranteed under the German constitution.[81] Second, they scrutinise a norm in a stricter manner when people belonging to the disadvantaged group have little or no influence over the feature chosen as the defining criterion of differentiation. In other words, if immutable characteristics were designated by the legislature as decisive for differentiation, the Constitutional Court will engage in thorough review of the measure.[82] The third consideration held to lead to stricter scrutiny was mentioned

[80] In the original:

> Aus dem allgemeinen Gleichheitssatz ergeben sich je nach Regelungsgegenstand und Differenzierungsmerkmalen unterschiedliche Grenzen für den Gesetzgeber, die vom bloßen Willkürverbot bis zu einer strengen Bindung an Verhältnismäßigkeitserfordernisse reichen. Die Abstufung der Anforderungen folgt aus dem Wortlaut und Sinn des Art. 3 I GG sowie aus seinem Zusammenhang mit anderen Verfassungsnormen (*BVerfGE* 92, 53 [68]).

See Bryde and Kleindiek (n 45) 39 and Kokott (n 1) 131.

[81] For example, it has been held that differentiating measures are subject to strict scrutiny in the event that they affect an individual's right of legal defence (protected by Art 19(4) Basic Law). *BVerfGE* 93, 99 (111); 50, 217 (231); see Kokott (n 1) 139. Similarly, if a legal differentiation imposes greater burden on one group than another in the realm of professional accreditations (guaranteed pursuant Art 12(1) Basic Law), strict scrutiny will be applied. *BVerfGE* 79, 212 (218); see Kokott (n 1) 138.

[82] Compare Kokott (n 1) 133. The underlying argumentation can be best understood when put in context. Besides the general principle of equality, that allows for differentiations where justified, Art 3 Basic Law stipulates absolute prohibitions of differentiation. Since it is stipulated in para 3 sentence 1 that '[n]o person shall be favored or disfavored because of sex, parentage, race, language, homeland and origin, faith, or religious or political opinions', differentiations that use one of the listed features as connecting factors may never be justified (certain derogations apply for equal treatment of men and women). The provision expresses that personal non-changeable attributes cannot serve as criteria of differentiation, as doing so would heighten the potential for discrimination of minorities. See for a similar argumentation *BVerfGE* 92, 26 (51 and 52); 88, 87 (96 and 97).

by the Federal Constitutional Court itself in an obiter dictum of its *Präklusion I* decision, which established the 'new formula'. There, the judges suggested employing different testing standards for cases dealing with differentiations between factual circumstances and cases concerning differences between individuals.[83] In the instance that a norm regulates human behaviour and differentiates amongst persons, strict scrutiny is indicated. Yet, if 'items' and not persons are the object of regulation, scrutiny at lesser intensity shall be performed.

This last delineation works on the premise that norms distinguishing between situations do not have the same capacity to influence, for better or worse, an individual's living conditions or relative standing in society as do norms distinguishing between persons. The Federal Constitutional Court held that, since differences of the former kind do not directly affect individuals, the margin of discretion granted to the legislature in the design of laws should be broader in instances where objective facts serve as criteria for differentiation.[84] In the end, within German legal circles, there is a commonly held understanding that these three aspects—freedom rights impact, reference to personal characteristics, and differentiation between norm addressees rather than situations—provide the basic structure informing equality review.[85]

Attempting a transposition of the narrative to European equality review, the thought of demanding stricter scrutiny in cases distinguishing between individuals and not between factual situations could potentially be translated without alteration. Further, the idea of requiring stricter scrutiny in the event that freedom rights are severely impacted may be adapted to fit EU law. Keeping in mind that, even after the introduction of the Charter of Fundamental Rights of the European Union (CFEU), not all human behaviour is protected under a European fundamental rights regime,[86] one may argue that strict scrutiny is required whenever differentiating measures touch upon fields of law covered by the Charter and/or belonging to the core of freedoms that advance the European integration project. Lastly, the application of strict scrutiny in cases where personal characteristics serve as criteria for differentiation could arguably be appropriate under European Union equality law too. For example, one could say that strict scrutiny must be

[83] *BVerfGE* 55, 72 (88); 74, 9 (24); 82, 126 (146); 87, 234 (255); 88, 87 (96). Bryde and Kleindiek (n 45) 39, with further references.

[84] Thus, the Court reasoned in *Präklusion I* that the difference in civil procedure under review concerned different stages of court proceedings and should be subject to low scrutiny (*BVerfGE* 55, 72 [88 and 89]). On the other hand, the Court's *Transsexuals I* decision, in which it had to decide on the compatibility of a law that allowed persons under the age of 25 to alter their first name from female to male or vice versa only in case of sex change surgery, with the German equality clause, serves as example of a pronounced application of heightened scrutiny. Drawing attention to the fact that the law distinguished between norm addressees and not between factual circumstances, the judges considered it necessary and appropriate to assess its legality under strict scrutiny (*BVerfGE* 88, 87 [96 and 97]).

[85] eg Jarass (n 57) marginal nos 20 ff, who also mentions complexity of the case as an additional factor. More nuanced Osterloh and Nußberger (n 2) marginal nos 31 f.

[86] Case C-617/10 *Åklagaren v Hans Åkerberg Fransson* [2013] ECLI:EU:C:2013:105, especially paras 19–21.

performed whenever differentiations can be connected to characteristics that are specifically listed in Article 21 CFEU or the special Equality Directives.[87]

B. Dismantling the Account

So much for the narrative and its transposition. But can it really explain the functioning of egalitarian review in its entirety? If so, is the more intriguing question not why these three factors and not others were chosen to establish the sliding scale of judicial scrutiny? If not, is there an alternative model that may provide a better account? Tackling these questions will be the subject of the following section.

To begin with there are good reasons to doubt that the narrative explains the courts' workings with regard to the principle of equality in an exhaustive manner. Commentators point out incongruities.[88] The explanation that a norm's deep impact on individual exercise of freedom leads to heightened scrutiny has repeatedly been a point of contention. The criticism stems from the following grounds: it is difficult to imagine a legislative act, capable of being subject to equality review, which does not affect individual freedom rights guarantees. Processes of judicialisation and constitutionalisation have defined the development of rights protection in the European Union. Ever more spheres of life are protected by fundamental rights (including EU law guarantees) and, as a consequence, all areas of law must hold up to comprehensive fundamental rights scrutiny. Further, law makers' decisions to distinguish between two groups or situations always take place in a particular context.[89] Each statutory differentiation is at the same time a fundamental rights impairment that requires justification.[90] In the end, the statement that one needs to pay attention to the impact of a particular instance of differentiation on the exercise of a person's liberties is of little importance when choosing the adequate standard of review, as (almost) all differentiations possess this potential. It can be reduced to a mere manifestation of the fact that equality and freedom rights protection are intertwined.[91] Consequently, a norm's 'freedom rights impact' remains an inappropriate tool when it comes to providing practical guidance in the choice of the correct level of judicial scrutiny.

In addition, there is some dispute as to the argumentative strength of the distinction between laws calling for differential treatment of objects, facts or situations and those demanding differential treatment of persons. One may rightly

[87] These characteristics comprise sex, race, colour, ethnic or social origin, genetic features, language, religion or belief, political or any other opinion, membership of a national minority, property, birth, disability, age or sexual orientation.

[88] See inter alia Kokott (n 1) 139. For Austria, Somek (n 60) 211 ff.

[89] See Heun (n 1) marginal no 20.

[90] See eg Epiney (n 61) 349 ff, especially 353.

[91] Osterloh and Nußberger (n 2) marginal no 18; C Spielmann, 'Die Verstärkungswirkung der Grundrechte' (2004) 44 *Juristische Schulung* 371.

question how this separation can be upheld, bearing in mind that 'law always regulates human behaviour'.[92] Even if a norm takes a factual condition as its point of reference for distinction, its impact is always felt by the individuals who find themselves in such circumstances. For instance, when a rule stipulates that cigarette packages may only be distributed if labelled with a warning, the objects of regulation are packages. Nevertheless, those affected by the norm are the producers who now have to label their products. Further, if a law provides for different consequences for late and incomplete submissions in a lawsuit, one may hold that it governs solely situations. Yet, the claimant or defendant whose plea is no longer taken into account will feel the norm's effects. So either directly through regulation of individual conduct or indirectly through the regulation of situations, individuals are the targets of law.[93]

With two of the explanations deconstructed, there is one left to explain the Court's workings in equality review. Can the remaining argument do the trick and offer a coherent account as to why the European Court of Justice engages in some cases in low scrutiny and in others in strict scrutiny equality review? To recall its content, it holds that laws are to be thoroughly reviewed if the statutory differentiation orients itself on group characteristics, on which the individual has little or no influence. This reference to 'immutable characteristics' bears the potential for nuanced reasoning, because it enables the judge to assess whether a person that has been disadvantaged by a norm has the means to either become part of the group of beneficiaries or leave the burdened group on her own. The less a person has the possibility to change the features that make her subject to disadvantageous treatment through individual behaviour, the greater the need for protection. Overall, this seems to be a plausible way of determining whether courts should engage in strict or lenient scrutiny.[94]

[92] Bryde and Kleindiek (n 45) 40.

[93] Not surprisingly, critics have noted the inconsistency of the Federal Constitutional Court in its application of the criterion. Osterloh and Nußberger (n 2) marginal no 90 argue that the differentiation has so far taken on little concrete form. In particular, Gubelt draws attention to a statement made by the judges in a case that concerned a law distinguishing between situations, but indirectly discerning between individuals (Gubelt (n 45) marginal no 14). There, the court held that 'neither strict scrutiny under proportionality standards is apt nor mere arbitrariness review sufficient … For that reason, the specifics of the regulated sphere are of particular importance for deciding the question whether the differentiation is justified' (*BVerfGE* 89, 365 [376]). In the original: 'Danach ist weder eine strenge Prüfung der Verhältnismäßigkeit geboten noch eine bloße Willkürkontrolle ausreichend … Deshalb kommt hier den Besonderheiten des geregelten Lebens- und Sachbereichs für die Frage, ob die Ungleichbehandlung gerechtfertigt ist, erhebliche Bedeutung zu'. Provocatively put, this statement, with its reliance on empty formulas, amounts to an admission by the Federal Constitutional Court: the distinction between laws on situations and laws on people, stipulated in the decision that established the 'new formula', is an ineffective criterion for the identification of the correct standard of scrutiny.

[94] As an aside, a curious finding of this critical assessment is that the criterion for choice of scrutiny, which is applied by two prestigious European Constitutional Courts and not refuted by this analysis, mirrors the one applied by the United States Supreme Court (see also Bryde and Kleindiek (n 45) 43, with further reference). There, the justices have created an equality review mechanism that, in contrast to its European equivalents, does not work on the rationale of infringement and justification but on a classification rationale. The court applies a sliding scale of review with strict scrutiny for cases in which the differentiation is connected to 'suspect classifications' such as race or gender, and heightened

Yet, even if one accepts the explanation calling for strict testing in light of 'immutable characteristics' as a convincing approach, certain issues make one wonder about its consistency. First, Kokott points out that there is—with regard to the German adjudication—ample evidence of decisions, in which the approach would have called for strict scrutiny, that have been decided pursuant to more lenient requirements.[95] One should not prematurely dismiss these cases as instances of bad decision making, in which the judges opted for the wrong intensity of assessment. Instead, these occurrences may well point to logical incoherence in the choice of equality scrutiny. Second, the reference to 'immutable characteristics' fails to account for the third identified strand in testing, namely intermediate scrutiny. It cannot give an explanation for why, within the realm of equality review, a test is applied that resembles means-ends-analysis, as we know it from freedom rights proportionality analysis. For example, the review in *Arcelor* cannot be explained with reference to the changeability or non-changeability of the unprivileged groups' characteristics because the judges held the differentiation to be justified by the need for a step-by-step introduction of a new regulatory scheme. To take the argument even further, nor does a 'reliance on immutable characteristics' explain the choice in scrutiny performed in cases of affirmative action. Here, 'immutable characteristics' such as gender are even perceived as the decisive aspects that trigger scrutiny of intermediate intensity. One should not understand this assessment as an argument against affirmative action. To the contrary, there are good reasons to depart from comparative evaluation in affirmative action cases and to instead review whether the end of achieving an emancipated society justifies differential treatment. The preceding analysis only pursued two interrelated objectives: First, it sought to illustrate the inconsistency of an approach which states that reliance on 'immutable characteristics' explains the choice in judicial scrutiny. Second, it intended to raise awareness of the fact that the intriguing question is not when 'immutable characteristics' can be detected, but what lies behind the reference to 'immutable characteristics'.

Due to these shortcomings, one may be well advised to not simply dismiss the third argument believed to explicate the diverse levels of intensity in review, but to question the analytical strength of the presented account altogether.[96] Looking at the deficiencies of the existing approaches, what shall replace them? In lieu of substituting them with another explanation that avails itself of purely legal language and judicial constructs, it may be of benefit to think beyond traditional interpretive constraints. For this, we should not only take into account the actors involved in the making and control of law, but award them a prominent place in

scrutiny in instances where 'discrete and insular minorities' are disadvantaged. In other words, European constitutional systems have, quite apart from developments on the new continent and following a different path, established means of review that in the end feature more similarities with equality review by the United States Supreme Court than one might expect at first sight.

[95] Kokott (n 1) 135.

[96] Building upon the tradition of legal realism.

the deliberations. If one ignores or neglects the question of *who* performs judicial review and *whose* work is being judged in the process of equality review, one's analysis of why judges exercise control at a particular level of scrutiny and not at another will be 'seriously incomplete'.[97] In short, one needs to factor in which social decision making processes, that is to say institutions,[98] take part in the egalitarian assessment of laws. The most appropriate way of doing so is via the application of comparative institutional analysis.

III. CHANGING PERSPECTIVES: A COMPARATIVE INSTITUTIONAL EXPLANATION

A. An Introduction into Comparative Institutional Analysis

The term 'comparative institutional analysis' comes with different connotations. Especially in the field of economics, it has come to denote an entire field dedicated to the study of institutions and their influence on economic development.[99] At present, there is extensive debate on the proper definition of 'institutions'.[100] Whereas for example North perceives institutions as 'humanly devised constraints that structure human interactions',[101] Scott considers institutions to 'comprise regulative, normative, and cultural-cognitive elements that, together with associated activities and resources, provide stability and meaning to social life'.[102] In contrast, this analysis employs the specific framework of comparative institutional analysis devised by Komesar. Under his approach, institutions denote decision making processes[103] and their study is directed to explaining '[m]ore particularly ... the way we choose to allocate authority to and among them'.[104] In its purest

[97] R Pierce, 'Book Review—A Comment on Imperfect Alternatives: Choosing Institutions in Law, Economics, and Public Policy' (1995) 83 *California Law Review* 941, 942; interpreting Komesar's work.

[98] See in that respect G Shaffer, 'Power, Governance and the WTO: A Comparative Institutional Approach' (2009) Minnesota Legal Studies Research Paper No 09-11, 2, papers.ssrn.com/sol3/papers.cfm?abstract_id=1349368, with reference to N Komesar, *Imperfect Alternatives: Choosing Institutions in Law, Economics, and Public Policy* (Chicago, University of Chicago Press, 1994) 9 and A Wendt, 'Anarchy is What States Make of it: the Social Construction of Power Politics' (1992) 46 *International Organizations* 391, 395.

[99] For an overview, see G Morgan, JL Campbell, C Crouch, OK Pedersen and R Whitley (eds), *The Oxford Handbook of Comparative Institutional Analysis* (Oxford, Oxford University Press, 2011).

[100] See M-L Djelic, 'Institutional Perspectives—Working Towards Coherence or Irreconcilable Diversity?' in G Morgan, JL Campbell, C Crouch, OK Pedersen and R Whitley (eds), *The Oxford Handbook of Comparative Institutional Analysis* (Oxford, Oxford University Press, 2011) 15, 25 f.

[101] D North, *Institutionen, institutioneller Wandel und Wirtschaftsleistung*, M Streissler tr (Tübingen, Mohr Siebeck, 1992) 4.

[102] WR Scott, *Institutions and Organizations. Ideas, Interests, and Identities* 4th edn (Los Angeles, Sage, 2014) 56.

[103] N Komesar, *Law's Limits* (Cambridge, Cambridge University Press, 2001) 3.

[104] Komesar (n 98) 3. Komesar's comparative institutional analysis is influenced by other institutional theories of law, as the one developed by JH Ely, *Democracy and Distrust* (Cambridge, Harvard University Press, 1980) or the one put forward by R Posner, *Economic Analysis of Law* 9th edn

form, this variant of comparative institutional analysis argues that the decision 'who decides is really a decision of *what* decides'.[105] Its main claim is that we cannot explain a finding's substantial content without looking at the process through which it came about and the actors involved in the enterprise. Komesar's theory is anchored on three basic propositions:

1. Institutional *choice* implies that one must decide between *alternative* institutions if one wants to allocate power among them. Single institutional analysis is insufficient to explain decision making processes. All institutional analysis must be comparative in nature.
2. Each institution comes with its own deficiencies and no decision making process is perfect. The task is to identify the institution that is able to perform the least imperfect decision making in a given situation. The assessment of institutional performance is 'tied to the pattern of participation of important institutional actors common to all the institutions',[106] such as voters, traders or citizens.
3. All institutions must make decisions, in which they reconcile multiple, often contradictory, interests and deal with complex themes. The least imperfect institution is the one that may ensure the most adequate representation of interests under such straining circumstances.

As can be seen from the last premise, comparative institutional analysis follows to a large extent a participation-centred approach. 'The actions of the mass of participants' are considered 'as the factor that, in general, best accounts for how institutions function'.[107] Consequently, the emphasis on participation not only ties the three propositions together—as the most balanced representation of interests in a situation defined by competing and complex stakes will guide the way to the discovery of the most adequate institution and hence the best possible solution—but also serves as a philosophical backbone to a theory focusing on processes. More precisely, the focus on representation shows that the theory itself is motivated by egalitarian concerns. In this context, one can detect an interesting interrelation between comparative institutional analysis and equality theory: according to the prominent strand in egalitarian thought advocated by Dworkin and presented in the previous chapter, equality demands are demands for equal respect.[108] Such equal respect is denied to people whose interests have not been taken into account in decision making processes to the degree they should have

(New York, Wolters Kluwer Law, 2014). However it differs from them in not focusing on the functioning of a single institution, but examines their comparative strengths and weaknesses; see Komesar (n 98) 6 f.

[105] Komesar (n 98) 3.

[106] Komesar (n 103) 30.

[107] ibid.

[108] See R Dworkin, *Taking Rights Seriously* (London, Duckworth, 1978) starting at 223. For further explication of the relation between equality and majority rule, see Sadurski (n 2) 41 ff.

and comparative institutional analysis contends that the process that ensures the most apt representation of interests in a given situation should take the decision.

Turning to the allocation of decision making authority between the judiciary and the political process, which is of interest for our analysis, Komesar argues that we may only correctly understand a constitutional court's rulings and a parliament's actions, if we assess the two institutions' strengths and weaknesses in comparative terms.[109] The comparative evaluation in this enquiry shall be guided by three parameters: 'Numbers, complexity' and 'representation of interests'.[110] In this depiction, numbers and complexity signify that institutions can be strained in different ways and to different extents depending on the dynamics of participation. Numbers are high if institutions are confronted with such an amount of cases that it becomes difficult to manage them. Complexity is high if many dispersed interests need to be reconciled. Under such strained circumstances, some institutions function better—or less imperfectly—than others. Obviously, the strong point of the political process is its rather comprehensive representation of interests. However, historical and current observations tell us that the ideal of rational decision making according to which all represented interests are taken into account is often not translated into reality. Instead, the political process is partially characterised by two types of fear: the power of the few over the many and the power of the many over the few.[111] The former has come to be known as *minoritarian bias* and describes the 'overrepresentation of concentrated interests'[112] in the decision making process. The latter constitutes *majoritarian bias* and denotes the 'overrepresentation of dispersed interests'.[113] In both instances, the political process malfunctions because certain interests command more weight in the decision making procedure than their stake holders should be entitled to according to democratic standards. Such imbalance can occur because the political process may be captured by small or large interest groups and because representation must not be equated with interest. So in the event of *minoritarian bias*, a small but organised group with high per capita stakes in a given subject may influence the process through lobbying to a greater extent than actually foreseen by the democratic ideal, leading to special interest legislation. In instances of *majoritarian bias*, the risk is that a large group with low per capita stakes decides to accomplish its desires although this leads to a disproportionate burden on a small group or weaker members of society (the tyranny of the majority). Both biases can lead to excess, with potentially damaging and even catastrophic effects.

However, the judicial process comes with its own imperfections. Strong on the appraisal of abstract concepts, its most significant weak points are the courts'

[109] Particularly Komesar (n 98) 196 f and ibid (n 103) 35 ff and 174 ff.

[110] For numbers and complexity, see eg Komesar (n 103) 6, 8, 24, 75, 84 f; for representation of interests, ibid 22.

[111] M Maduro, *We, the Court* (Oxford, Hart Publishing, 1998) 177, referring to Komesar (n 98) 53.

[112] Komesar (n 103) 22.

[113] ibid, 22.

limited possibilities for hearing a multiplicity of voices on a given issue, the constant shortage of financial and organisational resources and its at times inadequate substantive competence.[114] Concerning the subject matter of representation, the high costs of adjudication and the procedural burdens paired with the uncertainty of outcomes often turn law suits into unprofitable exercises for claimants. In addition, the more people are affected (that is to say the more interests to be reconciled with each other) and the more complex a situation, the more difficulties courts have to perform well. Speaking in terms of supply and demand, '[i]ncreasing numbers and complexity strain courts as the demand for law and rights increases and the capacity to supply them decreases'.[115] Snyder points out a further 'inbuilt deficiency' in the workings of the judiciary, namely that it relies on ad hoc claims to trigger proceedings.[116] As a result, it is difficult for courts to develop a coherent approach to expansive subject matters.

Having these imperfections in mind, Komesar stresses that looking at the workings of the adjudicative and political processes through the lens of comparative institutional analysis provides a tool for questioning and changing our way of thinking about law. Law is no longer a given that ought to be interpreted and legitimised only in its own language and logic. Rather, it needs to also be analysed in light of the 'processes that make, interpret and enforce law'[117] as these forces determine its constitution. Carrying the point further, the author remarks that 'identifying a goal tells us virtually nothing about law and rights'[118] and that 'it is impossible to further any goal without choosing the combination of institutions and institutional roles that are capable of furthering that goal'.[119]

B. Comparative Institutional Analysis and Equality Reasoning

Adopting this perspective may also help to enhance our understanding of equality reasoning, as it is applied by European courts and political processes.

Starting with the performance of the political process in equality matters, it has to be noted from the very outset that political decision making in many—if not in nearly all—cases involves differentiation. As soon as the legislature decides to become active and passes a law, it creates differences between those that are within the norm's scope and those left outside.[120] What is more, laws are by definition drafted to govern a multiplicity of isolated situations in an abstract manner.[121]

[114] Komesar (n 103) 59; Maduro (n 111) 59.

[115] Komesar (n 103) 4.

[116] F Snyder, 'The Effectiveness of European Community Law: Institutions, Processes, Tools and Techniques' (1993) 56 *ML Rev* 19, 40 and 51.

[117] Komesar (n 103) 3.

[118] ibid, 23.

[119] Pierce (n 97) 942.

[120] See eg Gusy (n 45) 2507; Haller (n 1) 204; Ipsen (n 64) 141.

[121] See H Maurer, *Staatsrecht I* 6th edn (Munich, Beck, 2010) § 17 marginal nos 7 ff.

Therefore, not only are the numbers of equality decisions high, but also within each of these decisions the legislature deals with a multitude of individual instances.

As far as the parameter of 'competence' is concerned, the political process has considerable means to address complex problem sets. Legislatures have (at least when construed in relative terms) ample financial resources and material support. For example, in the realm of EU social regulation, the Commission, Council and European Parliament have to take value-laden, ideologically grounded decisions with far reaching implications on persons' lives and the states' budgets. Yet, they are not alone in this task and can commission impact assessments or rely upon various other supports provided by their office staff and legal services.[122] As the legislature is allowed (or shall I rather say obliged) to look at the picture as a whole, in its decision making processes it is used to taking into account the consequences of law making on various areas and players. The political process is set up to make 'substantive social decisions'.[123] It has expertise in estimating if a law will lead to unfair outcomes—be it because it is drafted in under- or over-inclusive terms. Nevertheless, it can be strained when complexity is high; and complexity is increasing.[124] In light of this risk of overstrain, the question becomes when the political process is less strained than other institutions to make decisions on law's fairness.

Focusing on the theme of representation, it comes as no surprise that, as regards equality, majoritarian bias is the biggest concern.[125] Laws whose decision making process has been hijacked by an overrepresentation of the majority's interests are suspect to producing discriminatory outcomes. Majority groups have, both in the past and today, acted to single out minority groups in order to impose on them disproportionate burdens. They opt for the persecution of individuals who feature 'insular and discrete' characteristics (such as race, gender, or sexual orientation) that cannot or are unlikely to be adopted by the majority. As Komesar explicates, these 'insular and discrete' 'attributes make these minorities safe targets'.[126] On the other hand, capture of the political decision making process in equality affairs can also stem from minorities. It may happen that small, organised interest groups with high per capita stakes have overly proportionate influence on the law making process through extensive lobbying or vast media presence. Seen from the perspective of egalitarian concern, actions of small interest groups risk resulting in

[122] For the workings of impact assessment see European Commission, COM (2002) 276, *Impact Assessment* and Craig Robertson, 'Impact Assessment in the European Union' EIPAScope 2008, 17, www.eipa.eu/files/repository/eipascope/20080905132658_SCOPE2008-2_3_CraigRobertson.pdf.

[123] Komesar (n 103) 38.

[124] ibid, 4.

[125] See for the US Constitutional debate, the *Carolene Products* footnote which states in its third paragraph that stricter scrutiny is demanded if statutes are 'directed at particular religious, or national, or racial minorities; or whether prejudice against discrete and insular minorities may be a special condition' (*United States v Carolene Products Co* 304 US 144, 58 S Ct 778 at 784 n 4). Further, Komesar (n 98) 221 ff.

[126] ibid, 224.

undue preferential treatment to the disadvantage of the rest. Given that such over- or underrepresentation of interests can occur in any political setting, 'understanding the form as well as the extent of … political malfunction is crucial'.[127]

After one has established whether there is increased demand for judicial intervention in equality matters, one needs to assess in comparative terms whether courts are actually in a position to supply sound alternative decisions. In this exercise, an examination of a court's ability to rule on issues of equality according to the parameters of scale, competence and representation of interests ought to take place.[128] To begin with scale, courts are generally ill equipped to deal with high numbers. Looking at decision making in individual cases, they have fewer resources than the political process to undertake thorough investigations. Looking at overall decision making, when the amount of cases on a court's docket increases, it has few options besides deciding in less time (meaning after review at lower scrutiny) at its hands to meet greater demand. Further, in order to remain functioning, courts ought to factor into their assessment of cases whether their judgments invite additional cases in numbers which are difficult or impossible to deal with. As regards the theme of competence, the working methods of courts are designed to deal with singular disputes on a case-by-case basis.[129] Judges are less suited to engaging in full-scale assessments than the legislature, because they are assigned to decide only on the specific issues individual claimants bring to them. However, in the case of equality review, comprehensive evaluation might not be what is needed most. Instead, the important point is to assess whether a differential treatment is fair or not. For this exercise, it is sufficient if judges examine isolated cases—that come with specific circumstances and concern individual lives—and perceive them as representative models that pose the question of a norm's fairness in crystallised form. To then find a convincing answer is certainly difficult, but not necessarily complex in the sense of comprising deliberations in high numbers. Furthermore, judges are well prepared to think in interpretive or substantive terms, since they are trained in law. Dealing with the subject of fairness falls within the expertise of courts. Judges are competent to engage in reasoning as it is demanded in relation to the concepts of equality and non-discrimination. They employ the language of rights, which is based around notions of 'fairness', 'equality' and 'non-discrimination'.

This interpretation of the parameter of competence may be subject to criticism. One may object that this move introduces exactly the same interpretive considerations into institutional analysis which one set out to replace due to their inadequacy in foreseeing or explaining judicial decisions. Nevertheless, I would defend the above analysis on primarily two grounds. The alternative approach, namely an

[127] Komesar (n 103) 70.

[128] ibid; see also Somek (n 60) 638.

[129] See Snyder (n 116) 40. Class actions are a mentionable exception to the rule. However, expanded definitions of standing that allow more distantly or indirectly affected parties to be heard in court can still be reconciled with the traditional picture of singular dispute resolution.

outright rejection of interpretively informed institutional analysis, would come with its own deficiencies: first, leaving capacity for interpretive consideration completely aside in our consideration, we would be prevented from adequately picturing a defining element of judicial workings. Second, an allocation of decision making authority, completely independent of an assessment whether the achieved outcomes are fair or just, may have potentially devastating effects.[130] In this regard, my variation of comparative institutional choice deviates from its original conception. While it departs from the formulation devised by Komesar, it draws near the framework of voice, rights and expertise underlying Halberstam's theory on constitutional pluralism. The latter holds that in a situation of competing claims for decision making power, the authority within the system of that institution that best succeeds at vindicating the values of voice, expertise and the protection of rights 'becomes paramount'.[131] Therefore, Halberstam argues that our assessment of decisions—be they political or judicial—needs to square interpretation of the law in the books and institutional considerations.[132] A reading of 'competence' in comparative institutional analysis, stating that competence ought also to be measured in an institution's ability to make interpretive assessments, features the same rights component.

Alongside an assessment of the courts' performance as regards scale and competence, the theme of representation of interests ought to be addressed in a detailed comparative institutional analysis. On the one hand, judicial proceedings open up spaces in which underprivileged groups or otherwise underrepresented claimants can make their voice heard. On the other hand, the high costs of litigation and formalised trial procedures already often discourage the weakest members of society from taking legal action and hinder interest groups other than the claimants in submitting their arguments to the courts.[133] Further, specifically in relation to the European context and seen in comparison with the political process, the chain legitimising the office of judges at the European Court of Justice is longer, as they are assigned to office and do not act as elected representatives.[134] This limitation on input legitimacy needs to be compensated by an increase in output legitimacy. In other words, the judges' legitimacy strongly depends on the convincing strength of their argumentative reasoning and society's perception of their role and actions.[135] The more courts' decisions are comprehensible and sound,

[130] Besides, as argued in s III.A, comparative institutional analysis can well be interpreted as itself being grounded in legal theory, namely egalitarianism.

[131] D Halberstam, 'Constitutional Heterarchy: The Centrality of Conflict in the European Union and the United States' in J Dunoff and J Trachtman (eds), *Ruling the World? Constitutionalism, International Law and Global Governance* (Cambridge, Cambridge University Press, 2009) 326, 338.

[132] Further J Komárek, 'Institutional Dimension of Constitutional Pluralism' in M Avbelj and J Komárek (eds), *Constitutional Pluralism in Europe and Beyond* (Oxford, Hart Publishing, 2010).

[133] See Komesar (n 103) 35 ff.

[134] Their powers are legitimised by the electorate in a more indirect way, as they receive their offices upon 'common accord of the governments of the Member States' (Art 253(1) TFEU).

[135] It is further ensured by the fact that judges are 'chosen from persons whose independence is beyond doubt and who possess the qualifications required for appointment to the highest judicial

the more will they be accepted as integral players. Linking these ideas to equality review, the following emanates: if judges decide to assess legally introduced differentiations and potentially replace legislative decisions with their own, they will have to reason and balance interests well.

To summarise, if we compare the capacity of the political process and the courts to deal with the subject of equality and non-discrimination, we detect that as far as the theme of scale and competence is concerned, the former is generally more suited to decide on the topic than the latter. This is not to say that the legislature functions perfectly in that regard, but only that as a rule, it functions at high numbers and great complexity less imperfectly than courts.[136] As regards the issue of 'representation of interests' comparative institutional analysis claims that courts should become more active in equality review in the event that the dynamics of representation indicate greater involvement by decision makers other than political processes. This is the case if there is risk of either minoritarian or majoritarian bias—that is to say if certain stakeholders' interests have received considerably more attention than would have been appropriate.

Combining these findings, one can develop an idealised sketch of potential institutional choice constellations in issues touching upon equality. Of course, this sketch only serves as a rough proxy of the possible variations. Nevertheless, it seeks to convey how far one can conceptualise equality review in an alternative framework:

Table 1: decision-making allocation pursuant comparative institutional analysis parameters

	adequate representation of interests	misrepresentation of interests
high numbers and complexity	[1] political process	[2] political process / ECJ
low numbers and complexity	[3] ECJ / political process	[4] ECJ

The themes of 'scale and competence' and of 'representation of interests' either speak in favour of leaving decisions that cause differential treatment to the political process (table cell 1.1) or they call for judicial review of differentiating norms through the courts (table cell 1.4). It is also possible that according to one theme, allocation of powers to the court should be preferred, whereas under the other theme, decision making should be with the political process (table cells 1.2 and 1.3). This may happen if numbers and complexity in a particular case imply judi-

offices in their respective countries or who are jurisconsults of recognised competence' (Art 253(1) TFEU) and by the process of panel review assessing a candidate's suitability to perform the duties of a Judge at the European Court of Justice before his assignment (see especially Art 255 TFEU).

[136] Komesar points out that at high numbers and complexity, all institutions tend to deteriorate and that institutional choices are often close calls; Komesar (n 103) 24.

cial action, but the danger of political malfunction can be considered low (table cell 1.3) or if numbers and complexity are high, but overrepresentation of certain interests is likely at play (table cell 1.2). In other words, there are cases in which judges are more competent than the legislature to rule on equality aspects, but where the representation of interests in the political process seems to function correctly. Further, there are instances where the political process appears to be prone to majoritarian or minoritarian bias, yet the courts are ill equipped to address the substantive issues of a case on its docket.

C. Matching Theory with Facts

As depicted, if one applies comparative institutional analysis to judicial testing of the general principle of equality, one can group the constellations in such a way that there are three potential outcomes regarding the best allocation of authority: clear assignment to the political process, clear assignment to the courts and a mixed picture. How these findings relate to the trichotomy of testing standards in European equality review will be the subject of this section.[137]

I argue that these three options are to a certain extent mirrored in the three diverse testing standards of equality review. Comparative institutional analysis offers a framework for assessing when judges should engage in equality scrutiny at varying intensity, namely low, heightened and strict scrutiny. The European Court of Justice should perform—as it has already done in the past—equality review at a low level of intensity when the political decision making process was likely to function without bias and a variety of complex interests had to be reconciled (table cell 2.1). It should test—as it has done on occasion—measures according to an intermediate standard if the parameters of the framework are aligned in the following ways: (a) there was no indication of misrepresentation of interests in the political process, but the court had higher competence (table cell 2.3) or (b) the risk of the political process having been captured existed, but it nevertheless retained a greater ability to deal with the subject (table cell 2.2). Further the Luxembourg judges should engage in strict scrutiny review in the event that the political decision making process showed signs that it may have been distorted by

[137] It should be mentioned that this part of the thesis applies comparative institutional analysis to European equality law in a one-dimensional manner. That is to say it compares the workings of the judicial and the political process, but leaves out of the equation the interplay between Member States and European institutions. I opted for this depiction for two reasons: first, a substantial part of the depicted cases is concerned with the compatibility of secondary legislation with EU primary law, in which the vertical choice in authority allocation arises to a lesser extent or only indirectly. Second, in all of the cases which were presented in greater detail (apart from *Kind*, which concerned the legality of a regulation), the representation of interests at the national level resembles the one at the supra-national level, as nationality is not a distinctive criterion. Thus, a vertical comparative analysis would not have changed the picture.

bias and the question posed was of a sufficiently low degree of complexity that a court was competent to decide on it (table cell 2.4).

Table 2: levels of scrutiny pursuant comparative institutional analysis parameters

	adequate representation of interests	misrepresentation of interests
high numbers and complexity	[1] low scrutiny	[2] intermediate scrutiny
low numbers and complexity	[3] intermediate scrutiny	[4] high scrutiny

In greater detail, it was said that the political process performs better in decision making than the courts in the event that numbers and complexity are high and that interests are correctly (in the sense of proportionately) represented. Consequently, scrutiny of these actions should be low. Going back to the example of *Kind*,[138] the claimant in the case argued that a regulation that set out to create a common market for mutton and lamb meat was illegal. The firm contended that the introduction of premium payment requirements for exported lamb and mutton, which differed depending on the origin of the meat, was discriminatory. Faced with the question whether the regulation was in violation of the European general principle of equality, the European Court of Justice was confronted with the tension that is inherent to the project of integration: on the one hand, the Court persistently holds that like cases have to be treated alike and different cases differently. On the other hand, European integration pursues the aim of subjecting situations that were formerly different to uniform and therefore alike treatment. This harmonising idea also lies at the core of forming a common agricultural market. In order to circumvent having to address this dilemma head on, the European Court of Justice examined the regulation according to low scrutiny and detected no violation of the general principle of equality.

From a comparative institutional perspective, the Court was well advised not to scrutinise the norm in too much detail. Numbers and complexity spoke in favour of a low standard of review. The case was decided at a time when harmonisation of the agricultural market was one of the prime objectives of the European Union's political process. Had the Court opted for a more thorough review, it would have invited many more cases concerning the creation of a common agricultural market to reach its docket. Further, its time and ability to explore the overarching ideas in the creation of such common market were limited. The general principle of equality provided the Court with a tool to seriously undermine the dynamics of integration and the Court chose not to avail itself of it. Moreover, the parameter of interest representation indicated judicial self-restraint. At first sight, one might assume that the field of agricultural policy is prone to minoritarain bias and that

[138] *Julius Kind* (n 11).

the Court should have been more thoroughly involved for that reason. It is common knowledge that farmers exercise considerable pressure on Member State and European Union politicians to have their special interests overrepresented in decisions on agricultural policy.[139] Yet, the regulation at hand was designed to abolish the structures created under the influence of special interest groups and subject them to uniform treatment. Therefore, one can argue that the new provisions under review intended to remedy past over-influence of framers on agricultural regulation. Even though the circumstances in the area of agricultural policy were at the time of the *Kind* decision, as nowadays, far from ideal, there were intelligible reasons for the Court to believe that it would not be able to make for a less imperfect decision maker on such issues.

Concerning heightened scrutiny review, comparative institutional analysis indicated that the European Court of Justice should increase the intensity of control in equality cases, if the parameters of 'numbers and complexity' and 'representation of interests' offered a mixed picture of preferring allocating power at times to the political process and at other times to the judiciary. An examination of the *Arcelor* case,[140] in which the Court performed review at intermediate intensity, can be used to test this point.

To recall, in *Arcelor*, the Court assessed the compatibility of a provision that exempted the aluminium and plastics industry from the greenhouse gas emission trading scheme with the general principle of equality under heightened scrutiny. From an institutional choice perspective, the following arguments supported the judges' choice in scrutiny: to begin with the theme of complexity, the introduction of an emissions trading scheme to the European Union is an intricate exercise. Its design as well as the specifics of its implementation required yearlong planning by European and Member State administrations and intense deliberation by the involved political processes. Its aim to internalise the costs caused by pollution, which had up to the introduction of such scheme been externalised on third parties and the general public, was and still is difficult to achieve.[141] Consequently, the complexity of the issues surrounding the question of fair inclusion or exclusion of industries in the framework strained the Court in its decision making ability. In addition, as far as the theme of scale is concerned, strict scrutiny did not lend itself as a feasible alternative to the judges. To cite a number, 1,849 German enterprises took part in certificate allocation in the period between 2005 and 2007.[142] 799 of them lodged objections against decisions relating to their cases.[143] Extrapolating this figure to 28 Member States over a longer period of time, one sees the high

[139] See for a current example of the influence of agribusiness on the TTIP negotiations, Corporate Europe Observatory Study, www.corporateeurope.org/international-trade/2014/07/who-lobbies-most-ttip, with data annex.

[140] *Arcelor* (n 25).

[141] See R Pfromm, *Emmissionshandel und Beihilfenrecht* (Berlin, Duncker und Humblot, 2010) 22 ff.

[142] M Bongard, *Emissionshandel und effektiver Rechtsschutz: Ein unvereinbarer Gegensatz?* (Frankfurt, Peter Lang 2010) 2 with further references.

[143] ibid.

potential of cases reaching the European Court of Justice. Consequently, both scale and competence argued in favour of the Court exercising self-restraint.

However, the question that came before the Court was not whether externalised costs of pollution thus far incurred could be internalised, but whether the allocation of such costs amongst economic competitors was in accordance with the law. To this extent, the unequal distribution between the aluminium or plastics industry and the steel sector proved to be problematic. Assessing the risk of over- or underrepresentation of interests in the decision to only make the steel sector part of the emissions trading scheme, one must consider it as rather high. By being excluded from the scheme, manufacturers of plastic and aluminium goods obtain a competitive advantage whilst competing with steel producers for the same contracts. Not having to pay for emissions certificates they have lower production costs. It is at least imaginable that undue influence by lobbying groups representing the spared sectors led to this unbalanced imposition of financial burdens. Thus, there was an increased likelihood of minoritarian bias being at play. This combination of high numbers and complexity with indications of overrepresentation of special interests called for intermediate scrutiny. Choosing this middle ground left the European Court of Justice with sufficient room for the inclusion of impact assessments, as seen in political decision making.[144]

Lastly, comparative institutional analysis envisages a strict scrutiny equality review, when minority groups' interests are under- or over-represented and scale and competence lead courts to appear to be the more perfect (or rather, less imperfect) institution to decide on the appropriateness of differential treatment. As in the observations on the first two standards of testing, one can find examples in the European Court of Justice's equality adjudication, for which comparative institutional analysis envisaged strict scrutiny review and the Court followed such approach. In the depiction of the European Court of Justice's adjudication on equality matters, I cited among other decisions *Racke v Hauptzollamt Mainz*[145] as well as referred to cases on equal pay as examples of high intensity judicial review. Turning to *Racke*, the case concerned an allegation that—in the area of custom duties—imported liquor wines were subject to a different conversion rate into national currency than other wines. Employing a strict scrutiny review, the judges found the differentiation to be justified. Comparative institutional analysis supports their choice in scrutiny. First, there was a suspicion of minoritarian bias having impacted the law making process. The referring court thought it 'obvious that the application of two different exchange rates was bound to result in distortions of competition'.[146] In light of the fact that such distortion was apparent to the national court, the risk of political malfunction when passing the law can be considered rather high. It is feasible that liquor wine producers and importers

[144] For a comparative institutional analysis of European affirmative action law, see ch 6.
[145] *Racke* (n 22).
[146] ibid, para 4.

influenced the wording of the provision under review, so as to place other wine producers at a disadvantage. Second, numbers and complexity of the issue at stake did not reach a dimension that placed the political process at a comparative advantage to the European Court of Justice when deciding the case. The Court was competent to rule on the issue, as it concerned the very limited topic of monetary conversion rates in the context of wine imports. Far-reaching effects of the Court's decision were not to be expected. More importantly, the issue at hand could not be considered as a 'substantive social decision',[147] which would speak in favour of decision making allocation to the political process. Major changes to the social or economic set-up in the Member States were not to be expected from the Court's judgment on wine imports. Besides, compared to decisions as the just discussed *Arcelor* judgment on a green house gas emissions trading scheme, the risk of opening up new routes of litigation to the European Court of Justice and thereby overstraining its docket in the future with further similar cases was low. Hence, all parameters of comparative institutional analysis pointed towards the use of strict scrutiny by the Court.

The interplay between institutional choice and standard of review can also be seen in cases on equal pay. In this field of law, the Court subjects Member State provisions to strict scrutiny. To take the leading case in the field, *Defrenne*,[148] as an example, the claimant contended that she was discriminated against because she received lower pay for her work as a stewardess than her male colleagues while performing the same job. Reviewing the practice under strict scrutiny, the European Court of Justice held the differential treatment to be unjustified.

The institutional choice explanation for the Court's approach is as follows: measures that lead to lower pay for women are likely to have been passed under circumstances of majoritarian bias. They are further likely to prevail under conditions of political malfunction.[149] Women have less political representation than their number would suggest. In comparison to men, they are still too loosely organised as a group in order to have their interests as fully equal partners in the working life adequately represented. This underrepresentation can result in less favourable treatment than that of the traditionally established ruling group. Thus, doubts as to the correct representation of interests call for strict scrutiny assessment.

Moreover, numbers and complexity of the issue do at the current stage not indicate judicial self-restraint. The question of equal pay can easily be assessed, because it only requires us to analyse if a man and a woman performed the same job. Any deviations from equal pay can easily be detected as violations of the general principle of equality. Given this straightforward appraisal, one can consider the European Court of Justice as a suitable actor to address the issue with respect

[147] Komesar (n 103) 38.
[148] *Defrenne* (n 23).
[149] On the variant of political malfunction in the case of women, see ch 6 s IV.A.

to its complexity. Additionally, the numbers of further equal pay cases can be considered as not exceeding the amount of references the Court can handle. The reason for this estimation is the same as regards the complexity of the issue: the requirements set forth by the Court for equal pay are simple and easy to apply.

Table 3: exemplary cases in the comparative institutional analysis pattern

	adequate representation of interests	misrepresentation of interests
high numbers and complexity	[1] *Kind*—low scrutiny	[2] *Arcelor*—intermediate scrutiny
low numbers and complexity	[3] affirmative action—intermediate scrutiny	[4] *Racke* / equal pay—high scrutiny

In conclusion, the European Court of Justice's approach to examine equality cases at different levels of intensity can be conceptualised by means of comparative institutional analysis. As an analysis of exemplary equality decisions shows, the Court should range in its review from low to high scrutiny, depending on the risk of political malfunction and its own ability to deal with numbers and complexity of the cases before it.

IV. CONCLUSION

German legal doctrine has commonly argued that differences in equality testing by the Federal Constitutional Court can be explained with reference to three aspects of the norm under review: freedom rights impact, reference to personal characteristics and differentiation between persons instead of factual situations. It held that the more pronounced these elements, the stricter the scrutiny of these provisions. For the European legal discourse, this conceptualisation has been paraphrased as differentiation in equality review between 'economic equality' and 'social equality'.[150] The more a person is affected in the exercise of his (other) fundamental rights and in his personhood, the more he is affected in his social equality and the stricter a norm's review ought to be. Under the conception of social equality, a person's fundamental rights situation relative to that of other members of society is still the sole ground of reflection. Justifications are limited, as only reasons internal to the differentiation can count as valid arguments and scrutiny is strict. Under the conception of economic equality, on the other hand, the costs of equal treatment, such as administrative feasibility, may be taken into account as valid arguments. More justifications are then at the judges' disposal and scrutiny of differential treatment hence less intense.

[150] I am thankful to Síofra O'Leary for pointing out this connection.

The preceding paragraphs sought to offer an alternative account for the differing testing standards in European equality review; one that focuses on institutional analysis instead of textual interpretation. This is not to say that the European Court of Justice has consistently applied institutional choice in its non-discrimination case law or that the conceptualisation in terms of economic and social equality is irrelevant. Rather, it is meant to provide an additional perspective to perceive as well as criticise the Court's decisions. If applicants and observers of European equality law sense that interpretive accounts of the field yield incoherent or even contradictory results, comparative institutional analysis is a conceptual framework, which can contribute to our understanding of when the European Court of Justice should be more or less strict in its testing of equality cases.

4

Differential Treatment of EU Citizens

I. NON-DISCRIMINATION ON GROUNDS OF NATIONALITY: A LEITMOTIV OF THE TFEU

THE PRINCIPLE OF non-discrimination on grounds of nationality is one of the leading principles of EU law. Commentators on EU law avail themselves of descriptions heavy with meaning in order to stress its importance. In the past, it has been labelled a 'leitmotiv' of the Treaty on the Functioning of the European Union (TFEU)[1] as well as its 'Magna Charta'.[2] Even if one remains hesitant to embrace such categorisations wholeheartedly, it is fair to say that, from a historical perspective, the principle plays a key role in the evolution of EU law.[3] A Union that is geared towards eradicating barriers to the free movement of goods and people relies on the principle of equal treatment of its citizens to achieve its goals. Consequently, it is hardly surprising 'that prohibiting nationality discrimination' has been attributed 'a strong market integration rationale'.[4]

The reference above already points towards the difficulties attached to the application of the principle. First, since the principle displays a strong connection to the EU's integration project, questions as to the desirability of advancing EU integration are also questions on the interpretation of the guarantee of equal treatment irrespective of nationality. The issue as to whether there should be limits to integration can be rephrased as the query whether a state should be allowed to discriminate against nationals from other Member States so as to promote the interests of its own citizens. This leads over to a second central interrelated theme: asking about the permissibility of preferential treatment toward a state's own citizens also means investigating the relationship between the state and its citizens. Is there an intrinsic core to national citizenship, which is not at the disposal of

[1] See, eg A Epiney, 'Artikel 18 AEUV' in C Calliess and M Ruffert (eds), *EUV/AEUV* 4th edn (Munich, Beck, 2011) marginal no 1; M Holoubek, 'Artikel 18 AEUV' in J Schwarze, U Becker, A Hatje and J Schoo (eds), *EU-Kommentar* 3rd edn (Baden-Baden, Nomos, 2003) marginal no 3; A von Bogdandy, 'Artikel 18 AEUV. Diskriminierungsverbot' in E Grabitz, M Hilf and M Nettesheim (eds), *Das Recht der Europäischen Union* (Munich, Beck, 2016) marginal no 1.

[2] HP Ipsen, *Europäisches Gemeinschaftsrecht* (Tübingen, Mohr, 1972) 592.

[3] See T Tridimas, *The General Principles of EU Law* 2nd edn (Oxford, Oxford University Press, 2006) 118, who calls 'the right to equal treatment irrespective of nationality … the most important right conferred by substantive Community law'.

[4] M Bell, *Anti-Discrimination Law and the European Union* (Oxford, Oxford University Press, 2002) 43.

the logic of EU integration?[5] Moreover, as has been pointed out in the previous chapters, applying the principle of non-discrimination to individual cases is challenging. Not only is it a broad concept, it also depends upon underlying conceptions to endow it with meaning.[6]

The following chapter approaches these issues. More specifically, it seeks to examine the functioning of the non-discrimination principle on grounds of nationality as well as its associated questions from the perspective of institutional choice. It starts by introducing the principle and its application by the European Court of Justice in greater detail (section II). Then, the chapter analyses two areas of law, in which the strict application of the principle presents EU practitioners and academics with a problem. Although both feature instances of direct discrimination on grounds of nationality, few question their conformity with EU law. These areas are the grant of social security benefits to EU citizens coming from other Member States and voting rights for EU citizens in Member States other than their home state (section III). The last section reconceptualises the case law by the European Court of Justice with help of comparative institutional analysis presented in the previous chapter (section IV).

II. ARTICLE 18(1) TFEU: A RELATIVE RIGHT TO EQUAL TREATMENT

The prohibition of discrimination on grounds of nationality is prescribed by Article 18(1) TFEU, which states: 'Within the scope of application of the Treaties, and without prejudice to any special provisions contained therein, any discrimination on grounds of nationality shall be prohibited'. As the wording reveals, Article 18(1) TFEU contains the general principle of non-discrimination on grounds of nationality. In addition, the Treaty features special equal treatment provisions, which apply irrespective of nationality. The most prominent examples are the fundamental freedoms.[7] In the event that a measure falls within their scope of application, Article 18(1) TFEU is not consulted separately for the purposes of reviewing the measure in question.[8] However, in instances in which such nexus

[5] See J Shaw, 'EU Citizenship Rights and Political Rights in an Evolving European Union' (2006/2007) 75 *Fordham Law Review* 2549, 2578; see generally C Schönberger, *Unionsbürger* (Tübingen, Mohr Siebeck, 2005) 22 ff, especially 31 ff; on the elements of citizenship TH Marshall, *Citizenship and Social Class: and Other Essays* (London, Cambridge University Press, 1950) 10 ff.

[6] See ch 2.

[7] Art 40(2)(2) TFEU, prohibiting 'any discrimination between producers or consumers within the EU' is discussed as a further example, see R Streinz, 'Artikel 18 AEUV' in R Streinz (ed), *EUV/AEUV* 2nd edn (Munich, Beck, 2012) marginal no 15; see also Holoubek (n 1) marginal nos 50 f. If further provisions contain special prohibitions of discrimination on grounds of nationality has to be assessed 'depending on the specific content' of these provisions (ibid, marginal no 51).

[8] See, eg Case C-289/02 *AMOK Verlags GmbH v A & R Gastronomie GmbH* [2003] ECR I-15059, para 26; Case C-222/04 *Ministero dell'Economia e delle Finanze v Cassa di Risparmio di Firenze SpA, Fondazione Cassa di Risparmio di San Miniato and Cassa di Risparmio di San Miniato SpA* [2006] ECR I-289, para 99; Case C-40/05 *Kaj Lyyski v Umeå universitet* [2007] ECR I-99, para 34; Case C-222/07

to the fundamental freedoms cannot be established, but where the possibility of discrimination between EU citizens nonetheless exists, equality testing under Article 18(1) TFEU comes into play.

It should be noted from the outset that the volume of cases that could potentially arise pursuant the non-discrimination principle on grounds of nationality is vast. There are multiple reasons for this: first, the prohibition binds EU institutions as well as the Member States.[9] To what extent private entities are bound by the prohibition is subject of an ongoing debate.[10] Looking at the case law of the European Court of Justice on the free movement of workers, one may presume that a private party is bound by Article 18(1) TFEU, if it holds a position of power over the EU citizens comparable to the power of a state.[11] Second, as the scope of application of EU law expands, an ever-increasing number of situations fall within the ambit of the provision. The principle of non-discrimination on grounds of nationality covers any instances that feature a nexus to the Treaties. Given that EU secondary law has to be measured against the Treaty provisions, this implies that all EU legislative acts are subject to review. Besides, all situations, the '*facts and effects* of which are [not] confined within a single Member State'[12] but which display a cross border element must be in conformity with the equality provision.[13] Third, the principle applies to instances of 'overt' or direct as well as 'covert' or indirect discrimination.[14] According to the case law of the European

Unión de Televisiones Comerciales Asociadas (UTECA) v Administración General del Estado [2009] ECR I-1407, paras 37 ff.

[9] See, eg Epiney (n 1) marginal no 44.

[10] In favour von Bogdandy (n 1) marginal no 28; more reserved M Rossi, 'Das Diskriminierungsverbot nach Art 12 EGV' (2000) *Europarecht* 197, 216 f.

[11] See Epiney (n 1) marginal no 44 with reference to Case 36/74 *BNO Walrave and LJN Koch v Association Union cycliste internationale, Koninklijke Nederlandsche Wielren Unie and Federación Española Ciclismo* [1974] ECR 1405, para 25; Case C-415/93 *Union royale belge des sociétés de football association ASBL v Jean-Marc Bosman* [1995] ECR I-4921, paras 69 ff; Case C-438/05 *International Transport Workers' Federation and Finnish Seamen's Union v Viking Line ABP and OÜ Viking Line Eesti* [2007] ECR I-10779, paras 32 ff. For an institutional choice reading of the obligations of private parties to respect the fundamental freedoms, see P Caro de Sousa, *The European Fundamental Freedoms: A Contextual Approach* (Oxford, Oxford University Press, 2015) 200 ff.

[12] Case C-72/03 *Carbonati Apuani v Commune di Carrara* [2004] ECR I-8027, Opinion of AG Maduro, para 23 (emphasis added). See, eg Case 286/81 *Criminal proceedings against Oosthoek's Uitgeversmaatschappij BV* [1982] ECR 4575, para 9; Case 98/86 *Criminal proceedings against Arthur Mathot* [1987] ECR 809, paras 7–9; Case C-332/90 *Volker Steen v Deutsche Bundespost* [1992] ECR I-341, para 9; and Case C-108/98 *RI.SAN. Srl v Comune di Ischia, Italia Lavoro SpA and Ischia Ambiente SpA* [1999] ECR I-5219, para 23.

[13] For a detailed analysis of the purely internal rule, see ch 5.

[14] See for examples of direct discriminations Joined Cases C-92/92 and C-326/92 *Phil Collins v Imtrat Handelsgesellschaft mbH and Patricia Im- und Export Verwaltungsgesellschaft mbH and Leif Emanuel Kraul v EMI Electrola GmbH* [1993] ECR I-5145 para 33; Case C-122/96 *Stephen Austin Saldanha and MTS Securities Corporation v Hiross Holding AG* [1997] ECR I-5325 para 26; for examples of indirect discriminations Case C-85/96 *María Martínez Sala v Freistaat Bayern* [1998] ECR I-2691 paras 46 ff (residence permit); Case C-209/03 *The Queen, on the application of Dany Bidar v London Borough of Ealing and Secretary of State for Education and Skills* [2005] ECR I-2119 paras 28 ff (residence) or Case C-158/07 *Jacqueline Förster v Hoofddirectie van de Informatie Beheer Groep* [2008] ECR I-8507, paras 34 ff (residence).

Court of Justice, measures which explicitly differentiate between nationals of one Member State and nationals of others, are subject to review. Likewise, measures which rely on another aspect as a criterion of differentiation, but which 'lead to the same result' as those differentiating on the grounds of nationality, are tested for their compatibility with the norm.[15]

One development can be inferred from the list of reasons just given: as the EU's integration project progressed, the scope of application of the principle also expanded over time. With this expansion in scope the question whether the possibilities to justify discriminatory measures should be expanded has demanded greater attention. The European Court of Justice showed responsiveness to the raised concerns. With regard to indirect discrimination on grounds of nationality, it held that it may be justified 'if it is based on objective considerations independent of the nationality of the persons concerned and is proportionate to the legitimate aim of the national provisions'.[16]

Building on the above, EU lawyers asked if the justification for indirectly discriminatory measures could be transferred to instances of direct discrimination. The debate on this issue ensued under the heading: 'Is the right to non-discrimination on grounds of nationality an absolute or a relative right?'[17] Proponents of the idea that it was an absolute right argued that the wording of Article 18(1) TFEU left little room for alternative interpretations.[18] Adherents to the view that the article concerned a relative right saw less of a necessity to differentiate between direct and indirect discrimination. If ever more fields of law were subject to scrutiny under the principle of non-discrimination, then the possibility for justifying existing instances of discrimination should also be available in these fields. Moreover, it was put forward that the special non-discrimination provisions such as the freedom of movement for workers and services or the right of establishment allowed under certain conditions for justification of direct discrimination. Therefore, the argument goes, it is absurd to maintain the position that the more general clause allowed for fewer justifications than its more precise stipulations.[19]

The European Court of Justice gradually approached the issue. In *Gravier*,[20] decided in 1985, the Court did not take into consideration whether a directly

[15] eg Case 152/73 *Giovanni Maria Sotgiu v Deutsche Bundespost* [1974] ECR 153, para 11; Case C-175/88 *Biehl v Administration des contributions du grand-duché de Luxembourg* [1990] ECR I-1779 para 13; Case C-29/95 *Eckehard Pastoors and Trans-Cap GmbH v Belgian State* [1997] ECR I-285 para 16.

[16] eg Case C-274/96 *Criminal proceedings against Horst Otto Bickel and Ulrich Franz* [1998] ECR I-7637, para 27; *Bidar* (n 14) para 54; similar Case C-224/98 *Marie-Nathalie D'Hoop v Office national de l'emploi* [2002] ECR I-6191, para 36.

[17] Rossi (n 10) 212.

[18] K Feige, *Der Gleichheitssatz im Recht der EWG* (Tübingen, Mohr, 1973) 44 ff; see also A Mohn, *Der Gleichheitssatz im Gemeinschaftsrecht. Differenzierungen im europäischen Gemeinschaftsrecht und ihre Vereinbarkeit mit dem Gleichheitssatz* (Kehl, Engel, 1990) 10.

[19] For an overview, see Streinz (n 7) with further references.

[20] Case 293/83 *Françoise Gravier v City of Liège* [1985] ECR 593.

discriminatory norm could be justified. It argued that the Belgian practice, which required students from other Member States to pay a registration fee to be granted access to vocational training (whereas Belgian nationals were exempt from this obligation), constituted discrimination on grounds of nationality.[21] As a consequence—and without engaging in further review—the Court held the practice to be 'contrary to Article 7 of the Treaty [now Article 18(1) TFEU]'.[22] Straight-forward was also its reply in *Phil Collins*.[23] There, the Court decided that the German law, which granted German authors more comprehensive means of protection for their artistic works than nationals of other Member States, was incompatible with the EU principle of non-discrimination on grounds of nationality.[24] No mention was made of potential justifications.

Subsequently, the Court began to more openly address the idea that direct discriminations might also be justified. *James Wood*[25] is a decision that indicates this shift. The case concerned the unsuccessful request for compensation of Mr Wood, who had lost his daughter in a traffic accident. Mr Wood held British nationality, but had been living in France for over 20 years when he filed the request. Had he been a French citizen, he would have been entitled to compensation, but due to his British nationality, the French law denied him damages. In its examination, the European Court of Justice first established that the case constituted an instance of direct discrimination. It continued with a reference to the justification standard employed in instances of indirect discrimination and raised in the abstract the question as to whether objective and proportionate considerations 'independent of the nationality of the persons concerned' might justify the differentiation.[26] However, the introduction of the more permissive justification standard did not alter the outcome of the case. Ultimately, the Court held the French law to be contrary to the principle of non-discrimination on grounds of nationality.[27]

As the explications above show and as is common for EU law, adjudication on the principle of non-discrimination on grounds of nationality is in continuous flux. The principle's scope of application has widened while the means of its limitation have increased. For an analysis of how the principle functions, I consider it therefore especially interesting to focus the investigation on those areas which are currently in motion or show the biggest potential for evolution. These borderline

[21] ibid, paras 11 ff.
[22] ibid, para 26.
[23] *Phil Collins* (n 14).
[24] ibid, para 33. As the Court stated in unequivocal terms:

> Article 7 of the Treaty [now Art 18(1) TFEU] requires ... that persons in a situation governed by Community law be placed on a completely equal footing with nationals of the Member State concerned ... In so far as that principle is applicable, it therefore precludes a Member State from making the grant of an exclusive right subject to the requirement that the person concerned be a national of that State (ibid, para 32).

[25] Case C-164/07 *James Wood v Fonds de garantie des victimes des actes de terrorisme et d'autres infractions* [2008] ECR I-4143.
[26] ibid, para 13.
[27] ibid, para 16.

cases can tell us much about the elements of the principle which are still indeterminate and in need of specification.[28] In particular, two subjects come to mind. Both share that direct discrimination on grounds of nationality occurs and that the discrimination is (likely to be) considered justified.

III. CHALLENGES TO THE EQUAL TREATMENT OF EU CITIZENS

A. Enjoyment of Social Benefits in Host Member States

To begin with, an analysis of the adjudication on social benefits shows that the European Court of Justice assumes limits to equal treatment of EU citizens. As in other areas of EU citizenship law, a rather expansive phase in the European Court of Justice's case law on the issue was followed by more modest interpretations of the relevant EU provisions.[29] At first, the Court stated that EU citizens were entitled to the equal grant of certain national benefits. However, it then held other assistance measures to be legitimately reserved to a country's own nationals. Whilst some of the commentators remained sceptical towards the expansive phase,[30] others saw the later, more diffident decisions as an assault on the accomplished *acquis*.[31]

i. The Expansive Phase

The expansive phase can best be exemplified with the European Court of Justice's decisions in *Grzelczyk*,[32] *Trojani*[33] and *Bidar*.[34] All three cases concerned the question as to whether EU citizens were entitled to financial support in a Member State different from their own. In *Grzelczyk*, a French national pursuing his studies in Belgium applied unsuccessfully for Belgium minimum subsistence allowance (minimex). When asked about the conformity of the Belgium authorities' refusal to grant Mr Grzelczyk the allowance, the European Court of Justice first established that the refusal constituted a case of discrimination on grounds of

[28] See generally R Dworkin, 'Hard Cases' (1975) 88 *Harvard Law Review* 1057; ibid, *Taking Rights Seriously* 9th edn (London, Duckworth, 2000).

[29] See for the developments concerning the purely internal rule ch 5 s II.B.iii.

[30] eg K Hailbronner, 'Union Citizenship and Access to Social Benefits' (2005) 42 *Common Market Law Review* 1247, 1264 ff.

[31] eg A Farahat, 'Solidarität und Inklusion: Umstrittene Dimensionen der Unionsbürgerschaft' (2016) *Die öffentliche Verwaltung* 45, 49 ff; N Nic Shuibhne, 'Limits Rising, Duties Ascending: The Changing Legal Shape of Union Citizenship' (2015) 52 *CML Rev* 889. Arguing in this direction S Guibboni, 'Free Movement of Persons and European Solidarity Revisited' (2015) 7 *Perspectives on Federalism*, issue 3, 14 f.

[32] Case C-184/99 *Rudy Grzelczyk v Centre public d'aide sociale d'Ottignies-Louvain-la-Neuve* [2001] ECR I-6193.

[33] Case C-456/02 *Michel Trojani v Centre public d'aide sociale de Bruxelles (CPAS)* [2004] ECR I-7573.

[34] *Bidar* (n 14).

nationality.[35] Though it stated that in general such discriminations might be justified, it could not detect a satisfying justification in the present case. In particular, it ruled out the financial burden on the host state as an explanation for the differential treatment, as students in similar situations to that of Mr Grzelczyk were likely to rely on assistance only temporarily.[36] Continuing with *Trojani*, the European Court of Justice held that EU citizens entitled to residence in another Member State due to that state's national law could also 'rely on Article 12 EC [now Article 18 TFEU] in order to be granted a social assistance benefit'.[37] Accordingly, the European Court of Justice used the principle of non-discrimination on grounds of nationality 'as an instrument of social solidarity'.[38] Finally, the Court elaborated in *Bidar* in which instances Member States might justifiably deny EU citizens social benefits that they grant their own nationals. It started with the assumption that EU citizens lawfully resident in another Member State may rely on the right of non-discrimination on grounds of nationality.[39] The Court continued to hold that the right to equal treatment was a relative right and engaged in justificatory review. In this exercise, it argued that Member States were allowed to require from a person 'a certain degree of integration into the society of that State',[40] so as to be entitled to financial assistance. In the specific case, the Court found that Mr Bidar, a French national who had applied for a university student loan in the UK, had sufficient ties with the UK due to a period of secondary education in the country to be eligible for financial aid.[41]

We can gain two insights from an analysis of the cases: first, though the European Court of Justice stated that justification of differential treatment was possible, it nevertheless helped each litigant to back his individual claim for social security benefits with the means of EU law. Second, the Court argued in all cases that EU citizens were entitled to equal treatment under the Treaty provisions.[42] Consequently, it tested in each instance of differential treatment presented to it whether the differential treatment was justified pursuant the standard of Article 18(1) TFEU explained above.

ii. Defining the Limits to Social Benefits for Nationals of Other Member States

Under the impression of the expansive approach by the European Court of Justice in the above mentioned cases, the question arose under which circumstances the Court would hold a specific Member State social benefit, which reserved rights

[35] *Grzelczyk* (n 32) para 29.
[36] ibid, paras 44 f.
[37] *Trojani* (n 33) para 46.
[38] Tridimas (n 3) 134.
[39] *Bidar* (n 14) para 46.
[40] ibid, para 57.
[41] See ibid, para 62.
[42] *Grzelczyk* and *Bidar* were thus seen as 'aptly illustrat[ing] the impact of European citizenship on the interpretation of Article 12' (Tridimas (n 3) 128).

to the country's own nationals, to be in accordance with EU law. Were Member States still allowed to grant financial support to their own nationals without having to include citizens of other Member States living on their territory in the pool of eligible applicants, and if so, under which conditions? The intricate interplay between provisions of EU citizens' right to free movement and of the coordination of social security systems in EU secondary law further complicated the issue, because the question of EU citizens' differential treatment came to the fore in disputes surrounding the 'correct' interpretation of specific directive or regulation provisions. After a period of incrementalism, the European Court of Justice has defined its current approach more clearly. As of now, it allows for general limits to the grant of social benefits for EU foreigners. In this regard, a caveat must be mentioned: the decisions giving contours to the approach are fairly recent. Hence, this analysis can offer but a snapshot appraisal which might be subject to change in the future.

a. The Interim Phase

To sketch the development of the Court's adjudication, it first indicated more strongly than before that it was willing to accept limits to equal treatment of EU citizens with regard to social benefits not only in theory, but also in practice. To begin with, the European Court of Justice clarified in *Förster*[43] what it meant by its requirement in *Bidar*, that EU citizens studying in a Member State different from their own needed to 'have demonstrated a certain degree of integration into the society of that State'[44] in order to be eligible for a maintenance grant. It stated that a residence requirement of five years could not be regarded as 'excessive'.[45] In *Vatsouras and Koupatantze*,[46] the Court added another element to its social benefits adjudication. It decided on the compatibility of Article 24(2) of Directive 2004/38[47]—the Free Movement Directive—with primary EU non-discrimination law. The relevant article contains a derogation from the general principle of equal treatment and establishes that Member States are not required to grant social benefits to economically inactive EU foreigners under certain circumstances. Pressed on the issue whether Article 24(2) Directive 2004/38 was in conformity with the equal treatment provisions of Articles 12 and 39 TFEU, the Court answered in the affirmative. It stated that Member States were allowed to demand a 'real link'

[43] *Förster* (n 14).

[44] *Bidar* (n 14) para 57.

[45] *Förster* (n 14) para 54.

[46] Joined Cases C-22/08 and 23/08 *Athanasios Vatsouras and Josif Koupatantze v Arbeitsgemeinschaft (ARGE) Nürnberg 900* [2009] EU:C:2009:344.

[47] Dir 2004/38/EC of the European Parliament and of the Council of 29 April 2004 on the right of citizens of the Union and their family members to move and reside freely within the territory of the Member States amending Regulation (EEC) No 1612/68 and repealing Dirs 64/221/EEC, 68/360/EEC, 72/194/EEC, 73/148/EEC, 75/34/EEC, 75/35/EEC, 90/364/EEC, 90/365/EEC and 93/96/EEC [2004] OJ L158/77.

between the person seeking social assistance and the granting state.[48] Yet, the judgment remained ambiguous on other points. It sought to confine instances in which the derogation might apply to a minimum. The judges first stated that national authorities needed to observe the wide interpretation given to the definition of 'workers' under EU law; a group not subject to the derogation of Article 24(2) Directive 2004/38.[49] Second, they argued that any measure 'intended to facilitate access to employment' was not covered by the derogation, either.[50] So, although they repeated their insistence on 'sufficient ties' to the host state as a requisite for social benefits (in the narrow sense of the word), they were generous in pointing out other options to the avail of EU citizens for financial aid. Last, the European Court of Justice declared in *Brey* that Member States had to decide on an individual basis if they could deny pensioners from other Member States the grant of compensatory supplements in order to prevent their national social security systems from becoming overburdened.[51] Following the decision, there was uncertainty as to the scope of this statement. Were national authorities required under the logic of *Brey* to assess on a case by case basis if they could justifiably deny EU citizens from other Member States social benefits that they granted to their own nationals?

Looking for clarification and simplification, the European Court of Justice entered a new phase in its social benefits case law. Its decisions in *Dano*,[52] *Alimanovic*[53] and *García-Nieto*[54] illustrate its renewed effort to develop a coherent approach to the non-discriminatory grant of social benefits.

b. Setting out the Approach: *Dano*

Mrs Dano was a Romanian national who had moved to Germany with her underage son. Her prospects of finding employment in Germany were rather grim. She had received only limited primary education, no professional training and had not worked prior to her move to Germany.[55] Mrs Dano applied for social assistance under Book II of the German Social Code (*Sozialgesetzbuch Zweites Buch*), yet the German authorities denied her claim. Their argument was that she did not meet the requirements of the German provisions on social assistance for foreign nationals. Having established that, the competent court 'expresse[d]

[48] *Vatsouras and Koupatantze* (n 46) para 38, with reference to *D'Hoop* (n 16) and Case C-258/04 *Office national de l'emploi v Ioannis Ioannidis* [2005] ECR I-6191, para 30.

[49] *Vatsouras and Koupatantze* (n 46) paras 23 ff.

[50] ibid, para 45.

[51] Case C-140/12 *Pensionsversicherungsanstalt v Peter Brey* [2013] ECLI:EU:C:2013:565.

[52] Case C-333/13 *Elisabeta Dano and Florin Dano v Jobcenter Leipzig* [2014] ECLI:EU:C:2014:2358.

[53] Case C-67/14 *Jobcenter Berlin Neukölln v Nazifa Alimanovic and Others* [2015] ECLI:EU:C:2015:597.

[54] Case C-299/14 *Vestische Arbeit Jobcenter Kreis Recklinghausen v Jovanna García-Nieto and Others* [2016] ECLI:EU:C:2016:114.

[55] *Dano* (n 52) para 39.

doubts as to whether provisions of EU law … preclude[d] those provisions of German law'.[56]

More precisely, the national court asked whether Article 4 of Regulation 883/2004 on the coordination of social security systems—the Regulation's equal treatment provision for EU citizens[57]—prohibited Member States from excluding citizens from other Member States, who had not paid into the social security scheme beforehand, from receiving benefits.[58] Should this question be answered in the negative, the referring court asked whether the German law was incompatible with other EU non-discrimination laws, specifically Article 18 TFEU and/or Article 20(2)(2)(a) TFEU.[59,60]

In its reply to the national court, the European Court of Justice emphasised the 'fundamental status' of EU citizenship[61] and continued that '[e]very Union citizen may therefore rely on the prohibition of discrimination on grounds of nationality laid down in Article 18 TFEU in all situations falling within the scope *ratione materiae* of EU law'.[62] To adequately depict the Court's further reasoning, it is worth citing the passage in full:

> In this connection, it is to be noted that Article 18(1) TFEU prohibits any discrimination on grounds of nationality '[w]ithin the scope of application of the Treaties, and without prejudice to any special provisions contained therein'. The second subparagraph of Article 20(2) TFEU expressly states that the rights conferred on Union citizens by that article are to be exercised 'in accordance with the conditions and limits defined by the Treaties and by the measures adopted thereunder'. Furthermore, under Article 21(1) TFEU too the right of Union citizens to move and reside freely within the territory of the Member States is subject to compliance with the 'limitations and conditions laid down in the Treaties and by the measures adopted to give them effect'. …
>
> Thus, the principle of non-discrimination, laid down generally in Article 18 TFEU, is given more specific expression in Article 24 of Directive 2004/38 in relation to Union citizens who, like the applicants in the main proceedings, exercise their right to move and reside within the territory of the Member States. That principle is also given more specific expression in Article 4 of Regulation No 883/2004 in relation to Union citizens, such as the applicants in the main proceedings, who invoke in the host Member State the benefits referred to in Article 70(2) of the regulation.
>
> Accordingly, the Court should interpret Article 24 of Directive 2004/38 and Article 4 of Regulation No 883/2004.[63]

[56] ibid, para 43.

[57] Art 4 Reg 883/2004 states: 'Unless otherwise provided for by this Regulation, persons to whom this Regulation applies shall enjoy the same benefits and be subject to the same obligations under the legislation of any Member State as the nationals thereof'.

[58] *Dano* (n 52) para 45, question (2) referred.

[59] Art 20(2)(2)(a) TFEU states: 'They [citizens of the Union] shall have … the right to move and reside freely within the territory of the Member States'.

[60] *Dano* (n 52) para 45, question (3) referred.

[61] ibid, para 58.

[62] ibid, para 59.

[63] ibid, paras 60–62.

The Court further explained in its rather technical interpretation[64] of the two articles that only EU citizens covered by the Directive, respectively the Regulation, could rely on their protection. Therefore, only persons to whom the Free Movement Directive 2004/38 granted a right to reside in another Member State could invoke equal treatment under the provisions. Since a person in Mrs Dano's situation met none of the requirements, a person in her position was not eligible to qualify for equal treatment protection under Article 24 Directive 2004/38 or under Article 4 Regulation 883/2004.

How had the judges at the European Court of Justice reached their conclusion? As a first step, they had (correctly) argued that Article 24 Directive 2004/38 and Article 4 Regulation 883/2004 specify the EU's general principle of non-discrimination on grounds of nationality. Then, they had (correctly) argued that a person in Mrs Dano's situation was not within the scope *ratione personae* of Directive 2004/38 and could therefore not rely on the equal treatment provision of the directive.[65] Accordingly, the Court evaded deciding whether the differential treatment of Mrs Dano and a German citizen in the same position was justified under the Directive.

Irritation was caused by the reasoning of the Court ending there. Arguing that Article 24 Directive 2004/38 as well as Article 4 Regulation 883/2004 specify the general principle of non-discrimination on grounds of nationality does not establish that the norms deal with the issue conclusively. After having applied the facts of the case to the wording of the Directive and the Regulation, the next logical step would have been to test the compatibility of these EU secondary provisions—Article 24 Directive 2004/38 and Article 4 Regulation 883/2004—with EU primary law, especially Article 18 TFEU. In her comment on the case, Nic Shuibhne addresses the issue head on, asking what is left of the 'primary-ness' of Treaty articles under the approach taken by the Court in the given case.[66]

However, the Court was not wholly blind to the equality aspects of *Dano*, either. Its reasoning shows heightened awareness of *Dano*'s substantive equal treatment implications. Even though the Court deliberately avoided equality review by denying the applicability of the special equal treatment provisions, it touched upon the underlying egalitarian issue. In paragraph 74 of the decision, the Court stated that extending the right to social benefits to persons not covered by Directive 2004/38 'would run counter to the objective of the directive … namely preventing Union citizens who are nationals of other Member States from becoming an

[64] D Thym, 'EU-Freizügigkeit als rechtliche Konstruktion—nicht als sozial Imagination', www.verfassungsblog.de/eu-freizuegigkeit-als-rechtliche-konstruktion-nicht-als-soziale-imagination/.

[65] See D Düsterhaus, 'Timeo *Danones* et dona petentes. European Court of Justice (Grand Chamber), Judgment of 11 November 2014, Case C-333/13, *Elisabeta and Florin Dano v Jobcenter Leipzig*' (2015) 11 *European Constitutional Law Review* 121, 130.

[66] Nic Shuibhne (n 31) 909. See also Düsterhaus (n 65) 136. *Vatsouras and Koupatantze* (n 46) did not solve the issue entirely, as it only discussed the compatibility of Art 24(2) of Dir 2004/38/EC with primary law.

unreasonable burden on the social assistance system of the host Member State'.[67] Although the statement does not drive the Court's argument, it is interesting for two reasons: first, it serves as backup reasoning and signals that the Court, should it have been necessary to engage in thorough equality review, would have decided in favour of the Member State provision. Second, it indicates that the European Court of Justice would have used a quantitative argument to justify the differentiation, if called upon. The justification would have relied on no *internal* difference amongst free moving EU citizens without sufficient resources and nationals of the host Member State. Instead, it would have taken the achievement of an *external* aim into account. Thus, the Court's insinuated reasoning is a further example of equality review independent from comparison, which has been described above in chapter 3.[68]

c. Confirming the Approach: *Alimanovic* and *García-Nieto*

Whilst *Dano* was pending before the European Court of Justice, a similar case — *Alimanovic*[69]—reached the Court. It is the more relevant of the two as it concerned a more frequently arising situation that EU free movers could find themselves in. Whereas in *Dano*, Leipzig's Social Court of first instance applied an extreme case to its reference which served numerous prejudices against EU free movers—Eastern European 'welfare tourist' with low education[70]—the reference by the German Federal Social Court in *Alimanovic* was less biased.

Mrs Alimanovic, a Swedish national and mother of three, moved to Germany in 2010 after having already lived in the country previously. She found employment for the first 11 months of her stay. After termination of her work and a period of transitional allowance, she applied for social security benefits. The ensuing litigation dealt with the question whether Mrs Alimanovic and her children were entitled to such benefits. Due to the fact that Mrs Alimanovic had worked for less than a year since her return to Germany, they were not eligible under German law. However, as in Mrs Dano's case, the national court questioned the compatibility of German law with the EU guarantee not to be discriminated against due to one's nationality. In particular, the referring court asked whether the German measures were in conformity with the secondary norms of Article 4 Regulation 883/2004 and Article 24 Directive 2004/38 as well as Article 45(2) TFEU read in conjunction

[67] *Dano* (n 52) para 74.
[68] See ch 3, s I.C,iii.
[69] *Alimanovic* (n 53).
[70] On this highly problematic aspect of the reference, see, eg A Wallrabenstein, 'Wie Florin zwischen die Stühle rutschte—Die Unionsbürgerschaft und das menschenwürdige Existenzminimum' (2016) 71 *Juristenzeitung* 109, 120. For data on the exaggeration of the so-called 'threat of welfare tourism' see ICF GHK, 'A fact finding analysis on the impact on the Member States' social security systems of the entitlements of non-active intra-EU migrants to special non-contributory cash benefits and healthcare granted on the basis of residence', www.ec.europa.eu/employment_social/empl_portal/facebook/20131014%20GHK%20study%20web_EU%20migration.pdf.

with Article 18 TFEU.[71] So, differing from *Dano*, the preliminary reference dealt with the situation of an EU citizen with work experience who stood chances of being integrated into the labour market of the host Member State.

In its decision, the European Court of Justice first established that the social benefit Mrs Alimanovic sought to obtain was not 'intended to facilitate access to the labour market of a Member State'.[72] Therefore, the Court abstained from reviewing further whether or not German law was in accordance with the right of free moving workers not to be discriminated against. In this context, the judges took the wording of the referring court—which asked for an interpretation of Article 45(2) TFEU *in conjunction with* Article 18 TFEU—as an opportunity not to review the case pursuant primary law. Rather, they continued with an examination of Article 24 Directive 2004/38 and Article 4 Regulation 883/2004. In its next step, the Court reiterated that an EU citizen may only claim equal treatment with respect to social benefits in the event of rightful residence in the host state.[73] Having worked in Germany for less than a year and not owning sufficient resources to provide for herself, Mrs Alimanovic did not qualify for rightful residence under Directive 2004/38. The free movement Directive only provided her with 'subsidiary protection', since it guaranteed that she, as a job seeker, could not be expelled from Germany. Besides, Article 24(2) TFEU stipulates that the group of merely tolerated EU citizens is exempt from the right to equal entitlement of social benefits under the directive. Elaborating on this exemption to equal treatment, the European Court of Justice held that the German law denying Mrs Alimanovic social benefits was compatible with EU law.[74] Further, the Court moved away from its former finding in *Brey* that individual assessment of an EU citizen's entitlement to social benefits was required. Instead, it held that the directive provided a scheme for categorisation, which sufficiently took into account the different situations EU free movers could find themselves in.[75] So again, the Court found an EU citizen not to be eligible for social assistance in a host Member State.

A third case, namely *García-Nieto*,[76] topped off the line of cases on access to the German welfare system. Mrs García-Nieto, a Spanish national, moved with her daughter to Germany. Shortly thereafter her Spanish partner Mr Peña Cuevas, with whom she was connected neither through marriage nor through a civil partnership, also relocated to Germany from Spain with his son to join the family. When Mr Peña Cuevas applied for social benefits for the first three months of his stay following the move, the German authorities denied his claim. The case reached the European Court of Justice because the national court concerned with

[71] *Alimanovic* (n 53) para 38.

[72] ibid, para 46; with reference to *Vatsouras and Koupatantze* (n 46).

[73] *Alimanovic* (n 53) paras 49 f.

[74] ibid, paras 57 f.

[75] ibid, paras 59 ff; see Farahat (n 31) 49. Criticising the move away from individual assessment already in her discussion of *Dano*, Nic Shuibhne (n 31) 973.

[76] *García-Nieto* (n 54).

the case sought clarification on the point whether EU law allowed Member States to deny citizens from other Member States social benefits in the first three months of their stay in the territory of the host state.

It is unsurprising that the European Court of Justice declared the German limitation on equal access to social benefits to bear scrutiny. The Court stated that the exception was 'consistent with the objective of maintaining the financial equilibrium of the social assistance system of the Member States pursued by Directive 2004/38'.[77] It argued that since Member States committed themselves under the directive's regime to allow nationals of other Member States to reside in their territory for three months without having to prove sufficient resources, they could not be expected to also provide for these persons during the period of their stay.[78] Furthermore, the judges explicated that the directive contained no requirement according to which Member States were obliged to individually examine the situation of every EU citizen applicant for social benefits.[79] Relying on *Alimanovic*, the Court argued that the directive itself incorporated 'various factors characterising the individual situation of each applicant'.[80] In other words, the directive's categorisation of different classes of free moving citizens was again held to ensure individual consideration.

On a positive note, one may perceive *Alimanovic* and *García-Nieto* as two decisions that coherently continue the reasoning developed in *Dano*. The case line provides a practicable legal framework under which Member States and EU citizens alike can estimate which persons qualify for social benefits and which do not. Moreover, commentators interpreted the decisions as the Court's acknowledgements of Member State sovereignty.[81] At the time of the judgments, it was clear that there was sparse political will in some Member States—including Germany—to let EU citizens benefit unconditionally from social assistance.[82] It would have caused major distortion, had the European Court of Justice not exercised judicial self-restraint, but instead engaged in thorough equality review with the potential outcome of declaring the differentiation of social benefit applicants from other Member States and a country's own nationals as unjustified.

Yet the criticism of the Court's judgments was equally strong. The decisions were esteemed to have 'grave consequences for the solidarity and inclusive dimension of Union citizenship'.[83] Critics asked what was left of the 'fundamental status

[77] ibid, para 45.
[78] ibid.
[79] ibid, paras 46 ff.
[80] ibid, para 47.
[81] Thym (n 64).
[82] See the letter of 23 April 2013 to A Shatter, then President of the European Council for Justice and Home Affairs, by the interior ministers at the time J Mikl-Leitner, HP Friedrich, F Teeven and T May, docs.dpaq.de/3604-130415_letter_to_presidency_final_1_2.pdf.
[83] A Farahat, 'Der Umbau der europäischen Sozialbürgerschaft: Anmerkungen zum Urteil des EuGH in der Rechtssache Alimanovic', www.verfassungsblog.de/der-umbau-der-europaeischen-sozialbuergerschaft-anmerkungen-zum-urteil-des-eugh-in-der-rechtssache-alimanovic.

of EU citizenship' if Member States were allowed to treat certain EU citizens—free movers without sufficient resources—less favourably than their own nationals.[84] They combined their critique with the observation that the European Court of Justice followed a pattern of 'ebb and flow' in its case law,[85] thereby questioning how far the Court accomplished its task of providing legal certainty. Further, the Court was accused of introducing classes of EU citizens. According to this view, the decisions pitted the economic active citizen against the economic inactive one.[86] In general, one could witness the enhanced employment of conceptual pairs to describe the Court's adjudication: the economic citizen versus the economic inactive citizen just mentioned became associated with the rich enjoying EU rights versus the poor being denied protection. The decisions were also seen as evidence for the theory that the European Court of Justice was more favourable towards 'good' citizens compared with 'bad' citizens.[87] Finally, commentators argued that the Court's social benefit judgments embraced an integrational reading of the EU citizens' right to non-discrimination instead of a residential one.[88] Pursuant this interpretation, only EU foreigners who are already to some extent integrated in the host state or stand good chances of becoming well-integrated, are said to benefit from the EU principle of non-discrimination on grounds of nationality.

In the end, supporters and disapprovers of the *Dano*, *Alimanovic* and *García-Nieto* case line agree on one point: with its judgments, the European Court of Justice made clear that it sees limits in Member States' obligation to solidarity[89] and limits to EU citizens' right not to be discriminated against on grounds of their nationality.

B. Voting Rights in National Elections

A second area, in which limitations to the EU principle on non-discrimination on grounds of nationality might possibly emerge, is electoral laws within the EU and its Member States. As of now, no case has reached the European Court of Justice, which has been specifically concerned with EU citizens' differential treatment in national elections. Therefore, the Court has not had to decide if and under

[84] Düsterhaus (n 65) 138; Nic Shuibhne (n 31) 930 ff; Wallrabenstein (n 70) 117.

[85] Nic Shuibhne speaks of 'a profound shift in emphasis towards the rising significance of conditions and limits … in the application and interpretation of citizenship rights' (Nic Shuibhne (n 31) 891).

[86] On this point see Farahat (n 31) 55; Nic Shuibhne (n 31) 926 ff; D Thym, 'The Elusive Limits of Solidarity: Residence Rights of and Social Benefits for Economically Inactive Union Citizens' (2015) 52 *CML Rev* 17, 19 f and 33 ff; Wallrabenstein (n 70) 120; R Zahn, '"Common Sense" or Threat to EU Integration? The Court, Economically Inactive EU Citizens and Social Benefits' (2015) 44 *Industrial Law Journal* 573, 583.

[87] See Nic Shuibhne (n 31) 927.

[88] Thym (n 86) 38 with reference to *Dano*.

[89] Generally on this point P Hilpold, 'Die Unionsbürgerschaft—Entwicklung und Probleme' (2015) *Europarecht* 133, 146 f; Nic Shuibhne (n 31); Thym (n 86).

which circumstances Member States may confine participation in national elections to their own citizens. However, it is likely that the European Court of Justice will eventually have to address the question. Ultimately, it will in all probability consider Member State's limitation of voting rights to its own nationals to be in conformity with EU law. However the argumentative effort to justify the distinction between Member State's own nationals and EU citizens of other countries could potentially be considerable.

i. A Feasible Scenario before the European Court of Justice

What would a case on the compatibility of voting rights in national elections with EU law look like? Two scenarios are possible.

The first scenario involves an EU citizen moving from her home state to another Member State and seeking access to national elections in the host state. For example, if a French student moves to Germany to pursue her undergraduate studies, she may wish to participate in the elections to the Bundestag, the German Parliament. As of now, there are little means to her avail. The Federal Electoral Law (*Bundeswahlgesetz*) stipulates that only Germans are entitled to vote[90] (and eligible to be voted on).[91] Further, she cannot rely on an explicit voting right under the EU Treaties. Articles 20(2)(b), 22 TFEU state that EU citizens have 'the right to vote and to stand as candidates in elections to the European Parliament and in municipal elections in their Member State of residence, under the same conditions as nationals of that State'.[92] Articles 39 and 40 Charter of Fundamental Rights of the European Union (CFEU) repeat these guarantees. However, a right to access to national elections at the state-wide level has intentionally been omitted in the Treaties and the Charter. The only option left for her is to seek naturalisation according to the procedure laid down in the German Nationality Act (*Staatsangehörigkeitsgesetz*)[93] and to then take part in the elections. Yet, naturalisation is not only a long-standing process but also a step that affects a person's identity as well as her self- and external perception.[94]

Should the French student in question not wish to become a German national, yet would still like to vote for a Member of the Bundestag, she may construe the

[90] § 12 Bundeswahlgesetz, BGBl. I 1993, 1292. The norm refers to the definition of 'German' as it is set forth in Art 116(1) Basic Law:

> Unless otherwise provided by a law, a German within the meaning of this Basic Law is a person who possesses German citizenship or who has been admitted to the territory of the German Reich within the boundaries of 31 December 1937 as a refugee or expellee of German ethnic origin or as the spouse or descendant of such person.

[91] § 15 Bundeswahlgesetz, BGBl. I 1993, 1293.

[92] Art 20(2)(b) TFEU.

[93] RGBl 1913, 583 in the version of 1 November 2015 (BGBl I 2015, 1802).

[94] On the interrelation between citizenship and identity, see generally J Shotter, 'Psychology and Citizenship: Identity and Belonging' in BS Turner (ed), *Citizenship and Social Theory* (London, Sage, 1993); C Tilly (ed), *Citizenship, Identity and Social History* (Cambridge, Cambridge University Press, 1995).

following argument: as an EU citizen making use of her right to free movement, EU law grants her the right to non-discrimination on grounds of nationality. Living and studying in Germany, most of the laws by the German legislature affect her in the same way as German nationals. However, German law bars her from participation in the political process at the federal level due to her French citizenship. She could therefore contend that German law discriminates against her on grounds of her nationality and violates her right to equal treatment as an EU citizen under Article 18(1) TFEU.

A second similar scenario, under which the European Court of Justice might be confronted with a case on voting rights in national elections, is conceivable. It shall only be touched upon, since it does not concern discrimination on grounds of nationality—the specific subject of this chapter—but rather deals with free movement. A case may come before the Court in which an EU citizen challenges the conformity of voting laws in his home state with EU free-movement law. In several Member States, it is possible that citizens of that Member State can no longer participate in its national elections after having moved to another EU country. Bauböck gives examples for this:

> Ireland still does not grant an external franchise. The Greek constitution guarantees voting rights to Greeks living abroad, but the Greek parliament has never adopted the implementing legislation. Britain withdraws voting rights after fifteen years of residence outside the country. Italy allows those born abroad who have inherited their citizenship from Italian ancestors to vote in Italian elections but not those who have kept their residence in Italy and are merely temporarily absent on election day.[95]

A British national indeed attempted to proceed against the UK's '15 year rule', according to which British citizens are disenfranchised after having resided for more than 15 years outside the UK. In the case *R (on the application of James Alistair Preston)*,[96] the British claimant had moved from the UK to Spain over 15 years ago. When he applied for registration to the UK Parliament election, his application was dismissed due to the 15 year rule. In the ensuing litigation, the claimant put forward that 'the rule penalize[d] him for having exercised his directly effective fundamental right under EU law to move and to reside and work in another Member State'.[97] The Court of Appeal indicated (though not explicitly stated) that it considered the claimant's situation to be within the scope of EU law.[98] However, the judges did not regard the British rule as a restriction of EU law, because they deemed its deterrent effect as 'too speculative, remote and indefinite'.[99] Though thoroughly engaging in review pursuant to EU law, the Court of Appeal deemed it

[95] R Bauböck, 'EU Citizens should have Voting Rights in National Elections, but in which Country?', EUI Working Paper, RSCAS 2012/32, 3.

[96] *R (on the application of James Alistair Preston) v The Lord President of the Council* [2012] EWCA Civ 1378.

[97] ibid, para 8.

[98] ibid, paras 64 ff.

[99] ibid, para 80.

unnecessary to make a preliminary reference to the European Court of Justice in order to obtain guidance on the interpretation of relevant EU norms.

Thus, the European Court of Justice has up to this date not had to decide on the compatibility of Member State laws governing national elections with EU law. But this may well change in the future. There have already been signs of political activism on electoral rights in the EU. In 2004, the European Commission mentioned that it perceived a potential 'gap in electoral rights at the present level of Community law', since EU citizens having moved to a different Member State were not allowed to participate in national elections.[100] Additionally, a group filed a European Citizens' Initiative under the title 'Let me vote' in 2012.[101] Its object was '[t]o strengthen the rights listed in article 20(2) TFEU by granting EU citizens residing in another Member State the right to vote in all political elections in their country of residence, on the same conditions as the nationals of that State'.[102] In the end, it did not succeed in collecting the signatures necessary to make the European Commission start a legislative procedure on the proposal. But the existence of the mentioned initiative shows that there are interest groups within the EU that pursue the aim of voting rights for EU citizens in national elections of Member States other than their country of origin. After the failure of the initiative, its proponents may well look for other ways to achieve their objective. They could turn to national courts and construct a case in which an EU citizen desires the right to vote in national elections. In the event that they convince the national court of the relevance of EU law to the outcome of the case, that national court could approach the European Court of Justice under the preliminary reference procedure.

ii. Declining or Asserting Jurisdiction?

Suppose a case similar to that of the French student seeking the right to vote in German federal elections was on the docket of the European Court of Justice, which options would be at the judges' disposal?

A first option would be to deny its jurisdiction and dismiss the case for lack of applicability of EU law. The Court could reason that the deliberate choice by the Member States to mention voting rights for European Parliament and municipal elections in the Treaties but not to touch on voting rights for national elections meant that these rights were beyond the scope of EU law.[103] However, the European Court of Justice could also assert review. Under the logic of the 'interpretive' account, the French student in the hypothetical is an EU citizen who has

[100] European Commission, *Fourth Report on Citizenship of the Union (1 May 2001–30 April 2004)*, COM (2004) 695 final (26 October 2004), 8. See further Shaw (n 5) 2558 ff.

[101] According to the laws governing the European Citizens' initiative, Art 11(4) TEU, Art 24(1) TFEU and Reg (EU) 211/2011 of the European Parliament and of the Council of 16 February 2011 on the citizens' initiative, [2011] OJ L65/1.

[102] www.letmevote.eu/en/initiative.

[103] See also the reasoning in *R (on the application of James Alistair Preston) v The Lord President of the Council* [2012] EWCA Civ 1378, para 68.

made use of her right to free movement and legally resides in Germany. It is undisputed that, as a consequence, the European Union grants her the right to non-discrimination on grounds of nationality.[104] Thus far, the Court has subjected measures, such as the differential raising of student fees[105] or the difficult recognition of foreign diploma, to assessment.[106] On what grounds therefore could the Court then argue that the refusal of voting rights for EU citizens from other Member States was beyond its powers of review? Especially since lack of political participation in the host country could be perceived as a more severe limitation to EU citizens' rights than for example additional expenditures.

In addition, the European Court of Justice has in the past made decisions concerning the voting rights in elections to the European Parliament (EP).[107] In these judgments, it has issued statements on the general significance of political rights in the EU. The Court would run the risk of contradicting these statements, should it now consider national voting rights to be beyond its powers of review.

First, the case known under the name *Gibraltar*[108] dealt with the question whether qualifying Commonwealth citizens[109] living in Gibraltar, who are not EU citizens, should be allowed to vote in EP elections. Important details to the case are that Gibraltar is a British Crown Colony that is not part of the United Kingdom, but part of the European Union,[110] and that the UK had created the voting right 'to comply with the judgment of the European Court of Human Rights in *Matthews v the United Kingdom*'.[111] In the case before the ECtHR, the UK government had been held liable for 'failing to organise elections in Gibraltar for the European Parliament' in the past.[112] In its effort to remedy the violation, the UK extended the right to vote for European Parliament elections not only to EU citizens, but also to qualifying Commonwealth citizens residing in Gibraltar. The European Court of Justice held that it was within the competence of the Member States to determine who was eligible to vote and that the UK's extension of voting rights to Gibraltar's qualifying Commonwealth citizens did not breach Community law.[113] However,

[104] See, eg *Bickel and Franz* (n 16) para 16.

[105] See *Gravier* (n 20) para 11 ff.

[106] See, eg Case 71/76 *Jean Thieffry v Conseil de l'ordre des avocats à la cour de Paris* [1977] ECR 765, speaking of 'restriction'; Case 11/77 *Richard Hugh Patrick v Ministre des affaires culturelles* [1977] ECR 1199; Case C-71/76; Case C-340/89 *Irène Vlassopoulou v Ministerium für Justiz, Bundes- und Europaangelegenheiten Baden-Württemberg* [1991] ECR I-2357.

[107] Case C-145/04 *Kingdom of Spain v United Kingdom* [2006] ECR I-7917; Case C-300/04 *Eman and Sevinger v College van burgemeester en wethouders van Den Haag* [2006] ECR I-8055; Case C-650/13 *Thierry Delvigne v Commune de Lesparre-Médoc and Préfet de la Gironde*; ECLI:EU:C:2015:648.

[108] *Kingdom of Spain v United Kingdom* (n 107).

[109] The term denotes a group of persons, who 'do not require permission to enter or remain in the country [the UK] or have been granted it' (A Landsbergen and J Shaw, 'National Membership Models in a Multilevel Europe' (2010) 8 *International Journal of Constitutional Law* 50, 59).

[110] For a more detailed description of the relationship, see J Shaw, 'The Political Representation of Europe's Citizens: Developments' (2008) 4 *European Constitutional Law Review* 162, 170.

[111] *Kingdom of Spain v United Kingdom* (n 107) para 60. See for the ECtHR case *Matthews v United Kingdom* A no 24833/94 (1999) 28 EHRR 361.

[112] *Kingdom of Spain v United Kingdom* (n 107) para 11.

[113] ibid, paras 59 ff.

the judges' respect for national decisions on voting eligibility was not unfettered. They stated:

> [I]n the current state of Community law, the definition of the persons entitled to vote and to stand as a candidate in elections to the European Parliament falls within the competence of each Member State *in compliance with Community law*.[114]

Second, in the *Aruba* case,[115] decided on the same day as the *Gibraltar* case, the Court was presented with the question whether the citizenship provisions of the TFEU required 'that a citizen of the Union resident or living in an OCT [overseas country or territory] has the right to vote and to stand as a candidate in elections to the European Parliament'.[116] Under Dutch law, Dutch nationals residing in Aruba were excluded from participating in European Parliament elections. The Court repeated its statement that Member States were free to decide on the eligibility to vote in European Parliament elections, as long as they acted in compliance with Community law.[117] It ultimately held that the exclusion of Dutch nationals residing in Aruba was contrary to EU law due to a breach of the EU general principle of non-discrimination (not the more specific principle of non-discrimination on grounds of nationality).[118]

Third, lately, the European Court of Justice reinforced its claim for review of national laws regulating participation in European Parliament elections. In *Delvigne*,[119] a national court made a reference asking whether French electoral law was in compliance with the CFEU. In particular, Mr Delvigne contested the loss of his voting rights after having been given a sentence of 12 years for committing a serious crime.[120] Approaching the issue, the European Court of Justice showed little hesitance in establishing its jurisdiction. It referred to the 1976 EU Electoral Act,[121] as well as to the EU primary provision on universal and free suffrage (Article 14(3) TEU), to link Mr Delvigne's case to EU law. Using this as a starting

[114] ibid, para 78 (emphasis added).

[115] *Eman and Sevinger* (n 107).

[116] ibid, para 32.

[117] ibid, para 54.

[118] The Dutch law granted Netherlands nationals residing in Non-Member States the right to vote in European Parliament elections. By contrast, Netherlands nationals residing in the Antilles or Aruba were barred from participating in these elections. The European Court of Justice dismissed the arguments that were brought forward to justify the differentiation.

[119] *Delvigne* (n 107).

[120] More precisely, the situation under French law was the following: Art 28 of the French Criminal Code (laid down by the Law of 12 February 1810) valid until 1994 stipulated that '[a] sentence for a serious criminal offence will entail the loss of civic rights'. Laws, entering into force in 1994, eased the conditions for criminal offenders. Under the new law, courts now 'may rule that a person is to be deprived of … his civic rights for a period which may not exceed ten years' and any person, who has been deprived of his civil rights can apply to the court for lifting the deprivation.

[121] Act concerning the election of the members of the European Parliament by direct universal suffrage, annexed to Council Decision 76/787/ECSC, EEC, Euratom of 20 September 1976, [1976] OJ L278/1, as amended by Council Decision 2002/772/EC, Euratom of 25 June 2002 and 23 September 2002, [2002] OJ L283/1.

point, the Court stated that Member States 'implement … EU law within the meaning of Article 51 (1) of the Charter' when they determine under which conditions nationals of that state are barred from voting.[122] Therefore, the Court considered the French law to be subject to scrutiny under the CFEU. It then continued to state that Article 39(2) CFEU contained the individual right of Union citizens to elect members of the European Parliament in direct and universal suffrage.[123] Ultimately, it held the French law to be in accordance with Article 39(2) CFEU on substantive grounds.[124] So in a familiar move, the European Court of Justice first brought national legislation within its sphere of review to then grant Member States discretion in the specific design of the law.[125]

Gibraltar, *Aruba* and *Delvigne* all contain statements that indicate the importance the European Court of Justice attaches to the right to vote in European Parliamentary elections. In all cases, the Court claimed its right to review of national voting laws, despite the fact that in principle, EU law leaves the competence to decide on the electorate to the Member States. In *Aruba*, the Court even went as far as to hold a national provision on the composition of the electorate to be incompatible with EU law. Moreover, in *Delvigne*, the Court declared that the right to vote in European Parliament elections was a fundamental right protected by the Charter.[126] Notwithstanding the obvious difference between elections to the European Parliament and elections to national assemblies, the case law on the former has implications for the judicial evaluation of the latter. As Coutts explicates, if Member States have one voting law that covers national as well as European Parliament elections, 'potentially at least a whole range of national measures restricting voting rights [in national elections] could be subject to judicial review under Union law and especially a requirement of proportionality'.[127] In light of this case law, the Court could of course still decline review of electoral laws for national elections in an outright manner. Yet, this would stand in contrast to its assertive, rights-accentuating case law on voting provisions for European Parliament elections.

[122] *Delvigne* (n 107) para 33.

[123] ibid, para 44; see further S Coutts, 'Case C-650/13 Delvigne—A Political Citizenship?' www.europeanlawblog.eu/?p=2946.

[124] The French law was considered a proportionate limitation of voting rights because it 'took into account the nature and gravity of the criminal offence committed and the duration of the penalty' as well as provided affected persons with a means of review of their individual cases (*Delvigne* (n 107) paras 49 ff.).

[125] See Coutts (n 123).

[126] ibid. Therefore, the European Court of Justice holds a different view on the issue than the United Kingdom Supreme Court. The latter held in *R (on the application of Chester) v Secretary of State for Justice and McGeoch (AP) v The Lord President of the Council and another (Scotland)* [2013] UKSC 63, paras 56 ff that EU law guaranteed no autonomous right, that is to say a right independent from an egalitarian claim, to participate in European Parliament elections.

[127] Coutts (n 123).

iii. Justificatory Burdens

Reflecting further, in the event that the European Court of Justice asserted jurisdiction and found the principle of non-discrimination on grounds of nationality to be applicable to a voting rights case, the Court would have to determine whether the discrimination was justified. For this exercise, it would have to employ the justification standard presented above and inquire whether 'objective considerations independent of the nationality of the persons concerned and ... proportionate to the legitimate aim of the national provisions'[128] justified the differentiation. These deliberations are at the heart of the matter because—staying in the terminology of the interpretive account—there exists no 'consideration *independent of the nationality* of the persons concerned' that explained the denial of voting rights to non-nationals.

Practical reasons might be cited. States with a large population of EU foreigners such as Luxembourg may claim that they have to bar EU citizens from other Member States from national elections to ensure stability of the political process.[129] It may well be that equal participation of EU foreigners residing in a host state and citizens of that state in national elections will lead to considerable changes in the voting outcome. But the argument that one should forestall these changes is still connected, or dependent upon, the nationality of those excluded from national elections.

Otherwise, the claim could be made that different voting rights must be granted to a country's own nationals and those of other countries in order to protect a core of citizenship. The argument that states need to be able to reserve certain privileges to their own nationals is clearly not independent of the nationality of the persons concerned. It essentially holds that the criterion for differentiation—citizenship status—already comprises the justification for differentiation—protection of citizenship status. From the perspective of preserving an essence of citizenship, such reasoning is coherent since citizenship is a legal construct defined by 'the tension between internal inclusivity and external exclusivity'.[130] From the perspective of EU citizens' right to non-discrimination on grounds of nationality, the argument stays challenging. It boils down to the statement that there are inherent limits to the EU right to equal treatment irrespective of nationality.

[128] See eg *Bickel and Franz* (n 16) para 27; *D'Hoop* (n 16) para 36; *Bidar* (n 14) para 54; similar Case C-148/02 *Carlos Garcia Avello v Belgian State* [2003] ECR I-11613, para 31.

[129] Even as far as European Parliament elections are concerned, EU law permits Member States to derogate from EU citizens' universal suffrage in the event of a strong foreign community. In Luxembourg, the right to participate in the elections to the European Parliament organised by Luxembourg is reserved to long-time residents. See Art 14 Council Dir 93/109/EC laying down detailed arrangements for the exercise of the right to vote and stand as a candidate in elections to the European Parliament for citizens of the Union residing in a Member State of which they are not nationals [1993] OJ L329/34); see Landsbergen and Shaw (n 109) 54.

[130] J Shaw, 'The Political Representation of Europe's Citizens: Developments' (2008) 4 *European Constitutional Law Review* 162, 179.

C. The EU's Principle of Non-discrimination on Grounds of Nationality versus the Existence of the State

The issue of social benefits for EU citizens, similar to the issue of their voting rights in national elections, epitomises one, if not the fundamental, tension of EU law: at some point, the objective of non-discrimination on grounds of nationality clashes with the idea of the existence of the state. This is the case as 'the protection of nationals, even to the disadvantage of nationals of other Member States, not only forms part of the concept of state sovereignty, but is also a function of the State's existence'.[131] When and under what circumstances the clash occurs depends on the subject area. Strict pursuit of non-discrimination on grounds of nationality contravenes national social security law, under which welfare states provide their nationals (exclusively) with living basics. It also contravenes national electoral laws that pursue the idea of an electorate composed of a state's citizens.[132]

If one bears this conceptual tension in mind, the critique brought forward against the European Court of Justice's case law on social benefits (and the foreseeable critique against decisions on national elections, no matter what their conclusion) becomes more understandable: the 'ebb and flow'[133] in the adjudication is owed to the need of the Court to adjust to changed circumstances under a heightened degree of integration. The conceptual pairs employed in discussions on the case law—'good' versus 'bad' movement or the integration versus residence model of citizenship[134]—depict that EU citizens' complete equal treatment cannot be reconciled with our conventional conception of the state. Last, the doctrinal difficulties of EU equality law become more understandable. Testing standards that seek to justify differentiation between EU foreigners and a state's own nationals irrespective of nationality are bound to malfunction if there are inbuilt limits to non-discrimination.

In the future, the conceptual tension will remain and people will continue to disagree about the 'correct' handling of cases on social benefits or national voting rights. Proponents and opponents will have reasonable grounds for their opinion on both sides. Instead of assessing whether the European Court of Justice judged 'correctly' in the cases on social benefits or what its reasoning in a case on national voting rights should look like in substance, it makes sense therefore to shift the focus to the institutions that shape these laws. 'The goodness or badness' of the Court's decisions 'depends on the context in which they are envisioned'.[135]

[131] M Maduro, *We, the Court* (Oxford, Hart Publishing, 1998) 165.

[132] For alternative potential conceptions of an electorate, see generally CM Rodríguez, 'Noncitizen Voting and the Extraconstitutional Construction of the Polity' (2010) 8 *International Journal of Constitutional Law* 30.

[133] See Nic Shuibhne (n 31) 891.

[134] See s III.A.ii.b.

[135] N Komesar, *Law's Limits* (Cambridge, Cambridge University Press, 2001) 29, though his remark referred not to judicial decisions, but to the evaluation of informal arrangements.

Thus, the questions that underlie the further section are questions of institutional choice: if and when is the European Court of Justice the adequate actor to decide on social benefits or national voting rights?

IV. EQUAL TREATMENT OF EU CITIZENS: AN INSTITUTIONAL CHOICE RECONSTRUCTION

A. Representation of Interests in a Supranational Setting

The previous chapter on different standards of equality testing argued that comparative institutional analysis can contribute to explaining the workings of constitutional review. It sought to illustrate that the level of judicial scrutiny employed depends on a court's estimation of its role in terms of representation of interests, numbers and complexity relative to that of other decision making institutions. The following section explores what insights can be gained from reconceptualising the European Court of Justice's case law on social benefits as well as from analysing national electoral laws from the viewpoint of institutional choice. Within the framework of institutional choice, one assesses whether there is risk of the political process malfunctioning when addressing the issue. One further investigates on the demand side for judicial activity if the political process is in a position to deal with numbers and complexity of a given topic. On the supply side, one examines if judges are in a position to rule on an issue or if high numbers and complexity hinder them from replacing a decision of the political process for their own.

As already indicated above, comparative institutional analysis is not confined to studying horizontal power allocation; it is also a valid tool for explaining the distribution of decision making authority between vertically allocated players. Thus its explanatory strength can be deployed in the European context. In Union law and politics, the question whether the political process or the courts are better suited to make a decision[136] is joined by the question whether that decision shall be taken at the national or the supranational level. This second question addresses the choice facing any process of integration between uniform action at the European level and preservation of diversity and autonomy at the Member State level.

Maduro in his thesis *We, the Court*[137] was the first to employ an institutional choice analysis in the context of European Union law when he explained the free movement of goods case law of the European Court of Justice.[138] In this exercise, he adjusted the framework devised by Komesar to fit the European setting.

[136] A third place for power allocation named by Komesar is the markets, ibid, eg 12. This study focuses on the power play between the judiciary and the legislature merely for the reason that it is concerned with constitutional review.

[137] Maduro (n 131).

[138] See further P Caro de Sousa, *The European Fundamental Freedoms: A Contextual Approach* (Oxford, Oxford University Press, 2015).

The themes of interest representation, numbers and complexity remained, but were partially amended in order to account for the fact that decision making authority could now not only be distributed among the national political process and national courts, but also between the European legislature and judiciary. The themes of scale and competence did not have to be altered in order to accommodate the duplication of choices in power allocation, which was a result of the introduction of a supranational level. So even if one applies institutional analysis on vertical lines, one still needs to identify which actor is better suited (or less inappropriate) to deal with the complexity of particular decisions and which one has the resources to adequately (or less inadequately) make them. But Maduro introduced changes with respect to the parameter of interest representation; more particularly he modified the description of 'political malfunction' by dividing the forms of potential malfunction in the political process into sub-groups, namely (1) *vertical majoritarian bias,* (2) *vertical minoritarian bias,* (3) *horizontal majoritarian bias* and (4) *horizontal minoritarian bias.*[139] The first two categories are concerned with the 'balance of powers among States'.[140] Under *vertical majoritarian bias*, bigger or more influential Member States assert their interests at the expense of smaller Member States, although the impact felt by the latter is excessive when measured against the advantage of the former.[141] In contrast, *vertical minoritarian bias* 'consists of an inordinate power held by smaller States at the expense of larger States'.[142] As regards groups three and four in the scheme, they deal with the allocation of stakes and influence not between States, but throughout the European Union generally. The author states in his introduction of horizontal biases, 'majoritarian bias consists of an inordinate power of the majority, evenly spread throughout all States large and small, at the expense of the few; and minoritarian bias consists of the fear of the European Union political process being captured by supra-national interest groups'.[143]

The establishment of the concept of *vertical bias* is of particular importance in the European context. When decisions are taken at the national level, it is (still) often the case that the stakes of other Member States are not adequately taken into account due quite simply to the fact that national political processes are not designed to provide for broad representation of interests coming from other States. That other countries' citizens are affected by national measures, as well, is regularly not reflected in the decision making processes at Member State level. What is more, there were many norms passed within Member States before they joined the European Union, so that transnational considerations were absent in their deliberations. Consequently, there is an increased risk of disconnect between a measure's negative impact on individuals and those individuals' influence on the

139 ibid, 116 ff.
140 ibid, 117.
141 ibid.
142 ibid.
143 ibid.

decision. Let me explain the functioning of *vertical bias* with help of a classic case of free movement law, *Cassis-de-Dijon*.[144] A German law on liquor denomination stipulating that only spirits with an alcoholic strength over a certain threshold were allowed to be labeled liquor was under review. French Cassis was below the legally required level and therefore not entitled to wear the label. By its decision not to allow the selling of French cassis as liquor in Germany, the German legislature had not paid due account to the fact that the manufacture of liquor in France followed different rules and traditions. The interests of French producers were, if not entirely absent, at least heavily underrepresented in the German political process and the European Court of Justice granted protection in order to remedy this malfunction.

Further, an additional element of vertical bias can act out in national political processes. In a framework of shared competences and mutual loyalty, political processes often do not adequately take into account the interests of European actors, such as Commission, Council or Parliament, despite having committed themselves to do so. Instead, Member State actors perceive 'European interests', namely that of the Union or other Member States, as external. One may object to this depiction that under traditional international law, such disregard of 'external interests' is, except in instances in which this disregard results in *jus cogens* abuses or violations of treaty provisions, in conformity with the legal system.[145] In response to this, I would stress that one of the defining elements of European integration is the internalisation of such interests. A core aspect of the Union's constitutional nature is that national institutions are obliged to factor the interests of the Union and other Member States into account when making their decisions.

In view of these possibilities of malfunction in decision making processes throughout Europe, comparative institutional analysis holds that in the event that these external interests are not adequately appraised at the national level, European institutions may act as better (namely less imperfect) alternatives for decision making.[146] Whether the European legislature or the European Court of Justice should then be more suited to step in again depends on the factors of numbers, complexity and representation.

[144] Case 120/78 *Rewe-Zentral AG v Bundesmonopolverwaltung für Branntwein* [1979] ECR 649.

[145] On the *jus cogens* principle, see C Tomuschat and J-M Thouvenin (eds), *The Fundamental Rules of the International Legal Order: Jus Cogens and Obligations Erga Omnes* (Leiden, Martinus Nijhoff Publishers, 2006).

[146] This last line of argument reveals an interesting interconnection between institutional choice and the principle of subsidiarity. Pursuant the principle, Union organs shall only act

> in areas which do not fall within [their] exclusive competence … if and in so far as the objectives of the proposed action cannot be sufficiently achieved by the Member States … but can rather, by reason of the scale or effects of the proposed action, be better achieved at Union level (Art 5(3) TEU).

If one works under the premise that the furtherance of European integration is one of the objectives pursued by a measure, the parameters of institutional choice provide the framework for assessing whether the criteria for action at the supranational stage are met.

For the workings of the European Court of Justice, this means that it should become active in reviewing national measures, if firstly there is an increased risk of interests of other Member States, their citizens or the European Union being underrepresented and secondly if it is better suited than national institutions to weigh all interests involved. Relying on comparative institutional analysis, Maduro suggested 'that the Court of Justice should not second-guess national regulatory choices, but should instead ensure that there is no under-representation of the interests of nationals of other Member States in the national political process'.[147] The last paragraphs show the complexity of its work: the question of legal or illegal is intertwined with that on the correct decision maker and both inform the Court's actions. It must assess when it is the correct moment to replace the diverse weightings of interests in the Member States with uniform judgment.

B. Comparative Institutional Analysis of Social Benefits Adjudication

Applying the framework of institutional choice to national welfare laws, we must first determine (on the demand side of law) whether misrepresentation of interests is at play. A vertical bias, in the sense of some Member States pursuing their objectives at the expense of other Member States with help of their national laws is hard to detect. Obviously, a divide runs between the Member States with regard to the issue. It does not run between smaller and bigger Member States, but rather between countries with extensive welfare measures and those with less developed social security systems. Yet one cannot infer from this gap that some states designed their welfare laws to the detriment of others. This is due to the fact that the states whose social security systems are under scrutiny are those granting benefits. Behind their legislation does not lie, or if so only to a small extent, the incentive to obtain competitive advantages over other states. The primary reason for them to provide social benefits is their own citizens' sustenance. As long as harmonisation of the divergent social security systems within the EU is not pursued,

[147] Maduro (n 131) 173. One may ask in how far there is a real difference in decisional outcome between second-guessing regulatory choice and checking adequate representation of interests. Differently put, how often will the European Court of Justice arrive at the conclusion that European provisions were not violated according to its estimation although misrepresentation of interests of other Member States was present in the national decision making process? Drawing an analogy to German judicature on mistakes in the exercise of discretion, one recognises that the Court may well arrive at different results. German courts may control administrative decisions if misuse of discretion exists, that is to say if an institution fails to take interests into account that should have been regarded (H Maurer, *Allgemeines Verwaltungsrecht* 18th edn (Munich, Beck, 2011) 2011) para 7, marginal no 22). This kind of mistake in decision making is captured by the suggested control of adequate interest representation. In the event that the European Court of Justice then exercises its control, it may still arrive at the conclusion that, had the national institution taken these interests into account, its substantial decision was nevertheless reasonable. Thereby, national decisions are not automatically replaced with the Court's own ideas on the correct weighting of interests and Member State autonomy is respected to a greater extent than under the scrutinised 'second-guessing'.

discrepancies in the extent and amount of social benefit grants are bound to exist between the Member States.

As far as the detection of bias of one Member State against nationals of another Member State is concerned, the picture is less clear. If one looks at interest representation as dispersed amongst individual stake holders in the national political processes, there are indications of bias. Once they have arrived in Germany, persons such as the individuals in *Dano*, *Alimanovic* and *García-Nieto* belong to a minority group. Their interests are prone to underrepresentation. Though the topic of welfare benefits for EU citizens has featured prominently in German political debates for some years,[148] their options as directly affected individuals to shape the decisions by the political process have been negligible.[149] First, they were free movers coming from another Member State without the right to participate in national elections. Second, they had insufficient resources to provide for their own and were dependent on external financial support. Thus, they also belonged to an economically marginalised group. According to this reading, the majority by contrast consists of the nationals of the host Member State. Seen from this point of view, one may argue that the free moving EU citizens' interests in social benefit cases are underrepresented with the entailing risk of the majority exercising inordinate power at the expense of the minority. The majority may want to delimit the group of potential social benefit receivers for concern that the national welfare programmes financed by their taxes become overburdened.

According to the comparative law approach, the likelihood of political malfunction to the detriment of a particular group triggers the question whether the judicial process can provide for a more adequate and balanced interest representation. On the supply side of law, we need to assess whether a court, for the purposes of this investigation the European Court of Justice, is a suitable actor to substitute a decision of the political process. As explained above, the parameters of numbers and complexity guide this decision. In this exercise, one has to bear in mind that '[c]ourts are severely limited in significant ways'.[150] Their resources are limited[151] and detailed reasoning in their judgments often invites further litigants who wish to have clarified whether the rationale behind the judgment applies to their situation. In the European setting, an additional factor ought to be considered. When the European Court of Justice engages in review, the decision not only moves horizontally from the political to the judicial process, but also vertically from the Member States to the European Union. Thus, as soon as the supranational court becomes active, it replaces a decentralised national choice with a

[148] See, eg Deutscher Bundestag, 'Abschlussbericht des Staatssekretärsausschusses zu "Rechtsfragen und Herausforderungen bei der Inanspruchnahme der sozialen Sicherungssysteme durch Angehörige der EU-Mitgliedstaaten"', BT-Drs 18/2470.

[149] The options available might be recourse to the diplomatic missions of their home states or turning to support by NGOs.

[150] Komesar (n 135) 52.

[151] See ibid, 35 ff.

centralised European choice.[152] So even though direct discrimination on grounds of nationality is usually a clear indicator of substantive review, respect for autonomous national choices may call for judicial self-restraint. And as far as social benefits are concerned, numbers and complexity are high. Within the Member States, social assistance programmes can take on many forms: benefits can be allowances in kind or cash benefits, earmarked or at the recipient's free disposal, granted temporarily or without time limitations. If the Court showed increased activity in the area, many cases varying in their specifics would come to it. Soon enough the Court would develop an extensive social security jurisprudence in which it distinguished the facts of the cases from each other. Judging from the preliminary references that prominently mention cases such as *Vatsouras and Koupastanze*,[153] one can infer that the onset of this development has already occurred. In addition, one aspect of the law on social benefits is rather intricate: Though there exists information on how many EU citizens rely on welfare in host Member States, it is difficult to predict future developments. A far-reaching non-discriminatory approach by the European Court of Justice may lead to a significant increase in EU citizens' application for social benefits in countries other than their home state. This is not to say that the potential effects on Member State budgets should or must guide the decisions by the European Court of Justice. However, the aspect highlights that one can justifiably ask whether the Court is the adequate actor to make a decision on the issue. A certain reservation is all the more in place, since Member States have put the topic of social benefits for EU citizens on the EU's political agenda.[154]

Although the aspiration of this analysis is not to explicate the case law by the European Court of Justice on social benefits, but to offer a tool for its scrutiny, certain aspects of the Court's current approach towards social benefits become more comprehensible from an institutional choice point of view. The Court engaged neither in *Dano*, nor in *Alimanovic* or *García-Nieto* in substantive equality review. Instead, its reasoning focused on the scope *ratione personae* of secondary law equality provisions. Although, due to the primaryness of the Treaties, review should still have taken place pursuant the TFEU,[155] the Court opted for a formalistic interpretation of the relevant directive and regulation provisions. This 'technical reasoning'[156] that does not touch upon the constitutional principle of equal treatment indicates that the Court considered itself a less (or at least not more) adequate decision maker on the issue than national political processes.

Besides, under its current approach, the Court placed emphasis on the point that no individual assessment of each EU citizen's application for social assistance was

[152] See Maduro (n 131) 169.

[153] *Dano* (n 52) para 41; *Alimanovic* (n 53) para 34.

[154] See n 82.

[155] See Nic Shuibhne (n 31) 909.

[156] See Thym (n 64).

required.[157] With its acceptance of generalisations, the Court lowered the numbers and complexity of European social welfare cases. On the one hand, its decision to allow generalisations facilitates social assistance proceedings by national welfare administrators. As far as EU law is concerned, they are not obliged to assess the specific facts of each situation. One may rightly perceive this move as a decrease in individual rights protection. But given that resources are limited and decisions have to be taken under suboptimal circumstances,[158] easing the requirements on individual assessment keeps the case load manageable. On the other hand, accepting generalisations also reduces the burden on the docket of the Court itself. There is less potential for individual claimants to argue that the national authorities have insufficiently taken the specifics of their case into account. Less litigation in national courts translates into fewer preliminary references to the European Court of Justice. Thus, the supranational Court evades (or at least lessens the frequency of) having to judge whether EU law demands equal treatment due to the particularities of a case or not.

C. Comparative Institutional Analysis of National Electoral Laws

Moving from social benefit law to national electoral laws, can comparative institutional analysis offer insights into how the European Court of Justice should decide, if asked whether Member State voting laws were in conformity with EU law? I maintain that the approach provides an additional argument for the prompt dismissal of cases that seek to establish equal voting rights in national elections for EU citizens. As mentioned above, the European Court of Justice has two options to uphold the differential voting rights of a Member State's own nationals and EU foreigners. It can either decline its jurisdiction or consider the differentiation between the two groups justified. A comparative institutional choice analysis argues in favour of a dismissal of national voting rights cases at an early stage of reasoning.

Admittedly, one can arrive at the conclusion that the European Court of Justice should hold cases on national voting laws inadmissible without explicit recourse to institutional reasoning. Under the interpretive account, the Court could dismiss the case with reference to Article 20(2)(2)(b) TFEU, since the norm only stipulates voting rights for EU citizens that reside in another Member State than their country of origin in European Parliament as well as local elections. No mention is made of an EU right—in the form of a freedom right or a non-discrimination right—to participate in national elections. Given that Article 20(2)(2)(b) TFEU as well as the guarantee not to be discriminated against on grounds of nationality are both laid down in the TFEU and therefore of equal rank, the Court may legitimately prioritise the former over the latter.

[157] See s III.A.ii.c.

[158] Komesar (n 135) 11 ff.

But the grounds underlying such reasoning will relate to aspects of legitimacy and institutional balance between the Member States and the European Union. By dismissing a case on national voting rights, the European Court of Justice would evade opening a new frontier of conflict with national constitutional courts. For example, the German Federal Constitutional Court has held in the past that the Basic Law's stipulation that '[a]ll state authority is derived from the people' (Article 20(2)(1) Basic Law) entails a definition of the people.[159] Citing further constitutional provisions, the judges stated that 'the people' in Article 20 Basic Law meant the German people. As a consequence, it is doubtful if the German constitution allows for the participation of EU foreigners in national elections. As far as EU citizens' suffrage in local elections is concerned, the Basic Law had to be amended at the time of its introduction to allow for the change.[160] A similar amendment, which would allow for EU citizens' participation in German national elections, might not be possible. In the event that the set-up of the national electorate was protected by the constitution's eternity clause (Article 79(3) Basic Law), even the German *pouvoir constituant* could under German law not confer the right to vote to EU foreigners. Under these circumstances, already a move by the European Court of Justice to subject national electoral laws to scrutiny—irrespective of the review outcome—would evoke heavy criticism and opposition. The contest over supremacy in constitutional adjudication, which the two courts have been competing in for some time, would enter an additional round. What is more, it is highly unlikely that the Federal Constitutional Court would seek to conciliate its point of view on the sensitive matter of electoral design with that of the European Court of Justice.

A comparative institutional argument completes the picture. The lack of electoral rights might be considered as the prime example of majoritarian bias. The majority, composed of a Member State's own citizens, decides on its political representatives. The minority, composed of the EU citizens coming from other Member States, is affected by the decisions of that political process. Yet, it has no options to its avail to influence its composition. The demand side of law would therefore call for heightened awareness by alternative decision makers, particularly the European Union's judicial process. However, as far as the supply side of law is concerned, the European Court of Justice would have to fare better with regard to scale and competence in order to substitute Member States' political decisions on the electoral set-up for its own. Here, the problem of judicial intervention is evident: when could a supranational court argue that it was more apt 'to investigate, understand, and make the substantive social decisions'[161] concerning the grant of national electoral franchise than the Member States' constituent processes? The cases that called for intervention by the European Court of Justice would have to

[159] *BVerfGE* 83, 37 (50). See further Landsbergen and Shaw (n 109) 56 f.

[160] See Gesetz zur Änderung des Grundgesetzes of 21 December 1992, BGBl I 1992, 2086, amending Art 28(1) Basic Law.

[161] See Komesar (n 135) 38.

be examples of excessive political malfunction.[162] In the event that a Member State should completely negate the rights of EU citizens coming from other European countries, the Court might become active in order to ensure at least a minimum of EU foreigners' interest representation in national decision making processes. In less biased settings, it should refrain from intervening in national voting laws.

An additional institutional choice consideration speaks in favour of such judicial restraint. From the point of view of comparative institutional analysis, the question whether EU foreigners should be allowed to participate in national elections under the same conditions as a Member State's own nationals differs from the other egalitarian subject matters discussed in this book. In the electoral context, Komesar's statement that the decision 'who decides is really a decision of *what* decides'[163] needs to be rephrased: the decision 'who decides is really a decision of *who will* decide'. Any judgment by the European Court of Justice altering the electorate in national elections would change the institutional composition of an alternative—if not to say competing—decision maker. In principle, the Court has the power to alter electoral designs, as the decision in the *Aruba* case shows.[164] But from the perspective of institutional choice, it should use this power cautiously, as it alters long term the conditions of decisions making within the Member States and therefore also within the European Union.[165] Addressing differential voting rights and the potential malfunctions of national political processes associated therewith demands acknowledgement on part of the European Court of Justice of its own restraints and deficiencies. Outright declining review therefore seems to be the adequate choice.

V. CONCLUSION

This chapter has investigated how far comparative institutional arguments support or argue against heightened involvement by the European Court of Justice in social benefit cases and in the review of national voting rights. Though both subject matters can be phrased as questions about EU citizens' right to equal treatment, the chapter holds that it is important to take their institutional facets into account. Institutional considerations not only underpin the European Court of Justice's acceptance of generalised limits on equal access to social benefits, they

[162] See for a similar conclusion A von Bogdandy, M Kottmann, C Antpöhler, J Dickschen, S Hentrei and M Smrkolj, 'Reverse Solange—Protecting the Essence of Fundamental Rights against EU Member States' (2012) *CML Rev* 489.

[163] N Komesar, *Imperfect Alternatives: Choosing Institutions in Law, Economics, and Public Policy* (Chicago, University of Chicago Press 1994) 3.

[164] See s III.B.ii.

[165] Therefore, one may also argue that in *Aruba*, the European Court of Justice should not have subjected the Dutch electoral law to scrutiny and deemed the Dutch electoral law to be incompatible with the EU general principle of equality.

also point towards a hands-off approach in the event that the Court will have to deal with the compatibility of electoral laws in national elections with EU law.

As has been previously explained, the approach taken in this book is not to argue that institutional choice can explain every development in the European Court of Justice's case law on equal treatment. Instead, it sets out to explore to what extent comparative institutional assessment is a valid tool to analyse the Court's adjudication. In this exercise, the next chapter turns to a comparative institutional choice examination of reverse discrimination.

5

Reverse Discrimination

THE PREVIOUS CHAPTER showed that the European Court of Justice does not understand the Treaty on the Functioning of the European Union (TFEU)'s Articles of non-discrimination on grounds of nationality as absolute prohibitions. The next section examines a further aspect of European law and seeks to describe an additional mechanism employed by the Court to take institutional considerations into account in its judicial review. It is dedicated to an inquiry of reverse discrimination.

But before I explain in greater detail what reverse discrimination is about and how it relates to the broader theme of European equality law, let me briefly point out the structure of this chapter and its main finding as regards the relation of equality review and institutional reasoning. The first part of this chapter provides for a definition of the phenomenon, describes its origins and shows the extent to which reverse discrimination is interlinked with the general principle of equality. The second part deconstructs the case law of the European Court of Justice and reveals its multi-faceted nature. In the third and final part, comparative institutional analysis is used in order to reconceptualise the Court's approach towards the topic. In this context, I will argue mainly three points: first, explicit institutional considerations form part of the explanation for why the issue is debated in terms of the scope of applicability of European law and not in terms of equality. Second, considerations as to the balance of powers between European and Member State actors as well as its own capability to deal with the numbers and complexity of reverse discrimination should lead the Court to generally refrain from taking on such measures. Third, the Court should nevertheless sometimes be willing to engage in judicial review of reverse discriminations, if it perceives national political processes to be captured by minoritarian or majoritarian bias and has the ability to rule on a narrowly defined set of problems.

I. REVERSE DISCRIMINATION: ITS DEFINITION, EGALITARIAN TUNE AND RELEVANCE

A. Definition and Characteristics

Without exaggerating, reverse discrimination can be described as one of the prime paradoxes of European law and one of the most delicate issues facing the Court of

Justice. It describes a set of situations in which individuals being unable to rely on European law in a specific case have fewer rights or must bare greater legal burdens than people in a comparable situation who can rely on Union law.[1] In instances of reverse discrimination, some find themselves in a situation of comparable disadvantage to others simply because of the fact that they are solely subject to national law.[2] The phenomenon arises because of 'the application of two distinct but parallel regulatory regimes';[3] because not all individuals are entitled to enjoy European rights.

Without a more detailed explanation of the phenomenon's origins and its application the above description is not very enlightening. It is therefore useful to sketch its development in a few broad strokes. Reverse discrimination has occurred as a result of the application of the Treaty's free movement provisions. As O'Leary puts it, according to

> one of the orthodox, even sacred, tenets of European Union (EU) law, developed principally in the context of the rules on free movement of goods, persons and services, the latter cannot be invoked in respect of activities which have no bearing on any of the situations governed by EU law.[4]

Activities without a connecting factor to European law were traditionally those which did not involve movement from one State to another and were confined to one Member State. As a consequence situations arose in which some persons were protected by European free movement law, whereas others—those that stayed within their country of origin—were subject to national provisions. This led to the curious state of affairs, where it was possible that the protection under Union law for free movers was more far reaching than that granted by Member States to their own citizens under national law. The phenomenon of reverse discrimination was born.

Since the occurrence of the phenomenon depends on identifying those instances when people are able to rely on Union law, it is understandable that the debate on reverse discrimination is closely linked to that on the scope of application

[1] Eg A Balthasar, '"Inländerdiskriminierung" in der EU nach dem EG-Vertrag und aus österreichischer Sicht' (1998) 53 *Zeitschrift für öffentliches Recht* 143, 146; S O'Leary, 'The Past, Present and Future of the Purely Internal Rule in EU Law' in M Dougan, N Nic Shuibhne and E Spaventa (eds), *Modern Studies in European Law: Empowerment and Disempowerment of the European Citizen* (Oxford, Hart Publishing, 2012) 37, 38; C Ritter, 'Purely Internal Situations, Reverse Discrimination, Guimont, Dzodzi and Article 234' (2006) 31 *EL Rev* 690, 691.

[2] Of course, it should be mentioned that the ECHR, depending on the means of implementation chosen by Member States, is either directly or indirectly applicable to those situations.

[3] O'Leary (n 1) 38. Further E Cannizzaro, '"Reverse Discrimination" Through the Exercise of EC Competences' (1997) 17 *Yearbook of European Law* 29; A Epiney, *Umgekehrte Diskriminierungen* (Cologne, Karl Heymanns, 1995) 25; D Hanf, '"Reverse Discrimination" in EU Law: Constitutional Aberration, Constitutional Necessity, or Judicial Choice?' (2011) 18 *Maastricht Journal* 29, 32 ff; M Heintzen, 'Inländerdiskriminierung im Gemeinsamen Markt—dargestellt am Beispiel der Rechtsanwaltschaft' (1990) 1 *Europäisches Wirtschafts- und Steuerrecht* 82, 84.

[4] O'Leary (n 1) 37.

of Union law.[5] During the stage of legal integration that focused on creating an integrated market by means of free movement provisions, not only legal academia but also the European judiciary sought to establish a workable formula to delimitate European from national law. In this process, the Court developed the so-called 'purely internal rule' in order to determine whether Treaty guarantees were applicable or not in preliminary references concerning the interpretation of the four freedoms. It was applied for the first time in the case of *Saunders*,[6] when the Court was asked to determine whether a probation measure ordering a British national, Ms Saunders, to leave England and Wales and move back to Northern Ireland for three years was a violation of then Article 48 EEC Treaty. In its decision, the court declared that it was not for it to rule on the subject matter, holding that '[t]he provisions of the Treaty on freedom of movement for workers cannot ... be applied to situations which are wholly internal to a Member State, in other words, where there is no factor connecting them to any of the situations envisaged by Community law'.[7]

This statement came to be read as implying that the articles on free movement of goods, workers, establishment and services (and capital) were only applicable to situations that featured a cross-border element.[8] It was a reasonable and conclusive move at the time of the decision in *Saunders* to equate situations that were confined to one Member State with situations that lacked a link to European law. But, as we know with the benefit of hindsight, the application of the demarcation rule proved to be more complex than the statement indicates. Rather, defining what comes within the scope of Union law and what is left outside has become an intricate exercise.

To begin with, what constituted a 'purely internal situation' came to be defined more precisely by the Court as a situation whose '*facts and effects* ... are confined within a single Member State'.[9] With that said, the rule could no longer be

[5] See M Maduro, 'The Scope of European Remedies: The Case of Purely Internal Situations and Reverse Discrimination' in C Kilpatrick, T Novitz and P Skidmore (eds), *The Future of Remedies in Europe* (Oxford, Hart Publishing, 2000) 117, 118.

[6] Case 175/78 *The Queen v Vera Ann Saunders* [1979] ECR 1129. A Tryfonidou, *Reverse Discrimination in EC Law* (Alphen aan den Rijn, Kluwer Law International, 2009) 10; Maduro (n 5) 119; N Nic Shuibhne, 'Free Movement of Persons and the Wholly Internal Rule: Time to Move On? (2002) 39 *CML Rev* 731, 733 ff. But first mentioning in the obiter dictum of Case 115/78 *J Knoors v Staatssecretaris van Economische Zaken* [1979] ECR 399, see N Bernard, 'Discrimination and Free Movement in EC Law' (1996) 45 *International and Comparative Law Quarterly* 82, 86; O'Leary (n 1) 41.

[7] *Saunders* (n 6) para 11.

[8] Nic Shuibhne (n 6) 731.

[9] Case C-72/03 *Carbonati Apuani Srl v Commune di Carrara* [2004] ECR I-8027, Opinion of AG Maduro, para 23 (emphasis added). See, eg Case 286/81 *Criminal proceedings against Oosthoek's Uitgeversmaatschappij BV* [1982] ECR 4575, para 9; Case 98/86 *Criminal proceedings against Arthur Mathot* [1987] ECR 809, paras 7–9; Case C-332/90 *Volker Steen v Deutsche Bundespost* [1992] ECR I-341, para 9; and Case C-108/98 *RI.SAN. Srl v Comune di Ischia, Italia Lavoro SpA and Ischia Ambiente SpA* [1999] ECR I-5219, para 23. Taking a measure's effects from the very beginning into account, this works' depiction of the European Court of Justice's 'traditional approach' towards (non-)purely internal situation differs from the one defended by Tryfonidou, see Tryfonidou (n 6) 11 and 29 ff.

understood in territorial terms exclusively. Movement that had taken place across borders was just one possibility of triggering protection under free movement laws (*facts*). The other option for free movement law to apply was that the measure in question had the potential to impact future movement (*effects*). Jessurun d'Oliveira described this poignantly when he argued that according to this latter formulation of the purely internal rule, two criteria may serve as sufficient linking factors between a situation and freedom of movement provisions.[10] He categorised the first as 'geographical'[11] and stated that a case will come within the sphere of protection under the fundamental freedoms, if it features cross-border movement. He continued by describing the second criterion as teleological in character.[12] Pursuant to it, a measure will be subject to scrutiny under the four freedoms, if it has potentially deterrent effects on the exercise of free movement. Consequently, given that both—facts and effects—of a case need to be confined to one Member State so as to deem it to lie beyond the scope of application of European law, only the cumulative absence of the two aspects turns a situation into a 'purely internal' one.[13]

Second, the application of the purely internal rule proved to be more difficult due to the fact that the interpretation of the Treaty's free movement provisions widened considerably in the course of time. To sketch just the beginnings of a well-known development, the Court of Justice extended the scope of application of the four freedoms from the prohibition of direct discrimination to a prohibition of indirect discrimination,[14] so as to then abolish unjustified obstacles to these individuals' freedom of movement altogether.[15] This evolution has had two effects that are important in the context of reverse discrimination: the intensity of protection increased to such an extent that the level of protection granted under European provisions is at times higher than that conventionally granted at national levels. Maduro and Tryfonidou have labelled this effect as the grant of European 'bonus rights'[16] to free movers within the Union. As an additional consequence, the group of people not enjoying European protection has with each extension of the rights

[10] HU Jessurun d'Oliveira, 'Is Reverse Discrimination Still Possible under the Single European Act' in *Forty Years On: The Evolution of Postwar Private International Law in Europe: Symposium in Celebration of the 40th Anniversary of the Centre of Foreign Law and Private International Law, University of Amsterdam, on 27 October 1989* (Deventer, Kluwer Law International, 1990) 71, 73 ff. See for a discussion Maduro (n 5) 125.

[11] Jessurun d'Oliveira (n 10) 73 f.

[12] ibid.

[13] See Tryfonidou (n 6) 89.

[14] For examples of indirect discrimination see Case 124/81 *Commission v United Kingdom* [1983] ECR 203; Case C-415/93 *Union royale belge des sociétés de football association ASBL v Jean-Marc Bosman, Royal club liégeois SA v Jean-Marc Bosman and others and Union des associations européennes de football (UEFA) v Jean-Marc Bosman* [1995] ECR I-4921; see Matthias Herdegen, *Europarecht* 17th edn (Munich, Beck, 2015) 284 f.

[15] Case 8/74 *Procureur du Roi v Benoît and Gustave Dassonville* [1974] ECR 837; Case C-55/94 *Reinhard Gebhard v Consiglio dell'Ordine degli Avvocati e Procuratori di Milano* [1995] ECR I-4165.

[16] Maduro (n 5) 125; Tryfonidou (n 6) 18.

adjudication by the Court of Justice become smaller.[17] Considering these aspects together, if a Member State measure that poses an obstacle to the future movement of that state's own nationals triggers the application of EU law, what convincing justification is there left to argue that reverse discrimination is beyond the limits of scrutiny by the European Court?

At the current stage of development of European law, the question can be formulated in even more pressing terms. Given that the integration project has progressed since the creation of the purely internal rule and that the Maastricht Treaty has added a citizenship dimension to EU law, on what grounds should reverse discrimination be allowed to prevail? Taking up this last point, many scholars have illustrated that the problematic character of reverse discrimination can be seen even more clearly since the introduction of EU citizenship in European law.[18] Certain commentators argue that the status of being a European citizen should suffice to bring individuals, who experience reverse discrimination, within the scope of application of Union law.[19] Without wanting to anticipate the discussion of the case law of European citizenship and the purely internal rule that is yet to follow, Articles 18 and onwards TFEU have indeed proved to be the legal environment, recently utilised by the Court, to address the subject matter and modify its adjudication.

As the mention of 'citizenship' and 'four freedoms' in the last paragraphs already indicate, reverse discrimination can appear in the most diverse areas of life and in fact does so regularly. To give just a few examples, Italian pasta producers faced a situation of reverse discrimination because they were only allowed to label their products pasta if they were manufactured without the admixture of egg, whereas producers of other Member States had permission to sell their noodles containing egg under the heading of 'pasta' in Italy.[20] Following the *Cassis de Dijon* decision,[21] German liquor companies had to meet higher standards in manufacture of their spirits than producers from outside the country in order to be allowed to sell their products as spirits.[22] Furthermore, reverse discrimination does not only take place

[17] D Rabenschlag, *Leitbilder der Unionsbürgerschaft* (Baden-Baden, Nomos, 2009) 127, 129.

[18] eg A Lach, *Umgekehrte Diskriminierungen im Gemeinschaftsrecht* (Frankfurt, Peter Lang, 2008) 295 ff (especially 344); Nic Shuibhne (n 6) 748 f; ibid, '(Some of) The Kids Are All Right' (2012) 49 *CML Rev* 349; E Spaventa, 'Seeing the Wood Despite the Trees? On the Scope of Union Citizenship and Its Constitutional Effects' (2008) 45 *CML Rev* 13; Tryfonidou (n 6) 129 ff; R White, 'A Fresh Look at Reverse Discrimination' (1993) 18 *EL Rev* 527, 532. More critical, P van Elsuwege, 'Shifting the Boundaries? European Union Citizenship and the Scope of Application of EU Law—Case No C-34/09, *Gerardo Ruiz Zambrano v Office national de l'emploi*' (2011) 38 *Legal Issues of Economic Integration* 263, 273; AP van der Mei, 'Combating Reverse Discrimination: Who Should do the Job?' (2009) 16 *Maastricht Journal* 379 f.

[19] eg Nic Shuibhne (n 6) 731; Spaventa (n 18) 13.

[20] An effect of the decisions in Case 407/85 *3 GlockenGmbH and Gertraud Kritzinger v USL Centro-Sud and Provincia autonoma di Bolzano* [1988] ECR 4233 and Case 90/86 *Criminal proceedings against Zoni* [1988] 4285. See eg Epiney (n 3) 286.

[21] Case 120/78 *Rewe-Zentral AG v Bundesmonopolverwaltung für Branntwein (Cassis de Dijon)* [1979] ECR 649.

[22] A depiction of the consequences of the decision can be found in Lach (n 18) 352 f.

in connection with the marketing and distribution of goods, as two instances in the field of education show. In Scotland, students from other constituent parts of the United Kingdom have to pay higher university fees than their fellow students coming from other countries of the European Union.[23] In Germany, the law stipulates that craftsmen have to pass a masters' exam after three to five years of training in order to work as self-employed, with artisans having worked in other Member States being exempt from the examination requirement.[24] Moreover, reverse discrimination occurs to an increasing extent in the field of family reunification law. This has also been the area in which the European Court of Justice has become most active in addressing the problem, as will be shown in the following. Various Member States subject their own citizens to stricter regulation than nationals of other Member States in a comparable situation with regard to residence rights for spouses coming from outside the European Union.[25] If a German wants to apply for a permanent residence permit for her spouse, who happens to live in and hold citizenship of a non-EU country, it will be more difficult for her to obtain the authorisation than for a French or Czech living in Germany and pursuing the same aim.[26]

Furthermore, reverse discrimination touches not only upon diverse fields, but also upon some of the most fundamental issues of European law. Placing the phenomenon in a broader context, its handling has implications for ensuring a comprehensive level of fundamental rights protection within the European Union as well as for the respect of Member State competences and constitutional identities.[27] As the last chapter has already pointed out, one of the defining questions the European Court of Justice will have to deal with in the upcoming future is how to define the Union as a community, in which rights are extensively protected, whilst paying due regard to national particularities.[28] Reverse discrimination stands as another formulation of this question, since judges at the Luxembourg Court need to assess its conformity with European law in light of two aspects: on the one hand, does the status of European citizen in combination with the prohibition of discrimination on grounds of nationality require an end to reverse

[23] I McArdle, 'University Funding, Scotland and a Question of Equality' UK Human Rights Blog, www.ukhumanrightsblog.com/2011/08/22/university-funding-scotland-and-a-question-of-equality.

[24] On the issue: J Kormann and F Hüpers, 'Inländerdiskriminierung durch Meisterpflicht?' (2008) *Gewerbearchiv* 273; F Rieger, 'Ist die Inländerdiskriminierung noch mit dem Grundgesetz vereinbar?—Besprechung des Kammerbeschlusses zur Verfassungsmäßigkeit des Meisterzwangs' (2006) *Die Öffentliche Verwaltung* 685.

[25] In greater detail, see A Walter, *Reverse Discrimination and Family Reunification* (Oisterwijk, Wolf Legal Publishers, 2008).

[26] See ibid, 8 ff.

[27] See van Elsuwege (n 18) 273; AP van der Mei, 'The Outer Limits of the Prohibition of Discrimination on Grounds of Nationality: A Look Through the Lens of Union Citizenship' (2011) 18 *Maastricht Journal* 62, 83.

[28] O'Leary (n 1) 70 f. See the Heidelberg proposal as one suggestion for resolving the tension. A von Bogdandy, M Kottmann, C Antpöhler, J Dickschen, S Hentrei and M Smrkolj, 'Reverse Solange—Protecting the Essence of Fundamental Rights against EU Member States' (2012) 49 *CML Rev* 489.

discrimination? On the other hand, does the parallel alignment of competences for the European Union and the Member States not require a hands-off approach by the European judiciary towards the issue?

This introduction into the subject of reverse discrimination points to (at least) three factors shaping its debate:

1. Reverse discrimination is about rights. With respect to fundamental rights protection, it stands as an oddity in EU law.[29] The project of European integration, which is designed to establish equal opportunities for its constituents, brings about inequality.[30]
2. Reverse discrimination is about competences.[31] The differentiation has its root causes in the structural alignment of the Union's and the Member States' legal orders.[32] The logic of European integration at its current stage holds that Member States are free to govern those areas not yet harmonised under EU law, as long as they do so in a manner compatible with primary and secondary European law. According to the principle of regulatory competition, they are explicitly allowed to set regulatory standards that differ from those in force in other Member States.[33] In order to become more appealing to foreign investors, Member States are technically not prohibited by EU law from creating situations of reverse discriminations and to establish rules which privilege European movers over that group of their own citizens who do not feature a relation to EU free movement provisions. But generally, neither political processes nor courts plan to place those individuals that find themselves in purely internal situations at a disadvantage. Instead, reverse discrimination seems to 'merely happen'[34] in the event that out of two similar cases, one falls within the EU legal system and one into a Member State's legal system.

[29] M Jarvis, *The Application of EC Law by National Courts. The Free Movement of Goods* (Oxford, Oxford University Press, 1998) 154.

[30] Joined Cases 80/85 and 159/85 *Nederlandse Bakkerij Stichting and others v Edah BV* [1986] ECR 3359 (3375), Opinion AG Mischo, quoted in White, (n 18) 532; *Carbonati Apuani* (n 9) Opinion AG Maduro, para 63:

> [T]he aims of the Treaty have now been extended. I take the view that it is now clearly one of the fundamental objectives of the Community to ensure that no discrimination of any kind should arise as a result of the application of its own rules (fn omitted). Consequently, it must always be ensured, so far as possible, that the application of a Community rule does not give rise to the infringement of the principle of non-discrimination.

Jarvis (n 29) 154; Jessurun d'Oliveira (n 10) 84; Maduro (n 5) 126; G Nicolaysen, 'Inländerdiskriminierung im Warenverkehr' (1991) 26 *Europarecht* 95, 101; Tryfonidou (n 6) 197.

[31] Bernard (n 6) 82. See also Epiney (n 3) eg 235 f and 244; D Rabenschlag (n 17) 134; C Schönberger, *Unionsbüger* (Tübingen, Mohr Siebeck, 2005) 430.

[32] See Cannizzaro (n 3) 33; Hanf (n 3) especially 34; K Lenaerts, 'Federalism and the Rule of Law: Perspectives from the European Court of Justice' (2009/2010) 33 *Fordham International Law Journal* 1338, 1344; van der Mei (n 27) 75; S O'Leary, *The Evolving Concept of Community Citizenship: From Free Movement of Persons to Union Citizenship* (The Hague, Kluwer Law International, 1996) 276.

[33] See P Craig and G de Búrca, *EU Law. Text, Cases and Materials* 5th edn (Oxford, Oxford University Press, 2011) 685.

[34] See Maduro (n 5) 127; Nic Shuibhne (n 6) 738.

3. Since reverse discrimination arises from the partial application of European law, those rules that govern the delimitation of the supranational legal order from its national counterparts are of crucial importance to understanding the subject.

B. Reverse Discrimination: When Egalitarian and Institutional Concerns Meet

As this cursory listing shows, the phenomenon is characterised by its tension between egalitarian and institutional concerns. Arguing that all reverse discrimination must be abolished under a prohibition of discrimination based on nationality is inadequate, as it fails to pay attention to the demarcation of competences between the national and the European legal sphere. At the same time, arguing that reverse discrimination is an exclusively systemic problem arising out of the simultaneous application of two legal orders is insufficient as well, since it does not take seriously the fact that persons are treated unfavourably because of it.

This last point—the egalitarian facet of the subject—is worth reflecting upon in greater detail. This analysis takes the view that the issue is after all also a question of equality.[35] One should not forget that the phenomenon has been labelled 'reverse discrimination' with good cause. It is concerned with the differential treatment of two groups and persons affected by it, one of which takes offence at the relative effects that result from the application of the two different legal regimes. In situations of reverse discrimination in the market place, individuals are burdened because they are in a position of competitive disadvantage towards other producers and providers thereby decreasing their opportunities on the market. In addition in cases of reverse discrimination that touch on issues of most personal life (such as family reunification), the effect is such that some feel that they have unjustifiably been treated differently from others. Given the fact that the quintessential element of the principle of equality is that it is able to portray the relational aspect of fundamental rights within society, the egalitarian offence of reverse discrimination is clearly visible in the last sentence: for some face heavier burden or receive less benefits than others because they are only subject to national law, whilst the latter can rely on EU law, they feel as if official authorities do not treat them with equal concern and respect.[36]

On the other hand, it is just as crucial to point out the effects of an outright abolition of reverse discrimination. If one opted for the matter to be dealt with by the

[35] In this direction, Cannizzaro (n 3) 29 and 39 f; Epiney (n 3) 90 ff; Hanf (n 3) 46 ff; Lach (n 18) 220 ff; K Lackhoff and B Raczinski, 'Umgekehrte Diskriminierung' (1997) 8 *Europäisches Wirtschafts- und Steuerrecht* 109, 110. Of other opinion Schönberger, who does not see reverse discrimination as an issue of EU provisions on equality, see Schönberger (n 31) 291, 405; Rabenschlag (n 17) 132 f and N Graf Vitzthum, 'Die Entdeckung der Heimat der Unionsbürger—Anmerkungen zum Urteil des EuGH vom 8. März 2011, Rs. C-34/09—Zambrano' (2011) 46 *Europarecht* 550, 559.

[36] See R Dworkin, *Taking Rights Seriously* (London, Duckworth, 1978) starting at 223.

judiciary,[37] judgments on the illegality of reverse discrimination would introduce uniform regulation according to European standards.

Thus in the event that national courts decided to prohibit reverse discrimination, legal harmonisation would be introduced through the backdoor with help of the general principle of equality.[38] There are usually two measures by which discrimination may be remedied: if a norm is deemed invalid solely on the basis of its violation of the equality guarantee, one may restore an equal state by either making both groups of comparators subject to the stricter legislation or allowing both to enjoy the preferential treatment. The former alternative is not available in the case of reverse discrimination. As mentioned before, the disadvantageous treatment stems from national norms that impose stricter obligations than EU law. Harmonisation by the application of a national standard of rights protection would thus imply that EU law must not be applied in situations where this would grant preferential treatment to people being able to establish a cross-border link. Such practice would be in breach of the principle of supremacy of European law and would be considered an obstruction to the uniform enforcement of European norms within the Union and hence prohibited.

In case the European Court of Justice opted for an abolition of the purely internal rule thus rendering reverse discrimination obsolete, the scope of application of European law would widen considerably. Under the dynamics of integration, the interpretation of the four freedoms which has paved the way for granting 'bonus rights'[39] for mobile European citizens would not be constricted to prevent the discrimination. Instead, reverse discrimination, itself often brought about through an extensive interpretation of Treaty provisions, would be remedied by even more extensive interpretation. As a corollary, Member States would be partially deprived of their ability to regulate matters within their sphere of competence in accordance with their own preferences. European institutions would enter into fields of law that Member States explicitly wished to retain at a national level. The influence of the Luxembourg Court (and in its wake, of the political process in Brussels and Strasbourg) on national legislation would expand and as a consequence give rise to well-known critiques of European activism.[40] One needs only to refer to

[37] This implies a rejection of the idea that the decision on how to correctly proceed in instances of reverse discrimination should be left to the political process.

[38] See on this point, Cannizzaro (n 3) 30.

[39] Maduro (n 5) 125; Tryfonidou (n 6) 18.

[40] Ritter (n 1) 702. Further P van Elsuwege, 'European Union Citizenship and the Purely Internal Rule Revisited—Decision of 5 May 2011, Case C-434/09, *Shirley McCarthy v Secretary of State for the Home Department*' (2011) 7 *European Constitutional Law Review* 308, 322 mentions the 'allegation of an *ultra vires* application of EU law'. See also P van Elsuwege and D Kochenov, 'On the Limits of Judicial Intervention: EU Citizenship and Family Reunification Rights' (2011) 13 *European Journal of Migration and Law* 443, 450; K Hailbronner and D Thym, 'Case C-34/09, *Gerardo Ruiz Zambrano v Office national de l'emploi (ONEm)*, Judgment of the Court of Justice (Grand Chamber) of 8 March 2011, not yet reported' (2011) 48 *CML Rev* 1253, 1258. More differential in his appraisal P Craig, 'The ECJ and *Ultra Vires* Action: A Conceptual Analysis' (2011) 48 *CML Rev* 395, especially 412 ff. Less critically M Hailbronner and S Iglesias Sánchez, 'The European Court of Justice and Citizenship of the European

the catchwords such as 'legitimacy deficit'[41] and 'disempowerment of national parliaments'[42] to recognise the constitutional dimension of potential rulings on the subject matter. The more European actors interfered in instances of reverse discrimination, the more the balance with regard to the division of competences struck and stipulated in the Treaties would shift towards the European sphere.

Before the chapter turns to an examination of the case law of the European Court of Justice on the purely internal rule and reverse discrimination, I would like to mention two last preceding points: to begin with, reverse discrimination in the European Union should not be confused with the term reverse discrimination as is used in an American context.[43] As explained above, the former describes factual situations, in which the alignment of the national and the supranational, that is to say European, legal orders causes differential treatment with negative effects as unintended side-effects.[44] The latter is comprised of measures designed to provide for a targeted promotion of members of a historically disprivileged group. For that reason and in order to avoid terminological confusion, it is better to speak—with regard to the latter—of affirmative action.

Moreover, although one can think of many instances in which individuals not being able to rely on Union law are treated less favourably than persons that can, there are limits to when reverse discrimination can occur. Only rules of European primary or secondary law with direct effect and requiring a cross-border element are capable of giving rise to situations of reverse discrimination. Provisions applying to all persons (within the European Union) without exception cannot bring about reverse discrimination. For example, Article 157 TFEU stipulates the right to equal pay for men and women—a guarantee provided irrespective of the existence or nonexistence of a cross-border element.[45] In addition, a multitude of

Union: New Developments Towards a Truly Fundamental Status' (2011) 5 *Vienna Journal on International Constitutional Law* 498.

[41] For an overview: A Føllesdal, 'Survey Article: The Legitimacy Deficits of the European Union' (2006) 14 *The Journal of Political Philosophy* 441.

[42] On that point Spaventa (n 18) 37. See generally for the criticism the decisions by the Federal Constitutional Court on European integration, *BVerfGE* 89, 155 (*Maastricht*), *BVerfGE* 123, 267 (*Lisbon*), *BVerfGE* 129, 124 (*Financial Aid to Greece*) and *BVerfGE* 134, 366 (*OMT-Order*).

[43] See eg Lach (n 18) 10 f. Reverse discrimination in the US and in the EU context are common in that they both put persons who have been historically discriminated against in an advantageous situation. Originally, affirmative action was designed in the United States in order to ameliorate the situation of Blacks competing in the market place with Whites. It then extended to cover policies that aimed to counter the comparative disadvantage faced by other minorities, including women. At the roots of EU reverse discrimination also lies the idea of privilege of a group, which has traditionally been discriminated against, namely that of nationals coming from other Member States. These people had to make the experience that their living and working conditions abroad, which were shaped through the foreign state's law, were worse than those of persons staying in that respective state as their country of origin. As stated, the difference lies in the voluntariness with which the differential treatment is performed. But see C Riese and P Noll, 'Europarechtliche und verfassungsrechtliche Aspekte des Inländerdiskriminierung'(2007) *Neue Verwaltungszeitschrift* 516, 517.

[44] Maduro (n 5) 127; Nic Shuibhne (n 6) 738.

[45] Case 43/75 *Gabrielle Defrenne v Société anonyme belge de navigation aérienne Sabena* [1976] ECR 455. Maduro (n 5) 121.

directives and regulations of positive harmonisation govern situations regardless of movement. Hence, a great deal of European secondary law has always included the regulation of purely internal situations and never had—due to its institutional setup—the potential to create reverse discrimination.

II. THE EUROPEAN COURT OF JUSTICE'S HANDLING OF REVERSE DISCRIMINATION

In researching the case law of the European Court of Justice the impression may initially arise that the judges do not regard reverse discrimination as a pressing issue that needs to be attended to. The term 'reverse discrimination' appears in only 11 of the Court's judgments,[46] although it is employed as an established term in the academic discussion. Furthermore, in nine out of these 11 decisions, the Court mentions the keywords only when summarising the observations of the parties to the dispute or when restating the question of a referring court.[47] Only in two instances, namely the *Jakubowska* and the *Ordine degli Ingegneri di Verona* cases,[48] do the judgments allude to the concept in their reasoning. However, to infer from the paucity of explicit references by the Court that it refuses to look

[46] Joined Cases C-297/88 and C-197/89 *Massam Dzodzi v Belgian State* [1990] ECR I-3763; Case C-206/91 *Ettien Koua Poirrez v Caisse d'allocations familiales de la région parisienne, substituée par la Caisse d'allocations familiales de la Seine-Saint-Denis* [1992] ECR I-6685; Joined Case C-321/94, C-322/94, C-323/94 and C-324/94 *Criminal proceedings against Jacques Pistre and others* [1997] ECR I-2343; Case C-168/98 *Grand Duchy of Luxembourg v European Parliament and Council of the European Union* [2000] ECR I-9131; Case C-355/00 *Freskot AE v Elliniko Dimosio* [2003] ECR I-5263; Case C-445/03 *Commission of the European Communities v Grand Duchy of Luxembourg* [2004] ECR I-10191; Case C-127/08 *Blaise Baheten Metock and Others v Minister for Justice, Equality and Law Reform* [2008] ECR I-6241; Case C-225/09 *Edyta Joanna Jakubowska v Alessandro Maneggia* [2010] ECR I-12329; Case C-571/10 *Servet Kamberaj v Istituto per l'Edilizia sociale della Provincia autonoma di Bolzano (IPES) and Others* [2012] ECLI:EU:C:2012:233; Case C-84/11 *Marja-Liisa Susisalo, Olli Tuomaala and Merja Ritala* [2012] ECLI:EU:C:2012:374; Case C-111/12 *Ministero per i beni e le attività culturali and Others v Ordine degli Ingegneri di Verona e Provincia and Others* [2013] ECLI:EU:C:2013:100.

'Reverse discrimination' is mentioned in further decisions, eg Case T-24/91 *Carlos Gómez González and others v Council of the European Communities* [1992] II-1881; Case T-25/91 *Pilar Arto Hijos v Council of the European Communities* [1992] II-1907; Joined Cases C-231/06, C-232/06 and C-233/06 *Office national des pensions v Emilienne Jonkman and others v Office national des pensions* [2007] ECR I-5149 and Joined Cases 302/11—305/11 *Rosanna Valenza, Maria Laura Altavista, Laura Marsella, Simonetta Schettini and Sabrina Tomassini v Autorità Garante della Concorrenza e del Mercato* [2012] ECLI:EU:C:2012:646. However, there it is used in a different context, as the differential treatment does not distinguish between persons being able to rely on EU law and those who cannot.

[47] *Dzodzi* (n 46); *Poirrez* (n 46); *Pistre* (n 46); *Grand Duchy of Luxembourg v European Parliament and Council of the European Union* (n 46); *Freskot* (n 46); *Commission of the European Communities v Grand Duchy of Luxembourg* (n 46); *Metock* (n 46); *Kamberaj* (n 46) and *Susisalo, Tuomaala and Ritala* (n 46).

[48] *Jakubowska* (n 46) and *Ministero per i beni e le attività culturali* (n 46). In the cases, the judges do not examine the compatibility of reverse discrimination with European law, either, see for the former, para 63 and for the latter, para 38.

into the subject would misstate its case law.[49] In fact, it occupies itself with reverse discrimination on a regular basis. Key to understanding the adjudication by the Court of Justice is paying attention to the fact that it results from the partial application of EU law and by bearing in mind the nexus between the subject and the purely internal rule. The Court addresses the issue of reverse discrimination not as an issue that must be scrutinised under European equality guarantees, but concerns itself with the matter when it delimits European law's scope of application.

Looking into the cases at point, one can divide the approaches of the European Court of Justice roughly into three categories: the exclusionary, the inclusionary and the procedural approach.

First, the Court allows reverse discrimination to arise (or continue) when it denies its jurisdiction or the applicability of free movement law. This is the approach generally followed and occurs when the Court applies the purely internal rule in a strict manner (*exclusionary approach*). Second, the Court at times seeks to minimise the purely internal rule or introduce exceptions to it so as to judge upon cases that were traditionally considered to fall within the sphere of competences of the Member States and had potentially reversely discriminatory effects (*inclusionary approach*). Third, a procedural rule has been established that enables the judges to give advice to referring courts. Guided by the response given to the preliminary reference, these are then able to prohibit reverse discrimination pursuant to national norms (*procedural approach*). The three methods employed by the Court to deal with the subject matter are depicted in greater detail in the following passage.[50] Due to the amount of cases that touch upon the question of 'purely internal situations' and hence reverse discrimination, the presentation is limited to a discussion of singular decisions, which will serve as representatives of broader lines of argumentation.

A. The Exclusionary Approach

The European Court of Justice repeatedly receives requests by national courts under the preliminary ruling procedure (Article 267 TFEU) asking for advice in

[49] One further needs to recognise that the Advocate Generals have in numerous Opinions drawn the Court's attention to the subject matter. To name just some of the most prominent of their pieces: *Bakkerij Stichting* (n 30) Opinion of AG Mischo; Joined Cases C-515/99, C-519/99 to C-524/99 and C-526/99 to C-540/99 *Hans Reisch and Others* v *Bürgermeister der Landeshauptstadt Salzburg and Grundverkehrsbeauftragter des Landes Salzburg and Anton Lassacher and Others v Grundverkehrsbeauftragter des Landes Salzburg and Grundverkehrslandeskommission des Landes Salzburg* [2002] ECR I-2157, Opinion of AG Geelhoed; *Carbonati Apuani* (n 9) Opinion of AG Maduro; Case C-34/09 *Gerardo Ruiz Zambrano v Office national de l'emploi (ONEm)* [2011] ECR I-1177, Opinion of AG Sharpston.

[50] I would like to emphasise that this part of the analysis builds upon two excellent works on the topic of reverse discrimination, in which the authors sketch the developments with regard to the application of the purely internal rule. See Tryfonidou (n 6) and Lach (n 18) 107 ff.

handling cases that seem to have little or no connection to European law. In such instances, the Member State judges are generally aware that the 'facts and effects' of their case under review are confined to one country. Nevertheless, they experience a certain amount of discomfort in applying exclusively national law because they acknowledge that the protection of individual rights would be greater (under European law), if they were only able to establish the existence of a cross-border element. Most often, the European Court of Justice answers their inquiries with a reference to the purely internal rule laid down in *Saunders* and holds European law to be irrelevant for the decision of the case. It states that the referred situations do not fall within the scope of application of the free movement provisions and therefore dismisses the cases without undertaking any material assessment.

A first example of this approach can be found in *Mathot*.[51] Asked whether a Belgium provision imposing stricter labelling conditions on products manufactured in Belgium than on imported goods was contrary to the freedom of movement for goods (now Article 34 TFEU), the Court held:

> [I]t must be emphasized that the purpose of that provision is to eliminate obstacles to the importation of goods and not to ensure that goods of national origin always enjoy the same treatment as imported goods. A difference of treatment as between goods which is not capable of restricting imports or of prejudging the marketing of imported goods does not fall within the prohibition contained in that Article.[52]

Within its adjudication on the free movement of goods, the court confirmed its stance in *3 Glocken*, when it stated that it is within its competence to decide on the compatibility of an Italian law that made the selling of pasta products subject to restrictions, but that the effects of this judgment were confined to pasta imports from other Member States.[53]

Further evidence of the strict application of the purely internal rule can be found in the Court's decision on the *Flemish Welfare Case*.[54] In the case, the legality of a Flemish insurance scheme provision was at issue. The scheme's creators made the affiliation to it subject to the condition of residence in the Dutch-speaking part of Belgium. In its response to a preliminary reference, the Court found a violation of Article 45 TFEU (ex Article 39 EC), in so far as it was an obstacle to the free movement of workers who were either

> nationals of Member States other than the Kingdom of Belgium working in the Dutch-speaking region or in the bilingual region of Brussels-Capital but who live in another part of the national territory, [or] Belgian nationals in the same situation who have made use of their right to freedom of movement.[55]

[51] *Mathot* (n 9).
[52] ibid, para 7.
[53] *3 Glocken* (n 20) para 25 and *Zoni* (n 20) para 25. See Tryfonidou (n 6) 34.
[54] Case C-212/06 *Government of the French Community and Walloon Government v Flemish Government* [2008] ECR I-1683.
[55] ibid, para 41.

In its assessment, it explicitly excluded the situation of Belgian nationals who were living in the French- or German-speaking part of the country and working in the Flemish part or the Brussels region, but had never exercised their freedom of movement between different Member States.[56] In unequivocal terms, the court stated in paragraph 38 of the judgment: 'Community law clearly cannot be applied to such purely internal situations'.[57] Consequently, the verdict of the European Court of Justice confirmed a situation of reverse discrimination, in which all EU citizens were allowed to join the insurance scheme, except for Belgian nationals not residing in the Flemish or Brussels region (or not having made use of their freedom of movement).

Judgments in which the purely internal rule has been strictly applied are also to be found in the area of family reunification, such as *Morson and Jhanjan*.[58] The case concerned the rights of two Surinamese women that wanted to live with their children, who were of Dutch nationality, in the Netherlands. Given the fact that they had no right to stay pursuant to Dutch law, the *Hoge Raad* asked in a preliminary reference whether the women could rely on Article 10 of Regulation (EEC) No 1612/68 (which served as a specification of the freedom of movement for workers)[59] in order to receive a permanent residence permit in the Netherlands as dependants of their children. Employing a literal and teleological interpretation of the freedom of movement provisions, the Court argued that the situation of *Morson* and *Jhanjan* was not protected under Community law, as their children had never left their national country to work in other Member States.[60] Considering the fact that the case was decided in 1982 and that European law has widely advanced in the meantime, one may wonder if the Court would nowadays reach the same conclusions.

Affirmation for the case law's validity can also be found in a line of decisions concerning the interpretation of EU citizenship law, such as *McCarthy*,[61] *Dereci*,[62] *Iida*[63] and *Ymeraga*.[64] In *McCarthy*, it was disputed whether Mr McCarthy, a Jamaican national living with his wife—who holds dual citizenship of Ireland and the United Kingdom—in England, could rely on the rights to residence granted under Directive 2004/38/EC or on the EU citizenship provisions of the TFEU. Turning first to an interpretation of the Directive's articles, the Court held that it

[56] See ibid, para 37.

[57] ibid, para 38.

[58] Joined Cases 35 and 36/82 *Elestina Esselina Christina Morson v State of the Netherlands and Head of the Plaatselijke Politie within the meaning of the Vreemdelingenwet; Sweradjie Jhanjan v State of the Netherlands* [1982] ECR 3723.

[59] Reg (EEC) No 1612/68 of the Council of 15 October 1968 on freedom of movement for workers within the Community [1968] OJ L257/2.

[60] See ibid, paras 15 ff.

[61] Case C-434/09 *Shirley McCarthy v Secretary of State for the Home Department* [2011] ECR I-3375.

[62] Case C-256/11 *Murat Dereci and Others v Bundesministerium für Inneres* [2011] ECR I-11315.

[63] Case C-40/11 *Yoshikazu Iida v Stadt Ulm* [2012] ECLI:EU:C:2012:691.

[64] Case C-87/12 *Kreshnik Ymeraga and Others v Ministre du Travail, de l'Emploi et de l'Immigration* [2013] ECLI:EU:C:2013:291.

only stipulated residence rights for family members of Union citizens who exercised their freedom of movement for persons.[65] Mr McCarthy's situation was not covered by the Directive, because his wife had never gone to other Member States in a manner relevant for Union law purposes. Continuing with an assessment of primary law, the Court chose to address the issue in terms of European citizens' right to free movement, Article 21 TFEU. When judging the applicability of the article, it made reference to the purely internal rule.[66] It stated that due to the existence of EU citizenship, 'the situation of a Union citizen who, like Mrs McCarthy, has not made use of the right to freedom of movement cannot, for that reason alone, be assimilated to a purely internal situation'.[67] In a next step, it referred to the point that a situation may only be considered internal when not only its facts but also its *effects* are confined to one Member State[68] and held that the refusal to grant him residence would not hinder her possibilities to exercise her freedom of movement. But before doing so, the judges voiced an argument, which this analysis will turn to in greater detail in its discussion of the *inclusionary approach*. They held that the refusal did not deprive 'her of the genuine enjoyment of the substance of the rights associated with her status as a Union citizen'.[69]

Furthermore, the judges confirmed the validity of the exclusionary approach in its *Dereci* ruling.[70] Austria's highest administrative law court (*Verwaltungsgerichtshof*) asked under the preliminary reference procedure whether the situations of five cases on its docket were within the scope of application of European citizenship law. In all of the cases, the national court had to review decisions by the ministry of interior that denied residence permits to third country nationals. They shared the further feature that they were all concerned with the situation of third country nationals who had relatives with Austrian nationality. To take the case of Mr Dereci as an example, he had started a family with an Austrian citizen 'by whom he has three children who are also Austrian nationals and who are still minors'.[71] Confronted with the question whether protection under the European citizenship provisions was to be granted to families in situations such as the one of the Derecis, the European Court of Justice held that under certain conditions, 'Union law … does not preclude a Member State from refusing to allow a third country national to reside on its territory'[72] even if that person has dependent family with European citizenship in that country. The details of its argument were similar to the reasoning put forward in *McCarthy*: focusing on the applicability of

[65] ibid, para 35.

[66] ibid, para 45, referring to *Government of the French Community and Walloon Government v Flemish Government* (n 54) para 33 and *Metock* (n 46) para 77.

[67] *McCarthy* (n 61) para 46. See further Case C-403/03 *Egon Schempp v Finanzamt München V* [2005] ECR I-6421, para 22.

[68] *McCarthy* (n 61) paras 50 f.

[69] ibid, para 49.

[70] *Dereci and Others* (n 62).

[71] ibid, para 24.

[72] ibid, para 74.

primary law, the Court stated that free movement provisions only apply in situations that are not 'confined in all relevant respects within a single Member State'.[73] It then referred to the argument already raised in *McCarthy* that a situation lacking a free movement element is not to be equated with a purely internal situation.[74] In a next step, it turned more explicitly than in *McCarthy* to an examination of the provision guaranteeing the status—not the right of free movement—of European citizenship. It maintained that denying a person to live with his family members in one Member State was not sufficient to deprive those family members 'of the genuine enjoyment of the substance of the rights conferred by virtue of [their] status'[75] as Union citizens. Transferring this reasoning to the case of the Dereci family, the Court of Justice considered that Mr Dereci's children would not be refused enjoyment of their European citizen rights if their father had to leave the Union. The harsh reality is that—due to their mother's Austrian nationality—the Court was of the opinion that the children would not be forced to leave the Union territory in the event that their father was to be deported.

The case *Iida*[76] provides for an additional, albeit somewhat different, example of the exclusionary approach. Mr Iida, a Japanese national, had lived with his German wife and infant daughter in Germany. After his wife had moved together with their child to Austria, the couple permanently separated, and subsequently the question arose whether Mr Iida was allowed to stay in Germany. Acting under the premise that Mr Iida had no autonomous right of residence, the national court asked whether he had a derivative right pursuant to EU law.[77] The European Court of Justice judged that he did not. In essence, it argued that Mr Iida could not rely on EU law, since a refusal to grant him residence in Germany had no restricting effects on his spouse's and daughter's free movement. After all, the two of them had already exercised this freedom when they had moved to Austria.[78] This answer might seem counterintuitive given that Mr Iida's wife and daughter had undisputedly crossed the border between two Member States.[79] But in the logic of the court, the case lay beyond the boundaries of EU law since EU citizens' (Mr Iida's wife and daughter) right to free movement was not impacted. Accordingly, the

[73] ibid, para 60 with reference to *Government of the French Community and Walloon Government v Flemish Government* (n 54) para 33; *Metock* (n 46) para 77, and *McCarthy* (n 61) para 45.

[74] *Dereci and Others* (n 62) para 61.

[75] ibid, para 64.

[76] *Iida* (n 63). For discussions, see S Reynolds, 'Exploring the "Intrinsic Connection" between Free Movement and the Genuine Enjoyment Test: Reflections on EU Citizenship after *Iida*' (1013) 38 *EL Rev* 376 and A Tryfonidou, '(Further) Signs of a Turn of the Tide in the CJEU's Citizenship Jurisprudence, Case C-40/11 *Iida*, Judgment of 8 November 2012, not yet reported' (2013) 20 *Maastricht Journal* 302, 319.

[77] As the judges at the European Court of Justice point out, they are—after hearing the German government on the case—of the opinion that Mr Iida has a direct right of residence under German law in the event that he files the necessary applications, see ibid, paras 44 f and 75.

[78] ibid, para 74. Even more explicit, *Iida* (n 63) Opinion of AG Trstenjak, para 65.

[79] Tryfonidou goes as far as arguing that *Iida* 'appears to reinforce—rather than abolish—the internal frontiers within the EU' (Tryfonidou (n 76) 319).

Court referred Mr Iida to the German jurisdiction for the purpose of obtaining a residence permit.

That the Court continues to apply the exclusionary approach despite contrary evolutions in its EU citizenship adjudication can be inferred from its decision in *Ymeraga*,[80] whose facts were very similar to the ones in *Morson and Jhanjan*. Asked whether EU law conferred a right to stay to third-country national parents or adult siblings of an also adult EU citizen, who happens to live in his home state, the Court answered in the negative. Again, it stated that hindering family reunification in that particular situation did 'not have the effect of denying [the EU citizen] the genuine enjoyment of the substance of the rights conferred by virtue of his status'.[81]

One may critique the presented decisions on many grounds: would the Court have decided *Iida* otherwise had it not been so sure that Mr Iida could obtain a residence permit under German law?[82] Does Mr McCarthy's potential deportation really fail to impinge his wife's genuine enjoyment of rights as an EU citizen?[83] Or does the refusal of a residence permit for their father not hinder the Dereci children from enjoying the core of their rights as European citizens? Leaving these questions aside for the moment, the judgments make one point evident: as it stands, the Court still employs the *exclusionary approach* to bar situations from material review and the scope of Union law.

B. The Inclusionary Approach

However, in contrast to the examples given above, the Court does not always apply the principle in a rigid manner. There are cases whose 'facts and effects' an impartial observer might consider to be internal to one Member State, that have nevertheless been decided according to European standards. The *Ruiz Zambrano* decision,[84] drawing the attention of legal scholars since its pronouncement, is a prominent representative of the respective case law. But, as the following section shows, *Ruiz Zambrano* can be placed in a line of judgments in which the Court opted for review, although the connecting factors to European law were at best frail.[85] Overall, in order to bring situations within the scope of application of EU law, the Court avails itself of three techniques. It either (1) widens its perspective on the case from a specific to an abstract one, (2) widens its interpretation of the facts of a case so as to easier establish a nexus to European law, or most far-reaching, (3) widens its definition of the scope of application of EU law.

80 *Ymeraga and Others* (n 64).
81 ibid, para 42.
82 See n 77.
83 eg Nic Shiubhne (n 18) 349.
84 *Ruiz Zambrano* (n 49).
85 See van Elsuwege (n 40) 315.

i. The Abstract Link

A first strand of the 'inclusionary approach' is characterised by a narrowing of the purely internal rule, in so far as situations may come into the scope of EU law, which fail to show a *specific* connection to Union law but may be linked to the norms in the *abstract*.[86] *Pistre*[87] is a textbook example for the application of the technique. The case dealt with criminal proceedings which were brought against Mr Pistre, a French farmer, and colleagues of his, in France. They were charged of having labelled products manufactured by them in the French lowlands, with the adjunct 'montagne', although this denotation was reserved to food products produced in higher altitudes pursuant to national law. During the proceedings, the issue of the law's compatibility with the freedom of movement for goods arose,[88] particularly as it was impossible for producers from outside France to meet the requirements for 'montagne' labelling. Uncertain about the compatibility of the norm with Union law, the national court initiated a preliminary reference to the Court of Justice. Confronted with the subject, the judges in Luxembourg could have applied the purely internal rule in its rigid form and dismissed the case for lack of jurisdiction. After all, it dealt with proceedings against French nationals on French soil for the incorrect labelling of French food. But since the discriminatory effects of the regulation on imported products to France were clearly visible, the Court opted to adapt the purely internal rule instead of dismissing the case holding:

> In such a situation, the application of the national measure may also have effects on the free movement of goods between Member States, in particular when the measure in question facilitates the marketing of goods of domestic origin to the detriment of imported goods.[89]

In the passage, the Court moved from an interpretation of the specifics of the case to an abstract assessment of potentially inhibiting effects of the national measure on the free movement of goods. The result of this perspective change is that the application of Union law no longer depends on the existence of a specific cross-border element, but on the establishment of an abstract nexus between the measure under review and European free movement law. That *Pistre* cannot be considered a singular case is proven by judgments such as *Preussen Elektra*,[90] *Parking Brixen*,[91]

[86] See Lach (n 18) 178 ff; Tryfonidou (n 6) 80 ff.

[87] *Pistre* (n 46).

[88] For the sake of completion, the national court also posed the question whether the law was compatible with Art 2 of Council Regulation (EEC) No 2081/92 of 14 July 1992 on the protection of geographical indications and designations of origin for agricultural products and foodstuffs [1992] OJ L208/1. See ibid, especially paras 24–40.

[89] ibid, para 45.

[90] Case C-379/98 *Preussen Elektra AG v Schleswag AG* [2001] ECR I-2099, para 70; see Tryfonidou (n 6) 82 f.

[91] Case C-458/03 *Parking Brixen GmbH v Gemeinde Brixen and Stadtwerke Brixen AG* [2005] ECR I-8612, para 55; see Tryfonidou (n 6) 86.

Centro Europa[92] or *Venturini*.[93] In all of these cases, the Court did not consider the lack of a specific nexus to Union law a hindrance to its assessment and tested the national measures by reason of their abstract relevance for the free movement guarantees of the Treaty.[94]

ii. Stressing the Facts

Under a second strand of the *inclusionary approach*, the European Court of Justice interprets *specific* facts of a case extensively in order to establish a nexus to free movement provisions. Through this expansive reading cases that would otherwise have been considered outside the scope of application of Union law had the purely internal rule been applied strictly are considered covered by Union law. An initial example of this line of argument can be found in the *Singh* case.[95] Mr Singh, an Indian national, married a British citizen and subsequently moved with his wife for three years to Germany for the purposes of work. Two years after the couple's return to the United Kingdom, Mr Singh was refused indefinite leave to remain in the state.[96] During the appeals procedure, the national court inquired whether the fact that the couple had worked in another Member State brought the situation within the scope of EU law, even though it had to decide on the right to stay of a person married to a British national, residing on British soil.[97] In the decisive passage, the judges at the European Court of Justice held that the case fell within the scope of Union law stating that:

> [a] national of a Member State might be deterred from leaving his country of origin in order to pursue an activity as an employed or self-employed person as envisaged by the Treaty in the territory of another Member State if, on returning to the Member State of which he is a national in order to pursue an activity there as an employed or self-employed person, the conditions of his entry and residence were not at least equivalent to those which he would enjoy under the Treaty or secondary law in the territory of another Member State.[98]

Thus, applied to Mr and Mrs Singhs' situation, the British Mrs Singh would have been deterred from her move to Germany, had she known that she and her husband

[92] Case C-380/05 *Centro Europa 7 Srl v Ministero delle Comunicazioni and Others* [2008] ECR I-349, para 66. The Court established its jurisdiction in *Centro Europa* through an interesting combination of the abstract link to European law approach (*Pistre* case law) and the procedural approach; see further n 183.

[93] Joined Cases C-519/12, C-160/12 and C-161/12 *Alessandra Venturini et al v ASL et al* [2013] ECLI:EU:C:2013:791, para 25.

[94] Tryfonidou (n 6) 82 f. Therefore, H Weyer's estimation in 'Freier Warenverkehr, rein innerstaatliche Sachverhalte und umgekehrte Diskriminierung' (1998) 33 *Europarecht* 435 that *Pistre* abolishes to a good extent the purely internal rule in the field of free movement of goods has proven to be wrong.

[95] Case C-370/90 *The Queen v Immigration Appeal Tribunal and Surinder Singh, ex parte Secretary of State for Home Department* [1992] ECR I-4265.

[96] ibid, para 4.

[97] It should be mentioned that the couple had separated at the time the case reached the Court of Justice. However, as far as the reply to the preliminary reference is concerned, Mr and Mrs. Singhs' divorce was not a decisive issue in the Court's reasoning, ibid, para 12.

[98] ibid, para 19.

would not be entitled to European free movement protection upon their return to the United Kingdom. One may argue that the paragraph with its reference to the potentially deterring effects on free movement stands as a mere application of the purely internal rule. However, contrary to such an assessment the Singh judgment marks a substantial broadening of European law's scope of application. Not the deterring effect of the measure, but the mere exercise of movement in the past forms the point of departure in reasoning.[99] As Maduro points out: 'How can a national be deterred from leaving his country of origin if a State applies to him the same law it would have applied had he remained?'[100] Consequently, the formula does not aim at the protection of the freedom of movement of individuals, but stipulates that its past exercise renders European provisions applicable.[101] Developing the point further, Nic Shuibhne has raised the critique that 'the logic of Singh is potentially infinite'.[102] Given the fact that one can easily establish a link between a measure under review and cross-border movement in the past or its potential for hindrance of future movement, nearly all cases may come within the scope of EU law. As a result of this expansion, judicial review by the European Court of Justice is expanded. At the same time, the risk of reverse discrimination decreases because more situations are subject to the same standard of review, namely European law.[103] Despite the criticism concerning the formula's logic coherence, the judges have repeatedly applied it in the context of the demarcation of the scope of EU law, as the decisions in *Carpenter*,[104] *Eind*[105] or *S and G*[106] show.[107]

[99] Nic Shuibhne (n 6) 745 f; O'Leary (n 1) 47 f. See also Lach (n 18) 113. Against Tryfonidou (n 6) 100.

[100] Maduro (n 5) 124.

[101] Nic Shuibhne (n 6) 745.

[102] ibid, 746.

[103] See Tryfonidou (n 6) 95. Further (but with regard to a different extension of the scope of application of EU law) P van Elsuwege and D Kochenov, 'On the Limits of Judicial Intervention: EU Citizenship and Family Reunification Rights' (2011) 4 *European Journal of Migration and Law* 443, 456; van Elsuwege (n 18) 274.

[104] Case C-60/00 *Mary Carpenter v Secretary of State for the Home Department* [2002] ECR I-6279, especially para 39. In *Carpenter*, the European Court of Justice argued that a British national, who lives and works in the UK but provides services in other Member States occasionally, would be deterred from exercising his freedom of movement if his wife, herself national of the Philippines, was refused right to residence in the UK.

[105] Case C-291/05 *Minister voor Vreemdelingenzaken en Integratie v R N G Eind*, [2007] ECR I-10719, para 35. In *Eind*, a Dutch national sought a residence permit for his daughter of Surinamese origin in the Netherlands. The case was peculiar in that Mr Eind had moved to Great Britain for work purposes, where he was joined by his daughter directly from Surinam, and had then moved back to the Netherlands. Faced with the question whether the refusal to grant the daughter, Miss Eind, a Dutch residence permit upon her first entry into the Netherlands (and her father's respective re-entry) was in accordance with EU law, the judges held that

> [a] national of a Member State could be deterred from leaving that Member State in order to pursue gainful employment in the territory of another Member State if he does not have the certainty of being able to return to his Member State of origin (para 35).

[106] In Case C-457/12 *S v Minister voor Immigratie, Integratie en Asiel and Minister voor Immigratie, Integratie en Asiel v G* [2014] ECLI:EU:C:2014:136, the *Carpenter* reasoning was expanded to cover situations under the freedom of movement of workers provision, Art 45 TFEU.

[107] Tryfonidou (n 6) 100 ff.

Furthermore, the judges have dispensed with using the language of deterrence and proceeded to more explicitly arguing that persons may enjoy protection under European free movement law via a cross-border move per se—whether it is past or potential. For example, in *Ritter-Coulais*,[108] the Court of Justice held quite straightforwardly:

> It should be noted that any Community national who, irrespective of his place of residence and his nationality, has exercised the right to freedom of movement for workers and who has been employed in a Member State other than that of residence falls within the scope of Article 48 EC [now Article 54 TFEU].[109]

By this and similar expressions, the European Court of Justice signifies that Member State nationals acquire the 'status' of free mover through their movement from one state to another. Moreover such a status remains attached to their person and grants them future protection. The result proves the accuracy of previous criticisms in academic discussion[110] based on the Court's judgment in *Singh*: movement triggers protection under EU law, instead of EU law being applicable in order to protect free movement.

The cases that have so far been presented under the second heading of the *inclusionary approach* were decided under the regime of the four freedoms. One can detect a similar approach adopted by the Court in its decisions on European citizenship. Looking at the broader picture, the potential sphere of influence of EU law has grown vastly through the introduction of Union citizenship. Prior to its

[108] Case C-152/03 *Hans-Jürgen Ritter-Coulais and Monique Ritter-Coulais v Finanzamt Germersheim* [2006] ECR I-1711. In the preliminary reference, the European Court of Justice was asked if German nationals, residing in France and working in Germany, could rely on the freedom of establishment or the right to free movement of capital in order to file costs in their German income tax declaration that arouse out of their home use in France. For a more detailed discussion see Tryfonidou (n 6) 110 ff.

[109] ibid, para 31, with reference to Case C-385/00 *F.W.L. de Groot v Staatssecretaris van Financiën* [2002] ECR I-11819, para 76; Case C-209/01 *Theodor Schilling and Angelica Fleck-Schilling v Finanzamt Nürnberg-Süd* [2003] ECR I-13389, para 23.

See further Case C-212/05 *Gertraud Hartmann v Freistaat Bayern* [2007] ECR I-6303. In *Hartmann*, the judges decided that an Austrian national, who was married to a German husband working in Germany but living with his family in Austria, was entitled to receive child allowance benefits from the Federal Republic of Germany. They argued that the national law, which made the entitlement to child support subject to a residence requirement inside Germany, was in instances such as the one at hand, contrary to EU law. Though maybe not surprising in outcome, the judgment was striking because it relied on freedom of movement for workers provisions. Similar to *Singh* and *Carpenter*, the national measure did not deter Mr Hartmann from pursuing his work in Germany. Instead, the refusal to grant child allowance was connected to the fact that he had opted for living in Austria. Consequently, the nexus between the family's situation and freedom of movement for workers is limited to the circumstance that Mr Hartmann exercised his right to interstate movement for working purposes. In the words of the Court:

> That Mr Hartmann settled in Austria for reasons not connected with his employment does not justify refusing him the status of migrant worker which he acquired as from the time when, following the transfer of his residence to Austria, he made full use of his right to freedom of movement for workers by going to Germany to carry on an occupation there (para 18).

Also discussed in Tryfonidou (n 6) 112.

[110] eg Maduro (n 5) 124 f.

introduction an economic element was required for a situation to come within the scope of free movement law. Articles 18 and onwards TFEU grant European citizens protection of free movement without them having to establish a link to an economic enterprise.[111] As a result of this expansion cases such as *Garcia Avello*,[112] *Chen*,[113] *Alokpa*[114] or *O and B*[115] reached the Court of Justice. As far as the first two of these cases are concerned, although in both cases the individuals in question had never left their respective Member States, the judges engaged in a review of the national measures and held that the individuals were entitled to protection under EU citizenship law.

Garcia Avello concerned the case of two children living in Belgium with joint Belgian-Spanish nationality. Belgian authorities refused permission to the parents to use a double-barrelled name for the children, as was common in Spain. The case came before the European Court of Justice and it found that a connecting factor to European law was discernible in the link between the children's Spanish nationality and authorisation of a double surname. While not relying on the citizenship free movement provisions, the judges reached the conclusion that the family's situation was covered by Articles 18 and 20 TFEU.[116] Continuing in *Chen*, the Court also identified the situation as not being of purely internal nature. Mrs Chen, a Chinese national, was living and working for a limited amount of time without a permanent residence permit in the UK, when she gave birth to a daughter in Belfast. Due to the peculiarity of Irish nationality law at that time all persons born on the island Ireland had the right to Irish citizenship.[117] Accordingly Mrs Chen's daughter held Irish nationality. In the ensuing case the European Court of Justice faced the question as to whether Mrs Chen, as the mother and primary caretaker of an EU citizen living in another Member State than that of her nationality, enjoyed a right to stay in the UK pursuant to Union law. Citing

[111] Spaventa (n 18) 23.

[112] Case C-148/02 *Carlos Garcia Avello v Belgian State* [2003] ECR I-11613.

[113] Case C-200/02 *Kunqian Catherine Zhu and Man Lavette Chen v Secretary of State for the Home Department* [2004] ECR I-9925.

[114] Case C-86/12 *Adzo Domenyo Alokpa and Others v Ministre du Travail, de l'Emploi et de l'Immigration* [2013] ECLI:EU:C:2013:645.

[115] Case C-456/12 *O v Minister voor Immigratie, Integratie en Asiel and Minister voor Immigratie, Integratie en Asiel v B* [2014] ECLI:EU:C:2014:135.

[116] *Garcia Avello* (n 112). The Court stated that

> '[i]t is not permissible for a Member State to restrict the effects of the grant of the nationality of another Member State by imposing an additional condition for recognition of that nationality with a view to the exercise of the fundamental freedoms provided for in the Treaty (see in particular, to that effect, Case C-369/90 *Mario Vicente Micheletti and others v Delegación del Gobierno en Cantabria* [1992] ECR I-4239, para 10)' (para 28).

[117] As reaction to the *Chen* decision, the Irish law has been amended by s 4 of the Irish Nationality and Citizenship Act 2004, introducing additional requirements for the acquisition of the Irish citizenship. See Hailbronner and Thym (n 40) 1265 as well as A Landsbergen and N Miller, 'European Citizenship Rights in Internal Situations: An Ambiguous Revolution?—Decision of 8 March 2011, Case C-34/09 *Gerardo Ruiz Zambrano v Office national de l'emploi (ONEM)*' (2011) 7 *European Constitutional Law Review* 287, 302.

Garcia Avello, the Court argued that, although mother and daughter (the latter in her status as an EU citizen) had never left the territory of the United Kingdom, both were entitled to protection under EU citizenship law due to the daughter's Irish nationality and the existence of sufficient personal financial resources.[118] The reasoning first developed in *Chen* was further pursued in *Alokpa*.[119] There, the European Court of Justice considered a right to stay for a Togolese woman, who was raising her two children in Luxembourg as a single mother. The peculiarity of the case was that both children held French nationality, due to their father's citizenship, but had never left the state of Luxembourg.[120]

As the above presented examples illustrate, the forecast of the *Singh* logic being 'potentially infinite'[121] proved to be true. The open-endedness of *Singh*, in combination with further developments in EU citizenship adjudication (more thoroughly explained below), came to haunt the Court. As a reaction, it redefined certain limits when establishing the existence of a cross-border element.[122] In *O and B*, the Court upheld its statement

> that [a] third-country national must, when the Union citizen [spouse] returns to the Member State of which he is a national, be entitled, under Union law, to a derived right of residence in the latter State (see *Singh*, para 25, and *Eind*, para 45). If that third-country national did not have such a right, a worker who is a Union citizen could be discouraged from leaving the Member State of which he is a national.[123]

Yet, by analogy to Directive 2004/38,[124] the judges argued that the movement of the EU citizen to another Member State than his country of origin had to be of a period of 'sufficiently genuine [time] so as to enable that citizen to create or strengthen family life'.[125]

Even though one can conclude from these remarks that the Court has taken on the task of re-establishing clearer contours to the purely internal rule, the trend

[118] *Zhu and Chen* (n 113) paras 19 f. In a similar vein it is worthwhile noting to the European Court of Justice's decision in the *Metock* case (n 46). In that case judges held that third country nationals married to Union citizens 'residing in [a] Member State but not possessing its nationality' (para 48) were covered by the protection of Directive 2004/38 on the right of citizens of the Union and their family members to move and reside freely within the territory of the Member States. The Court declared that a national measure requiring third country nationals to have held previous lawful residence in another Member State to come within the scope of protection of the directive was incompatible with Union law (paras 48–80). Disregarding the question of whether the Union citizen spouse had moved across borders, the Court found that if such third country nationals were not entitled to enjoy the protection of the directive, their Union citizen spouse would be discouraged 'from exercising his right of entry into and residence in [a] Member State' (para 63) different from his country of origin. A nexus between the third country national in such a situation and the directive was thereby established.

[119] *Alokpa and Others* (n 114).

[120] Ultimately, the European Court of Justice left it to the national court to decide if Mrs Alokpa was entitled to a right of residence pursuant to EU law. Unlike *Chen*, it was not obvious in the case if Mrs Alokpa had sufficient resources to provide for her family; ibid, para 30.

[121] Nic Shuibhne (n 6) 746.

[122] Tryfonidou (n 76) 313.

[123] *O and B* (n 115) para 46.

[124] ibid, para 50.

[125] ibid, para 51.

remains that it is, at times, very permissive in interpreting the facts when establishing the existence of a cross-border element. As was already emphasised above, the result is not only that situations are less often considered to be confined to one Member State but also that the likelihood of reverse discrimination decreases.

iii. Reinterpreting the Rule

Under the *inclusionary approach*, the European Court of Justice applies a third technique to bring cases within the scope of Union law. This method is likely to be the most difficult to fit into a coherent picture of the Court's powers to review national measures. The judges restrict themselves to an assessment of the specifics of the case (contrary to their actions under the first strand of the *inclusionary approach*) and abstain from interpreting its facts in an extensive manner (contrary to their performance under the second strand of the *inclusionary approach*). Instead, they engage in an undertaking I would term the 'conceptual reinterpretation of the purely internal rule'. It occurs in two fields of European law that have little in common apart from the Court's use of them to modify its interpretation of the purely internal rule: customs law and, once again, European citizenship law.

Starting with the first category of cases, the modification strategy has been pursued in decisions that deal with customs imposed on products moving within a single Member State.[126] In *Lancry*,[127] the Court established that dues charged on goods because these goods enter a 'region from another part of the same state'[128] are prohibited under the provisions on the establishment of a customs union. *Lancry* concerned a French provision, which allowed for the levying of a dock due (*octroi de mer*) on all products shipped to the French overseas departments. The Court had already held in *Legros*—a case that concerned products coming from other Member States than France to the *territoire de la Réunion*—that this due had to be considered as a 'charge having an effect equivalent to a customs duty'.[129] Thus, in *Lancry*, the Court was asked to clarify to what extent this judgment was applicable to products sent from mainland France to the overseas departments. In its reply it stated that EU law also prohibits charges equivalent to customs duties, which are charged on goods originating in France. Although these goods technically never left France and one could reasonably argue that the 'facts and effects of the case' were confined to one Member State, the judges held EU law to be applicable. Their assessment was based on three grounds:[130] first, they argued that

[126] On this line of cases and the determination of the scope of application of EU law see Tryfonidou (n 6) 72 ff.

[127] Joined Cases C-363/93, C-407/93, C-408/93, C-409/93, C-410/93 and C-411/93 *Lancry SA v Direction Générale des Douanes* [1994] ECR I-3957.

[128] ibid, para 32.

[129] Case C-163/90 *Administration des Douanes et Droits Indirects v Léopold Legros and others* [1992] ECR I-4625, para 18.

[130] Also discussed in Lach (n 18) 188 ff.

there was an element of cross border movement to the case and that a customs union was undermined just as much by frontiers internal to a Member State as by those that may exist between Member States.[131] Second, they stated that 'it would be inconsistent to hold, on the one hand, that dock dues constitute charges having equivalent effect in so far as they are levied on goods from other Member States and to concede, on the other, that those dues do not constitute charges having equivalent effect where they are levied on goods from metropolitan France';[132] thereby addressing the issue of reverse discrimination. Third, they reasoned that 'it would be very difficult, if not impossible, in practical terms, to distinguish between products of domestic origin and products originating in other Member States'.[133] Therefore, the Court of Justice reserved itself the right to review customs, which were imposed on goods circulating within one single Member State, with regard to their compatibility with Union law.

The final argumentation was used once again in *Simitzi v Kos*[134] and was extended to cover charges 'levied on goods dispatched from one region to other regions of the same State'.[135] Furthermore, the judgments in *Carbonati Apuani*[136] and *Jersey Potatoes*[137] also made ample reference to *Lancry*.[138] In *Carbonati Apuani*, it was decided that charges imposed on marble transported from one Italian municipality to other regions of the same Member State were contrary to EU customs law. Regarding *Jersey Potatoes*, the judges concluded that an export framework system, which required potato growers from the Isle of Jersey to pay mandatory contributions if they wanted to export their produce to other destinations in the United Kingdom, was a breach of then Article 23 EC (now Article 28 TFEU).

This line of cases has been commented on as marking a departure from the purely internal rule in tariff cases.[139] It was argued that the rule was dismissed for the sake of a uniform treatment of customs (or measures having equivalent effect thereof) inside the European Union, without privileging goods imported from other Member States. However, certain developments have led one to question whether this idea was the driving force behind the Court's decisions. What is remarkable about the reasoning in the *Carbonati Apuani* and the *Jersey Potatoes* judgments is that the argument on the inconsistency of an approach distinguishing between charges with nexus to movement between two Member States and charges related to movement within one state alone is no longer explicitly

[131] *Lancry* (n 127) paras 27 ff.
[132] ibid, para 30.
[133] ibid, para 31.
[134] Joined Cases C-485/93 and C-486/93 *Maria Simitzi v Dimos Kos* [1995] ECR I-2655.
[135] ibid, para 26.
[136] *Carbonati Apuani* (n 9).
[137] Case C-293/02 *Jersey Produce Marketing Organisation Ltd v States of Jersey and Jersey Potato Export Marketing Board* [2005] ECR I-9543.
[138] *Carbonati Apuani* (n 9) paras 22 ff; *Jersey Produce* (n 137) para 62. Tryfonidou (n 6) 74 f.
[139] A Tryfonidou, 'Carbonati Apuani Srl v Commune di Carrara: Should we Reverse "Reverse Discrimination"?' (2005) 16 *The King's College Law Journal* 373, 376 ff. More nuanced, ibid (n 6) 20 f.

mentioned.[140] As a consequence, any direct reference to the establishment of reverse discrimination is removed from the decision's grounds. Instead the Court stresses the arguments relating to cross-border movement (although confined to frontiers within one country) and impracticality to distinguish between goods destined to stay within one Member State and products chosen to be further transported to other places in the European Union.[141] One may interpret this shift of analytical emphasis in the following way. In its case law on interstate customs, the European Court of Justice is not so much interested in setting the purely internal rule aside, but in redefining its conception. To recall, pursuant the traditional principle, a situation is considered purely internal in the event that 'its facts and effects ... are confined within a single Member State'.[142] If one now looks at the argument on indistinguishableness, one will recognise that the Court—contrary to the first two strands of the inclusionary approach—still examines the specific charges in question. Yet, one will further detect that it conducts an expansive reading of what it considers to be an effect that is *not* confined to one Member State. It is not the direct implications of a measure that are assessed but rather its indirect, long-term effects on interstate trade.[143] There is an extension in the interpretation of what is considered to be an element, which sufficiently links a situation to Union law.

One additional factor must be kept in mind when deciding whether the Court of Justice actually dismissed the purely internal rule in the above mentioned cases. They were all decided under the rules on the establishment of a customs union.[144] One can argue that the specific feature of levying charges on goods due to their movement across frontiers makes a measure per se subject to EU law scrutiny. The physical aspect of a border—even if it is a border internal to one Member State—is in stark opposition to the idea of a non-fragmented European territory.[145] In addition, the Union has exclusive competence in the area of a customs union (Article 3(1)(a) TFEU). Given that such action is so contrary to the spirit and the wording of the Treaties, one can claim that the impact of tariffs or equivalent measures can never be considered as confined to one Member State. The Court's remarks in paragraph 23 of the *Carbonati Apuani* decision point towards such understanding, when the judges state that the aim of the Treaty is to establish an internal market and that 'Article 14(2) EC [now Article 26(2) TFEU] defines the internal market as "an area without internal frontiers in which the free movement of goods, persons,

[140] In *Jersey Potatoes*, this move by the Court is logical only because the provision under review regulated exclusively the dispatch of potatoes from the Island of Jersey to mainland Great Britain, see Tryfonidou (n 6) 75.

[141] *Carbonati Apuani* (n 9) para 26; *Jersey Produce* (n 137) paras 65 and 79 ff.

[142] eg *Oosthoek's Uitgeversmaatschappij* (n 9) para 9; *Mathot* (n 9) paras 7–9; *Steen* (n 9) para 9; and *RI.SAN.* (n 9) para 23.

[143] Tryfonidou (n 6) 207.

[144] Further, *Jersey Produce* (n 137) also discussed the compatibility of the Jersey Potato Export Marketing Scheme Act 2001 with Art 35 TFEU (ex Art 29 EC).

[145] My thanks to Loïc Azoulai for pointing out this aspect. On the issue, Tryfonidou (n 139) 378.

services and capital is ensured", without drawing any distinction between inter-State frontiers and frontiers within a State'.[146] Hence, a more plausible reading of the case law is that the Court of Justice merely modified the purely internal rule in the case of customs so as to accommodate for the peculiarities of the subject matter.

An even more far reaching modification in defining the limits of Union law has been undertaken in the *Ruiz Zambrano* judgment. As the following paragraphs show, one may read the decision as the Court's introduction of a second option besides the cross-border element to bring cases within the scope of application of European citizenship law. Alternatively, one can understand it as a form of conceptual reinterpretation.

Mr Ruiz Zambrano is a Colombian national who moved with his (also Colombian) wife to Belgium in 1999. During his stay in Belgium, his wife gave birth to two children who both obtained Belgian nationality. In this period, Mr Ruiz Zambrano worked full-time, contributed to the state's unemployment fund and was nonetheless refused a residence permit on multiple occasions.[147] Upon finding himself unemployed, the National Employment Office refused payment of benefits on the grounds that his presence in Belgium was irregular. In the proceedings, the Court of Justice had to decide whether the TFEU provisions on European Union citizenship conferred a right of residence on a third country national, who is the primary caretaker of children with European citizenship, and whether these norms exempted 'him from having to obtain a work permit in that Member State'.[148] These questions were of complex nature, because the Ruiz Zambrano children had never made use of their European movement rights. Accordingly one could have argued that their situation was of 'purely internal' nature.[149] In its reply the Luxembourg Court found that the children, and Mr Ruiz Zambrano as a relative in the ascending line, could rely on Article 20 TFEU, and held that Mr Ruiz Zambrano was to be granted residence and work permits. More specifically, the judges argued that 'citizenship of the Union is intended to be the fundamental status of nationals of the Member States'[150] and that further,

[146] *Carbonati Apuani* (n 9) para 23.

[147] An action for annulment of one of the refusal decisions was still pending at the time of reference, see *Ruiz Zambrano* (n 49) Opinion of AG Sharpston, para 21.

[148] *Ruiz Zambrano* (n 49) para 36. In full, para 36 states:

> By its questions, which it is appropriate to consider together, the referring court asks, essentially, whether the provisions of the TFEU on European Union citizenship are to be interpreted as meaning that they confer on a relative in the ascending line who is a third country national, upon whom his minor children, who are European Union citizens, are dependent, a right of residence in the Member State of which they are nationals and in which they reside, and also exempt him from having to obtain a work permit in that Member State.

[149] This was the appraisal of all Member State governments and of the European Commission that submitted observations to the Court of Justice in the proceedings; see ibid, para 37.

[150] ibid, para 41 with reference to Case C-184/99 *Rudy Grzelczyk v Centre public d'aide sociale d'Ottignies-Louvain-la-Neuve* [2001] ECR I-6193, para 31; Case C-413/99 *Baumbast and R v Secretary of State for the Home Department* [2002] ECR I-7091, para 82; *Garcia Avello* (n 112) para 22; *Zhu and Chen* (n 113) para 25 and Case C-135/08 *Janko Rottmann v Freistaat Bayern* [2010] ECR I-1449, para 43.

'Article 20 TFEU precludes national measures which have the effect of depriving citizens of the Union of the genuine enjoyment of the substance of the rights conferred by virtue of their status as citizens of the Union'.[151] As a refusal to grant their father residence in Belgium would have implied the children's forced departure from the '*territory of the Union*',[152] the Court considered such measure to be contrary to EU law.

Following the decision, two questions emerged: first, on what grounds can one distinguish the later decisions of *McCarthy*, *Dereci* and *Iida*, which all involved minor children and were found not to lie within the scope of Union law, from *Ruiz Zambrano*? Second, and more generally, is the purely internal rule as such still valid in the area of European citizenship?

a. Excursus: *Ruiz Zambrano* and its Follow-up Cases

Turning to the question whether one can account for the difference in outcome between *Ruiz Zambrano, McCarthy, Dereci* and *Iida*, two explanations are conceivable, namely (a) that the Court examined the cases pursuant different articles or (b) that the factor linking the situation to the territory of the Union was stronger in *Ruiz Zambrano* than in the other cases.

In the first reactions to *Ruiz Zambrano* and *McCarthy*, which the Court issued in an interval of two months, scholars suggested that the difference between granting protection to the Ruiz Zambrano family whilst denying it to the McCarthys was owed to the fact that the Court once examined the situation under Article 20 TFEU, the provision on citizenship status, and once under Article 21 TFEU, the citizen free movement provision.[153] They stressed in particular the connection the Court made in the *Ruiz Zambrano* judgment to one of its former decisions on the status of citizenship, *Rottmann*.[154]

The case concerned an Austrian citizen who naturalised in Germany and as a legal consequence lost his Austrian citizenship through the procedure. In his application for German nationality Mr Rottmann did not disclose the fact that an arrest warrant was pending against him in Austria—information he was required to reveal. When the German administration was informed about his fraudulent acquisition of nationality, it withdrew its decision on naturalisation pursuant Paragraph 48(1) *Verwaltungsverfahrensgesetz*, rendering Mr Rottmann stateless. In the following judicial procedures, the question arose whether such action, stripping Mr Rottmann not only of his German, but also his EU citizenship, was in accordance with EU law. Confronted with the issue, the European Court of Justice had to assess whether the situation fell within the scope of application of

[151] *Ruiz Zambrano* (n 49) para 42.
[152] ibid, para 44, emphasis added.
[153] O'Leary (n 1) 60. Solely mentioning the difference, Nic Shiubhne (n 18) 357.
[154] *Rottmann* (n 150).

EU law. Instead of analysing in depth the question whether relevant cross-border movement took place, it held that the situation was subject to EU scrutiny 'by reason of its nature and its consequences'.[155] The judges established the nexus to EU citizenship protection because the national measure placed Mr Rottmann 'in a position capable of causing him to lose the status conferred by Article 17 EC [now Article 20 TFEU]'.[156]

Even at that stage commentators argued that the case constituted an 'overhaul of the legal construction of the wholly internal situations'[157] and that the Court's approach pursuing the establishment of a cross-border situation 'has been trashed in *Rottmann*'.[158] A less revolutionary reading of the case suggests that it was not in fact about the purely internal rule (and thus not about the prevention of reverse discrimination). Instead, the peculiar character of the case with the clear risk of stripping an individual of his *status* as a European citizen justified an examination by the court.[159] The question of status, Member State nationality and supranational citizenship were so strongly linked to each other that *Rottmann* represented a true *Sonderfall*, which allowed for the establishment of a nexus to EU law without need for reliance on the purely internal rule.

Even if one does not read *Rottmann* as marking a departure of the purely internal rule, it is correct that its reasoning was transferred to the situation of *Ruiz Zambrano*, where not only the status itself, but the exercise of rights connected to that status was at stake. Consequently, the Court took the step to hold that some national measures may infringe the rights related to European citizenship to such an extent that the status provision of Article 20 TFEU offers protection—irrespective of the application of the purely internal rule. Against this background, one might argue that *McCarthy* was decided differently since the judges examined the case not under aspects of status, but free movement (Article 21 TFEU).

However, particularly in light of *Dereci*, this explanation based on the status-free movement distinction must be dismissed. To begin with *Dereci*, the next decision in line, it does not fit the picture where protection under free movement as well as under status was considered and ultimately denied. The same holds true for the decision in *Iida*, where the Court jointly assessed the compatibility of the national norms with Articles 20 and 21 TFEU.[160] In addition, it appears rather

[155] ibid, para 42.

[156] ibid.

[157] D Kochenov, 'Comment on Case C-135/08, *Janko Rottmann v Freistaat Bayern*, Judgment of the Court (Grand Chamber) of 2 March 2010, not yet reported' (2010) 47 *CML Rev* 1831, 1836. More cautiously, Jessurun d'Oliveira argues that after *Rottmann*, 'the concept of the "internal case" has become very elusive if not illusionary' (HU Jessurun d'Oliveira, 'Decision of 2 March 2010, Case C-315/08 *Janko Rottmann v Freistaat Bayern—Case Note 1* – Decoupling Nationality and Union Citizenship?' (2011) 7 *European Constitutional Law Review* 138, 141).

[158] Kochenov (n 157) 1841. Though he then proceeds by arguing that the issue of 'status' was of fundamental importance for the decision.

[159] Nevertheless, *Rottmann* remains revolutionary in the sense that it reverses the relationship between EU and Member State citizenship: 'The nationality law of the member states becomes dependent on the fortunes of Union citizenship' (Jessurun d'Oliveira (n 157) 141).

[160] *Iida* (n 63) paras 66 ff.

formalistic to argue that the choice in the provision selected as the basis of review explains the different outcomes. In this context, the real question that the judgments need to be measured against is why the Court opted to address the issue in terms of status in one case, in terms of free movement in another and in terms of a combination of both in a third.

This leads over to a second possible account arguing that the difference in outcome can be explained on factual grounds.[161] One may claim that the Court saw a stronger connection to the European Union in *Ruiz Zambrano* than in the other two cases. The Court perceived the choice in *Ruiz Zambrano* to be the following: either, protection under Union law is granted or Belgian law applies and the children holding the European citizenship will be forced to leave the territory of the Union.[162] With regard to the situation of Mrs McCarthy, the Court argued that the refusal to grant her husband permanent residence did not result in the necessary consequence of Mrs McCarthy having to leave the territory of the Union.[163] Similarly in *Dereci*, the situations were depicted in such a light, that the option for the EU citizens (not for their dependent third-country national relatives) existed to stay in the Union.[164] Differently put, '"mere" economic dependency or desire to keep a family together will not suffice'[165] to bring a situation within the scope of EU citizenship law. Instead, 'actual (im)possibility with respect of staying in the territory of the Union'[166] is a necessary requirement for granting protection. In following cases, the Court put it even more markedly by arguing that a right of residence is exceptionally granted to a third-country national family member if otherwise the Union 'citizen would be obliged in practice to leave the territory of the European Union altogether'.[167]

The last point—the importance of the territorial element[168]—hints at the response to the question of how far the European Court of Justice abandons with

[161] This stands in a certain contradiction to the principle that the European Court of Justice gives in the preliminary reference procedure abstract replies as to the interpretation of primary and secondary Union law. Although this is contrary to the ideal of general review, the Court made 'fact-finding statements' (Nic Shiubhne (n 18) 371) in the decisions under review. Given that it engaged in factual assessments, it is reasonable to discuss the cases with regard to their factual differences.

[162] *Ruiz Zambrano* (n 49) para 44. However, this choice between EU protection and forced leave seems to have been overstated. As AG Sharpston remarked in her Opinion, Belgium had in the meantime granted Mr Zambrano a provisional and renewable residence permit (ibid, Opinion of the AG Sharpston, para 32).

[163] *McCarthy* (n 61) para 49.

[164] *Dereci and Others* (n 62) paras 66 ff.

[165] Nic Shiubhne (n 18) 367.

[166] ibid.

[167] *Iida* (n 63) para 71; interestingly, the European Court of Justice abstains from using *Ruiz Zambrano* as a reference for this statement and prefers referring to *Dereci*. See further *Alokpa and Others* (n 114) para 33 and *Ymeraga and Others* (n 64) para 36.

[168] Azoulai proposes an alternative reading of the territorial argument in *Zambrano*. He states that it needs to be understood as a 'central reference … to a new common space, a space of distribution of rights and common values' (L Azoulai, 'A Comment on the Ruiz Zambrano Judgment: a Genuine European Integration', www.eudo-citizenship.eu/search-results/457-a-comment-on-the-ruiz-zambrano-judgment-a-genuine-european-integration).

its new line of cases the purely internal rule. Even when it reviews whether the 'genuine enjoyment of the substance of the rights conferred by virtue of their status as citizens of the Union'[169] is secured, it examines if there is a territorial aspect to the case. Only if EU citizens were otherwise forced to leave the territory of the Union, does the Court provide protection under the citizenship provisions. In this respect, the just discussed cases are in the tradition of the Court's adjudication on the purely internal rule.[170] The novelties are that the cross-border element does not concern frontiers between Member States (the standard case for the application of EU movement law) but the Union's external borders and that the review focuses on the status of European citizenship instead of the right to free movement.

Consequently, one may interpret the cases as a modification rather than an abolition of the purely internal rule.[171] The introductory remarks on reverse discrimination highlighted that a situation is considered purely internal and outside the scope of free movement law if its 'facts and effects are confined to one Member State'. Commonly, the need to establish the existence of a move between two Member States in order for EU law to apply was inferred from this statement. However, this interpretation curtails the purely internal rule. Negatively defined, it states that all those situations that are not confined to one Member State must not be considered purely internal. Under this logic situations (such as the one of the Ruiz Zambrano family) in which EU citizens may be obliged to leave their own Member States fall within the scope of EU law.

In summary, the 'genuine enjoyment' test as it is currently applied[172] modifies the purely internal rule. It maintains that EU citizens can only rely on EU citizenship norms, if they otherwise have to leave the external borders of the Union.

C. The Procedural Approach

So far, the depiction of the handling of reverse discrimination by the European Court of Justice has centred on the Court's reasoning as regards the substantial existence of purely internal situations. But before material aspects of a case—including the question whether a situation falls qua *ratione personae* and *ratione materiae* into the scope of application of EU law—are addressed, the judges must

[169] *Ruiz Zambrano* (n 49) para 42.

[170] Van Elsuwege argues in (n 40) 315 that the *McCarthy* judgment 'goes hand in hand with a teleological interpretation of the cross-border requirement'. Assessing *Ruiz Zambrano* as a departure of the purely internal rule: van Elsuwege and Kochenov (n 103) 451; Hailbronner and Thym (n 40) 1253.

[171] Hailbronner and Iglesias Sánchez (n 40) 510 speak of 're-conceptualizing'.

[172] Notwithstanding, the wording of the 'genuine enjoyment test' leaves room for broader interpretation. The Court has equipped itself with a tool to engage in review of situations that were previously outside its reach. But before its application can be thoroughly evaluated, one will need to wait for additional cases to come. See van Elsuwege and Kochenov (n 103) 451; A Wiesbrock, 'The Zambrano Case: Relying on Union citizenship Rights in "Internal Situations"', www.eudo-citizenship.eu/search-results/449-the-zambrano-case-relying-on-union-citizenship-rights-in-internal-situations.

decide if procedural requirements are met. More specifically, they must assess if preliminary references, under which most questions touching upon the phenomenon reach the court, are admissible. This stage in the reasoning of the Court allows for further techniques to either include or exclude situations from assessment according to European norms. In its procedural review, the Court has over time become more generous in holding cases to fall within its jurisdiction.[173]

Typical of the development of its position on the issue are two judgments: *Dzodzi*[174] and *Guimont.*[175] The first case concerned the review of a Belgian law on family reunification. Although the Court of Justice considered the situation at hand, which led the national court to ask a preliminary reference, to be confined to Belgium and thus 'purely internal',[176] it argued that it was nevertheless 'obliged to give a ruling'.[177] The judges reached this conclusion because the Belgian court sought an interpretation of the EU legislation to which the national law made reference.[178] Addressing the procedural question, the European Court of Justice first stated the familiar phrase that

> it is solely for the national courts before which the dispute has been brought, and which must bear the responsibility for the subsequent judicial decision, to determine in the light of the special features of each case both the need for a preliminary ruling in order to enable them to deliver judgment and the relevance of the questions which they submit to the Court.[179]

It then continued that no norm in EU law spoke against the Court having jurisdiction 'for a preliminary ruling on a Community provision in the specific case where the national law of a Member State refers to the content of that provision in order to determine rules applicable to a situation which is purely internal to that State'.[180] In other words, the Court assumed in *Dzodzi* a jurisdiction in purely internal situations, in so far as (a) the national norm in question refers directly and unconditionally to EU law and (b) the interpretation of the respective European law is relevant for the assessment of the situation.[181]

[173] Lach (n 18) 170 ff; Tryfonidou (n 6) 121 ff.
[174] *Dzodzi* (n 46).
[175] Case C-448/98 *Criminal proceedings against Jean-Pierre Guimont* [2000] ECR I-10663. For a more recent example of the reasoning, see *Venturini et al* (n 93) especially para 28.
[176] See *Dzodzi* (n 46) para 28.
[177] ibid, para 35.
[178] Lach (n 18) 155.
[179] ibid, para 34.
[180] ibid, para 36.
[181] See Lach (n 18) 156. Over time, the so-called 'Dzodzi jurisprudence' (Tryfonidou (n 6) 123) has been modified as to also affirm jurisdiction over instances, whose governing norms are less directly connected to EU law: eg preliminary references are already admissible, if judicial custom demands that the national norm's interpretation depends upon EU law interpretation (Lach (n 18) 161). See eg Case C-28/95 *A Leur-Bloem v Inspecteur der Belastingdienst/Ondernemingen Amsterdam 2* [1997] ECR I-4161, para 32; Case C-1/99 *Kofisa Italia Srl v Ministero delle Finanze* [2001] ECR I-207, para 32; Case C-222/01 *British American Tobacco Manufacturing BV v Hauptzollamt Krefeld* [2004] ECR I-4683, para 40; Case C-3/04 *Poseidon Chartering BV v Marianne Zeeschip VOF and Others* [2006] ECR I-2505, para 16; and Case C-280/06 *Autorità Garante della Concorrenza e del Mercato and Others v ETI SpA and Others* [2007] ECR I-10893, para 21.

How this line of reasoning influences the Court's handling of the purely internal rule and reverse discrimination was shown in *Guimont*. In the case, a French court asked for the correct interpretation of the freedom of movement for goods with regard to a (national) regulation on the manufacturing of cheese. Problematic about this preliminary reference was that the situation in question concerned criminal proceedings against French producers, pursuant French legislation, on French territory. Eschewing a clear answer as to whether they considered the situation to be purely internal,[182] the judges based the exercise of their jurisdiction on one principal argument. They argued that

> a reply might be useful to [the national court] if its national law were to require, in proceedings such as those in this case, that a national producer must be allowed to enjoy the same rights as those which a producer of another Member State would derive from Community law in the same situation.[183]

Differently put, the judges, working under the assumption that French law could potentially prohibit reverse discrimination, issued a decision on the conformity of the measure with Article 34 TFEU (ex Article 28 EC) in order that the national court could assess whether it was dealing with a situation of reverse discrimination and initiate the steps necessary pursuant French law.

To recapitulate: under the procedural approach, the Court of Justice replies to references of purely internal nature, by giving a decision on the conformity of the measure with EU law, had there been a nexus between the national measure and the supranational norms. The reach of such rulings is confined to issues featuring a cross-border element. At the national level however, judges are equipped with the

It remains to be seen in how far Case C-482/10 *Teresa Cicala v Regione Siciliana* [2011] ECR I-14139 presents a departure or evolution of the case law. The Court seems to imply in para 19 that the two conditions do not have to be fulfilled concurrently, but that condition number two is rather a result of the first condition. In the original:

> Thus, an interpretation, by the Court, of provisions of EU law in purely internal situations is justified because they are made applicable by national law in a direct and unconditional way (see, to that effect, Case C-346/93 *Kleinwort Benson* [1995] ECR I-615, para 16, and Case C-280/06 *ETI and Others* [2007] ECR I-10893, para 25), in order to ensure that internal situations and situations governed by EU law are treated in the same way (see, to that effect, [Case C-3/04] *Poseidon Chartering BV v Marianne Zeeschip VOF and Others* [2006] ECR I-2505] para 17, and Case C-217/05 *Confederación Española de Empresarios de Estaciones de Servicio* [2006] ECR I-11987, para 22).

But see Ritter (n 1) 698, who argues that under *Dzodzi*, 'the Court does not actually check whether national law prohibits reverse discrimination'.

[182] *Guimont* (n 175) paras 13–21.

[183] ibid, para 23. Further, *Reisch and Others* (n 49) para 22; Case C-6/01 *Anomar and Others v Portugal* [2003] ECR I-8621, paras 39–41; Case C-451/03 *Servizi Ausiliari Dottori Commercialisti Srl v Giuseppe Calafiori* [2006] ECR I-2941, para 29; Joined Cases C-94/04 and C-202/04 *Federico Cipolla v Rosaria Fazari, née Portolese and Stefano Macrino and Claudia Capoparte v Roberto Meloni* [2006] ECR I-11421, para 30; Joined Cases C-570/07 and C-571/07 *José Manuel Blanco Pérez and María del Pilar Chao Gómez v Consejería de Salud y Servicios Sanitarios and Others* [2010] ECR I-4629, para 36.

In addition, the Court established its jurisdiction in *Centro Europa* through an interesting combination of the abstract link to European law approach (*Pistre* case law) and the procedural approach; see *Centro Europa* (n 92) paras 66–69.

European Court of Justice's interpretation of Union law in order to perform their assessment of the purely internal situation of the case according to national law.

D. Outlook

Where does this examination leave us? Its principle findings are: the European Court of Justice does not address reverse discrimination under the European equality provisions, but approaches the subject when delimiting its scope of application. In this demarcation exercise, the Court by and large still applies the purely internal rule. Thus, it is still a valid tool (in the legal and the practical sense of the term).

However, its secondary finding is that the procedural as well as substantial borders of the rule have been stretched to such an extent that the Court's reference to the rule appears artificial or even arbitrary. The varied approaches show that the judges have difficulties in drawing a clear line between situations subject to EU law scrutiny and those left to the Member States to decide.[184] A cursory explanation for this lack of methodological contours is the tension felt by the judges between preventing reverse discrimination occurring and respecting Member State competences.[185] Yet, greater insight might be gained from a detailed rather than sweeping assessment. The more intriguing questions resulting from this analysis are therefore: when is the Court willing to consider a situation to be in the scope of EU law and when not? And which parameters guide its decision? The next section turns to these questions.

III. THE FUNDAMENTAL BOUNDARIES CONCERN—OR INSTITUTIONAL CHOICE IN THE SUPRANATIONAL CONTEXT

In his excellent piece 'Fundamental Rights and Fundamental Boundaries: On the Conflict of Standards and Values in the Protection of Human Rights in the European Legal Space'[186] Weiler wrote about the Union law's defining struggle to ensure 'unity in diversity' in fundamental rights protection. As already revealed by the title, the piece is focused on the conflict between granting adequate fundamental rights protection in the Union and respect for self-determination in the Member States. He argues that rights protection in a transnational setting must not only be informed by rights considerations, but also by regard for 'the

[184] See Hanf (n 3) 37. See also Nic Shuibhne (n 6) 737.

[185] On this argument, see Hanf (n 3) 29.

[186] JHH Weiler, 'Fundamental Rights and Fundamental Boundaries: On the Conflict of Standards and Values in the Protection of Human Rights in the European Legal Space' in ibid, *The Constitution of Europe—'Do the New Clothes have an Emperor?' and other Essays on European Integration*, Essay Collection (Cambridge, Cambridge University Press, 1999) 102.

principle of enumerated powers or limited competences which are designed to guarantee that in certain areas communities (rather than individuals) should be free to make their own social choices without interference from above'.[187] Weiler thereby directly addresses the tension manifest in the handling of reverse discrimination between promoting equal treatment and accommodating institutional concerns.

With regard to the approaches employed by the European Court of Justice towards reverse discrimination, one can observe the following. The purely internal rule has been modified and pushed to its limits to such an extent that one may fear it will implode under the pressure of cases reaching the Luxembourg Court.[188] Moreover, it is so difficult to give a coherent account of the amassed case law that commentators resort to explaining it in terms of 'turn[s] of the tide'.[189] In the next passage, I seek to ascertain whether the framework of comparative institutional analysis, presented in the previous chapter, can be of guidance in conceptualising the European Court of Justice's adjudication on reverse discrimination.[190]

A. *Guimont*'s Underlying Institutional Choices

As depicted above, the Court of Justice has developed different techniques to deal with the phenomenon. When explaining its *procedural* approach, the judges stated (when commenting on their jurisdiction) that they will analyse a situation before them in so far as a connection to European law exists and let the Member State courts decide which conclusions to draw from this information for their judgments according to national law. Under the *inclusionary* and *exclusionary* approaches, the Court will comment on a situation or abstain from doing so, if it considers a case to feature a sufficient nexus with Union law, respectively if it deems it to be purely internal.

Guimont epitomises the first method and shall now serve as object for analysis from an institutional choice perspective. To recall, in criminal proceedings against Mr Guimont and other cheese producers, the question arose as to whether the French regulation stipulating that only cheese with rind was allowed to be labelled *Emmenthal* was in conformity with European law.

Beginning with an examination of the parameter 'interest representation', one could classify the risk of the French political process malfunctioning to the disadvantage of Mr Guimont and his fellow producers as rather low. Given that

[187] ibid, 103 f.

[188] AG Wahl himself addressed the risk of docket overload in the context of a narrow interpretation of the purely internal rule, see *Venturini et al* (n 93) Opinion of AG Wahl, paras 20 ff.

[189] Tryfonidou (n 76).

[190] In this respect, I would like to mention that Maduro has performed a comparative institutional choice towards reverse discrimination in Maduro (n 5) 134 ff. Also thinking in comparative institutional terms: P Caro de Sousa, *The European Fundamental Freedoms: A Contextual Approach* (Oxford, Oxford University Press, 2015) 183 ff; Nic Shuibhne (n 6) 767 ff.

the producers were of French nationality and had influence on the legislature through their electoral vote, there is little reason for concern that their interests were underrepresented. Instead, it is likely that French farmers and dairy factories, represented through their lobbies, were given more opportunities than the general public to influence the draft of the decree that eventually came before the Court.[191] As a consequence, one cannot speak of bias working against the French cheese producers. Nevertheless, bias might have existed in a different form, that is against producers coming from outside France. One may assume that, comparable to the situation in *Cassis de Dijon*, considerations on the traditions and situation of producers of other Member States were taken into account to a lesser extent. Therefore, interests of stakeholders 'external' to the French political process might have been underrepresented during the passage of the law.

As regards the aspects of scale and competence, one can make the following observation: an assessment in terms of scale, meaning in terms of 'the resources and budget available to the judiciary and the constraints on the expansion of the size of the adjudicative process',[192] actually argues against involvement by the European Court of Justice. Except for the fact that national courts have to create hypothetical situations with a connection to EU law that might lead to reverse discrimination, the procedural approach provides for no filters to keep cases away from the Court. Many cases that were previously beyond the reach of the Court are now within the scope of its review. How the judges want to manage such increase of preliminary references on the Court's docket has been insufficiently addressed.

With respect to competence, the question referred to the European Court of Justice was whether the French law was contrary to the EU guarantee of free movement of goods. There, the Luxembourg Court was in a position of greater relative expertise than the national referring court to assess the issue in terms of right to free movement. It had (and still has) the potential to remedy possible misrepresentations of European interests. On the other hand, balancing French interests may well have been better performed at the national level, because the French courts were more familiar with the particularities of the situation of French farmers. Facing this challenge of providing its expertise to the case whilst not overstepping its limits, the European Court of Justice opted for split assessment. As far as the decree had effects on free movers between the Member States, the Court scrutinised the norm. With respect to the law's other potential shortcomings, it remained silent and affirmed the referring court's competence to decide upon the issue. This way, the Court sought to show its respect for Member State competences and to thereby legitimise its decision. In terms of institutional choice, it

[191] Decree No 88-1206 of 30 December 1988 applying the Law of 1 August 1905 on frauds and falsifications relating to products or services and the Law of 2 July 1935 on the organization and restructuring of the milk market as regards cheeses, Official Journal of the French Republic of 31 December 1988, p 16753.

[192] Neil Komesar, *Law's Limits* (Cambridge, Cambridge University Press, 2001) 38.

allocated decision making on the purely internal elements of the case to institutions at the national level whilst deciding on the part of the reference which concerned the assessment of cross-border situations. The attempt to strike a balance between judicial intervention and restraint is obvious. However, one may still critique the approach chosen by the Court of Justice in institutional terms. The risk remains that the procedural approach may invite too many preliminary references for the European Court of Justice to deal with. Demand for decisions by the European Court of Justice will, with all likelihood, not lessen in the future. Even assuming it has the competence to rule on all these cases, the number of cases can eventually overburden the Court. With this in mind the Court may have been well advised to wait for a case with a more direct free movement nexus before testing the French manufacturing law.

B. The Inclusionary and Exclusionary Approach in Terms of Institutional Choice

Following the comparative institutional analysis of the *Guimont* line of cases the question of how far the institutional choice framework can contribute to explaining the case law on reverse discrimination that focuses on the application of the purely internal rule (*inclusionary* and *exclusionary* approaches) will be examined. This work upholds the claim that our understanding of the Court's approaches can greatly benefit from an observation of the topic through the lens of institutional comparison. In this context, one needs to recall that the purely internal rule, as it stands, is an expression of institutional considerations.[193] Its purpose is to delimit the spheres of decision making in a multi-layered legal order. It is designed for ensuring the proper demarcation of competences between the European Union and its Member States. It identifies the separate spheres of action for different institutional players and serves as a mechanism to keep cases off the docket of the European Court of Justice.

Under the first approach featured in the descriptive part of this chapter, the *exclusionary* approach, the Court of Justice applies the purely internal rule in a strict manner and allows reverse discrimination to persist in the respective situations. The analysis presented the cases *Saunders*, *Mathot*, *Flemish Welfare*, *Morson and Jhanjan*, as well as *McCarthy*, *Dereci*, *Iida* and *Ymeraga* as examples of this approach in the demarcation of European and national law. The familiar interpretive explanation for why the Court perceived these cases to fall outside the scope of application of free movement law was that their 'facts and effects are confined to one Member State'.[194] Additionally, the last four cases—decided after

[193] Caro de Sousa (n 190) 185.

[194] *Saunders* (n 6) para 11; *Morson and Jhanjan* (n 58); *Mathot* (n 9) para 7; *Government of the French Community and Walloon Government v Flemish Government* (n 54) paras 37 f; *McCarthy* (n 61); and *Dereci and Others* (n 62) paras 61. In the latter two cases, the Court gave the lack of an impediment

Ruiz Zambrano—were seen as not depriving European citizens of the 'genuine enjoyment of the substance of their rights' conferred upon them by their status.[195]

The above mentioned cases shall now be examined with the help of the institutional choice framework in order to assess whether a more coherent account of the Court's adjudication can be developed. In this process, I would like to again shift the perspective away from textual interpretation towards an analysis of the decisions according to the parameters of interest representation, numbers and complexity. Looking first at *Saunders*, the case concerned a British national's proceedings against a British probation measure. As regards the risk of the political process malfunctioning, there is no indication that Mrs Saunders' stakes were insufficiently taken into account in the national decision making process. Instead, one may assume that her British nationality equipped her with the means to influence the decision.[196] Against this argument, one could object that her means of influence were rather minimal. In addition, one needs to bear in mind that criminal offenders can become exposed to majoritarian bias. The desire for security of the majority is (even though vague and not substantially theorised) strong to the extent that laws regulating punishment run the risk of not taking into account the interests of sentenced persons. However, given that this analysis is comparative in character, we need to ask whether a supranational actor like the Court of Justice would have succeeded in providing a more adequate representation of her interest than national institutions. The answer is that one can remain sceptical about the Court's abilities to do so. This leads to the assessment of the case in terms of the complexity of the decision. In light of the importance society attaches to criminal law not only in terms of its own security, but also in more general terms of its self-perception, the European Court of Justice is a rather unsuited player for intervention.[197] Although the numbers of cases that would have been attracted by giving a substantive ruling in *Saunders* can be considered as rather low, 'complexity' and 'interest representation' suggest that the European Court would not have been in a better position than national institutions to decide on the subject.

To take *Flemish Welfare* as a second example, the case concerned the legality of a Flemish insurance scheme that excluded Walloons from participating. There was risk of the political process malfunction because of the particularities of Belgian

'of the genuine enjoyment of the substance of the rights conferred by virtue of the status of Union citizenship' as an additional rationale for the denial of protection under Arts 18 ff TFEU.

[195] *McCarthy* (n 61) para 49; *Dereci and Others* (n 62) para 74; *Iida* (n 63) para 76 and C *Ymeraga and Others* (n 64) para 42.

[196] Strikingly, Lenaerts links the Court's refusal to hear cases of purely internal situations to interest representation. He writes 'Yet, it is very unlikely for reverse discrimination to be left unaddressed (fn omitted). Since non-movers tend to be nationals, they have access to the national or regional political process to claim the extension of EU rights to all citizens' (Lenaerts (n 32) 1341).

[197] Notwithstanding the increased integration in the Area of Freedom, Security and Justice at the European level, see generally Craig and de Búrca (n 33) 923 ff.

politics.[198] The scheme was instituted by the Flemish political process. Due to electoral arrangements and distribution of regulatory powers in Belgium, it is conceivable that Walloon interests were underrepresented in the scheme's drafting. In the end, the fact that they were not allowed to become members of the scheme is indicative of their stakes not receiving proper weight. The same estimation holds true for the assessment of representation of foreign interests in the decision on the insurance scheme. Nationals from other Member States most likely had their interests underrepresented as well because they were likewise excluded from the scheme. With regard to their situation, the Court of Justice opted for intervention. This raises the question whether the Court acted correctly by reviewing only part of the issue in *Flemish Welfare.* As regards the situation of movers, the European Court of Justice is a competent forum for stakeholders whose interests are external to a Member State's decision making process. The same reasoning applies less so for stakeholders whose interests are internal and underrepresented. In these instances, the political malfunction must be either extensive or resemble very much the one encountered by persons outside Member States for the supranational Court to replace a substantive social decision for its own. This resemblance exists with regard to the Belgian insurance scheme.

But to conclude from this that the European Court of Justice should undertake to decide the case would neglect assessment of the topic in terms of numbers and complexity. As Komesar has pointed out in his works, the different parameters of institutional choice interact with each other.[199] Interest representation is linked to complexity. The Flemish Welfare case is complex for two reasons, with only the first complexity also being relevant in the transnational context. The case concerned the design of an insurance scheme. Considering that the arrangement of social security systems is an intricate exercise requiring that many specific facts be taken into account, it becomes evident that the European Court was facing thorough and far-reaching substantial questions.[200] Moreover, the fact that the case arose in Belgium, suffering as it does from its own imperfections, poses challenges to the judges at the European Court of Justice. Relations between the country's Walloon and Flemish part are tense. Had the Court decided on the situation of Walloon applicants to the insurance scheme, it would have involved itself in the very sensitive Belgian issue of regional autonomy. At the current stage of integration, the European Court of Justice is not in an appropriate position to do so

[198] Belgium is a federal state with three distinct regions: Flanders, Wallonia and Brussels-Capital. Whereas the majority of the Flemish community speaks Dutch as their first language, the majority of the Walloon community has French as their mother tongue. In Brussels Capital, the constellation is now diverse. Eventually (roughly beginning in the early 18th century), a conflict rooted in linguistic and socio-economic reasons developed between the various groups. Extensive federalisation was seen as a way to resolve the dilemma, but instead entailed greater compartmentalisation of interests and an increased risk of under-representation of the stakes of the respective minority.

[199] See, eg Komesar (n 192) 38.

[200] On the difficulty for the European Court of Justice to rule on social security issues, see Lenaerts (n 32) 1370.

and is aware of its limitations. If one takes into account the additional fact that application of the judgment to the situation of (non-mobile) Walloons would have attracted further references, the Court's restraint to rule in the issue becomes understandable.

Thirdly, one can scrutinise the family reunification judgments *Morson and Jhanjan, McCarthy, Dereci, Iida* and *Ymeraga* in institutional terms. In these cases, the Court of Justice denied the applicability of Union law by referring to the purely internal rule. Scrutinising the parties' representation of interests in the cases at hand, one may correctly hold the view that the interests of the third country nationals wishing to stay within the Union were likely to be under-represented in the national decision making processes; though one must view *Iida* as an exception to the appraisal. As the judges stressed in Iida, they were of the opinion that Mr Iida continued to have the option to apply successfully with the German authorities for a residence permit pursuant to German law.[201] Consequently, to their mind, national institutions could still take Mr Iida's situation adequately into account.

Even though one may assess the respective third-country nationals' interest representation at the Member State level as meagre, the comparative question to ask, with regard to the remaining cases, is whether their interests would have been better represented within European decision making processes. Here, the answer must be that there is no guarantee either that European actors can ensure adequate representation of their stakes. The interests of third-country nationals are also external to European Union decision making so that one must be cautious to simply assume that their interests are better represented at the supranational sphere. More promising is a comparative evaluation that takes the legal situation of the relative who holds EU citizenship as starting point for the inquiry. In all of the other cases, *Morson and Jhanjan, McCarthy, Dereci* and *Ymeraga*, the relatives serving as potential connectors to European law protection were citizens of the Member States enforcing their restrictive laws. Under ideal conditions, they had the chance of having their interest represented in the national political process.[202] Yet, as reality unfortunately teaches us, people entering into relationships with foreigners often become a marginalised group within societies themselves and subject to majoritarian bias. Their vote is but an insufficient representation of their interest in allowing family reunifications at a larger scale. 'The concept[] of majoritarian … bias capture[s] the pervasive sense that … counting noses without considering the degree or extent of impacts … can create injustice'.[203] The question is then how far the European Court of Justice is, in

[201] *Iida* (n 63) paras 44 f and 75.

[202] In this respect, Schönberger opposes protection under EU citizenship law against reverse discrimination because citizens of a Member State are free to create change by influencing the political process in that state, see Schönberger (n 31) 431.

[203] Komesar (n 192) 65.

comparative terms, a more appropriate institution than national political processes or courts to make the decision. There, one needs to bear in mind that granting residence permits is in terms of numbers and complexity an intricate process. The Court is, especially in instances that involve dependence on national welfare systems,[204] in a relatively weak position to decide on such issues. Not only could it be overburdened with making such substantive social decisions, but additionally its acceptance by actors in the Member States could decrease if it decided in favour of far-reaching intervention in this field of law. With these considerations in mind it becomes plausible that the Court, as a supranational judicial body, was hesitant to substitute national political decisions for its own.

Nevertheless, two reservations are in place: first, the situation of the family lending its name to the *Dereci* case involved minor children. When their father applied for residence in Austria, the children did not have the means to have their interests represented in the country, except for the abstract link of their mother's Austrian nationality. There was an even further increased likelihood of majoritarian bias acting to their disadvantage. In light of the odds that their interests were so under-represented, the European Court of Justice should have gotten involved as a better and alternative decision maker. Second, I consider the other cases to have been decided wrongly, too. The risk of political bias was of such nature and intensity that the European Court should have addressed this issue. However, as explained in an earlier part of this thesis, different persons follow different institutional preferences and it seems that the Court opted for a more cautious assessment of its own role.

In the end, the institutional choice framework provides for an alternative account of when the European Court of Justice should refrain from exercising scrutiny. The interpretive paradigm holds that EU law should be inapplicable in the discussed cases, because the 'facts and effects of a situation were confined within one State'. (Yet, one can already call into doubt whether *Morson and Jhanjan*, *McCarthy*, *Dereci* or *Ymeraga* were 'confined to one state', given the fact that they dealt with the legality of orders denying leaves for stay and forcing people to move or remain in foreign countries.) In contrast, the institutional choice paradigm holds that the European Court of Justice should dismiss cases which are commonly deemed to be on the outer margins of the purely internal rule if the parameters of interest representation, numbers and complexity speak in favour of the Court exercising restraint.

The display of judicial restraint under the exclusionary approach is in conformity with Komesar's institutional choice finding that '[m]ost courts allocate decision making to the political process'[205]—in the case of reverse discrimination to

[204] See ch 4.
[205] Komesar (n 192) 84.

Member State political processes. In the very different context of US zoning laws, the author continued to argue the following:

> But this decision not to decide is an unstable equilibrium. There remains a serious distrust of local zoning that manifests in various ways. There will be hit-and-miss activism in which courts strike down particularly offensive pieces of legislation and then, recognizing the long-term costs of this activism, retreat back into dormancy.[206]

It is striking how much of this conclusion can be transferred to the European Court of Justice's handling of reverse discrimination. Even under the exclusionary approach, the Court's unease about the existence of reverse discrimination and its distrust towards the Member States in attending to the issue are manifest. For instance, Advocate Generals turn to the issue regularly in great detail. More importantly, the Court has entered into a phase of hit-and-miss activism, in which it takes on cases under the inclusionary approach that it used to consider beyond its realm. The intriguing question is therefore if comparative institutional analysis can help to account for those decisions, in which the judges go to great lengths to hold European law applicable.

To begin with the investigation, I would refer to a series of cases presented in the second section of this chapter, in which the European Court of Justice chose to widen its perspective when examining if a situation falls within the scope of European law. Following this approach, the Court examined the case *Pistre*. It found the situation that prompted the preliminary reference to be within the scope of application of EU law although it concerned a French producer's challenge to a French manufacturing regulation. As the preceding analysis pointed out, one cannot reasonably establish a cross-border element to the case by looking only at the specific facts of the case.[207] However nor does comparative institutional analysis succeed in explaining why the Court found EU law to be applicable if one limits the assessment to Mr Pistre's specific situation. After all, there are no indications of the French political process malfunctioning in the matter. Rather it may be assumed that Mr Pistre had adequate means for making his interests heard. Yet, if one examines the case in the abstract, comparative institutional analysis affirms the finding that the Court had reasons to engage in review. When seen in the abstract, there was plausible risk of underrepresentation of foreign interests. The fact that only French producers could meet the law's requirements indicates that the concerns of producers from outside France were not fully taken account of.

But can this move to the abstract really be sustained? The Court's precise argument was that the law's applicability *only* to French products led to the discrimination of foreign products. '[T]he application of the measure, even if restricted to domestic producers, in itself creates and maintains a difference of treatment between those two categories of goods [domestic and imported goods], hindering,

206 ibid.

207 See also Tryfonidou (n 6) 80 ff.

at least potentially, intra-Community trade'.[208] Hence, the French law differs from most other norms under review, in so far as it cannot be only partially disapplied to producers making use of their right to free movement of goods. In the logic of the Court, it had to examine a situation, whose specifics were confined to France, in order to stop the discrimination occurring. Translated into comparative institutional terms, the European Court of Justice might not have been confronted with a situation that called for activism in order to ensure adequate representation of Mr Pistre's interests, but with a situation in which it saw an increased need for the protection of interests held by foreign stakeholders.

The reasoning is problematic in approaching the subject from the point of view of a desired outcome. Under the inclusionary approach as applied in *Pistre*, one is willing to establish a cross-border link or look at the representation of interests in the abstract in order to open up review according to EU law. A more appropriate solution would be to concede that also on comparative institutional grounds the purely internal rule should not have been applied in *Pistre*. Instead, the Court should have waited for a comparable situation, involving a disprivileged cheese producer from another Member State, to come before the Court before issuing a decision.

Continuing with the analysis, the European Court of Justice opted in a second line of cases for an extensive reading of facts, so as to establish a cross-border element in particular situations. To begin with *Singh*, *Eind*, *Carpenter*, *Ritter-Coulais*, *Hartmann*, *S and G* and *O and B*, the Court argued that cases are not of purely internal nature, when the parties have exercised their right to free movement in the past. In response, it was said that the Court sees the four freedoms (plus nowadays Article 21 TFEU) as provisions that not only protect free movement, but also grant 'bonus rights' to persons having made use thereof in the past.[209] As I will argue in the following, the previously mentioned cases can be assessed in comparative institutional terms. In all of them, the institutional logic for the Court to become active or remain inactive is the same as in 'conventional' cross-border situations.

According to the comparative institutional approach to free movement adjudication, the European Court of Justice should review national measures if it believes the interests of nationals of other Member States to be underrepresented.[210] The reasoning behind the suggestion is that people with lesser ties to a Member State's political process are barred to the same extent from having their interests represented as those with closer connections. People who have moved from their home state to another country area are also barred from enjoying the same amount of interest representation they did prior to going abroad. Furthermore, these individuals might have not been able to represent their interests adequately when

[208] *Pistre* (n 46) para 45.
[209] The term 'bonus rights' has been adopted from Maduro (n 5) 125 and Tryfonidou (n 6) 18.
[210] M Maduro, *We, the Court* (Oxford, Hart Publishing, 1998) 173.

still living in their home states, as they were not then conscious about becoming free movers. Whether past cross-border movement serves as connecting factor or whether the protection of present or future movement is at stake, the logic of interest representation remains unchanged: greater detachment from national institutions results in less influence on those institutions' decisions. In *Singh*, *Eind*, *Carpenter*, *Ritter-Coulais*, *Hartmann* and *S and G*, people had relocated or at least spent a considerable amount of time in a different Member State, but were still subject to regulations of their home countries. Thus, they faced an increased risk of exposure to majoritarian bias. The parameter of 'interest representation' spoke in favour of judicial intervention by the Court of Justice. Moreover, the Court had expertise in substituting national decisions on the treatment of cross-border movers; after all, this was its main business. Consequently, the Court could be seen as an appropriate player to remedy the under-representation of interests of those EU citizens that had crossed the Union's internal borders.[211]

The situation presented itself differently in *O and B*. There, the connection of the EU citizens to another Member State was loose. They were still living in their home state and only visited their spouses in other Member States occasionally and for short periods of time, such as weekends or vacations. Having the centre of their lives still in the state of their nationality, there was less risk of under-representation of their interests in their home states. The Court itself alluded to this fact when it stated that 'the residence of the Union citizen in the host Member State has [to be] sufficiently genuine'[212] for the Union citizen to rely upon EU law. Consequently, according to the logic of institutional choice, the Court rightly exercised restraint when reviewing the situations in *O and B*.

[211] As far as *Singh* is concerned, it may be argued that the case was not concerned with the adequate or inadequate representation of Mr and Mrs Singh's interests. In the proceedings on Mr Singh's leave to stay, the interests, which were inadequately taken into account and served as connecting factors to European law, were those of Mrs Singh as a British citizen. The rights of her husband were not or could not be better or worse represented at the European level, given the fact that he is Indian and not a constituent of the UK's or EU's democratic institutions. The reference to Mrs Singh's situation may be called into doubt by the fact that the couple divorced after their return to the UK. However, the European Court of Justice explicitly stated that

> although the marriage was dissolved by the decree absolute of divorce delivered in 1989, that is not relevant to the question referred for a preliminary ruling, which concerns the basis of the right of residence of the person concerned during the period before the date of that decree (*Singh* (n 95) para 12).

Consequently, also in *Singh*, the Court examined the legal situation of Mrs Singh and the representation of her interests in order to determine whether EU law should be held applicable.

As regards a comparative institutional reading of *Carpenter*, the remarks on *Dereci* are instructive. The cases are compatible as in both decisions, one parent is a third country national and the other citizen of the Member State with the restrictive laws in place. In this context, it is interesting to note and a point of critique that *Dereci* is more restrictive with respect to the enjoyment of EU rights than the earlier decided *Carpenter* judgment.

[212] *O and B* (n 115) para 51.

Applying the comparative institutional logic to *Ruiz Zambrano* and *Chen*, the Court's decision to review the cases pursuant to EU law becomes also more plausible.[213] To recall, in these cases, the Court of Justice decided that third country nationals with children holding EU citizenship had the right to stay in a Member State their children had never left. In its judgments, the Court focused on the children's situation to then argue that their enjoyment of rights (granted under European law) depended upon their parents' right of residence as caretakers. Examining the decisions from an institutional point of view, one can make the following observations: even though the children held the respective Member States' nationalities, their interests were prone to underrepresentation in the national decision making processes. Their age prevented them from participating in their home countries' political processes. Granted, that minors do not play an active part in political decision making is the normal state of affairs. However, their interests are theoretically represented by their parents. Such delegation of representation could not take place in *Chen* or *Ruiz Zambrano*. Due to the fact that their parents were not represented in the national institutions, there was the risk that their interests were also only imperfectly taken account of.[214] The political processes in Belgium and the United Kingdom were in jeopardy of malfunction, because they could not ensure adequate representation of some of their own citizens' interests. Consequently, the parameter of 'interest representation' signalled towards greater involvement by other institutions, namely judicial bodies.

The next question to address is therefore on what grounds the European Court of Justice as a supranational court should have gotten involved in the issue. Part of the explanation might be that there was not only distrust in the functioning of the national political, but also judicial, processes. Reading the reasoning in *Ruiz Zambrano*, one detects that the European judges conceived an imminent risk that the children would be expelled if they had not intervened.[215] Although this risk was unfounded given the case history (Mr Ruiz Zambrano had in the meantime been granted a preliminary residence permit), one notices the judges' supposition that there was a lack of sensitivity on the side of the Belgian judiciary for the situation of the Ruiz Zambrano family. Another part of the explanation for why the European Court of Justice considered itself to be a suitable decision maker might be that there had been a detectable trend in European states not to compel one's own nationals to leave the country. The deliberations could have been to the effect that if other Member States ensured that their own nationals could not be forced to leave their home country, protection in Belgium or the United Kingdom should not deviate too much from this norm. Under the combined impression of political

[213] For another institutional analysis of the *Ruiz Zambrano* case, see Hailbronner and Iglesias Sánchez (n 40) 525 ff.

[214] ibid, 525.

[215] *Ruiz Zambrano* (n 49) para 44.

malfunction and a predominant different approach in the Union, it was plausible for the Court to opt for review and therefore uniform treatment of the issue in the European Union.

Admittedly, with regard to certain cases—*Garcia Avello* and *Alokpa* at point—comparative institutional analysis can only offer limited additional insights. Concerning *Garcia Avello*, the ruling dealt with a Belgian provision that prohibited children from taking on a double name, composed of their parents' last names, even if one of their parents held the nationality of another Member State. This mode of naming is tradition in countries such as Spain, but rather unknown in Belgium. Assessing the Belgian law in terms of interest representation, one can establish that the newly born children affected by the law had of course no options to influence it. One may even hold that their parents' potential influence was also decreased (compared to that of parents who both have Belgian passports), because the parent holding a foreign nationality was barred from having his interests represented. However, such argumentation seems to stretch the logic of institutional choice beyond its limits. Therefore, reasons other than institutional concerns—such as the symbolic effects of naming being influenced by Union law—might have played a more prominent role in the Court's decision. Additionally, this analysis is incapable of providing a sound institutional choice account of the *Alokpa* decision when seen in the context of the Court's earlier judgment *Chen*. Both cases concerned the rights of third-country-national primary care takers of minor EU citizens who happened to live in Member States other than those of their nationality. Whereas a right to residence under EU law was granted to Mrs Chen, the Court was more hesitant to expand this protection to Mrs Alokpa. Given the divergent outcome of the cases, comparative institutional analysis would have to detect, for their explanation, a difference between the two in terms of interest representation, numbers or complexity. To me, such a difference is not clearly discernible, and the differentiation is rather owed to a different assessment of Mrs Chen's and Mrs Alokpa's ability to financially provide for their families. One might rephrase this circumstance in institutional terms by holding that—with respect to numbers—Member States would be stressed beyond capacity when granting residence rights to individuals in a situation comparable to that of the Alokpa family. However, this would merely reformulate and make less, instead of more, explicit the motives of the Court for being hesitant in considering Mrs Alokpa's situation to be covered by EU law.

Despite these open questions, the analysis maintains that there is added value in conceptualising reverse discrimination adjudication in terms of institutional choice. As argued from the outset, the approach is not meant to offer a wholesale explanation to EU equality law, but a tool for critique or a means to think anew about certain constellations. Last, the *Lancry* case-law, pursuant to which charges (with equivalent effects to customs duties) levied on intrastate trade are forbidden, shall therefore be analysed by means of institutional comparison. With respect to the existence of minoritarian or majoritarian bias, one may hold at first sight the view that there was no malfunction of the political process, which authorised the internal toll collection. There is no indication that the interests of traders moving goods within their home state were insufficiently represented or that they were barred from participating in the decision making process. If one defines 'interests' more broadly as 'European interests', including those of European Union institutions, one may nevertheless arrive at the conclusion that misrepresentation occurred, since such definition would comprise the interest in trade between different Member States. That the Court of Justice assumed such omission of 'European' interests in the passage of national toll collection provisions is hinted at in paragraph 65 of the *Jersey Potatoes* judgment. In the passage, it argued that the charges levied on potatoes for reason of their trade within the United Kingdom would result in hindrances of out-of-state trade, as the 'potatoes, once within the United Kingdom, might then be re-exported to other Member States, with the result that the contribution in question may be levied on goods which … are in fact exported to other Member States'.[216] In light of the fact that risk of political malfunction is conceivable, one needs to assess whether the European Court of Justice was a competent actor to supply a decision on the topic. Speaking in favour of intervention is the fact that the reference centred around the question on the abolition of tariffs; one of the European Union's main objectives. The Court therefore had expertise in dealing with the theme. With regard to the parameter of scale, the findings are mixed. On the one hand, one could argue that the amount of tariffs internal to a country is limited and that the Court broadened its review in *Lancry* to include a confined area of law. On the other hand, one could argue that even though the judgments applied to a limited subject-matter, they invited further references to the Court of Justice.

In the end, comparative institutional analysis might be unable to give a universal account of the respective case law with all its turns and developments. But it can provide an undisguised view of the institutional concerns—risk of national decision making processes malfunctioning, ability to rule on an issue, overburdening its own docket—which in the end inform the Court's decision to consider a situation as either purely internal or not. This does not to mean that such deliberations are clearly mirrored in the Court's judgments—to the contrary, one will find little evidence of explicit institutional reasoning (*Guimont* being a noticeable example). Instead, comparative institutional reasoning has found its way into the creation of the purely internal rule and into the interpretations given to it albeit not in the form of a necessarily deliberative process. More explicitly, the

[216] *Jersey Produce* (n 137) para 65.

'cross-border element' bears a comparative institutional connotation. According to the interpretation it has been given by the Court, the element serves as a proxy for the lack of representation of individuals' interests in the political process at the Member State level: the easier it is for a person to establish a cross-border element in her case, the less means of representation she has had in the national decision making process.

Having looked at the European Court of Justice's case law on reverse discrimination through the lens of institutional choice, the next chapter addresses another major egalitarian topic that the Court is confronted with: affirmative action for women.

6

Affirmative Action for Women

IN AN ANALYSIS that is concerned with the intricacies of European equality reasoning, affirmative action is the fourth subject that, in addition to different testing standards, discrimination on grounds of nationality and reverse discrimination, deserves closer attention. This is for two reasons. First, the European Union has for some time been engaged in an effort to introduce quotas for female executives in the private sector.[1] In November 2012, the Commission presented a proposal for a directive that aims at achieving a 40 per cent representation rate of women on corporate boards.[2] At the moment of writing, the European Parliament had approved of the proposal with minor alterations[3] and the Council of the EU is currently attending to the proposition.[4] In the event that the legislation is successfully enacted, the question of how well the norms can be reconciled with the existing EU affirmative action jurisprudence inevitably arises. Besides, numerous Member States (France, Spain, Italy, Belgium, the Netherlands[5] and Germany)[6] have implemented laws to increase women's participation in supervisory committees. Consequently, the European Court of Justice will most likely have to decide on the compatibility of specific national affirmative action arrangements with EU law. Second, the subject is of particular interest as adjudication on affirmative action illustrates better than any other issue the tensions that define equality reasoning. When deciding on affirmative action, judges at the European Court of

[1] On the plan, see V Reding, 'Gesetzliche Frauenquote?' (2011) *Zivilrechtliche Praxis* 127, as well as European Commission, 'Women on Boards: Commission proposes 40% objective', www.ec.europa.eu/justice/newsroom/gender-equality/news/121114_en.htm., for background information.

[2] European Commission, proposal for a Directive of the European Parliament and of the Council on Improving the gender balance among non-executive directors of companies listed on stock exchanges and related measures, COM(2012)0614 final.

[3] European Parliament legislative resolution of 20 November 2013 on the proposal for a Directive of the European parliament and of the Council on improving the gender balance among non-executive directors of companies listed on stock exchanges and related measures (COM[2012]0614—C7-0382/2012—2012/0299[COD]).

[4] European Commission, 'Factsheet: Gender balance on corporate boards—Europe is cracking the glass ceiling' (October 2015) 5, ec.europa.eu/justice/gender-equality/files/womenonboards/factsheet_women_on_boards_web_2015-10_en.pdf.

[5] J Suk, 'Democratic Deficits and Gender Quotas: The evolution of the proposed EU Directive on gender balance on corporate boards', *Foundation for Law, Justice, and Society Policy Brief*, 17 June 2014, 1.

[6] The parliamentary vote of the German Bundestag on the proposal BT-Drucksache 18/4053 and 18/3784 took place on 6 March 2015. See further Bundestag, 'Frauenquote für die Top-Positionen beschlossen', www.bundestag.de/dokumente/textarchiv/2015/kw10_de_frauenquote/363058.

Justice find themselves in a constant struggle to reconcile many competing visions of equality. Indeed the most prominent conflict revealed by the issue of reverse discrimination can be characterised as a tension between discriminating against singular individuals in order to achieve greater fairness in treatment overall.[7]

Before I elaborate on these tensions, I would like to outline in greater detail the theme of affirmative action. In its most basic definition, affirmative action is meant to describe 'a set of actions designed to eliminate existing and continuing discrimination, to remedy lingering effects of past discrimination, and to create systems and procedures to prevent future discrimination'.[8] As Advocate General Tesauro pointed out in one of his opinions, affirmative action may come in different forms. Focusing on schemes that seek to eliminate disadvantages faced by women in the workplace, he distinguished between three kinds, depending on the degree and form of intervention sought by the measures. Since his analysis provides a clear picture of the various modes of affirmative—or in his words 'positive action'[9]—it is worth citing the passage at full length:

> Positive action may assume several forms. A first model aims to remove, not discrimination in the legal sense, but a condition of disadvantage which characterizes women's presence on the employment market. In this case, the objective is to eliminate the causes of the fewer employment and career opportunities which (still) beset female employment by taking action with respect, among other things, to vocational guidance and training. A second model of positive action may be discerned in actions designed to foster balance between family and career responsibilities and a better distribution of those responsibilities between the two sexes. In that case, priority is given to measures relating to the arrangement of working hours, the development of child-care structures, the return to work of women who have devoted themselves to bringing up their children, and social security and fiscal offsetting policies which take account of family duties. In both those cases, positive action, albeit entailing the adoption of specific measures for women alone, designed in particular to foster the employment of women, has the aim of achieving equal opportunities and, in the final analysis, the attainment of substantive equality. However, the results will certainly not be immediate in terms of a quantitative increase in female employment.
>
> A third model of positive action is that of action as a remedy for the persistent effects of historical discrimination of legal significance; in this case, the action takes on a

[7] S Fredman, 'After *Kalanke* and *Marschall*: Affirming Affirmative Action' (1998) 1 *Cambridge Yearbook of European Legal Studies* 199; see further D Caruso, 'Limits of the Classic Method: Positive Action in the European Union After the New Equality Directives' (2003) 44 *Harvard International Law Journal* 331, 350; U Maidowski, *Umgekehrte Diskriminierung* (Berlin, Duncker und Humblot, 1989) 44. K Thomas, 'The Political Economy of Recognition: Affirmative Action Discourse and Constitutional Equality in Germany and the USA' (1998/1999) 5 *Columbia Journal of European Law* 329, 341 speaks of the 'root tension'. Generally on the struggle between competing visions of equality see D Rae, *Equalities* (Cambridge, Harvard University Press, 1981) especially 5, 19.

[8] B Garner (ed), *Black's Law Dictionary* 3rd edn (St Paul, Thomson West, 2006) 24.

[9] Advocate General Tesauro uses these terms interchangeably, see Case C-450/93 *Eckhard Kalanke v Freie Hansestadt Bremen* [1995] ECR I-3051, Opinion of AG Tesauro, para 8. On the terminology of positive action see L Waddington and M Bell, 'Exploring the Boundaries of Positive Action under EU Law: A Search for Conceptual Clarity' (2011) 48 *CML Rev* 1503, 1507 ff.

compensatory nature, with the result that preferential treatment in favour of disadvantaged categories is legitimized, in particular through systems of quotas and goals.[10]

My analysis is only concerned with the third and most far reaching model of affirmative action. It puts persons who have been historically discriminated against in an advantageous situation. Originally, affirmative action was designed in the United States in order to ameliorate the situation of Blacks competing in the market place with Whites.[11] It was then extended to cover policies that aimed to counter the comparative disadvantage faced by other minorities, including women. Around the 1980s, beginning with efforts to increase the presence of women in the workplace, affirmative action found its way into European legal systems. Since then, many Member States have been allowing for the preferential treatment of women in the hiring and promotion of public service employees. As far as the private sector is concerned, countries have been much more hesitant to introduce preferential quotas and goals. Given that such reforms are often considered and frequently fiercely resisted, a lively debate on the pros and cons of affirmative actions, as well as on their legality or illegality, has been taking place in Europe. Defendants of quotas and goals argue in line with Advocate General Tesauro that they need to be employed in order to compensate for past discrimination. In a forward-looking way, they further claim that affirmative action needs to be undertaken as socially entrenched and systemic discrimination will only be overcome by strong efforts.[12] By contrast, opponents of the practices maintain that such action generally amounts to prohibited 'reverse discrimination'.[13] They argue that any discrimination, even if it is performed with the intent to create a *fairer* state of affairs within a society, contradicts the concept of equality. In their opinion, affirmative practices violate the very concept they are said to promote.

Overall and as I will explain throughout this chapter both these public discussions and the case law of the European Court of Justice are characterised by three conceptual tensions and the attempt to resolve them. These tensions are (1) an individualistic versus a group conception of the European equality guarantee,

[10] *Kalanke* (n 9) Opinion of AG Tesauro, para 9. Critiquing the formulation E Ellis and P Watson, *EU Anti-Discrimination Law* 2nd edn (Oxford, Oxford University Press, 2012) 425.

[11] Starting with the Executive Order 10925 issue by JF Kennedy in March 1961, which stipulated that federal contractors were prohibited to discriminate against minorities. See A Peters, *Women, Quotas and Constitutions—A Comparative Study of Affirmative Action for Women under American, German, EC and International Law* (The Hague, Kluwer Law International, 1999) 31.

[12] For comprehensive analysis see Fredman (n 7) 199. Critically on the backward- and forward-looking justification of affirmative action, G Sher, 'Reverse Discrimination, the Future, and the Past' (1979) 90 *Ethics* 81.

[13] See for this critical understanding, C Starck, 'Artikel 3' in H von Mangoldt, F Klein and C Starck (eds), *Grundgesetzkommentar* 6th edn (Munich, Franz Vahlen, 2010) marginal nos 311 ff. Using the term 'reverse discrimination' but not adopting it as their own, Maidowski (n 7) 45 and D Schwartz, 'The Case of the Vanishing Protected Class: Reflections on Reverse Discrimination, Affirmative Action, and Racial Balancing' (2000) 2 *Wisconsin Law Review* 657.

(2) a formal versus a substantive conception of equality,[14] and (3) an understanding of law as neutral versus an understanding of law as a tool for social change.[15]

In greater detail, one's assessment of goals and quotas depends—among other factors—on one's predisposition to perceive equality as a group right. In the event that one defends an individualistic notion of the right to equality, one will be hesitant to accept affirmative action practices that leave certain persons worse off. If, however, one holds the opinion that an individual's place in society is to a smaller or larger extent shaped and destined by the characteristics of the group he belongs to, one will be more accepting of preferential treatment for minorities. Second, one's reception of affirmative action depends on which of the competing visions of equality one is inclined to follow. Adherents to formal equality will object to affirmative measures, since they call precisely for differential treatment of persons in comparable situations; whereas advocates of a substantive notion of equality are likely to consider affirmative action to be justified and legal. Third and related to the points just mentioned, one's stance on affirmative action will be dependent on one's receptiveness towards the idea of using law as a tool for social engineering.[16] The more one is willing to perceive law as an instrument that should be used to bring about societal change, the more likely will one be to accept affirmative action as an approach reconcilable with the concept of equality.[17]

This chapter intends to show how these tensions inform European affirmative action adjudication. Moreover, I seek to demonstrate over the following pages that comparative institutional analysis provides a framework not only for judges but also for scholars to conceptualise these tensions. I argue that affirmative action will better be understood, if more attention is paid to the questions of *who* restructures under the heading of affirmative action and *whose* framework is the object of restructuring in such exercise. In a first part, the Court's case law on women's quota shall be analysed. The passage is not intended to act as a simple summary of the developments that led to the Court's current approach on affirmative action, rather it seeks to connect the judges' decisions with the diverse conceptions of non-discrimination law mentioned above. In a second part, a comparison of the European case law on women's quotas with judgments by the United States

[14] E Landau and Y Beigbeder, *From ILO Standards to EU Law. The Case of Equality between Men and Women at Work* (Leiden, Nijhoff Publishers, 2008) 235.

[15] See, eg Fredman (n 7) 200 ff and 207; A Peters, 'The Many Meanings of Equality and Positive Action in Favour of Women under European Community Law—A Conceptual Analysis' (1996) 2 *European Law Journal* 177 and generally Rae (n 7) 81. Seeing any binary construction of the European notion of equality critically L Charpentier, 'The European Court of Justice and the Rhetoric of Affirmative Action' (1998) 4 *European Law Journal* 167, 179.

[16] I use the term 'social engineering' in a neutral way, without giving it any negative connotation. On that point, see R Siegel, 'Why Equal Protection No Longer Protects: The Evolving Forms of Status-Enforcing State Action' (1997) 49 *Stanford Law Review* 1111, 1143.

[17] For a transformative account of equality law, see R Post, 'Prejudicial Appearances: The Logic of American Antidiscrimination Law' (2000) 88 *California Law Review* 1.

Supreme Court on affirmative action shall be undertaken. In particular, I will examine how far the more advanced discussion on the subject matter in the United States can be utilised for an assessment of affirmative action under European law. In a last step, I will again use the framework of institutional choice in order to investigate to which extent judges should be driven by institutional considerations when navigating between the extremes of existing equality conceptions.

I. THE EUROPEAN UNION JURISPRUDENCE

But before entering the discussion on the Court's decisions, it is helpful to briefly describe the statutory framework, in which the European adjudication on affirmative action for women takes place. References to an intention to realise equality between men and women can be found throughout the Treaties. Article 3(3) Treaty on European Union (TEU) mentions gender equality as one of the prevailing values 'common to the Member States'. Article 8 Treaty on the Functioning of the European Union (TFEU) stipulates that '[i]n all its activities, the Union shall aim to eliminate inequalities, and to promote equality, between men and women'. More specifically, Article 157(1) TFEU outlines the principle of equal pay for men and women and has been attributed direct effect.[18] Further, the same provision's paragraph four, which was introduced to EU primary law with the entering into force of the Treaty of Amsterdam, states that

> [w]ith a view to ensuring full equality in practice between men and women in working life, the principle of equal treatment shall not prevent any Member State from maintaining or adopting measures providing for specific advantages in order to make it easier for the underrepresented sex to pursue a vocational activity or to prevent or compensate for disadvantages in professional careers.[19]

In the same spirit, the Charter of Fundamental Rights of the European Union (CFEU) contains Article 23 that deals specifically with the equality between men and women. In its second sentence, the rule states, in similar wording to that of Article 157(4) TFEU, that '[t]he principle of equality shall not prevent the maintenance or adoption of measures providing for specific advantages in favour of the under-represented sex'. Alongside the Treaties and the Charter, European secondary legislation also deals with the subject of gender equality. Initially, Council Directive 76/207/EEC[20] dealt with the implementation of the principle of equal

[18] Art 157(1) TFEU states: 'Each Member State shall ensure that the principle of equal pay for male and female workers for equal work or work of equal value is applied'. On the point Ellis and Watson (n 10) 246 ff.

[19] Art 157(4) TFEU. In addition, it is written in Art 153(1)(i) TFEU that 'the Union shall support and complement the activities of the Member States in [the field of] equality between men and women with regard to labour market opportunities and treatment at work'.

[20] Dir 76/207/EEC of 9 February 1976 on the implementation of the principle of equal treatment for men and women as regards access to employment, vocational training and promotion, and working conditions [1976] OJ L39/40.

pay between men and women. Considered too unspecific in certain of its definitions and occasionally outdated, it was amended by Directive 2002/73/EC[21] and complemented once more by Directive 2006/54/EC dealing with equal treatment of men and women in employment and occupational social security.[22] These, in combination with Article 157 TFEU, now constitute the body of law against which affirmative action for women must be assessed in the European Union's system.

A. *Kalanke* and the Restrictive Approach

The first time the European Court of Justice dealt with the issue of women's quotas was in *Kalanke v Freie Hansestadt Bremen*.[23] The case concerned the compatibility of a law by the city of Bremen[24] with the Directive on equal treatment of men and women in employment matters. Pursuant to the norm, preference in promotion was to be granted to the city's female employees, subject to the condition that they

[21] Dir 2002/73/EC of the European Parliament and of the Council of 23 September 2002 amending Council Dir 76/207/EEC on the implementation of the principle of equal treatment for men and women as regards access to employment, vocational training and promotion, and working conditions [2002] OJ L269/15.

[22] Dir 2006/54/EC of the European Parliament and of the Council of 5 July 2006 on the implementation of the principle of equal opportunities and equal treatment of men and women in matters of employment and occupation (recast) [2006] OJ L204/23. See B de Witte, 'From a "Common Principle of Equality" to "European Antidiscrimination Law"' (2010) 53 *American Behavioral Scientist* 1715, 1719. For the sake of completion, Dir 2004/113/EC of December 2004 implementing the principle of equal treatment between men and women in the access to and the supply of goods and services [2004] OJ L373/37 was also introduced in the antidiscrimination canon.

[23] *Kalanke* (n 9).

[24] Para 4 Landesgleichstellungsgsesetz of 20 November 1990 (Bremen Law on Equal Treatment for Men and Women in the Public Service, Bremer Gesetzblatt 433) stating:

> Appointment, assignment to an official post and promotion
>
> (1) In the case of an appointment (including establishment as a civil servant or judge) which is not made for training purposes, women who have the same qualifications as men applying for the same post are to be given priority in sectors where they are under-represented.
>
> (2) In the case of an assignment to a position in a higher pay, remuneration and salary bracket, women who have the same qualifications as men applying for the same post are to be given priority if they are under-represented. This also applies in the case of assignment to a different official post and promotion
>
> ...
>
> (4) Qualifications are to be evaluated exclusively in accordance with the requirements of the occupation, post to be filled or career bracket. Specific experience and capabilities, such as those acquired as a result of family work, social commitment or unpaid activity, are part of the qualifications within the meaning of subparagraphs (1) and (2) if they are of use in performing the duties of the position in question.
>
> (5) There is under-representation if women do not make up at least half of the staff in the individual pay, remuneration and salary brackets in the relevant personnel group within a department. This also applies to the function levels provided for in the organization chart' (see Case C-450/93 *Eckhard Kalanke v Freie Hansestadt Bremen* [1995] ECR I-3051, para 3).

had the same qualifications as men applying for the post, until they were no longer under-represented in the respective sectors.

In the case before the Court, Mr Kalanke, an employee of the city of Bremen, claimed that he had been discriminated against when his equally qualified female colleague was promoted to a higher rank in compliance with the city's law. He argued that this practice and the Bremen statute were contrary to EU law. The case was particular in that the norm imposed a *Frauenquote*[25] for hiring and promotion, requiring that an unconditional preference be given to the applicant of the underrepresented sex (in the case that a female and a male applicant were equally qualified).

In its decision the Court held such a rule, which 'automatically give[s] priority to women in sectors where they are under-represented', is contrary to EU law.[26] More specifically, the judges stated that Bremen's quota regime was a derogation of the individual right to non-discrimination 'whatsoever on grounds of sex'[27] and that it needed to be measured against the requirements of Article 2(4) of the Directive on equal working conditions. As a derogation to an individual right, they further proclaimed that it had to be interpreted strictly.[28] Pursuant to this strict reading, they considered that '[n]ational rules which guarantee women absolute and unconditional priority for appointment or promotion go beyond promoting equal opportunities and overstep the limits of the exception contained in Article 2(4) of the Directive'.[29] As can be seen from this crucial passage of the Court's judgment, the decision was explicitly grounded in two main ideas, namely that the right to equal treatment is an individual right and that it is to be understood as a right that may not exceed the limits of equality of opportunity.[30] More subtly, the judges affirmed with their reading of the equal treatment guarantee the principle that positions should be assigned strictly according to merit.

Looking at *Kalanke*, the question of why the European Court of Justice relied on an individualistic point of view and insisted on a reading of equality as being

[25] For the classification of different types of quotas followed by this analysis, see D Schiek, 'Positive Action in Community Law' (1996) 25 *Industrial Law Journal* 239, 241; E Szyszczak, 'Positive Action After *Kalanke*' (1996) 59 *ML Rev* 876, 878 f.

[26] *Kalanke* (n 9) para 24.

[27] Art 2(I) Dir 76/207/EEC, referred to in *Kalanke* (n 9) para 15.

[28] *Kalanke* (n 9) para 21.

[29] ibid, para 22.

[30] See Caruso (n 7) 339. This analysis takes the view that the themes of 'equality as equality of opportunity' and 'equality as an individual right' are interrelated, yet distinct subject matters. It is correct that equality of opportunity or formal equality corresponds with the view of equality being an individual right. The questions asked in the context are: 'Why has one person been treated differently from another?' or 'Are there reasons that justify granting certain benefits to an individual, in order to let him reach the same starting point as others?' However, when one considers the notion of substantial equality, it is not necessarily related to a group-based perception. In ch 2, it was argued that substantial equality sets out to protect 'equality of results', so that persons with different background or talents may end up in the same (hopefully beneficial) situation. Hence, substantial equality allows for greater intervention by the state. This can, but need not necessarily, coincide with a group-based view of equality. For that reason, the themes of 'individual right' and 'equality of opportunity' are discussed independently of each other.

confined to 'equality of opportunity' in its assessment of the quota arises. First, an understanding of the right to equality as an individual right is more easily reconcilable with the traditional understanding of fundamental rights as being primarily designed to protect persons from unjustified infringements by state actors. Furthermore, the approach was in line with the procedural requirements of direct and individual concern, valid at the time of the *Kalanke* decision, that needed to be fulfilled in order to be granted standing.[31] Second, a simple answer to the question why the judges focused on the right to 'equal opportunity' is that the literal interpretation of the Directive called for it.[32] Its Article 2(4) allows for 'measures to promote equal opportunity for men and women'. Hence, the discourse centres on that particular conception. In addition, arguing that the city of Bremen's rule went further than the derogation provided allowed the judges to maintain that EU equality law was not intended to do away with the idea that hiring and promotion should primarily be based on an assessment of merit.

Nevertheless, one may question whether the Court's reasoning was convincing and in particular if the Court, still reasoning in terms of 'equality of opportunity', could have arrived at a different conclusion. The decision is criticised mainly on three grounds, two of which are directed against the judgment's underlying rationale and one of which opposes the ruling on a more fundamental level.[33] The first point concerns the subject matter of an individual's right to equality. Fredman raises the argument that there was no such right of the male applicant that could have been violated by the quota.[34] She argues that in a situation such as the one in *Kalanke*, where both candidates were of equal qualification, '[n]either applicant had the "right" to the promotion'.[35] Although Fredman is correct in saying that Mr Kalanke had no right to promotion, it is unclear what this implies for his right to equal treatment. The fact remains that Mr Kalanke contended that his right to have the same chance for promotion as his female co-applicant had not been duly respected.[36] Therefore, the argument fails to invalidate the Court's findings. A further critique concerning the logic behind the conception of 'equality of opportunity' could call into doubt the argumentative strength of the reasoning in *Kalanke*. Maintaining equal opportunities is not the compelling reason

[31] See Case 25/62 *Plaumann & Co v Commission* [1963] ECR special edn 95; but see for a relaxation of the standing requirements Art 263(4) TFEU. On the development C Nowak, 'Rechtsschutz im europäischen Verwaltungsrecht' in J Terhechte (ed), *Verwaltungsrecht der Europäischen Union* (Baden-Baden, Nomos, 2011) 459, 480 ff.

[32] See Fredman (n 7) 203.

[33] GF Mancini and S O'Leary, 'The New Frontiers of Sex Equality Law in the European Union' (1999) 24 *EL Rev* 331, 342 further critique that the *Kalanke* decision contravenes with the European Court of Justice's adjudication on indirect discrimination and its group oriented construction.

[34] Fredman (n 7) 204.

[35] ibid. For a similar theoretical discussion in the American scholarship M Rosenfeld, *Affirmative Action and Justice. A Philosophical and Constitutional Inquiry* (New Haven, Yale University Press, 1993) 100.

[36] Fredman seems to see that inconsistency herself. Fredman (n 7) 204. Agreeing Rosenfeld (n 35) 101.

against quota provisions it is often described as. The distinction between equal opportunities and substantial equality, understood as equality of result, is not as clear-cut as it might seem. As argued by Strauss, drawing the line between actions that equip persons with the same opportunities to, for example, compete in the job market and actions that provide persons with the same results in promotion or job acquisition can be rather complex.[37] Therefore, since the difference between equality of opportunity and substantial equality is a matter of degree, it becomes difficult to distinguish between the two conceptions. In the end, it would appear that the Court's reliance on the former conception was mere façade; a pretence which allows it to evade answering the real question on affirmative action, namely whether some should be disprivileged for overall greater societal fairness. More fundamentally, the judges have been criticised not so much for (alleged) shortcomings in the coherence of *Kalanke*, but for their approach towards the subject in general. After the Court issued the judgment, several leading authors in European equality law scrutinised the case as portraying an outdated, formalistic view of the right to equality.[38] They argued that the Court had failed to pay attention to the remedial function of affirmative action and its ability to overcome socially entrenched discrimination. It was said to have inadequately taken into account the fact that quotas attempted to remedy the inequalities resulting from structures of working life that placed women in a situation of disadvantage. Further, they claimed that the Court had missed the opportunity to recognise the nature of equality as a group-based right and to acknowledge the capacity of affirmative action laws to accomplish social equality. Positioning the judgment in the even larger picture of the Court of Justice's role in European integration, an additional point of contention is apparent: one may in the first place criticise that a European institution has become active in reviewing Member State measures designed to promote equality. Shouldn't Member States enjoy a greater margin of discretion when making these equality judgments?

B. *Marschall*, *Badeck* and Greater Openness towards Affirmative Action

Two years after *Kalanke*, the Court ruled on another preliminary reference that dealt with the issue of affirmative action for women and used the occasion to accommodate part of the critique that had been raised towards its ruling in *Kalanke*.

[37] See ch 2 for a more detailed discussion.

[38] Mancini and O'Leary (n 33) 343; Peters (n 15) 192; arguing in the same direction S Prechal, 'Comment on Case C-450/93, *Eckhard Kalanke v. Freie Hansestadt Bremen* [1995] ECR I-3051' (1996) 33 *CML Rev* 1245 and implicitly critiquing the decision ibid, 'Equality of Treatment, Non-Discrimination and Social Policy: Achievements in Three Themes' (2004) 41 *CML Rev* 533, 539 f.

In *Marschall*,[39] the question was again whether a national provision that introduced quotas for women in job promotion was contrary to EU equal treatment law. The norm in question—a law by the German Land Nordrhein-Westfalen—stipulated that women should be given priority for promotion in sectors where they were underrepresented. This should be the rule 'in the event of [the candidates'] equal suitability, competence and professional performance, unless reasons specific to an individual [male] candidate tilt the balance in his favour'.[40] So compared with the measure under review in *Kalanke*, the rule contained a more flexible regime. Whereas the law in *Kalanke* made it mandatory that preference was to be given to female applicants equally qualified as their male competitors, the norm in *Marschall* allowed for a man be chosen over women candidates under certain conditions. It provided for considerations which were special or unique to the situation of the male applicant to be taken into account to the extent that the male's entitlement for preferential treatment could potentially trump the female co-applicant's eligibility. Such reasons could be his role as a single parent or his status as a disabled person. The European Court of Justice identified this 'saving clause', allowing for an individual assessment of the male candidate's situation, as the element that distinguished the case from *Kalanke*.[41] Thus, it found such a national measure to be in conformity with European Union law. In its decisive passage, the judgment reads:

> [S]ince Article 2(4) [of Directive 76/207/EEC] constitutes a derogation from an individual right laid down by the Directive, such a national measure specifically favouring female candidates cannot guarantee absolute and unconditional priority for women in the event of a promotion without going beyond the limits of the exception laid down in that provision (Kalanke, paragraphs 21 and 22).
>
> Unlike the rules at issue in Kalanke, a national rule which, as in the case in point in the main proceedings, contains a saving clause does not exceed those limits.[42]

The Court continued to hold that quotas are only in accordance with EU law, if the criteria of their saving clauses 'are not such as to discriminate against the female candidates'.[43]

Analysing the judgment, it becomes apparent that *Marschall* only takes on its real significance when contrasted with *Kalanke*. More remarkable than the decisions'

[39] Case C-409/95 *Hellmut Marschall v Land Nordrhein Westfalen* [1997] ECR I-6363. For discussion, see, eg D Schiek, 'More Positive Action in Community Law' (1998) 27 *Industrial Law Journal* 155.

[40] Para 25(5) of the *Beamtengesetz für das Land Nordrhein-Westfalen*, in the version published on 1 May 1981, as last amended by para 1 of the 7th law amending certain rules relating to the civil service, of 7 February 1995, GV NW 102 (*Marschall* [n 39] para 3).

[41] *Marschall* (n 39). See C Barnard, 'The Principle of Equality in the Community Context: *P, Grant, Kalanke* and *Marschall*: Four Uneasy Bedfellows?' (1998) 57 *Cambridge Law Journal* 352, 370; G Kucsko-Stadlmayer, 'Gleichstellung von Frauen und Männern an vollrechtsfähigen Universitäten' (2007) 6 *Zeitschrift für Hochschulrecht* 8, 12; Landau and Beigbeder (n 14) 232; Mancini and O'Leary (n 33) 346.

[42] *Marschall* (n 39) paras 32 and 33 at the beginning.

[43] ibid, para 33 at the end, respectively para 35.

differing outcomes is the difference in reasoning. If one takes as a starting point that the theoretical debate on affirmative action is structured into the three subject areas of 'varying conceptions of equality', 'individual versus group right to equal treatment' and 'law as a tool to bring about social change' mentioned at the beginning of this chapter, one discovers that—in comparison to the case decided in the European Court of Justice's earlier quota case—the emphasis in reasoning has shifted.[44] In fact, as regards the variety of positions on the correct meaning of equality, the discussion on equal opportunity was taken up in the decision only in a cursory manner.[45] To recall, in *Kalanke*, the notion of equality of opportunity had been important. The Court had stressed that the quota scheme by the city of Bremen went 'beyond promoting equal opportunities' and thus overstepped 'the limits of the exception in Article 2(4) of the Directive'[46] on equal treatment of men and women. In *Marschall*, on the other hand, the conception was only mentioned when the Court summarised the parties' submissions and quoted the directive's wording.[47] Engagement with the conception of equality remained absent from the grounds of the judgment. The judges' reasoning instead focused on the theme of equality as an individual right and addressed the topic that discrimination of women in the workplace may be so profound that accelerated efforts are needed to overcome it.

As far as equality as an individual right is concerned, the notion entered the decision at two points. Just as in *Kalanke*, the Court stated that equality is an individual right and that EU provisions allowing for an active promotion of equality of men and women in working life constitute derogations thereof.[48] In addition, the judges stressed that the mandatory, objective, individual assessment of male applicants within the scheme of affirmative action plays an important role in ensuring that the quota scheme remains compatible with European law.[49] They maintained that the saving clause ensures the consideration of the male candidates' interests in the decision making process. With its focus on the saving clause, the Court of Justice signified that it considered a limitation of an individual's right to equal treatment for the benefit of a traditionally discriminated group acceptable only under certain conditions. More pointedly formulated, the Court was unwilling to wholly embrace the notion that affirmative action justifies individual discrimination.[50]

Regarding the potential of the law as a tool for social engineering, the decision touched upon the topic more explicitly in two paragraphs. In paragraph 29 we

[44] See Thomas (n 7) 361 ff.

[45] Thomas argues that the Court went as far as 'ignor[ing] the concept altogether' (ibid, 362).

[46] *Kalanke* (n 9) para 22.

[47] *Marschall* (n 39) paras 12, 14, 19, 22 and 25.

[48] See ibid, para 32.

[49] See ibid, para 33.

[50] M Zuleeg, 'Gender Equality and Affirmative Action Under the Law of the European Union' (1998) 5 *Columbia Journal of European Law* 319, 326 writes about the 'key role of the individual right'. Compare Thomas (n 7) 363, who considers 'insistence' by the European Court of Justice on the individual rights aspect as 'merely gestural'.

find an acknowledgment that there is a traditional tendency in hiring processes to prefer male to female applicants, 'even where [they] are equally qualified'.[51] The Court acknowledges that stereotypes on women's ability to fully participate in working life persist and that often the belief persists that women are less capable of commitment to their jobs due to family duties and child caring obligations or to be present less due to pregnancy, childbirth and breastfeeding.[52] Further, paragraph 31 of the judgment states that quota rules 'may counteract the prejudicial effects on female candidates of [discriminatory] attitudes and behaviour'.[53] These references are important for two reasons: first, through mentioning them the Court draws attention to the role of the market as the leading decision making institution in employment. The judges go further in stating the well-known fact that hiring and promotion decisions are primarily based on the supply and demand of labour. They point to the risks of market malfunction in employment decisions, if hiring choices are informed by prejudice and stereotypes. Moreover, they show the Court's awareness of the fact that equality before the law must not be equated with equality in social life. The judges thus shared the view that in order to achieve equality in the working environment it may not be sufficient to grant men and women the same rights. Further, they recognised that traditional role allocations and gender stereotypes may call for intervention by the legislature.

Although or precisely because the outcome in *Marschall* differed from the conclusions in *Kalanke*, the decision was subject to criticism. Supporters of affirmative action—whilst recognising the development the adjudication had undergone in this area of law—criticised the lack of a clear commitment on behalf of the Court to the empowerment of women in the workplace. They had hoped for a full embrace of quota regimes[54] and were disappointed by the fact that the European Court of Justice made its finding of compatibility subject to two conditions. It found Member State quotas to be in accordance with Union law only if they first included provisions that allowed only for preferential treatment of women who were equally qualified as their male competitors and second contained rules such as the aforementioned saving clause. Unsurprisingly, opponents to affirmative action also disapproved of the decision, since it allowed for the existence and application of quotas.[55]

Apart from these broader critiques, *Marschall* could be questioned in terms of doctrinal coherence. It made explicit reference to passages of the *Kalanke*

[51] *Marschall* (n 39) para 29.

[52] ibid.

[53] ibid, para 31.

[54] For discussion, see, eg A Numhauser-Henning, 'Swedish Sex Equality Law before the European Court of Justice' (2001) 30 *Industrial Law Journal* 121.

[55] See B Schubert, *Affirmative Action und Reverse Discrimination* (Baden-Baden, Nomos, 2003) 102 with reference to eg M Sachs, '*Anmerkungen zu Marschall*' (1998) 103 *Deutsches Verwaltungsblatt* 183, 185.

judgment, only to then deviate from the standards that the previous decision established. When the Court laid out the standard of scrutiny to be applied, it argued just as in *Kalanke* that the article of the directive allowing for preferential treatment of women was a derogation of an individual right.[56] The judges continued by stating that therefore, 'a national measure specifically favouring female candidates cannot guarantee absolute and unconditional priority for women'[57] and cited *Kalanke* as a reference. However, in *Kalanke*, the Court had explicitly said that a derogation from an individual right called for strict scrutiny.[58] This mention of 'strict scrutiny' is absent in *Marschall*. In addition, the comparable passage in *Kalanke* linked the idea of a derogation that requires strict scrutiny testing with the conception of equality of opportunity. As the preceding part of the cases' examination described, *Marschall* relies to a much lesser extent on equality of opportunity. As a result, the reference to its previous decision on women's quotas seeks to convey a continuity that is more desired than real in the Court's adjudication.[59]

Nonetheless, the European Court of Justice did come closer to establishing consistency in its case law on women's quota in its judgment on *Badeck*,[60] decided three years after *Marschall*. Again, the judges had to review the compatibility of a women's advancement plan by a German Land (this time Hessen) with EU law. The plan provided for a range of measures to promote women's careers in public employment, amongst them the introduction of binding targets for female employment and a standard to preferentially allocate training positions to female candidates. Asked about the compatibility of the quota regime, which the Land Hessen had intended as a tool to fulfil the law's binding targets, the judges reiterated the conditions they had set out in *Marschall*.[61] Scrutinising the norm pursuant to these requirements, they came to the conclusion that it was compatible with EU law, because it did not 'determine from the outset that the outcome of each selection procedure must, in a stalemate situation where the candidates have equal qualifications, necessarily favour the woman candidate'.[62]

Turning to the question whether it was contrary to European equality law to allocate at least 50 per cent of the professional training places to women, the Court could not rely on its existing adjudication to the same extent. In contrast to the question which concerned the quota for women in hiring and advancement, this inquiry dealt with the education of potential candidates for public posts in the future. Based on the training aspect, the Court reasoned that the preferential

[56] *Marschall* (n 39) para 32.

[57] ibid.

[58] Strict scrutiny in the EU law context must not be wholly equated with strict scrutiny in the US law context, see ch 3 s I.A.ii.

[59] Schubert (n 55) 105 speaks of the creation of legal uncertainty.

[60] Case C-158/97 *Georg Badeck and Others, interveners: Hessische Ministerpräsident and Landesanwalt beim Staatsgerichtshof des Landes Hessen* [2000] ECR I-1875.

[61] ibid, paras 18 ff.

[62] ibid, para 28.

treatment of women was justified. More precisely, it stated that '[t]he provision at issue … forms part of a restricted concept of equality of opportunity'.[63] Even though the measure allowed for preference to be granted to less qualified female candidates, this was only the case for training places.[64] Further, male candidates still had the option of receiving the same education in the private sector.[65]

In terms of the decision's effect on doctrinal coherence the impact was twofold. On the one hand, the Court affirmed the line of argumentation, which it had set out in *Marschall*. By doing so, it brought a coherence to the case law that had been absent after the first two decisions on the issue. On the other hand, the Court's re-strengthened reliance on equality of opportunity opened up new questions concerning the legality of affirmative action. Does the Court's conception of equality of opportunity imply that quotas in education have to be judged differently than quotas in hiring[66] or in corporate board representation?[67] If so, where and for which reasons does the Court draw the line?

C. *Abrahamsson* and Balancing the Court's Adjudication

Abrahamsson[68] offered the Court of Justice a fourth occasion to clearly articulate its stance towards affirmative action. It rounds off the phase of European Union affirmative action jurisprudence, in which the Court of Justice developed not only its position towards, but also its technique of addressing the subject. *Abrahamsson* dealt with the compatibility of a Swedish affirmative action law with Articles 2(1) and 2(4) of Directive 76/207/EEC as well as then Article 141(4) EC (now Article 157(4) TFEU). The case concerned the awarding procedure of a chair at the University of Goteborg. After the favoured candidate declined the post, the offer of appointment was not made to the candidate considered by the selection committee to be second best for the job. Instead the job was offered to the third ranking candidate. The reason for doing so was that the former was a man whilst

[63] ibid, para 52.
[64] ibid. See generally Waddington and Bell (n 10) 601 f.
[65] ibid, para 53.
[66] Selanec deduces this from the European Court of Justice's decision in *Badeck and Others* (n 60), see G Selanec, 'Executive Summary' in European Network of Legal Experts in the Field of Gender Equality (ed), *Positive Action Measures to Ensure Full Equality in Practice between men and Women, including on Company Boards* (2012) 1, 12, www.ec.europa.eu/justice/gender-equality/files/gender_balance_decision_making/report_gender-balance_2012_en.pdf.
[67] In *Badeck and Others* (n 60) paras 64–66, the Court already concerned itself with the question whether quotas for the constellation of commissions, advisory boards, boards of directors and supervisory boards and other collective bodies were in accordance with EU equality law. The Court evaded ruling on this controversial issue by stating (a) that the national measure under review was 'not compulsory' and (b) that implementation of the measure 'would in any event require an amendment to the relevant [national] law' (ibid, para 65). Therefore, the reasoning in *Badeck* gives little indication as to the potential outcome of decisions by the European Court of Justice on the compatibility of quotas for women on boards with EU law. See also Selanec (n 66) 13.
[68] Case C-407/98 *Katarina Abrahamsson and Leif Anderson v Elisabet Fogelqvist* [2000] ECR I-5539.

the latter was a woman and that Swedish law contained affirmative action norms in order to facilitate participation of women in academia. Faced with a claim by the rejected candidates, the national court[69] filed a preliminary reference asking whether European equality law precluded 'legislation under which an applicant of the under-represented sex possessing sufficient qualifications for a public post is to be selected in priority over an applicant of the opposite sex who would otherwise have been selected'.[70]

Contrary to the cases that had previously appeared before the Court, the judges in *Abrahamsson* did not have to assess the legality of a 'tie-break' rule requiring preference to be given to a female applicant in the event that she is as qualified as her male contestants. Instead, they had to decide if a strict quota granting preference to a less qualified woman was in accordance with EU law.[71] In the end, the Court held the measure to be incompatible with EU law. In a two-tiered examination, it firstly explained that the law could not be considered as a derogation of the principle of equal treatment allowed under Article 2(4) of Directive 76/207/EEC and secondly stated that it was not protected by Article 141(4) EC (now Article 157(4) TFEU), either.[72]

An aspect of the case worth pointing out is the individualist reasoning underlying the decision or, more accurately, the crack in individualist reasoning that appears in the judgment. On the surface, the decision seems to be an affirmation of the point of view that equality is an individual right and that group-based notions of it ought to be rejected. For example, one of the judgment's decisive passages reads that the measure is incompatible with EU law because the appointment of the female candidate 'is ultimately based on the mere fact of belonging to the under-represented sex'.[73] With this statement, the Court rejects the notion that a woman has a right to preferential treatment based on her status as a woman. The passage continues by applying the formula first coined in *Marschall* and refined in *Badeck* to the facts of the case. It found that 'candidatures [under the measure] are not subjected to an objective assessment taking account of the specific personal situations of all the candidates'.[74] However, the individualist approach to equality

[69] The question arose whether the referring *Överklagandenämnden för Högskolan* could be considered a court or tribunal under Union law. After examination the European Court of Justice found it to be 'a court or tribunal within the meaning of [then] Article 177 of the [EC]' (Case C-450/93 *Eckhard Kalanke v Freie Hansestadt Bremen* [1995] ECR I-3051, paras 28 ff).

[70] ibid, para 27, question 1. Numhauser-Henning points out that the question referred to the European Court of Justice slightly misrepresented the actual workings of Swedish affirmative action. He explains that at the time of inquiry Art 15(a) of ch 4 of reg 1993:100 stipulated that 'a candidate belonging to the underrepresented sex and possessing sufficient qualifications for the post may be chosen in preference to a candidate belonging to the opposite sex who would otherwise have been chosen'. Thus, the national court phrased its reference imprecisely, giving the judges in Luxembourg the impression that the rule required, instead of allowed for preferential treatment of female candidates. See Numhauser-Henning (n 54) 122.

[71] Landau and Beigbeder (n 14) 235. On the classification of different quota schemes, see n 25.

[72] See *Abrahamsson* (n 68) paras 44 ff.

[73] ibid, para 53.

[74] ibid.

does not constitute a common thread running throughout the judgment. In the end, the court turns to assessing the question whether a milder form of the quota regime might be in conformity with EU law. It considers preferential promotion of women to be allowed, 'provided that the candidates possess equivalent or substantially equivalent merits, where the candidatures are subjected to an objective assessment which takes account of the specific personal situations of all the candidates'.[75] Thus, it repeats its request for an individual assessment, but rephrases its requirement of equal qualification. By allowing women, who 'possess … substantially equivalent merits' to benefit from quotas, the European Court of Justice essentially opens the door for affirmative action that goes beyond tie-breaking provisions. If preferential treatment of less-qualified candidates was in *Badeck* still limited to training positions, *Abrahamsson* extended it to the 'real' public job market of hiring and promotion. The result is that gender after all becomes a valid selection criterion. Thus, although the *Abrahamsson* decision is restrictive of affirmative action as concerns the case's outcome, it takes a more liberal point of view regarding its potential.

This finding is further supported by the fact that the conception of 'equality of opportunity', so heavily relied upon in *Kalanke*, is mentioned only in passing.[76] A consequence of this shift is that the *Abrahamsson* judgment leaves greater scope than previous decisions of the Court to deviate from the principle that positions should be assigned according to merit only. Availing oneself of the standard metaphor, the Court could have argued that under the Swedish regulation, candidates were not 'competing on a leveled playing field'[77] arguing that in order to obtain a position, women had to demonstrate fewer achievements in their careers than their male competitors. Likewise relying on 'equality of opportunity', the Court could have stated that the scheme guaranteed equal hiring chances to all applicants. It could have done so by moving its consideration of the correct starting point to a prior point in time. It would then have had to argue that it was, due to systemic discrimination, much harder for a woman to reach her level of qualification than for a man to reach his. Accordingly her achievements had to be given greater weight in any assessment. To avoid confusion, the judges abstained from entering into such a debate and stated clearly that they perceived the specific rule in question, which allowed for preference to be given to less competent candidates, to be incompatible with European law. However it was precisely in avoiding the debate on the correct reading of 'equality of opportunity' that the Court lessened its focus on merit based assessment in affirmative action law and provided space for more comprehensive evaluations.

[75] ibid, para 62.
[76] ibid, para 42.
[77] eg J Roemer, *Equality of Opportunity* (Cambridge, Harvard University Press, 1998) 1.

D. Synthesis

Considering the above four cases, the adjudication of the European Court of Justice can be summarised as follows.

Affirmative action for women is in accordance with European Union law, if it grants preference only to women, who possess substantially equivalent merit as their male co-applicants, and if the decision is based on an objective, individual assessment.[78]

Subsequent cases in the area have not led to a modification of this stance.[79] From the above statement one cannot detect a clear-cut preference or position by the Court on any of the three themes identified as cornerstones to the affirmative action debate. It highlights the importance of equality as an individual right, whilst showing itself open towards a group-based reading. It stresses the conception of equality as 'equal opportunity', only to disengage from a thorough interpretation of the term (or its application to the facts) in later cases. It mentions the potential of affirmative action to overcome entrenched discrimination, only to strike down laws that seek to bring about this change.[80]

What shall we make of this mixed picture? My first response is that this mélange should not be seen as a problem, but as the Court's solution. If we understand this lack of clear definition not as incoherence, but as openness, we can acknowledge that the Court deliberately chooses to move between equality's different conceptions in order to accommodate social and political developments as well as nuances in the design of the various schemes.

Second, I have to confess that I deliberately chose a misleading wording. It is not 'the Court' as a single entity that proclaims 'one interpretation' of the law. Rather, given that the European Court of Justice does not issue separate opinions, decisions are compromises between the different views held by judges. The various, sometimes contradicting aspects in the European affirmative action case law are an indication that judges hold different views on the legality (and desirability) of quotas and goals.

Third, looking to the experience of affirmative action in the United States could help us to better understand European adjudication on the matter. Not only has the judiciary on the other side of the Atlantic greater expertise in dealing with the legal aspects of the issue than its European counterpart, but the scholarly debate

[78] See, eg A Epiney, 'Neuere Rechtsprechung des EuGH in den Bereichen institutionelles Recht, allgemeines Verwaltungsrecht, Grundfreiheiten, Umwelt- und Gleichstellungsrecht' (2001) 20 *Neue Verwaltungszeitschrift* 524, 535.

[79] eg Case C-366/99 *Joseph Griesmar v Ministre de l'Economie, des Finances et de l'Industrie et Ministre de la Fonction publique, de la Réforme de l'Etat et de la Décentralisation* [2001] ECR I-9383; Case C-476/99 *H. Lommers v Minister van Landbouw, Natuurbeheer en Visserij* [2002] ECR I-2891; Case C-319/03 *Serge Briheche v Ministre de l'Intérieur, Ministre de l'Éducation nationale and Ministre de la Justice* [2004] ECR I-8807.

[80] As described, this does not happen in all instances, but has been the case in *Kalanke* (n 9) and *Abrahamsson* (n 68).

on its normative foundations, as well as effects, is also much further advanced in the United States.[81] However, before we turn to a discussion of the American case law, it must be stated clearly that it will be a highly selective exercise. The next pages are neither intended nor able to provide a fully-fledged comparison of American and European case law.[82]

II. THE AMERICAN EXPERIENCE

Not only has affirmative action in the United States existed for a longer period of time than its counterparts in European Member States but it is also more extensive in scope. Due to the institutionalised, persistent and infamous discrimination of the Black minority in the United States, efforts to abolish discriminatory laws and practices have been one of the key issues in American constitutional thought, practice and identity building. Turning to its historical roots, the notion of 'affirmative action' firstly appears in an executive order issued by President Kennedy in 1961. The order stipulated that governmental actors 'will take affirmative action to ensure that applicants are employed, and that employees are treated during employment, without regard to their race, creed, color, or national origin'.[83] As is evident from this excerpt, affirmative action was originally concerned with putting an end to segregation on the lines of race and national origin. Over time, its meaning changed to cover not actions undertaken to abolish different treatment of Blacks and Whites, but programmes that privileged members of a racial minority over Whites in an effort to counter entrenched discrimination. It was only after the concept had been established in the legal and political debate on desegregation that women's rights movements[84] expanded it to include actions that promote gender equality, a move that was subsequently followed by politicians and judges. Up to this point, affirmative action was primarily connected with equality between Blacks and Whites and only subsequently associated with equality between men and women. This mirrors the case law on affirmative action before the United States Supreme Court. Whereas a number of cases on affirmative action schemes have been concerned with preferential treatment of racial minorities, the Supreme Court Justices have only decided on the legality of an affirmative action favouring women in a single case.[85]

For this reason, a seriously incomplete picture of the American case law would be presented if one limited the description to affirmative action on grounds of

[81] It is important to note that there are prominent counterexamples, such as works by Fredman or Schiek.

[82] For this, see Schubert (n 55).

[83] Executive Order 10925 establishing the President's Committee on Equal Employment Opportunity, pt III, s 301(1) sentence 2.

[84] See generally Peters (n 11) 103 ff, though the author is somewhat critical of the analogy.

[85] *Johnson v Transportation Agency, Santa Clara County, California* 480 US 616 (1987) and S Ct 1442 (1987).

gender. On the other hand, the situation also calls for prudent assessment and awareness of differences between the two cases so as not to draw over-reaching conclusions from the case law on racial affirmative action for women's equality claims. Careful consideration is required of both the similarities and the differences between racial minorities and women. The two groups share the experience of being traditionally discriminated against. Their discriminations are based on the same ideology of 'white supremacy',[86] meaning that they had to suffer from the exercise of a feeling of superiority by a majority of men with European descent towards persons of colour or women. This sentiment of 'white supremacy' was expressed in rules that excluded people of other origins and women from the public sphere and deprived them of economic opportunities. Laws were designed so as to maintain the privileges of white men and to deny other groups adequate representation in the political process. Yet, the situation of women also considerably differed from that of racial minorities. The most obvious difference between the groups is that women have always been and continue to be represented in all social classes and come from all racial and national backgrounds. Thus, one may not infer from a woman's status that she has been socio-economically discriminated in the same way as members of other groups. As indicated by Mayeri in her book *Reasoning from Race* quoting the political scientist La Rue: '[A]ny attempt to analogize black oppression with the plight of the American white woman has the validity of comparing the neck of a hanging man with the hands of an amateur mountain climber with rope burns'.[87]

In this context, one needs to also address the issue of whether women can adequately be defined as a minority; after all, they make up for more than half of the population.[88] Working with the definition of a minority as denominating 'a group of people who differ … from a larger group of which it is a part', women do not meet the criterion of being outnumbered.[89] Thus, on numerical grounds, they cannot be seen as forming a minority. Furthermore, if one is also of the opinion that minorities are characterised by their social exclusion, women cannot be seen as belonging to a minority under this criterion. As the preceding passage indicated, they do not form an insular and discrete group.[90] On the other hand, women are not in a position to exercise their powers, as majorities under normal circumstances normally are. Up to this day, they are underrepresented in the workplace and in the public sphere and experience discrimination.

[86] eg Schubert (n 55) 156.

[87] S Mayeri, *Reasoning from Race. Feminism, Law, and the Civil Rights Revolution* (Cambridge, Harvard University Press, 2011) 49 f with reference to L La Rue, 'The Black Movement and Women's Liberation' (1970) 1(7) *The Black Scholar* 36.

[88] Though this thesis does not share its conclusions, see on the point for the German debate the work of Maidowski (n 7) 137.

[89] Mayeri (n 87) 77 with further reference.

[90] Referring to *United States v Carolene Products Co* 304 US 144, 58 S Ct 778 at 784 fn 4. Further JH Ely, *Democracy and Distrust. A Theory of Judicial Review* (Cambridge, Harvard University Press, 1980) 164.

However, the discrimination experienced by women is more subtle, as their role as child bearer and (prime) caretaker subjects them to a subordinate position in private and public life.[91] Considering all these factors, I would argue that women are not a minority, but form a discriminated subgroup belonging both to social minorities and majorities. Though my assessment will most likely be contested—either because it is seen as pure semantics or because the preceding analysis is not shared—I maintain that this is the most adequate way of describing the current state of affairs. Furthermore, this categorisation will become important for the comparative institutional analysis at the end of this chapter.

Returning to the comparison between the experiences of discrimination suffered by the Black community and women in the United States, the aforementioned author Mayeri illustrates in her work that the social movements in the United States on non-discrimination of both groups are intertwined and cross-fertilised each other.[92] Further, she describes that the United States Supreme Court follows similar lines of reasoning when scrutinising norms under equality guarantees.[93] In light of this latter finding, the next section presents the affirmative action jurisprudence of the United States Supreme Court in greater detail. It will be seen that the Supreme Court has placed an emphasis on assessing whether equality ought to be understood as an individualist or a group-based right and focused on evaluating which standard of scrutiny to apply.

A. Race Conscious Affirmative Action

Starting with an account of the leading cases on race based affirmative action before the Supreme Court, one should first point out that the adjudication is separated into two lines of cases, namely those concerned with educational affirmative action and those dealing with affirmative action in public employment and government contracting.

i. Race Conscious Affirmative Action in Education

The United States Supreme Court first considered the legality of an affirmative action scheme in the 1978 case of *Regents of University of California v Bakke*.[94] The Medical School at UC Davis had implemented a scheme under which 16 per cent

[91] Mayeri (n 87) 77 ff.

[92] ibid.

[93] ibid, 58 ff.

[94] *Regents of the University of California v Allan Bakke*, 438 US 265 (1978). Already four years earlier, the case *DeFunis v Odegaard*, 416 US 312 (1974) had reached the Supreme Court. It concerned a law school admission scheme, which granted preference to members of racial minorities. Then '[t]he Court sidestepped the controversy, declaring the case moot' (R Siegel, 'Equality Talk: Antisubordination and Anticlassification Values in Constitutional Struggles over Brown' (2004) 117 *Harvard Law Review* 1470, 1527).

of places were reserved to minorities. Allan Bakke, a white applicant to the school claimed that the university had wrongfully denied him a place and discriminated against him, when they rejected him and offered spots to persons 'with significantly lower scores'[95] and grade point averages. When issuing the decision, the Supreme Court was deeply divided on the question whether the affirmative programme by UC Davis could be reconciled with the right to equality. Four justices argued in favour of its legality, four against it and Justice Powell offered a separate opinion, which not only decided the case but has come to define the discourse surrounding affirmative action in the United States up till the present day.[96] In the end, the Court held the programme in that case be forbidden, yet at the same time found that other forms of affirmative action might well be reconciled with equality provisions. In an attempt to find a middle ground between the opposing views, Justice Powell argued that preferential treatment of racial minorities is permitted, so long as race is not the sole decisive factor in the decision, but merely considered 'as a plus'.[97] He stated that it would be irreconcilable with the right to equality to set aside a specific number of places for persons belonging to one specific group. Nonetheless, he said that educational facilities had a justified interest in fostering diversity at their institutions.[98] Therefore, such institutions were allowed to take an applicant's ethnic background into account in their admissions process, but needed to ensure that other applicant's specific features, talents, etc were also adequately considered.[99]

As can be seen from this summary, Justice Powell espoused an individualist conception of equality.[100] For him, it was crucial that estimation of each individual's talents and abilities formed the basis of any admissions decision. Although he agreed that the exclusion experienced by Blacks traced back to their belonging to a certain group, he argued that '[it] is the individual who is entitled to judicial protection'.[101] By holding that race should be considered as *one* decisive factor *amongst others* in the decision making process, he gave further expression to his individualistic point of view. Thus, when he required affirmative action programmes to be narrowly tailored in order to find them in accordance with equality guarantees, he aimed to protect those programmes which were able to reconcile collective advancement of minorities with concern for individual situations.

[95] *Regents of the University of California v Allan Bakke* 438 U.S. 265 (1978) at 266.

[96] See *Grutter v Bollinger* 123 S Ct 2325 (2003) at 2329, where his opinion was referred to as 'the touchstone of constitutional analysis of race-conscious admissions policies' (Rosenfeld (n 35) 168).

[97] *Regents of the University of California v Allan Bakke* 438 US 265 (1978) at 317.

[98] ibid, at 318. See R Siegel, 'From Colorblindness to Antibalkanization: An Emerging Ground of Decision in Race Equality Cases' (2011) 120 *Yale Law Journal* 1278, 1294.

[99] Among other examples, he states that students who have been brought up on farms contribute with their experience to the education at Harvard College, see *Regents of the University of California v Allan Bakke* 438 US 265 (1978) at 316.

[100] See Siegel (n 94) 1530 ff. Here, 'strict scrutiny' is used as common in the United States legal context.

[101] *Regents of the University of California v Allan Bakke*, 438 US 265 (1978) at 299.

Another topic that featured prominently in the separate opinions is the choice of scrutiny in affirmative action review.[102] As the chapter on different testing standards in the European context demonstrated, choice of scrutiny sets the course for any further examination under equality provisions. The stricter the testing standard, the fewer justifications will be accepted as capable of justifying the preferential treatment. Whereas five Justices, including Justice Powell, argued that racial or ethnic classifications were always subject to strict scrutiny, the remaining four contended that affirmative action ought to be judged pursuant to a less intense standard.[103] Consequently, strict scrutiny was set as the rule in review of educational affirmative action and only Justice Powell's differentiated ruling allowed him to reach the conclusion that the scheme at UC Davis was nevertheless justified.

Over time, the Supreme Court heard further cases on affirmative action in education and modified its position. Examples of this development include the judgments in *Grutter v Bollinger*[104] and *Gratz v Bollinger*,[105] both decided in 2003. In *Grutter v Bollinger*, the Supreme Court reviewed the admissions scheme of the University of Michigan Law School. After summarising its affirmative action jurisprudence up to that point it applied its approach to the case. The scheme allowed for variables intended to ensure diversity of the student body, such as an individual's predicted commitment to the academic and social life at the Law School, to be taken into account. An additional variable was the applicant's ethnic background. Had the candidate been part of a minority group, preference could be given to him or her. The Supreme Court decided in a five to four ruling that the admissions programme was in accordance with the American constitution's equal protection clause, the Fourteenth Amendment.[106] Justice O'Connor, writing for the majority, started by stressing that the equality clause 'protect[s] persons, not groups'.[107] In doing so, she referred to the case *Adarand Constructors, Inc v Pena*[108] decided in 1995, in which the Court for the first time found that the constitution required an

[102] See Siegel (n 98) 1293 ff.

[103] *Regents of the University of California v Allan Bakke*, 438 US 265 (1978) at 291 (Powell opinion) and at 361 ff; see Thomas (n 7) 337 f.

[104] *Grutter v Bollinger* 123 S Ct 2325 (2003).

[105] *Gratz v Bollinger* 123 S Ct 2411 (2003).

[106] The Fourteenth Amendment to the United States Constitution states in excerpts:

> Section 1: All persons born or naturalized in the United States, and subject to the jurisdiction thereof, are citizens of the United States and of the State wherein they reside. No State shall make or enforce any law which shall abridge the privileges or immunities of citizens of the United States; nor shall any State deprive any person of life, liberty, or property, without due process of law; nor deny to any person within its jurisdiction the equal protection of the laws
>
> ...
>
> Section 5: The Congress shall have power to enforce, by appropriate legislation, the provisions of this article.

[107] *Grutter v Bollinger* 123 S Ct 2325 (2003) at 2337.

[108] *Adarand Constructors, Inc v Frederico Pena, Secretary of Transportation*, 515 US 200 (1995) and 115 S Ct 2097 (1995); Siegel (n 94) 1539, fn 236.

individual reading of the equality principle. She further stated, citing *Richmond v JA Croson Co*[109] as an additional source alongside *Adarand Constructors, Inc v Pena*,[110] that any form of racial classification 'must be analyzed … under strict scrutiny'.[111] However she also argued that strict scrutiny in theory must not mean 'fatal in fact'[112] and that, as long as it was narrowly tailored, a compelling state interest advanced by a governmental institution could allow for affirmative action. Applying these standards to the case, the Justices forming the majority held that ensuring a diverse student body was a compelling interest and that the scheme, which granted preference to minority candidates, since it allowed for additional individual features to be taken into account, was sufficiently limited in design and thus permissible. The admissions practice in *Gratz v Bollinger*, on the other hand, was considered to overstep the boundaries of permissible affirmative action under the equal protection clause. The University of Michigan's College of Literature, Science and the Arts assigned places according to a point scheme. The plan gave points for SAT scores, high school grades, and—in a category labelled 'miscellaneous'—for membership of an ethnic minority. Under the scheme, the number of points awarded for ethnic affiliation could have considerable influence on a person's chances of admission. For this reason, the majority of Justices held the scheme not to be 'narrowly tailored' and considered the practice unconstitutional.

The diversity argument, espoused in *Grutter v Bollinger* and *Gratz v Bollinger*, was further stressed in *Fisher I*[113] when the Supreme Court took to scrutinising the Texan law that granted admission to each student ranked among the top 10 per cent of his high school class to the University of Texas, Austin. The law worked to the benefit of minorities because it offered students from less competitive high schools (often in urban centres) a way of acceptance to the university, which might have been barred under the parallel admissions process focusing on SAT scores, etc. In the majority opinion, the Justices stated that the university must demonstrate that it cannot achieve diversity through other, non-race sensitive means before applying a measure such as the one in question.[114] Arguing that the lower court had failed to assess under strict scrutiny if such other options were to the university's avail, the Supreme Court remanded the case back.[115]

[109] *City of Richmond v J A Croson Co*, 488 US 469 (1989) and 109 S Ct 706 (1989).

[110] *Grutter v Bollinger*, 123 S Ct 2325 (2003) at 2329 and 2337.

[111] ibid.

[112] ibid, at 2338; again citing *Adarand Constructors, Inc v Frederico Pena, Secretary of Transportation*, 515 US 200 (1995) and 115 S Ct 2097 (1995) at 2101.

[113] *Fisher v University of Texas at Austin et al*, 133 S Ct 2411 (2013), for a comment on the case and a critique of the diversity rationale as applied by the United States Supreme Court, see P Schuck, 'Assessing Affirmative Action' (2014) *National Affairs*, 76.

[114] ibid, at 2420. See R Siegel, 'Race-Conscious but Race-Neutral: The Constitutionality of Disparate Impact in the Roberts Court' (2014) 66 *Alabama Law Review* 653, 655 f.

[115] *Fisher v University of Texas at Austin et al* 133 S Ct 2411 (2013). In 2015, the case returned to the Supreme Court. Oral arguments were heard on 9 December 2015 and the Justices again faced the options to either further rely on the diversity argument or to restate their stance on affirmative action. With its decision of 23 June 2016, the Court opted for the former.

In the meantime, the United States Supreme Court has also attended to the matter of a law banning, instead of allowing, affirmative action. The case at point is *Schuette v Coalition to Defend Affirmative Action*,[116] decided in 2013. In the wake of *Grutter v Bollinger*, upholding the affirmative action scheme of the University of Michigan Law School, an initiative succeeded in amending Michigan's constitution so as to ban affirmative action by public institutions.[117] Reviewing the case, the Supreme Court had to decide, in particular, whether the United States Constitution allowed for a state to preclude public universities from considering race or sex in their admission processes. In a six to two decision,[118] the Justices held that the federal constitution did not prohibit such a ban. In essence, the majority of Justices based their decision on the ground that the ban did not inflict 'hurt or injury'[119] on racial minorities, but merely repealed legislation inuring to them. From the outset, the Justices in the majority stressed that the case was 'not about the constitutionality, or the merits, of race-conscious admissions policies in higher education'[120] so as to distinguish *Schuette* from the line of cases where the Court reviewed the legality of affirmative action policies. Seen in this light, the case is actually different from those previously described. However, in its decision, the Court also made a broader point that has a bearing on affirmative action schemes, as will be explicated more thoroughly below.[121] *Schuette* 'implicitly overrul[ed]'[122] the political process theory, as it was put forward in the Supreme Court decision *Washington v Seattle School District No 1*,[123] in the realm of affirmative action. In *Washington v Seattle School District No 1*, the Court stated

> that where a government policy 'inures primarily to the benefit of the minority' and 'minorities ... consider' the policy to be 'in their interests,' then any state action that 'place[s] effective decision making authority over' that policy 'at a different level of government' must be reviewed under strict scrutiny.[124]

For a (anti-subordination) critique of the case see M Barnes, E Chemerinsky and A Onwuachi-Willig, 'Judging Opportunity Lost: Assessing the Viability of Race-Based Affirmative Action after Fisher v University of Texas' (2015) 62 *UCLA Law Review* 271, 288 ff.

[116] *Schuette v Calition to Defend Affirmative Action, Integration, and Immigrant Rights and Fight for Equality By Any Means Necessary (BAMN)* 134 S Ct 1623 (2014).

[117] M Rose, 'Proposal 2 and the Ban on Affirmative Action: An Uncertain Future for the University of Michigan in its Quest for Diversity' (2008) 17 *Boston University Public Interest Law Journal* 309, 316 ff.

[118] Justice Kagan excused herself as she had been concerned with the case previously during her time as United States Solicitor General.

[119] *Schuette v Calition to Defend Affirmative Action, Integration, and Immigrant Rights and Fight for Equality By Any Means Necessary (BAMN)* 134 S Ct 1623 (2014), at 1637.

[120] ibid, at 1630.

[121] See s IV.A.

[122] Denniston goes as far as arguing that the Court majority rejected the political process theory as a whole; L Denniston, 'Opinion analysis: Affirmative action—up to the voters', www.scotusblog.com/2014/04/opinion-analysis-affirmative-action-up-to-the-voters.

[123] *Washington v Seattle School District No 1*, 102 S Ct 3187 (1982).

[124] *Schuette v Coalition to Defend Affirmative Action, Integration, and Immigrant Rights and Fight for Equality By Any Means Necessary (BAMN)* 134 S Ct 1623 (2014), at 1634, with reference to *Washington v Seattle School District No 1*, 102 S Ct 3187 (1982), at 3197.

According to this statement, the situation in *Schuette* would have had to be reviewed under strict scrutiny, because the decision on the criteria for university admissions was partially shifted from local universities' admissions boards to the state's *pouvoir constituant*.[125] However, with its focus on inflicted hurt or injury, the majority came to a different conclusion, did not apply the standard demanded by the political process theory and effectively curtailed the prescribed requirement of strict scrutiny review.[126] Therefore, the ruling has the perverse effect of making prohibitions of affirmative action subject to a lesser standard of review than measures allowing for preferential treatment of minority groups.

As this short depiction shows, the United States case law on affirmative action has stabilised to some extent in so far as the Supreme Court's jurisprudence centres on the themes of 'testing standard', 'individualist versus collective conception of the equality principle' and 'realization of diversity'.[127] Testing ought to be performed under strict scrutiny—unless the case concerns the prohibition of affirmative action—but may nevertheless result in deeming an affirmative action programme constitutional. The right to equality is considered an individual right but that does not necessarily imply that affirmative action violates this individual right. Affirmative action is perceived as an adequate tool to ensure the existence of diverse student bodies in higher education, but not as a means to remedy harm inflicted in the past. However the effects of this harmonisation are less significant than one might suspect. The conflict has shifted to assessing when affirmative action is narrowly tailored and the dispute on the correct understanding of the right to equality is relocated to this alternative context.

ii. Race Conscious Affirmative Action in Public Employment and Government Contracting

Pursuant the second line of cases, the Supreme Court reviewed affirmative action programmes in employment and government contracting. The case law comprises decisions that deal with affirmative action schemes created by private employers on a voluntary basis, as well as decisions on affirmative action in federal employment. As the Supreme Court has dealt with a considerable amount of cases on this issue the following analysis focuses exclusively on some of the more prominent federal employment decisions.[128]

[125] See Justice Sotomayor's dissent in *Schuette v Coalition to Defend Affirmative Action, Integration, and Immigrant Rights and Fight for Equality By Any Means Necessary (BAMN)* 134 S Ct 1623 (2014), starting at 1651.

[126] See further C D'Alessio, 'A Bridge Too Far: The Limits of the Political Process Doctrine in *Schuette v Coalition to Defend Affirmative Action*' (2013) 9 *Duke Journal of Constitutional Law and Public Policy* 103, 111 (written before the decision by the United States Supreme Court).

[127] See D Sabbagh, *Equality and Transparency: A Strategic Perspective on Affirmative Action in American Law* (New York, Palgrave Macmillan, 2007) 31 ff.

[128] For a decision on voluntary affirmative action by private parties, see eg *United Steelworkers v Weber*, 443 US 193, 93 S Ct 705 (1979).

In *Fullilove v Klutznick*,[129] the Justices assessed the constitutionality of a federal law, which stipulated 'that at least 10 percent of federal funds granted for local public works projects must be used to obtain services of minority groups, defined as United States citizens who are Negroes, Spanish-speaking, Orientals, Indians, Eskimos and Aleuts'.[130] With a vote of six to three, the Justices found the provision to be in accordance with the right to equal treatment. The majority based its assessment mainly on the argument that the provision was passed by Congress, which was vested with the powers 'to enforce … the equal protection guarantees of the Fourteenth Amendment'.[131] Thus, the Justices argued, the Constitution conceded ample discretion to the federal legislature in designing affirmative action campaigns. One could even say that, coated in constitutional language, they employed an institutional argument when writing that the checks imposed by the judiciary on Congress were less strict than those imposed on other public or private bodies. Apparently, the Justices perceived Congress with its broad constituency as a less imperfect decision maker to implement non-discrimination decisions than smaller, more local entities. In addition, they argued that the level of 10 per cent of funds set aside by the program met the requirement of narrow tailoring, that is to say that affirmative action ought to be 'narrowly tailored to achieve … the goal of equality of economic opportunity'.[132] Given that the Supreme Court upheld the measure and granted the political process leeway in the composition of affirmative action schemes, the judgment was interpreted as leaving substantial room for the implementation of advancement measures in public employment.[133]

Richmond v JA Croson Co[134] demonstrated however that the reach of the decision was more limited than was first assumed.[135] The case concerned a plan of the city of Richmond, Virginia, requiring principal contractors in city construction 'to subcontract at least 30 percent of the dollar amount of each contract to one or more Minority Business Enterprises'.[136] In a narrow five to four vote, the Supreme Court decided that the programme was not protected by the equal protection clause. In a first step, the Justices distinguished the case from *Fullilove* and held that a state or federal entity other than Congress lacked the 'specific constitutional mandate to enforce the dictates of the Fourteenth Amendment'.[137] Once again, the institutional facet of their assessment came to the fore in the reasoning. Then, the Justices

[129] *Fullilove v Klutznick* 448 US 448, 100 S Ct 2758 (1980).

[130] L Fisher and K Harriger, *American Constitutional Law*, vol 2 (Durham, Carolina Academic Press, 2011) 815.

[131] *Fullilove v Klutznick* 448 US 448, 100 S Ct 2758 (1980) at 2760.

[132] ibid, at 2761.

[133] D Days, 'Fullilove' (1986/1987) 96 *Yale Law Journal* 453, 454.

[134] *City of Richmond v J A Croson Co*, 488 US 469 (1989) and 109 S Ct 706 (1989).

[135] See, eg P Rubio, *A History of Affirmative Action, 1619–2000* (Jackson, University Press of Mississippi, 2001) 175 with further reference.

[136] Fisher (n 130) 817. In the plan, Minority Business Enterprises are described as businesses that are owned and controlled to a majority by Black, Spanish-speaking, Oriental, Indian, Eskimo or Aleut citizens.

[137] *City of Richmond v J A Croson Co*, 488 US 469 (1989) and 109 S Ct 706 (1989) at 720.

stated that the city's claim to address past social discrimination with its plan was an insufficiently 'compelling interest' for instructing construction contractors as to who they may hire. Further, Justice O'Connor wrote in the majority opinion that the quota was not 'narrowly tailored'.[138] She deemed a 30 per cent set-aside to be excessive and stated that the provision was over-inclusive, because minority groups that had no history of past discrimination in the city of Richmond, such as the Aleuts, could benefit from it.[139] With respect to the last point, one notes that the Court's majority relied on the remedial aspect of affirmative action when reaching its conclusion and left out of its assessment the policy's more forward looking element of changing future social practice. Moreover, although the Court was eager to stress that it only struck down the specific measure under review and that the Constitution still allowed for the option of affirmative action by institutions other than Congress, its ruling nevertheless limited the leeway of the political process with regards to preferential treatment of minorities. With *Richmond* as a precedent, affirmative action of public institutions other than Congress has become subject to strict scrutiny review.

When a further case—*Adarand Constructors, Inc v Pena*[140]—reached the Court, the Justices did not expand on the difference in affirmative action enacted by Congress and other federal or state entities. Instead, it held *Fullilove* to be no longer controlling and insisted on strict scrutiny for preferences in federal and state contracting alike.[141] The case at hand concerned a clause in federal agency contracts allowing for a higher compensation for contractors where they engaged minority business enterprises as subcontractors. Asked whether the clause illegally discriminated against subcontractors without substantial minority composition, the Tenth Circuit upheld the clause. In doing so, it relied on the precedents of *Fullilove* and *Metro Broadcasting*.[142] The Supreme Court vacated the decision, demanded strict scrutiny review in all instances of affirmative action in employment and remanded the case to the lower court for further proceedings.[143] Apart from the entrenchment of a high level of scrutiny in affirmative action cases, the decision is noticeable for its individualistic undertone. The Court had in past cases been willing to show concern for the specific situation of minorities. *Adarand* however stands as an example of a conception of American equality law that denies

[138] ibid, especially at 730.

[139] ibid, at 728. It needs to be mentioned that the dissent by Justices Marshall, Brennan and Blackmun critically pointed out that the affirmative action scheme was indistinguishable in all meaningful respects from—and in fact was patterned upon—the federal set-aside plan which this Court upheld in *Fullilove v Klutznick* 448 US 448, 100 S Ct 2758 (1980), *City of Richmond v J A Croson Co*, 488 US 469 (1989) and 109 S Ct 706 (1989) at 740.

[140] *Adarand Constructors, Inc v Frederico Pena, Secretary of Transportation*, 515 US 200 (1995) and 115 S Ct 2097 (1995).

[141] ibid, at 2101.

[142] Fisher (n 130) 819.

[143] Thereby overruling *Richmond v Croson* and *Adarand v Pena;* see Rubio (n 135) 175 with further reference.

any group-based roots. Accordingly, Whites enjoy the same protection under the equality clause as Blacks or other ethnic minorities. In the words of the Justice O'Connor,

> [this] means that whenever the government treats any person unequally because of his or her race, that person has suffered an injury that falls squarely within the language and spirit of the Constitution's guarantee of equal protection.[144]

As one can see it has also become increasingly difficult to establish and maintain affirmative action programmes for ethnic minorities in the realm of American public employment and government contracting.

B. Gender Conscious Affirmative Action

In stark contrast to the Supreme Court's repeated and intense dealings with the subject of racial and ethnic affirmative action, the Court has been less involved with the preferential treatment of women. It took to the issue in *Johnson v Transportation Agency*.[145] The Santa Clara County Transportation Agency adopted an affirmative action plan, according to which it was authorised to take the sex of a qualified applicant as one aspect amongst others into account in promotion procedures for 'positions within a traditionally segregated job classification in which women have been significantly underrepresented'.[146] When the Agency advertised for a new road dispatcher, it made use of the discretion granted by the plan. Relying on the fact that the position was classified as that of a skilled craft worker and that none of the 238 skilled craft workers at the agency at that time were women, it preferred a female candidate to a male, although the woman had received a lower test score on the job interview than the man. By choosing a (according to the test results) less skilled woman over a man, the Agency went further in its promotion procedure than applying a tie-break rule. When confronted with the issue whether the woman's preferential treatment was illegal, a majority of Justices held that it did not violate anti-discrimination law.

The Court reviewed the plan with regard to its compatibility with Title VII of the Civil Rights Act of 1964, the American subconstitutional law which for the first time granted significant rights of non-discrimination in the context of employment. They thereby refrained from engaging in a direct debate as to the constitutionality of the measure under the Fourteenth Amendment.[147] This choice of Title

[144] *Adarand Constructors, Inc v Frederico Pena, Secretary of Transportation*, 515 US 200 (1995) and 115 S Ct 2097 (1995) at 2114. The passage continues: 'It says nothing about the ultimate validity of any particular law; that determination is the job of the court applying strict scrutiny'.

[145] *Johnson v Transportation Agency, Santa Clara County, California* 480 US 616 (1987) and S Ct 1442 (1987).

[146] ibid, at 1443.

[147] The reason given by the Court is that '[n]o constitutional issue was either raised or addressed in the litigation below,' *Johnson v Transportation Agency, Santa Clara County, California* 480 US 616 (1987) and S Ct 1442 (1987) at 620/1446, fn 2. Critical, Schubert (n 55) 152 and 156.

VII as the norm guiding the review is linked to the question of the correct standard of scrutiny for gender based affirmative action. Had the Court turned towards the Fourteenth Amendment, it would have had to consider whether strict or intermediate scrutiny represented the correct level of review. By scrutinising the preferential treatment under Title VII, the Justices could abstain from deciding the issue of scrutiny and limit their assessment to examining whether the employer 'had a firm basis for believing that remedial action was required'.[148] Consequently, they could evade the question if the Transport Agency, as a governmental body, had a 'compelling interest' to prefer the female candidate over the male, which would have come up under constitutional review. Instead, testing under Title VII enabled them to bypass the thorny debate and apply a lower standard of scrutiny.[149] In the end, a majority of Justices argued that there was such 'manifest imbalance' in the representation of men and women in the Skilled Craft job category, that the Agency could legitimately assume that affirmative measures were necessary to counter the underrepresentation of women.[150]

Furthermore, the Justices investigated if the affirmative action plan 'unnecessarily trammel[ed] male employees' rights or create[d] an absolute bar to their advancement'.[151] As this statement shows, the Supreme Court was concerned about the measure's impact on the career chances of the male employees, especially of the one denied the promotion. In their assessment, the majority of Justices drew a comparison to the 'race plus' argument introduced by Justice Powell in *Bakke*.[152] They argued that the Transport Agency had considered the applicants' gender only as one factor amongst many in making its decision. Other aspects, which might have presented the male applicant's situation in a different light, could have changed the outcome of the promotion decision. With the evaluation that the promotion practice considered gender merely as a 'plus', the majority arrived at the conclusion that the plan did not excessively burden male applicants. Again, the Supreme Court's interest in interpreting equality law so as to avoid individual hardship is apparent. While the Court acknowledged that government employers have reasons to remedy the underrepresentation of women in the workplace and considered the affirmative action justified, it still attempted to reconcile its judgment with an individualistic conception of equality law.

However, if one wants to understand *Johnson*'s implications for today's discussion on the legality of affirmative action in the United States, one needs to bear

[148] *Johnson v Transportation Agency, Santa Clara County, California* 480 US 616 (1987) and S Ct 1442 (1987) at 1461.

[149] For a critique of the deeply troubling effect that affirmative action for Blacks is subject to strict scrutiny, whilst that for women is subject only to intermediate scrutiny, see Rosenfeld (n 35) 154.

[150] *Johnson v Transportation Agency, Santa Clara County, California* 480 US 616 (1987) and S Ct 1442 (1987) at 1442 (direct quote); at 1451 ff (reasoning).

[151] ibid, at 1445.

[152] D Bellam, 'Affirmative Action: Purveyor of Preferential Treatment or Guarantor of Equal Opportunity—A Call for a Revisioning of Affirmative Action' (1997) 18 *Berkeley Journal of Employment and Labor Law* 1, 4 and 15.

in mind that the judgment was passed in 1986. As presented above, the Court has since then issued decisions that show a greater reluctance on the side of the Justices to embrace affirmative action schemes (see *Adarand*). Given the fact that the Court has become more restrictive in its acceptance of affirmative action, it may well be the case that it would decide otherwise today if presented with the issue.

C. The Mediating Principle in United States Affirmative Action Case Law

Assessing the United States Supreme Court's case law on affirmative action, one element remains present: the consistent inconsistency with which the Court has been, and continues to be, deeply divided on the question of whether affirmative action is prohibited by the American equality clause. It decided multiple cases on a five to four vote and in *Bakke*—undoubtedly the pioneering case in the field—the Justices were not even able to produce a majority leaning one way or the other. This discordance is epitomised by the Court's decision in *Ricci*.[153] 'Divided five to four',[154] the Supreme Court held that the decision by the city of New Haven to reschedule an exam for the staffing of vacant positions in its fire department was in violation of US equality law. After the city had found out that minority candidates had disproportionately underperformed in the test, it choose to redesign the exam and to question the candidates once again, in order not to discriminate against any applicant. Although the case did not concern affirmative action in the sense of quotas or promotion plans, but focused on race conscious action,[155] it raised similar issues. In particular, it asked if a measure that is intended to remedy existing discrimination can become discriminatory itself and if so, if it is compatible with the principle of equality. The more recent cases *Fisher I* and *Schuette*—decided seven to one, respectively six to two—seem to indicate greater consensus among the Justices on the appraisal of race conscious policies. However, such assessment would be premature: *Fisher I* was referred to a lower court for further examination and has since returned to the docket of the Supreme Court.[156] In *Fisher II*, the Court was again divided on the issue of affirmative action in college admission, with the unusual majority of four to three upholding the admission scheme.[157] Moreover, *Schuette* contains three concurrences as well as one strong dissent by two Justices.

[153] *Ricci v DeStefano* 129 S Ct 2658, 2664 (2009). For a discussion, see M Selmi, 'Indirect Discrimination and the Anti-Discrimination Mandate' in D Hellman and S Moreau (eds), *Philosophical Foundations of Discrimination Law* (Oxford, Oxford University Press, 2013) 250, 261 ff.

[154] Siegel (n 98) 1325.

[155] My thanks to Pamela Karlan for pointing out this aspect.

[156] *Fisher v University of Texas at Austin et al*, Case 14-981, docketed 13 February 2015.

[157] ibid.

Thus, the question on the compatibility of affirmative action with the principle of equality still looms large in both American case law and academic debates. Moreover the responses depend to a significant extent on which conception of equality one is inclined to take. In American constitutional law, the Supreme Court Justices are said to hold competing visions, which '[o]ver the decades, observers of the Court have come to describe ... in binary terms':[158] the colour-blind approach versus the anti-subordination approach.

As the denomination of the former already reveals, one group of Justices is believed to be of the opinion that the equal protection clause prohibits harming any individual due to his or her colour, that is classification by race.[159] According to this view, the Constitution entitles Whites as much as Blacks or any other minority group to be protected against discrimination. Translated to the domain of affirmative action for women, the logic holds that anti-discrimination law is gender-blind and that no person may be disadvantaged because she has been classified as woman or he has been classified as a man. According to the conceptual dichotomy put forward, the latter group is said to perceive American equal protection law as an expression of a concept of anti-subordination.[160] Under this perception, the equal protection clause terminates the discrimination suffered by Blacks and other minority groups over a long period of time. It seeks to abolish discrimination on grounds of 'class, not classification'.[161] Fiss, a prominent advocate of the anti-subordination theory, argued that the Fourteenth Amendment prohibits the aggravation or perpetuation of the subordinate position of a specially disadvantaged group.[162] As one can infer from the remark, proponents of the anti-subordination principle seek an interpretation of the anti-discrimination clause that views instances of discrimination in their social context. As far as affirmative action on grounds of race is concerned, as Whites have not been subject to an entrenched disadvantage their less favourable treatment vis-à-vis

[158] Siegel (n 98) 1281. In J Balkin and R Siegel, 'The American Civil Rights Tradition: Anticlassification or Antisubordination?' (2003) 58 *University of Miami Law Review* 9 (especially 28 and 32) and Siegel (n 94) 1477 and 1533, the authors point out that the relation between the two approaches is more complex and intertwined than generally assumed.

[159] P Brest, 'The Supreme Court, 1975 Term-Foreword: In Defense of the Antidiscrimination Principle' (1976) 90 *Harvard Law Review* 1 coined this definition, though he also pointed out that he did not want to prejudge by this definition the legality of affirmative action. See for further depiction of this view O Fiss, 'Groups and the Equal Protection Clause' (1976) 5 *Philosophy and Public Affairs* 107, 108 ff; Post (n 17) 11; Rosenfeld (n 35) 21; R Siegel, 'Discrimination in the Eyes of the Law: How "Color Blindness" Discourse Disrupts and Rationalizes Social Stratification' (2000) 88 *California Law Review* 77, 92; ibid (n 98) 1281 and 1287; J Suk, 'Quotas and Consequences: A Transnational Re-evaluation' in D Hellman and S Moreau (eds), *Philosophical Foundations of Discrimination Law* (Oxford, Oxford University Press, 2013) 228, 229 f.

[160] Fiss (n 159). The author employs the labels of 'antidiscrimination' and 'group-disadvantaging' principle to define the same dichotomy. See also Siegel (n 98) 1281 and ibid (n 94) 1470 ff.

[161] MA Case, 'Reflections on Constitutionalizing Women's Equality' (2002) 90 *California Law Review* 765, 782, citing K Sullivan. The author applies the phrase in the context of discussing different ideas for the protection of gender equality.

[162] Fiss (n 159) 157.

persons of a different ethnicity may be allowed. In terms of gender equality, the anti-subordination principle holds that the law may not treat women in such a way that maintains their position of disadvantage but that it can be justified to treat men less favourably than women. To my mind, this second approach can once again be divided into two subcategories—one focusing on the idea of compensating past wrongs through affirmative action, the other putting its emphasis on overcoming structural biases via the means of affirmative action. Depending on which variant proponents of the anti-subordination theory are more inclined to follow, their justifications for affirmative action are either grounded more in arguments relying on the past or on arguments depicting present circumstances.

Looking at the Supreme Court's affirmative action case law, the controversy surrounding these two competing visions—of colour- or gender blindness and anti-subordination—finds expression in the reoccurring disputes on (a) the individual versus the group oriented character of equality guarantees and (b) the correct standard of scrutiny in testing. The colour-blindness principle is commonly associated with an individualist perception of equality as it holds that each person is entitled to an individual assessment without regard to stereotypes, namely ethnic or gender generalisations. Further, it is linked to the demand for strict scrutiny of affirmative action, since it permits only a limited range of reasons to act as justification for unfavourable treatment to anyone. In contrast, the anti-subordination principle is associated with a collective reading of equality and the call for a more lenient standard of review. Not only does it take the socio-historic situation of the group of which the (allegedly) discriminated person is a member into account[163] but it also seeks to leave room for justifying differential and simultaneously favourable treatment of minorities under a less rigorous standard of review.[164] Nevertheless, its variant that stresses the structural aspects of discrimination is able to accommodate an individualistic perception of equality. Whilst it acknowledges that patterns of discrimination are deeply entrenched in society, it leaves ample room for factoring in how far an individual is actually negatively affected by belonging to a group that is subject to structural bias.

In light of these broader tensions, one may claim that the American debate on affirmative action takes place under similar conditions to those experienced

[163] See Sabbagh (n 127) 60.

[164] However in reality the lines between the different conceptions and categorisations are often less well defined than the Justices' opinions and theoretical debates would have one believe. On the one hand, even proponents of equality as an individual right need to acknowledge that each individual is also characterised by his or her multiple collective identities. Though a person is more than the sum of her race, gender, sexual orientation, religious belief or *Weltanschauung*, these elements contribute to this person's definition, and more importantly, to her *self*-definition. Individual rights protection always also means protection of collective identities. On the other hand, defenders of an anti-subordination perspective also feel concerned about the potentially negative effects that affirmative action can have on people belonging to minority groups. See Balkin and Siegel (n 158) especially 28 and 32 and Siegel (n 94) 1477 and 1533. See generally R Primus, 'Equal Protection and Disparate Impact: Round Three' (2003) 117 *Harvard Law Review* 494, 554.

by the European Court of Justice when dealing with the issue.[165] Although the discourse is structured in slightly different terms, the lines of argument resemble those applied in EU cases. Most clearly, the tension between an individual and a collective understanding of the right to equality are featured in the same way as in Europe. But the choice between intense or intermediate scrutiny can also be conceptualised in terms of the tensions expounded at the beginning of this chapter. Strict scrutiny is an expression of a formal conception of the law as well as of a conception that requires law to be neutral. It allows for the acceptance of fewer arguments capable of justifying affirmative action. Due to this greater argumentative burden, it becomes more difficult to justify why differential treatment should be allowed in one instance whilst it is strictly forbidden in the other. Intermediate scrutiny with its approval of an extended range of justifications is consequently an expression not only of a substantive notion of equality but also of a conception of law as a medium for social change. In contrast to strict scrutiny review, it allows for consideration of more arguments in favour of differential treatment. It is therefore easier for courts to articulate the wider beneficial social effects of affirmative action when applying intermediate instead of strict scrutiny.

Given that these tensions also exist in US equality adjudication, that the convictions underlying the colour-blindness and the anti-subordination approach are so far apart, and that the Supreme Court has struggled for decades to definitely embrace one view over the other, the intermediate position plays a crucial role. Opinions reconciling the competing visions most coherently gained acceptance. To take Justice Powell's opinion in the *Bakke* case as an example, it left sufficient room for affirmative action whilst imposing strict enough restrictions on such procedures to ensure respect for individual situations. Furthermore, strict scrutiny prevailed as the testing standard to be applied in race conscious affirmative action only because the Court stressed that this does not mean fatal in fact, proving this point by upholding the admission scheme of the University of Michigan Law School under strict scrutiny in *Grutter*.

This existence of a position mediating between colour-blindness and anti-subordination has led analysts of the case law to reach the conclusion that the classically described dichotomy is overstated and ought to be replaced by tripartite division. Under this new conceptualisation, the additional position is defined as the 'anti-balkanization' approach.[166] It argues that the American case law on equal protection needs to be understood as prohibiting differentiations amongst minority and majority groups that disturb social cohesion.[167] To explain the approach in greater detail, Siegel wrote on anti-balkanisation and differentiation on grounds of race:

[165] See, eg S Foster, 'Difference and Equality: A Critical Assessment of the Concept of "Diversity"' (1993) *Wisconsin Law Review* 105, 147 ff.

[166] Siegel (n 98) 1281. See further Suk (n 159) 235 f, who argues that the anti-balkanisation approach is of consequentialist nature.

[167] ibid, 1281 and 1300 ff.

> Because Justices reasoning from an antibalkanization perspective understand that pervasive racial stratification can engender anomie and leave some groups feeling like outsiders or nonparticipants, the Justices permit and sometimes encourage government to act in ways that promote racial integration … Because Justices reasoning from an antibalkanization perspective understand that interventions promoting racial integration can become a locus of racial conflict, they insist that race-conscious interventions undertaken for compelling public-regarding purposes must nonetheless anticipate and endeavour to ameliorate race-conscious resentments.[168]

Discrimination will be considered wrong, if it makes people feel excluded due to their race, gender or other characteristics. However, it will be viewed as legal if the intention behind it is 'benign' (in the sense that it aims to ameliorate the situation of traditionally discriminated groups) and its execution does not convey a feeling of inferiority on anyone. Assessing whether it defends an individualist or rather a collectivist understanding of equality, I would argue that it does a bit of both. On the one hand, it is grounded on a group-based conception of equality because it sees social stratification along the lines of membership as the prime evil of discrimination. In line with this conviction, the approach does not value individualism for individualism's sake.[169] On the other hand, it shows concern for the situation of the individual complainant, who has experienced disadvantages due to affirmative action. Phrased in terms of the anti-subordination–anti-classification divide, the approach combines elements of both perspectives, since it is sociologically embedded as the former and shows the concern for the individual complainant of the latter.[170]

Moreover, not only does it achieve the above mentioned combination but also includes aspects of institutional comparison in its framework. If one takes the reasoning to its natural conclusion judges should intervene if they have reason to believe that a decision of differential treatment has been taken with insufficient inclusion of all stakeholders involved. In the review of equality cases, courts shall grant greater discretion to institutions that have succeeded in achieving a high level of inclusion of all affected groups. Conversely, if institutions have been exclusionary in their decision making and made people feel like outsiders, courts shall become more active in substituting such institutions' decisions for their own.

Yet, just as with conceptions of anti-classification and anti-subordination, one needs to be aware of difficulties that come with embracing the notion of anti-balkanisation. The approach is somewhat problematic in its subjectivity. The conception holds that discrimination should only be forbidden if it brings about citizens' heightened racial consciousness and makes people feel like 'nonparticipants'. For affirmative action cases before the Supreme Court, this means that each measure would have had to be judged illegal because in each instance there was

[168] ibid, 1300.
[169] ibid, 1282.
[170] ibid, 1300 f.

a claimant who felt aggrieved and excluded enough to file a lawsuit. The Justices would only be able to consider affirmative action to be in accordance with American anti-discrimination law, if they examined whether a claimant could *justifiably* have this sentiment of exclusion. Such move would merely shift the assessment of differential treatment to be justified or not to a different point in the equality review.[171] This last point of critique should not cast doubt on the benefits of the concept. The approach is highly valuable in terms of depicting and scrutinising the affirmative action debate, as it seeks to overcome the stale division between anti-subordination and colour-blindness approaches.

III. TRANSLATING THE AMERICAN EXPERIENCE TO THE EUROPEAN DEBATE

With this description of the American debate in mind the question interesting to ask is: how far can such a mediating principle be detected in the case law of the European Court of affirmative action or be made applicable to the Union's anti-discrimination law?

A. The Mediating Principle in European Union Affirmative Action Case Law

It is probably best to start the enquiry by recalling that affirmative action adjudication is taking place within a state of conceptual tensions. In the United States, the Supreme Court has been confronted with finding a line between individualist and collectivist, formal and substantial, conservative and progressive readings of the right to equality. In the European Union, the European Court of Justice sees itself challenged with these same choices. The way in which it has sought to work with these tensions shall briefly be recalled.

Starting with *Kalanke*, the judges based their decision considerably on their interpretation of the concept of equality of opportunity. In doing so, they relied on a mediating notion of equality, located somewhere between its formal and substantive conception. Consequently, one may argue, the Court followed neither the approach that limited its reference to 'equality before the law' nor one that pursued the aim of equal gender representation even at the cost of individual discrimination.

In *Marschall*—the second case before the Court which concerned affirmative action schemes—the judges employed a different technique to come to terms with the tensions characterising the subject matter. To recall, the decision held

[171] Siegel points out a further problematic aspect herself. She argues that the Justices' opinions, which can be read as statements of the anti-balkanisation approach, need to establish more 'clearly … how antibalkanization is connected to equality' (ibid, 1351).

that the affirmative action scheme of Nordrhein-Westphalen was in accordance with European equality law, because of a savings clause ensuring that it was still possible to grant preference to male competitors in exceptional circumstances. In its grounds, the Court stressed the importance of equality as an individual right, whilst acknowledging the highly reputable aim of the affirmative action legislation in question. It managed to address both conceptions without giving an impression of incoherence by modifying the testing standard of its equality review in a by now familiar fashion. The judges replaced the question of whether there were 'such differences between the men and women applying for the promotion that they justified the preferential treatment of the female candidates' with the question whether the measure was 'proportional in light of the aim of furthering women's representation on the workplace'.[172] This use of a proportionality analysis allowed the Court to reason in such a way as to take adequate notice of the mitigating measures included in the affirmative action scheme. It could argue that the scheme was proportional *strictu sensu*, because it offered enough flexibility to take into account that women's preferential treatment can at times excessively burden male co-applicants. Under a comparative testing it would have been difficult to factor in these deliberations.[173]

In *Badeck*, the Court's line of argumentation was divided. With respect to the quota regime for hiring and promotion under review, it followed the guidelines it developed in *Marschall*. However with regard to the promotion scheme for professional training, the judges relied once more to a greater extent on the conception of equality of opportunity.

Abrahamsson, the fourth case that was discussed in greater detail, is also characterised by an attempt to square the competing visions. Again, the Court set out to strike a balance between outlawing measures designed to promote women and having individual men bear the costs for granting such a preference. This time, the judges went further than in their previous decisions in their acceptance of affirmative action. As explained above in greater detail the specific measure was found to be contrary to EU law because it did not allow for sufficient consideration of the individual situations of applicants. Notwithstanding this, the Court also indicated that it was generally open to the idea of finding affirmative action for women to be legal, even in a situation where a female job candidate was less qualified than her male competitors.[174] Consequently, the Court accepted the potential of affirmative action legislation to counter deep-seeded discrimination against women as

[172] For this reason, Schiek perceives the *Marschall* decision as a judgment that 'cannot be reconciled with the … approach to equal treatment as a symmetric right,' Schiek (n 39) 155. In full, Schiek states that the judgment 'cannot be reconciled with the *formal* approach to equal treatment as a symmetric right' (emphasis added). It is correct that formal equality coincided with a symmetric vision of the right. However, this statement seems to imply a juxtaposition with the substantial equality as an asymmetric right. For reasons explained above, see n 30, this need not be the case.

[173] After all, the savings clause did not change the elementary distinction in treatment between male and female applicants.

[174] See *Abrahamsson* (n 68) para 62.

a group whilst at the same time still stressing the importance of equality as an individual right.

To summarise, the European Court of Justice has reached its decisions on affirmative action by constantly juggling between the three tensions laid out at the beginning of the chapter.[175] It has striven to mediate between equality's formal with its substantial reading, its individualist with its collectivist understanding, its affirming with its transformative interpretation and to reconcile all these positions. This claiming of the middle ground comes close to the anti-balkanisation approach suggested in the American debate. In a comparable fashion to the developments in American constitutional law, the European Court of Justice interprets the right to equal treatment in a manner that allows for affirmative action whilst remaining with the perspective required by an individualist notion of equality. In particular, the concern for an individual assessment in hiring decisions plays a prominent part in both jurisdictions. In the United States, it is expressed by the fact that minority status may be taken into account in recruitment procedures only as a 'plus factor' alongside other features that are unrelated to status. Within European law, it is articulated by the reliance on soft quota mechanisms and savings clauses in order to find affirmative action compatible with the general principle of equality.

B. Affirmative versus Transformative

Despite (or because of) the judiciary's efforts to do justice to both the traditional and the progressive understanding of equality, the fact remains that decisions by the European Court of Justice on affirmative action are often objected to as going beyond the letter of equality laws or criticised for falling short of realising equality.[176] Looking at the fervour of the debate on mandatory quotas for women on boards, one sees that the opposition between these two standpoints informs the dispute surrounding affirmative action in Europe up to the present day. For reasons of simplification, I will refer to these opposing points of view in the following as the 'conservative' versus the 'progressive'.[177]

This division is problematic in that both approaches leave little room for factoring in or simply addressing the motives of the other party. Adherents to the conservative perception of equality are often reluctant to admit that granting women the same rights as men has had little success in increasing their

[175] Shaw offers an alternative account for the Court's moves. She states that the European Court of Justice is meandering between its 'legal and [its] political role in its case law on gender equality', see J Shaw, 'Gender and the Court of Justice' in G de Búrca and JHH Weiler (eds), *The European Court of Justice* (Oxford, Oxford University Press, 2001) 87.

[176] See s I. For the second stance see further eg A Brzezińska, 'Gender Equality in the Case Law of the European Court of Justice' (2009) IES Working Paper 2/2009, especially 6, 17, www.ies.be/files/IES%20Working%20paper%202_2009%20Agata%20Brzezin%CC%81ska.pdf.

[177] I thereby apply the denomination by Siegel (n 98) 1282.

representation in the workplace. They seem to recognise only insufficiently that discriminatory practices run deep within society and may call for greater action to overcome them. Yet defenders of a more progressive notion of equality as well have made little effort to include the concerns of people with a more conservative understanding of equality. At times, they show little willingness to address the self-contradictory nature of affirmative action.[178] Employing discrimination in order to combat discrimination is simply seen as a necessary means to achieve the aim of greater equality and it is maintained that individual hardship suffered by some men must simply be accepted. As a result, observers of the debate are left with the feeling that the two camps talk past each other.

A possible explanation for this impression is that the opposing arguments do indeed have their origins in different strands of reasoning. Conservatives like to stay within the realms of the existing legal framework, whereas progressives want to overcome exactly these structures. In the context of affirmative action, the conservative impression of the 'existing legal framework' is informed by two factors in particular. First it relies on an understanding of the equality guarantee as equality before the law (only). Second there is the principle that hiring decisions should be based strictly on assessments of merit. For conservatives, this means that they may consider preferential treatment of women in the workplace legal, as long as at least one of the two conditions is met: only women can perform the job adequately[179] or the scheme does not supplant the principle of hiring persons according to their merit. The thinking of progressives, on the other hand, is not restricted by such concerns. The main reason for this is that their position on affirmative action is commonly informed by feminist theory. With it goes a broader critique aiming specifically against traditional, man-made interpretations of law and holds that our legal frameworks do not take the position of women adequately into account.[180] 'Equality' and 'merit' have been given their meaning by men and their traditional conceptions disadvantage women by neglecting their social roles.[181] Therefore, feminist theory advocates a more significant change in thinking: law itself ought to be newly conceptualised in order to abolish entrenched discrimination.

Fraser expressed this distinction eloquently, when she referred to 'two broad approaches to remedying injustice',[182] which she labelled 'affirmative' and 'transformative'. She wrote:

> By affirmative remedies for injustice I mean remedies aimed at correcting inequitable outcomes of social arrangements without disturbing the underlying framework that

[178] See N Fraser, *Justice Interruptus. Critical Reflection on the 'Postsocialist' Condition* (New York, Routledge, 1997) 25.

[179] This 'derogation' from the requirement of equal treatment is regularly featured in provisions as *lege lata*, see, eg Art 1(6) of Dir 2002/73/EC.

[180] The works by C MacKinnon, such as *Toward a Feminist Theory of the State* (Cambridge, Harvard University Press, 1989) are pioneer works for the field of feminist legal theory.

[181] See generally A Somek, *Engineering Equality. An Essay on European Anti-Discrimination Law* (Oxford, Oxford University Press, 2011) 162 and 174 with further references.

[182] Fraser (n 178) 23.

generates them. By transformative remedies, in contrast, I mean remedies aimed at correcting inequitable outcomes precisely by restructuring the underlying generative framework.[183]

Applied to the affirmative action debate, conservatives pursue an 'affirmative' approach and progressives a 'transformative' approach. The first group can accept actions to improve representation of women at the workplace, as long as these do not put the underlying rationale of the regulatory scheme into question. The second group, however, accepts endeavours that go beyond the restraints of merit based assessments, thereby also changing the conception of equal treatment. Consequently and as the last paragraphs tried to show, one can see that the talking past each other is partially a result of the 'affirmative'–'transformative' divide. Whereas the latter approach includes a desire to restructure a given social framework, the former seeks to work within its existing conditions.

However, there might be another factor driving the discourse on both sides: *who* restructures and *whose* framework is the object of the restructuring is of key importance. As I will develop in the following section, institutional comparison can help examine the division in approaches on affirmative action and disclose some of the considerations that are left under-articulated in judicial reasoning on the topic. Once again, the institutions involved in the decision making process become the focus of attention. To what extent is the European Court of Justice the appropriate actor to rule on the legality of affirmative action? And when should it substitute a reading of equality, given by the legislature of a Member State or the European Union, for its own interpretation of the principle? When investigating these issues, we return to analysing the role of institutional choice in equality reasoning, more particular, in affirmative action adjudication.

IV. COMPARATIVE INSTITUTIONAL ANALYSIS OF AFFIRMATIVE ACTION

To approach the issue from a slightly different angle, when one looks at the length of and the intensity of the debate on affirmative action it becomes evident that under current circumstances, reasonable people are unlikely to agree any time soon on its correct handling. With valid arguments on both sides, it is safe to say that neither conservatives nor progressives will abandon their position in the near future. The tensions characterising affirmative action law will remain.

In light of these findings, this book claims that comparative institutional analysis offers an alternative perspective on the European affirmative action debate. As I will explain in the remaining part of this chapter, the case law by the European Court of Justice on goals and quotas becomes more understandable if it is conceptualised not so much in terms of competing conceptions of equality, but rather in terms of the strengths and weaknesses of the institutions holding these

[183] ibid.

different opinions. In this exercise, the analytical scheme devised by Komesar will again serve as model for my examination. The next paragraphs are therefore a comparative assessment of the ability to insure adequate interest representation as well as to deal with numbers and complexity of affirmative action of the European Court of Justice vis-à-vis that of the European political process, Member State legislatures or national constitutional courts.

A. Ely's Influence

It should be pointed out that my analysis is not the first of its kind. John Hart Ely's paper 'The Constitutionality of Reverse Racial Discrimination' and seminal piece 'Democracy and Distrust'[184] led the way for institutional approaches towards affirmative action jurisprudence. In his article published in 1974 ('The Constitutionality of Reverse Racial Discrimination'), Ely set out to scrutinise the United States Supreme Court case law on race conscious action with respect to the Black minority from an institutional point of view. Building upon this work, his later and more comprehensive book on American constitutional law and institutional choice dedicates a section to an examination of the Court's affirmative action adjudication in *Bakke*. As Ely describes in these analyses, an interpretation of the constitution guided by institutional considerations can provide a framework for coherently addressing the issue of affirmative action. He further claimed that 'a difficult moral question does not necessarily generate a difficult constitutional question'.[185]

Within this contextualisation, treating discrimination of Whites differently from discrimination of Blacks is consistent with a singular conception of the American equal treatment guarantee. His main argument is that we should show little concern if a majority opts to grant preference or advantages to a minority because 'it is not "suspect" in a constitutional sense for a majority, any majority, to discriminate against itself'.[186] In institutional terms, this means that there is no misrepresentation of interests that should trigger strict scrutiny review by the courts. Whereas discrimination cases are usually defined by the imposition of burden and hardship on a minority by the majority, affirmative action cases that aim at privileging one or multiple racial minorities function differently because the majority opted to place a discriminatory burden on itself. In greater detail, he writes:

> When the group that controls the decision making process classifies so as to advantage a minority and disadvantage itself, the reasons for being unusually suspicious, and,

[184] JH Ely, 'The Constitutionality of Reverse Racial Discrimination' (1974) 41 *University of Chicago Law Review* 723; ibid (n 90). Further institutional analyses are by B Doherty, 'Creative Advocacy in Defense of Affirmative Action: A Comparative Institutional Analysis of Proposition 209' (1999) *Wisconsin Law Review* 91 and Schwartz (n 13) 657. Further agreeing W Sadurski, *Equality and Legitimacy* (Oxford, Oxford University Press, 2008) 140.

[185] Ely (n 90) 170.

[186] Ely (n 184) 727.

> consequently, employing a stringent brand of review are lacking. A White majority is unlikely to disadvantage itself for reasons of racial prejudice; nor is it likely to be tempted to either underestimate the needs and deserts of Whites relative to those of others, or to overestimate the costs of devising an alternative classification that would extend to certain Whites the advantages generally extended to Blacks.[187]

In the United States, Ely's theory has been subject to criticism. To take the Supreme Court's decision in *Schuette* as an example, there the majority opinion put an institutional reading of American equality law in question. The Court held that the political process theory[188] does not apply to reversals of affirmative action measures. To recall, that theory builds upon an institutional reading of equality law because it states that strict scrutiny review must be performed when the authority to make decisions on measures designed to benefit minorities is moved from one institution to another. Consequently, the limitation of its application, which the majority Justices undertook in *Schuette*, was also an expression of their reluctance towards institutional readings of equality law. This becomes even more evident when one looks at their reasons for dismissing the political process theory. They argued that the theory would require the Court to determine a person's interests in terms of his belonging to a certain stakeholder group and thus—with respect to affirmative action—according to racial stereotypes.[189]

However, this argumentation denies the realities of discrimination, as Justice Sotomayor forcefully establishes in her dissent. An individual belonging to a minority is discriminated against because he is part of that minority.[190] Further, it is in certain instances easy to establish the group interest of a minority: for example, the interest not to be discriminated against and to have equal access to educational facilities.[191] An institutionally informed reading of equality, such as the one offered by Ely or expressed in the political process theory, at least offers ways to grasp the comprehensive nature of discrimination. So although Ely's work has met dissent, this analysis maintains that one can make use of his work for the purpose of scrutinising EU equality law. However, I would like to highlight three differences between my examination and Ely's analysis before applying the comparative

[187] ibid, 735.

[188] The political process theory states that any state action that assigns to a different level of government decision making authority over a policy primarily inuring to the benefit of the minority must be subject to strict scrutiny review.

[189] *Schuette v Calition to Defend Affirmative Action, Integration, and Immigrant Rights and Fight for Equality By Any Means Necessary (BAMN)* 134 S Ct 1623 (2014), at 1634 f.

[190] ibid, at 1672. In this respect, Sabbagh writes that 'as a practical matter' it 'is simply impossible' to only take an applicant's individuality into account, see Sabbagh (n 127) 57. Speaking of the falseness of the colour-blind approach Sadurski (n 184) 114.

[191] What is meant by 'equal access'—whether this calls for strictly merit-based assessment or for a certain compensation of fewer opportunities in the past—is then again predetermined by one's own understanding of the equality guarantee; see D'Alessio (n 126) 119 f.; G Spann, 'Proposition 209' (1997) 47 *Duke Law Journal* 187, 261.

institutional choice framework to decisions by the European Court of Justice on gender quotas and goals.

A first difference is a difference in approach. As has been established in chapter 3, this discussion follows closely the framework devised by Komesar. The author explicates in *Imperfect Alternatives* that Ely's work is single institutional analysis whereas—as the name already reveals—comparative institutional analysis is comparative in nature.[192] Ely focuses on the shortcoming of the political process that has come to be described as the 'tyranny of the majority'. However, as Komesar mentions, not only does a further political malfunction in the form of special interest legislation need to be confronted but also deficits in the working procedures of courts need to be taken into account.[193] Courts face problems of numbers and complexity parallel to those of the political process when making decisions. They may not be apt to deal with cases that involve many actors or have far reaching effects into areas of life that cannot be easily foreseen at the time of decision making. In this respect, comparative institutional analysis goes further than Ely's approach because it weighs the political and adjudicative processes' strengths and weaknesses against each other.

The second and third differences concern the object of study. This analysis deals with European Union law. Even though Ely's work on the American system already factored in that decision making power is not only horizontally but also vertically divided between the federal level and the States, an examination of the handling of affirmative action in Europe needs to pay attention to the peculiarities of the division of power in the European Union. Furthermore and more importantly, the differing situation of Blacks in America—that formed the starting point of Ely's investigation in 'The Constitutionality of Reverse Racial Discrimination' — and women in Europe with regard to affirmative action needs to be taken into account. To recall, Ely considered that courts should not object to affirmative action schemes on grounds of race, because there were no grounds of suspicion if a majority voluntarily discriminated against itself in order to privilege members of a minority. However we cannot transfer this idea to affirmative action on grounds of gender without making some adaptations.[194] As pointed out above, women are not a numerically underrepresented group. To the contrary, they form the majority of people. Under ideal conditions of the institutional choice model, this would imply that women were in a position to assert their claims. In addition, it would mean that the reason for considering affirmative action as unsuspicious is absent in the case of preferential treatment of women. As I will argue in the following, one does not have to go so far as to deny any parallels between the institutional choice assessment of affirmative action on grounds of race and that

[192] For Komesar's discussion on the work of Ely, see N Komesar, *Imperfect Alternatives: Choosing Institutions in Law, Economics, and Public Policy* (Chicago, University of Chicago Press, 1994) 197 ff.

[193] It needs to be mentioned that Ely's work also features certain comparative elements, see, eg ibid (n 90) 103 or 168.

[194] Analysing this aspect, ibid, 164 ff.

on grounds of sex. My claim is rather that though women do not constitute a minority there is also a variant of political malfunction at play in their case. Due to developed and entrenched structures they are barred from actualising their potential to influence decision making. In this respect, they resemble a group, which Komesar refers to as the 'dormant majority'.[195] The latter group is characterised by the fact that its members are in a position to exercise power, but abstain from doing so as the individual member's stakes are too low to engage in the costly enterprise of influencing decision making. Women can best be understood not as a dormant, but as a 'benumbed majority'. Social habitus and tradition have put them in a position where they cannot make their voice as powerfully heard as their number would suggest, conditions that are only slowly changing.[196]

Nevertheless, even if we make room for these differences, affirmative action for Blacks and women share those features that drive Ely's analysis. First, both groups have under normal conditions suffered from the effects of political malfunction. This malfunction is exceptionally inoperative in preferential treatment schemes on their behalf. Second, both situations entail a politically powerful social group that opts for its own discrimination.

B. The Assessment

If we now look at European affirmative action adjudication with the modifications of Ely's model in mind, the following picture emerges. Alongside the European Court of Justice, national constitutional courts as well as the European and Member State political processes are in a position to make decisions on the issue. Evidence of political malfunction when legislatures decided to grant women preferential treatment would speak in favour of judicial intervention. However, as was mentioned above, the malfunction normally at play in legislation discriminating on grounds of gender is absent in the case of affirmative action. Instead, a political process dominated by men chooses to break up discriminatory structures by making it legally binding to grant preference to women in hiring and promotion. Such functioning of the political process—or at least the lack of severe malfunctioning—argues for judicial restraint in the review of affirmative action cases. Under these circumstances, judges should refrain from strict scrutiny and allow for a number of justifications of affirmative action. Simply put, if those in power decide to discriminate against themselves, they should be allowed to do so.

Some may object to this argumentation along the following lines: those in power may well not be the ones affected by affirmative action. Instead the group we classify as men is itself comprised of multiple entities and could abuse such

[195] On this point, see N Komesar, *Law's Limits* (Cambridge, Cambridge University Press, 2001) eg 62 f.

[196] See Ely (n 90) 165.

schemes in order to discriminate against one of its own sub-groups.[197] Places that might have been filled with men of migrant background now go to upper class girls. The possibility of less powerful groups being pitted against each other by means of affirmative action is certainly a danger of which we should be aware. However, the situation needs to be examined on an individual case basis.

Looking at the schemes that came under review by the European Court of Justice, I cannot detect such a burdened sub-group. The affected claimants brought action against affirmative action because they felt discriminated against on grounds of their gender. Their argumentation was aimed at establishing sex based discrimination and no mention was made of them being discriminated against on any grounds other than their sex. In other words, they did not identify themselves as being members of a specifically targeted sub-group of men. Further, persons who could be subjected to disadvantageous treatment under the reviewed schemes were members of a broadly defined group of male government employees. One cannot discern a minority within the majority—defined by class, race, religious or other status—that was particularly likely to be affected.

Therefore, the general picture of decisions on affirmative action for women in Europe is that severe malfunction of the political processes cannot be detected. Interest representation works adequately within the Member States opting for preferential treatment. As long as this is the case, respective decisions should be left to the discretion of the Member States and be taken at the national level. The European Court of Justice should not stand in the way of such developments.

Nevertheless, as far as promotion of affirmative action is concerned, a stronger role for the European institutions would lend itself as an option under the following scenario. If a trend was to be detected whereby quotas and goals were introduced in numerous Member States, European decision makers could play a more active role in allowing for such promotional efforts to take place in those Member States still hesitant in their introduction.[198]

Besides, changing circumstances may call for increased judicial intervention in the future. Gender roles have been changing quickly over the last number of decades. It is imaginable, not to mention desirable, that men and women will reach a status of true equality. In the event that women will no longer be a 'benumbed majority'—forced by antiquated perceptions of their role in society into a position inferior to men—our assessment of interest representation needs to change. Should they no longer be a group that is underrepresented in political decision making, one must see affirmative actions burdening male individuals in a more critical light.

[197] See for a discussion of this point of view Ely (n 184) 736 f. Also mentioned by Schwartz (n 13) 670.

[198] European Commission, proposal for a Directive of the European Parliament and of the Council on Improving the gender balance among non-executive directors of companies listed on stock exchanges and related measures, COM(2012)0614 final is an expression of such development.

However, in order to determine the function comparative institutional analysis ideally ascribes to the Luxembourg Court in affirmative action cases, one must not only examine whether the political decision-making process has malfunctioned, but also investigate whether the Court is an adequate alternative in terms of scale and competence. Numbers and complexity of affirmative action would have to be of such nature that the judges were able to deal with them. To recall, the comparative institutional model argues that courts suffer more under growing numbers than the political process.[199] Their organisational structure and limited resources have the effect of making them less suited (or more unsuited) actors to balance the diverse interests of multiple stakeholders. Starting with numbers, we can see that the Court of Justice is already in a position where quite specific inquiries on affirmative action schemes reach its docket. In *Abrahamsson*, a Swedish promotion regulation for filling university posts was under review. In *Kalanke*, it was the promotion scheme for civil servants in the city of Bremen. As it is common practice, the judges set out to establish criteria which ought to be met by affirmative actions in order to be in accordance with European Union law. But the multitude of conceivable programmes has posed difficulties for the Court in determining comprehensive criteria without closing off the possibility of future developments in the field.

Regarding complexity, there is one point at which the European Court of Justice has an advantage over other institutions in Europe to rule on affirmative action. It can raise concerns about the potential negative effects of affirmative action, in the event that a thus far dormant majority becomes active, more easily than the national or supranational legislature. The reason for this is that the Court will be more secluded from the pressures being exerted.[200] Should circumstances change for the benefit of women (as outlined above) judges will be in a more comfortable position than politicians to address the risk of entrenching stereotypes within society that comes with preferential treatment for women.[201] The introduction of affirmative action can have negative effects for the women working in the immediate context of its enforcement as well as for society as a whole.[202] As for women on the job, they are often confronted with the stigma of being the 'quota-woman', who owes her position solely to her sex. Regarding the social component, affirmative action helps to maintain sex based differentiation, that is to say exactly the kind of classification one thought of as already overcome. It makes a person's sexual status relevant—indeed the decisive factor—in hiring and promotion procedures, instead of rendering it meaningless.[203] Furthermore, judges can engage with the

[199] Komesar's statement in *Law's Limits* (n 195) 158 could be interpreted this way. 'As numbers and complexity continue to grow, simple rules are replaced by flexible standards and judicial balancing. Judicial activity increases, but judicial protections and judicial activism may decrease'.

[200] Of course, this is not to be understood as an attack on political discourse. Similar Ely (n 90) 103.

[201] ibid.

[202] Listing the utilitarian arguments against affirmative action, Rosenfeld (n 35) 108 ff; see also on the point Peters (n 15) 187.

[203] Rosenfeld (n 35) 109.

concerns that surround the 'effectiveness' of affirmative action for women. There have been studies conducted for the private sector that show that a larger number of women in leading positions are beneficial to a company's performance.[204] However other investigations do indicate that a firm's reputation decreases due to the introduction of quotas and that the quality of work may suffer because positions are not filled with the most competent applicants.[205] (The last point, however, fails to apply to instances of strict quota adaptation.) Against this background, the Court of Justice can potentially show its competence to balance competing arguments under the Socratic method.[206]

Besides, the findings of chapter 3, that the judiciary's strength is its capacity to perform interpretive evaluations, should be kept in mind. Judges are trained in assessing legal claims and can deploy their abilities in deciding on the legality of affirmative action schemes. It is within their expertise to examine whether constitutional guarantees have been violated and whether these violations may be justified. The deliberative processes of Courts, distinct from those of the political process, enable judges to look at the issue from another perspective; ideally one that is more in tune with egalitarian theory.

On the other hand, the description of European Union and American case law on affirmative action has hopefully demonstrated what an intricate undertaking it is to design and implement affirmative action schemes. It is a complex exercise to deploy law as a tool for social engineering and the reach of its effects are not easy to predict. Consequently, in terms of complexity, it is advisable for judges to exercise judicial restraint when assessing affirmative action and to move the debate forward only in those instances, where severe disregard of individual rights becomes obvious.[207]

Looking at *Kalanke*, the first case in which the Court of Justice pronounced on the issue, one cannot detect that the judges were concerned about taking on a more reserved role compared to that of other institutions. Instead, they were keen to establish a considerable sphere of influence for themselves on matters of affirmative action. Only in the following decisions did the judges begin exercising greater self-restraint without going as far as exercising low scrutiny. Their way to do so was twofold: they not only engaged in non-comparative equality testing but also formulated requirements that affirmative action schemes needed to fulfil in order to be held compatible with European Union law.[208]

[204] McKinsey, 'Women Matter—Gender Diversity, a Corporate Performance Driver', www.raeng.org.uk/publications/other/women-matter-oct-2007, 12 ff.

[205] 'The Wrong Way to Promote Women' *The Economist* (London, 23 July 2011) 9 f and 'Still Lonely at the Top', ibid (London, 23 July 2011) 54 ff.

[206] See generally M Kumm, 'Institutionalising Socratic Contestation: The Rationalist Human Rights Paradigm, Legitimate Authority and the Point of Judicial Review' (2007) 1 *European Journal of Legal Studies* 1.

[207] Mancini and O'Leary (n 33) 336.

[208] Similar, Caruso (n 7) 334 and 350. Evaluating the Court's review as proportionality analysis, eg S Pager, 'Strictness and Subsidiarity: An Institutional Perspective on Affirmative Action at the

The Court performed means-ends analysis of quotas and goals instead of a strict comparison between the situation of those men disadvantaged by affirmative action and the women benefiting from it. It examined the potential of affirmative action schemes to bring about social change as well as to contribute to women's emancipation and then contrasted these aspects against the schemes' negative effects on men. Further, it stipulated in its case law that one important condition for holding an affirmative action scheme legal was its capacity to take into account individual situations through hardship clauses. By doing so, it averted the danger highlighted above that gender quotas and goals can potentially operate at the expense of men who are members of disadvantaged groups such as racial minorities. By making an individual assessment of all candidates in job decisions a mandatory element of affirmative action, it ensured heightened control in those instances, in which there is a risk that the interests of male subgroups are underrepresented.

The interpretive paradigm can hardly capture these moves by the European Court of Justice. Yet, the conclusion we reach from this observation is not that the Court's adjudication on affirmative action is misguided or lacking in theoretical substantiation. Instead, it shows that the interpretive account is too limited in its vision to explain the background considerations driving affirmative action reasoning. 'Courts regularly consider the constraints of their institutional position in the course of crafting doctrine'[209] and, as institutional comparativists would add, the constraints of alternative decision makers. Consequently, an institutional assessment helps us understand and scrutinise the case law before us. In this respect, it would be wrong to assume that comparative institutional analysis can explain everything about European affirmative action adjudication. However, as the preceding analysis reveals, the approach provides us with an alternative conceptualisation of the issues before the European Court of Justice and commentators when debating affirmative action. This institutional choice conceptualisation offers a framework in which to navigate between equality as a group right and equality as an individual right, between formal equality and substantive equality, and, last but not least, between equality law as neutral and equality law as an emancipatory tool.

European Court of Justice' (2003) 26 *Boston College International and Comparative Law Review* 35, 60 ff.

Analysing the *Marschall* decision, Charpentier writes that the requirements of quota schemes have been formulated in such a way that

> the words of the provison literally denote affirmative action's irreducibility to the legal concepts that attempt to define it, or, in other words, the tension and the necessary convergence of the sphere of the legal and the sphere of the cultural and political which affirmative action itself exemplifies (Charpentier (n 15) 187).

Though not assuming an institutional perspective, he also highlights that the Court of Justice's adjudication on affirmative action cannot be explained in strictly interpretive terms.

[209] R Post and R Siegel, 'Equal Protection by Law: Federal Antidiscrimination Legislation After *Morrison* and *Kimel*' (2000) 110 *Yale Law Journal* 441, 467.

7

Conclusion

THE FIRST CHAPTER depicted the problem of human rights reasoning in the supranational context where different layers of interpretation and different actors at each level compete for the 'right' or at least the final right of interpretation. It then continued to examine this theme more particularly with respect to the reasoning on the EU general principle of equality. First, it illustrated what idea of equality lies at the core of political philosophy. In this exercise, I was looking for the egalitarian notions that should ideally inform the traditional human rights paradigm of interpretation. Next, the book turned to subjects of European equality review—different standards of scrutiny, permitted differentiation on grounds of nationality, reverse discrimination, affirmative action—that are difficult to explain solely by reference within the context of the prevailing framework. Their traditional interpretational account was deconstructed. Then, the case law on the respective issues was subjected to comparative institutional analysis, in order to show how this alternative conceptualisation can provide insights into the decision making process of courts and help us to better understand the functioning of equality review.

This last chapter now seeks to connect the findings developed in the case law analysis of chapters 3 to 6 with the larger themes of legal theory addressed at the outset of the examination. Its overall purpose is to address the question of how to define the relationship between interpretational rights reasoning and institutional reasoning. Different solutions will be suggested. In the end, I argue that equality doctrine needs to change in a way that can better reconcile interpretational and institutional reasoning. This can be achieved by a combined review of the objects and the subjects of comparison—by scrutinising not only the role of the compared, but also that of the comparator.

I. BREAKING DOWN THE DIVIDES

According to the traditional interpretive paradigm one can conceptualise equality in many different ways. Equality can be formal, substantive, economic or social; it can imply equal treatment or equality of results. All of these labels (and the many more left unmentioned in this short list) create a paradox. On the one hand, they are valuable devices to describe some of the pressing issues surrounding the general principle of equality. The variety of terms employed illustrates the intellectual richness of the principle. Equality can play a role in the most diverse settings, ranging from business life to the most personal affairs. It is only natural that one would seek to describe the concept in terms of particular adjectives in order to make it easily understandable and more fitting in specific contexts.[1] Furthermore, the different labels express that equality guarantees depend on other norms for their content[2] and contextualise them.

On the other hand, this multiplicity of labels reinforces the impression that depending on the context, different notions of equality are at work within European equality law. Egalitarian discourse seems to constantly demand from its participants and observers a choice in direction: either one follows a progressive reading of equality and focuses on its ability to create social change or one follows a traditional reading that mainly seeks to ensure equal application of laws. This perceived necessity to choose a particular direction turns into the belief that one theory alone cannot adequately explain the workings of the general principle of equality.

As this book aimed to demonstrate throughout its chapters, this alleged incoherence is a result of the limited perspective from which European equality law is viewed. The field's inconsistency is—even if not entirely eliminated—diminished if one looks at it from the additional point of view of comparative institutional analysis. To spin the argument further: the distinction commonly drawn between the substantial and the institutional facet of constitutional law, is—to say the least—overstated and has started to impede our understanding of the law instead of advancing it.[3] This is not to deny that constitutional judges and scholars are aware of the linkages between formal and substantive constitutional law and stress the fact that they ought to be considered in unison. Thus the German arbitrariness formula has been understood as a solution dressed in terms of competencies to the equality clause's conceptual openness.[4] But when and how such transcriptions of institutional conceptions into substantive constitutional law take place has seldom been subject to closer examination.[5] Moreover, it is common for judges at

[1] Amongst freedom rights, only the general freedom of action (*allgemeine Handlungsfreiheit*) has a comparable universality. However few Member States recognise it as a fundamental right and it has so far not been protected under European Union law.

[2] E Chemerinsky, 'In Defense of Equality: a Reply to Professor Westen' (1983) 81 *Michigan Law Review* 575, 578 f; L Osterloh and A Nußberger, 'Artikel 3' in M Sachs (ed), *Grundgesetz Kommentar* 7th edn (Munich, Beck, 2014) marginal no 5.

[3] Constitutional texts can in most cases be broken down into a substantial part dedicated to fundamental rights and an institutional part laying down a state's institutional set-up. But rather than stressing the interlinkages between the two segments, constitutional scholarship in the past has often exaggerated the partition and entrenched it in lawyers' minds. For example in German law schools it is common to teach constitutional law in two separate entities, namely *Grundrechte* (fundamental rights) and *Staatsrecht* (state law).

[4] Osterloh and Nußberger (n 2) marginal no 10; further C Starck, 'Artikel 3' in H von Mangoldt, F Klein and C Starck (eds), *Bonner Grundgesetzkommentar* 6th edn (Munich, Franz Vahlen, 2010) marginal no 12.

[5] Of course, notable exceptions are eg the aforementioned works by JH Ely, *Democracy and Distrust. A Theory of Judicial Review* (Cambridge, Harvard University Press, 1980) and G Leibholz, *Die Gleichheit vor dem Gesetz. Eine Studie auf rechtsvergleichender und rechtsphilosophischer Grundlage* (Berlin, Otto Liebmann, 1925).

the European Court of Justice to state that the legislature enjoys a wide margin of discretion in the design of laws. However, this statement is often made without subsequent reasoning showing a sufficient connection to it. Consequently, our understanding of the ways in which institutional considerations are translated and introduced into judicial reasoning can be expanded.

Some readers will not be convinced by the argument. They may reply that even if one accepts the proposition that equality law is shaped by institutional considerations, this still does not explain the incoherence of the principle's application. Assuming that institutional choices are the underlying causes for example for the choice of scrutiny in equality review, these decisions would follow uniform rules and clear patterns of judicial engagement should be detectable. If interpretive explanations and justifications are perceived as translations of institutional choices and do so in the entire field of equality law, shouldn't consistency prevail? To this question, I would respond that equality law is viewed as fragmented and incoherent because these translations have taken on a life of their own. They have been used and cited, without the users being aware of their institutional background. This 'non-reflective' usage has brought about decisions, in which their interpretive content is no longer in line with their institutional origins.

Let me explain this point with the help of two examples: the framing of the purely internal rule (or what is left of it)[6] and the conditions set for the acceptance of affirmative action schemes.[7] Looking at the purely internal rule, its translation of institutional considerations into a judicial formula is obvious. By stating that European provisions 'cannot ... be applied to situations which are wholly internal to a Member State, in other words, where there is no factor connecting them to any of the situations envisaged by Community law',[8] the judges at the European Court of Justice established a standard to delimitate their scope of review from that of national courts. At the time of its creation, the 'purely internal rule' proved to be a workable definition, since it succeeded in depicting the (then existing) limits of European Union law and power balance between the Union and its Member States. The fundamental freedoms had not yet developed into prohibitions that covered any restrictions on the freedom of movement,[9] internal market integration was less advanced than today and European citizenship was still an ideal for the distant future. However, due to the evolution of European law, the existence of shared competences and the changes in decision making power within the Union, the expression has lost much of its significance and is unable to depict the current allocation of decision making power in Europe.[10] It stands as a vestige of prior

[6] On that point, see ch 5.

[7] In greater detail, see ch 6.

[8] Case 175/78 *The Queen v Vera Ann Saunders* [1979] ECR 1129, para 11.

[9] With the notable exception of Art 34 TFEU; Case 8/74 *Procureur du Roi v Benoît and Gustave Dassonville* [1974] ECR 837.

[10] Similarly, O'Leary points out 'that the objectives and aims with respect to which [the Court] is now assessing the scope of application of EU law have altered substantially since its early decisions in

stages of development. Nevertheless, since the discussion on reverse discrimination is still about the contours of the purely internal rule, it lets the application of Union law look incoherent.

To present a second example, differentiation on grounds of sex was judged to be strictly prohibited[11] at a time when women were still actively discriminated against by the legal system, for example because it allocated to them the role of housewife.[12] In those instances, women were neither adequately represented when the laws were passed nor had the political power to overturn them, so that greater engagement by courts was adequate. Now, affirmative action programmes call for differentiation on grounds of sex in order to privilege women. The institutional argument that the judiciary should play a dominant role due to malfunction of the political process is therefore no longer evident. Yet, within interpretive (or substantive) constitutional law, the rationale has been established that *any* discrimination on grounds of sex was unconstitutional. As a consequence, the case law of constitutional courts appears to be incoherent in the event that judges start arguing that certain discriminations (affirmative action) are in accordance with the general principle of equality.

In the end, if there is one thing comparative institutional analysis to European equality law accomplishes, it is furthering our understanding of the subject matter by opening up an additional perspective for looking at it.

II. THE FOUR CONCEIVABLE RELATIONS BETWEEN EQUALITY REVIEW AND INSTITUTIONAL CHOICE

Over the last chapters, the European Court of Justice's adjudication on certain equality matters was deconstructed and reconceptualised by employing comparative institutional analysis. Through these reconstructions via the lens of comparative institutional analysis the thesis sought to critique European equality jurisprudence as well as show that there is more coherence to it than generally considered. So far, the goal has been to improve our understanding of the workings of this field of law. However the question that still needs to be addressed—the

Knoors and *Saunders*' (S O'Leary, 'The Past, Present and Future of the Purely Internal Rule in EU Law' in M Dougan, N Nic Shuibhne and E Spaventa (eds), *Modern Studies in European Law: Empowerment and Disempowerment of the European Citizen* (Oxford, Hart Publishing, 2012) 37, 56).

[11] One needs to note exceptions that continue to exist, such as Art 2(2) Dir 76/207/EEC in its consolidated version, which permits differentiations in labour relations, if 'by reason of their nature or the context in which they are carried out, the sex of the worker constitutes a determining factor'.

[12] Looking at the German experience, the Basic Law in its original 1949 version introduced the prohibition of discrimination between men and women (Art 3(2) Basic Law). Nevertheless, paras 1356 and 1357 BGB stipulated up to 1977 that in order to work women had to obtain the consent of their husbands and that the prime obligation of women was to fulfil their domestic duties; see M-A Grimme, *Die Entwicklung der Emanzipation der Frau on der Familiengeschichte bis zum Gleichberechtigungsgesetz 1957* (Frankfurt, Peter Lang, 2003) 142.

elephant in the room so to speak—is: what shall we make of the fact that institutional considerations are part and parcel of equality review?

Accordingly, the last part shall be dedicated to answering this inquiry. The following examination is not supposed to call into question the findings of the preceding chapters, but seeks to put the work into the broader picture of legal theory. In my opinion, no less than four different approaches present themselves as answers: *business as usual*, *rejection*, *embrace* and *adaptation*.

A. Business as Usual

A first option is to continue examining and discussing matters that concern the general principle of equality under the interpretive paradigm, whilst being aware of the institutional elements involved in their shaping. This way, one can employ the same review methods and language that has been used in the past to review equality cases. The big advantage of remaining within the interpretive paradigm is that it ensures continuity not only in equality adjudication, but also in the accompanying scholarly debate.

Critics of institutional choice will most likely argue that this is the most appropriate way to proceed. They will highlight that there is no need to alter European equality doctrine because the field of law can be explained in its own terms and has the ability to reproduce itself from within.[13] In line with the previously mentioned critique of comparative institutional analysis, they could state: 'Even if one acknowledges that institutional thinking forms equality law, the case law by the European Court of Justice and by national constitutional courts shows that those concerns are translated into judicial reasoning in a sensible way'. Therefore, the argument developed over the last chapters that institutional considerations become interpretational considerations could serve as prime justification for their position.

However, two points speak against upholding the status quo in European equality doctrine: the first refers back to the previously discussed aspect that misunderstanding persists if one continues to veil translations of institutional considerations. The more one stays within the interpretive paradigm, the less people will be aware of the institutional elements that shape the law. As is already the case the interpretive illusion will be perceived as the interpretive reality. Additionally concerns with regard to its legitimacy are heightened if European equality law continues to insufficiently reflect the fact that institutional considerations are at play. One parameter the law must be measured against is its intelligibility.[14] This requirement is not of minor importance, but at the base of the postulation that all

[13] See in general N Luhmann, *Das Recht der Gesellschaft* (Frankfurt, Suhrkamp, 1993) especially 38 ff.

[14] See generally A Burghart, *Die Pflicht zum guten Gesetz* (Berlin, Duncker und Humblot, 1996) 61 ff; J Lücke, 'Die Allgemeine Gesetzgebungsordnung' (2001) 16 *Zeitschrift für Gesetzgebung* 1, 7 ff;

democratic institutions ought to abide by the rules and obey the law.[15] If people are not able to identify the reasons that led to a certain judicial outcome, then these rulings fall short of meeting the standards set for decision making in democracies.[16] For these reasons, continuing to blur underlying institutional choices and to perform business as usual should be discarded.

B. Rejection

A second reaction is dismissing institutional considerations in judicial reasoning altogether. Opponents to institutional reasoning in law could argue the following: 'Just because one is able to interpret institutional choices into equality adjudication does not mean that we need to accept them as valid points'. In their opinion, the only acceptable form of legal reasoning is normative reasoning. Fundamental rights review ought to be performed in view of one objective, namely finding the 'right' normative answer to a legal problem. In the instance of equality adjudication, judges should reflect exclusively upon the differences between the compared persons in order to determine whether the differentiation in question is justified. Contemplation as regards general objectives pursued with the differentiation, as well as thoughts on the role of the legislature (which opted for the differentiation), would be left outside.

This second approach comes with one advantage over the option discussed above. It will be remembered that the principle of equality states in its most basic form that all persons deserve *equal* respect. It expresses that no person may be treated worse than any other, unless this differential treatment is justified. Furthermore, it embodies the *relational* side of fundamental rights and is comparative in nature.[17] Consequently, the only adequate question that one needs to pose in the context of equality is: do the differences between the persons compared justify their differential treatment?

However, as this thesis sought to illustrate, due to institutional considerations, equality review is influenced in such a way that questions on the aims of discrimination, as well as on the limited ability of courts to decide on certain egalitarian issues, appear in the tests developed for the principle.

By rejecting institutional considerations, equality review would be realigned with its egalitarian roots. The approach calls for an assessment of cases in light of

G Folke Schuppert, 'Gute Gesetzgebung. Bausteine einer kritischen Gesetzgebungslehre' (2003) 18 *Zeitschrift für Gesetzgebung* special edn 1, especially 8 and 11.

[15] Lücke (n 14) 8.

[16] See ibid.

[17] In this spirit, Somek argues that any account of European anti-discrimination law that fails to 'reconstruct the normative significance of anti-discrimination law from within', is bound to remain insufficient, A Somek, *Engineering Equality. An Essay on European Anti-Discrimination Law* (Oxford, Oxford University Press, 2011) 100.

the core content of equality and bars continued conflation of comparative equality assessments and non-comparative proportionality analysis (examinations as to a norm's *Sachgerechtigkeit*).[18] In other words, if judges at the European Court of Justice (or, for that matter, judges at Member State courts) followed this option, they could counter the criticism so poignantly phrased by Somek and alluded to at the very beginning of this inquiry: the approach would serve as a tool to address the normative deficiency attributed to European equality law by the author.[19]

Although this proposal has an undeniable appeal, two points—one practical, one theoretical—raise questions regarding its feasibility. As regards the practical aspect, the approach states that judges have to subject all cases that potentially involve infringements of the general principle of equality to comparative review. Under the present framework, this implies that all these cases would have to be reviewed according to strict scrutiny.[20] However, intensive testing of high numbers of equality cases could well strain courts beyond their logistical capacities.[21] Admittedly, one could modify the intensity with which the comparisons ought to be performed, however even if this was done it remains questionable if comprehensive comparative review is feasible.

Moreover, expecting judges to only employ interpretive reasoning raises theoretical problems. To begin with, such approach would alleviate the 'choice of comparator problem' addressed in chapter 3. As was explained in that passage, courts have little guidance in making the choice of whom to compare. In the event that one rejects the possibility that comparative institutional analysis may influence such decisions, judges have even less guidance in determining the objects of their comparison.

This reflection leads to a broader conundrum, what we could call the intrinsic dilemma of interpretive theory. How do judges know the 'right' answer? In the case of equality how do they know what is 'fair'? Furthermore, on the basis of what reasons do we think that judges have the 'right' answer to the question whether two persons may be treated differently? Hence if institutional arguments are rejected outright the question of the legitimacy of judicial review poses itself in even more potent form than is already the case. On this point, I refrain from entering into an in depth discussion as to the adequacy of judicial review, which is beyond the scope of this thesis.[22] Instead, I limit myself to pointing out that demands for strictly interpretive review would call for the establishment of a reign by judges. They would act as philosopher kings, just as Plato imagined in *The Republic* when

[18] On this point A Somek, *Rationalität und Diskriminierung. Zur Bindung der Gesetzgebung an das Gleichheitsrecht* (Vienna, Springer, 2001) eg 3, 39, 42.

[19] See for Somek's critique, Somek (n 17) especially 12, 84 and 177.

[20] On that point, see ch 3.

[21] See also N Komesar's, *Law's Limits* (Cambridge, Cambridge University Press, 2001) 4.

[22] For this, see J Waldron, 'The Core of the Case Against Judicial Review' (2006) 115 *Yale Law Journal* 1346.

he was describing his Utopia Kallipolis.[23] Whether this rule by philosophers is an ideal to be aspired to or merely a cherished illusion is in the eye of the beholder.[24]

C. Embrace

An alternative way of dealing with the fact that institutional considerations shape legal reasoning is taking an extreme position and advocating a sweeping embrace of a strictly institutional approach to law. Under this option, institutional choice acts as the single explanatory theory to European equality law. Judges no longer look through a 'substantive' lens to examine whether differential treatment is justified, but turn explicitly to an examination as to the correct functioning of the political process in introducing, respectively upholding, differentiations. In other words, this approach calls for the application by judges of institutional choice in its pure form without taking a 'detour' via interpretive translations in their reasoning.

But do we really want to abandon the interpretive paradigm in its entirety? After all if one thinks this proposition to its logical conclusion judges would have to forego all normative thought. Certainly, opponents of institutional analysis to law argue that such an approach should be rejected as prizing process over substance.[25] An institutional analyst convinced of the theory in its most rigid form would counter that this juxtaposition between process and substance is already misleading, as there is no distinction between the two concepts. Instead, all substance is process. However I remain doubtful that this answer would satisfy all critics. Rather I believe that one needs to provide a justification for a strict institutional analysis that does not deprive its opponents of their terms to depict the problem.

Accordingly, one can continue the argument between the two contrasting points of view by altering the depiction of the relation between substance and process. Adherents of an interpretive approach to law could maintain that comparative institutional analysis itself is ideologically loaded because the choice for a participation oriented theory of law 'entail[s] a value determination'.[26] As soon as one bestows courts with the task of remedying political malfunction, they would say, one makes the value choice that participation is an important good that deserves protection. Furthermore, the sceptics could insist that comparative institutional analysis is limited to helping decision makers ascertain whether they are more perfect (less imperfect) institutions than their alternatives for taking the

[23] Plato, *Der Staat*, Friedrich Schleiermacher tr, 2nd edn (Darmstadt, Wissenschaftliche Buchgesellschaft, 2001) bk V, 473.d.

[24] Plato himself points out this tension, see ibid, bk V, 472.d–473.e.

[25] On this point, already Ely (n 5) 181 ff.

[26] H Wellington, *Interpreting the Constitution. The Supreme Court and the Process of Adjudication* (New Haven, Yale University Press, 1990) 67. Note however that the author phrases the finding more cautiously stating only that this 'may entail a value determination'.

decision. What it cannot do, however, is guide those actors in their substantive value judgements.

Institutional theorists could counter this critique in the following way: what may at first sight look like logical inconsistencies to the analysis can be explained within our approach. But in order to accomplish this, we soften our original position that 'all substance is process'. To begin with, we do not deny that interpretive choices play a role in decision making. However, we think that they take up less space in the process than generally assumed. The main reason for us holding this conviction is that many of the decisions considered to be of interpretive nature are actually infused with institutional considerations. In this respect, we adapt our previous statement that 'all substance is process' to the less sweeping proposition that 'not all substance is process, but [that] much substance is process'. Additionally, we agree that a basic belief in the value of participation is at the roots of comparative institutional analysis. The approach proposes 'participation' as one of the key factors according to which institutional fitness is to be measured, because it is an inherently democratic theory of law. Insofar, it is correct to argue that constructing the analysis around the notion of participation is our own ideological choice.

Yet, (even) acknowledging that there is an ideological basis to comparative institutional analysis does not contradict the theory. To the contrary, the importance attached to the value of participation expresses the motive behind moving to an institutional theory. The reason for doing so is that institutional theory can accommodate two interconnected aspects that characterise Western democratic societies, namely value pluralism and the acceptance of reasonable disagreement. With the exception of a few abhorrent ideas,[27] people are allowed to cherish different values and to hold diverse points of view. If one takes this pluralism seriously and wants to protect it from undue interference, then substitution of others' value

[27] See the unsatisfying, as limited, picture Leff draws for the human relation towards law and ethics in the closing of Arthur Leff's article 'Unspeakable Ethics, Unnatural Law' (1979) *Duke Law Journal* 1229, 1249:

> All I can say is this: it looks as if we are all we have. Given what we know about ourselves and each other, this is an extraordinarily unappetizing prospect; looking around the world, it appears that if all men are brothers, the ruling model is Cain and Abel. Neither reason, nor love, nor even terror, seems to have worked to make us "good," and worse than that, there is no reason why anything should. Only if ethics were something unspeakable by us, could law be unnatural, and therefore unchallengeable. As things now stand, everything is up for grabs.
>
> Nevertheless:
>
> Napalming babies is bad.
>
> Starving the poor is wicked.
>
> Buying and selling each other is depraved.
>
> Those who stood up and died resisting Hitler, Stalin, Amin and Pol Pot—and General Custer too—have earned salvation.

assessments for one's own ideas of what is right and just can only be possible under very limited conditions. These conditions are what institutional choice defines as 'adequate representation', 'scale' and 'competence'. Moreover, the consequence of approving value pluralism is acceptance of reasonable disagreement. If a society agrees on the point that there are instances in which its members can justifiably hold different opinions on a given subject, then shifting an analysis from values to process presents itself as a reasonable choice. In disputes on the interpretation of fundamental rights—think of the general principle of equality and the correct take on affirmative action for women—there may be valid arguments that point to more than one direction. It is then adequate to move from the question of 'what to decide' to the one on 'who should decide'.

However, as soon as comparative institutional analysts soften their position in the way explained above and concede that they themselves make value judgements, it becomes evident that institutional choice cannot replace value based reasoning in its entirety.

Besides, the option of 'full embrace' can be challenged on a further point. Imagine a situation in which the political process functions perfectly fine, but passes a monstrous law. Would adherents to institutional law recommend that it ought to be upheld because parliament was in a comparatively better situation than courts to take the decision? Ely saw this problem and addressed it in the concluding part to *Democracy and Distrust*, when he engaged with a hypothesis posed by his colleague Wellington. Although the concrete hypothesis does not involve equality issues, it is worth reciting it since it highlights the bigger problem underlying institutional rights theory. The colleague had thought up 'a statute making it a crime for any person to remove another person's gall bladder, except to save that person's life'.[28] Reflecting on the kind of advice institutional analysts should give to judges confronted with such a law, Ely responded in a twofold manner: on one hand he argued that such 'law couldn't conceivably pass'.[29] In a functioning democracy, preposterous regulations would not be adopted or would be quickly repealed. For that matter, he thought it useless to dwell on this problem for too long. Second, he stated in response to the gall bladder example: 'If this law is really dangerous,

Those who acquiesced deserve to be damned.

There is in the world such a thing as evil.

[All together now:] Sez who?

God help us.

[28] H Wellington, 'Common Law Rules and Constitutional Double Standards: Some Notes on Adjudication' (1973) 83 *Yale Law Journal* 221, 304 f, quoted in Ely (n 5) 182. There is also the hypothetical question whether, under an institutional approach, judges would have to uphold a law providing for the Holocaust. Ely correctly explains that this is not the case as such a law would be an example of majoritarian tyranny over minorities. Consequently, institutional theories would demand strict scrutiny by courts and substitution of the political process' decision. See Ely (n 5) 181 f.

[29] Ely (n 5) 182.

I suppose I don't obey it'.[30] Following up on this remark, he drew a parallel between the discussion on the correct dealings with the gall bladder law and the American abolitionist debate on whether 'a judge [should] distort the (pre-Civil War) Constitution by pretending it doesn't support slavery, or resign from the bench'.[31] In both instances, the question is how a judge should go about a law he considers to be outright wrong and deeply immoral. In the end, Ely stated that he would most likely side with judges that opt to stay on the bench and engage 'in a little judicial civil disobedience'.[32] It is this last positioning that presents a challenge to institutional theory.

To put Ely's statements in a bigger picture, debates on the question whether judges within a legal system are obliged to uphold laws, even if they think that they are incorrect, have also taken place in continental Europe in addition to the United States. There were discussions in the context of defining the nature of law, with legal positivists arguing that law is a set of norms passed according to certain established standards and recognised within a society[33] and adherents to a natural theory of law stating that law out of tune with morality cannot exist.[34] Whereas positivists argue that judges reviewing a law that they consider to be deeply immoral need to either uphold it (if it has passed the standard set by the rule of recognition) or leave the bench, proponents of natural law argue that judges can stay on the bench and refuse to apply such immoral norms, because they are ultimately bound by principles that go beyond the letter of law. Ely seems to follow the latter suggestion making him a natural law theorist. But if he is a natural law theorist, why would he want to exclude all moral thought from judicial reasoning and intentionally limit judges' possibilities to align their decisions with their inner convictions?

Accordingly, also in the context of the monstrous law, institutional analysts are unwilling to exclude value judgements at all times. In the end, the argument for the theory's 'full embrace'—as in replacing legal-interpretive for institutional analysis—needs to be dismissed on the ground that institutional analysis itself relies on value choices.

D. Adaptation

Having ruled out both the outright rejection and the full embrace of an institutional analysis to law, it remains to be seen whether one can make use of an intermediate position to explain the functioning of European equality review. This

30 ibid, 182 f.

31 ibid, 183.

32 ibid, 183.

33 eg HLA Hart, *The Concept of Law* 2nd edn (Oxford, Calendron Law Series Oxford University Press, 1997).

34 eg G Radbruch, 'Statutory Lawlessness and Supra-Statutory Law (1946)' (B Litschewski Paulson and S Paulson trs) (2006) 26 *Oxford Journal of Legal Studies* 1.

view must be informed by two elements. First the approach must strike a balance between the 'interpretive' fundamental rights paradigm and the institutionally enriched rationalist fundamental rights paradigm. As set out in the introduction, the 'interpretive' paradigm states that law can be properly understood exclusively through the semantic, systemic, historic and teleological interpretation of norms. In contrast, the institutional-rationalist paradigm argues that in a context where many different actors compete for law's interpretation, the processes and actors of interpretation must also be taken into account. Thus, the substantial side of the general principle of equality must be assessed in light of its formal element. Second, it must provide for transparency in the decision making process so as to counter the critique that institutional considerations are not articulated clearly enough in judges' reasoning.

Many scholars have reflected on these points. Some of them have remained at the stage of formulating a demand for greater interaction,[35] whilst others have come up with elaborate theories that seek to square institutional with interpretive thought.[36] Instead of discussing the relative strengths and weaknesses of those theories (an exercise which would call for at least another book), I intend to limit my examination to reconciling interpretive equality review with comparative institutional analysis.

In this context, I suggest adapting the existing doctrine of equality review in order to include institutional considerations. If our conventional analytical tools fail to comprehensively explain the functioning of the general principle of equality, it would seem we are using the wrong methods for their analysis. In this case it is not so much the outcomes of equality decisions as our analytical approach towards them that would have to be criticised.

i. *First Order—Second Order Questions*

A first technique is for judges to ask the institutional questions before turning to the interpretive inquiry. These questions are:

$Q_{\text{institutional}}$: Is the subject matter under review prone to political malfunction? Are we as a court, according to the factors of numbers and complexity, a more competent institution than the political process to decide on the matter?

$Q_{\text{interpretive}}$: If yes, do the differences amongst the compared persons justify their differential treatment?[37]

[35] See n 5. Also B Friedman, 'The Politics of Judicial Review' (2005) 84 *Texas Law Review* 257, 329 ff.

[36] See D Halberstam, 'Constitutional Heterarchy: The Centrality of Conflict in the European Union and the United States' in J Dunoff and J Trachtman (eds), *Ruling the World? Constitutionalism, International Law and Global Governance* (Cambridge, Cambridge University Press, 2009) 326; J Komárek, 'Institutional Dimension of Constitutional Pluralism' in M Avbelj and J Komárek (eds), *Constitutional Pluralism in Europe and Beyond* (Oxford, Hart Publishing, 2010).

[37] Respectively: if yes, do the similarities of the groups affected by the law justify their equal treatment?

Under this model, equality review would be split into first order questions dealing with an equality issue's institutional implications and a second order question on the fairness of a person's treatment relative to that of other individuals.[38] In the event that they consider their relative institutional strength to make the decision strong they should continue with their examination. In the event that they consider it weak they should abstain from intense review, and only provide reasons for their institutional assessment. This way, judges at the European Court of Justice as well as at national constitutional courts would have to clearly articulate the reasons that make them believe they have the competence to rule on an issue. In this context, 'competence' must not be understood as denoting the allocation of competences, as regulated by the European Treaties. Instead, it is meant to describe the court's ability in terms of expertise and resources to deal with a given equality matter.

The divide between first and second order questions and the resulting pressure for clear articulation of institutional assessments would counteract the conflation of institutional and interpretive arguments in judicial review. There would be no point in veiling institutional thoughts in 'interpretive' or 'substantive' speech, because judges would be allowed to openly reason in comparative institutional terms. Likewise, interpretive evaluation would be freed of those institutional determinations that have interfered with comparison.

To elaborate further on this last point, chapter 3 of this thesis pointed out that the testing standards for the EU general principle of equality can be detached from the principle's conceptual premises. Comparison and relational reasoning is substituted for means-ends-balancing and proportionality analysis. For example, judges assess under the heading of equality whether discriminations pursue objective aims, such as limiting administrative burden or maintaining existing power allocations (reverse discrimination). As this thesis sought to demonstrate, the discrepancies between the theoretical ideal of equality and its functioning in judicial practice are owed to the institutional constraints faced by courts. If one addresses these constraints explicitly, by differentiating between institutional assessment as first order review and interpretive assessment as second order review, one will create room for equality reasoning that is more in line with legal philosophy than prevailing techniques.

In my opinion, this approach is preferable to the thus far presented methods of squaring interpretive with institutional thought for two reasons. First, it helps to provide for a clarity in European equality review that is currently said to be lacking. Second, it makes evident the potential and limitations of comparative institutional analysis. At its first level, the analysis provides the framework for comparing institutions' strengths and weaknesses. It identifies the institution that is the best, according to the factors of interest representation, numbers and complexity, to decide on an issue. What it does not do is offer a guarantee that the institution

[38] See Somek (n 18) 215 and 229 (placing the questions in reverse order).

thus identified will produce the best outcome. But the best institution is *more likely* to produce the best outcome. Therefore, comparative institutional analysis minimises the risk of bad decisions. At the second level, the analysis turns to the interpretive assessment of a subject matter. With this move, it ensures that value determinations and interest balancing stay at the core of judicial review.

Nevertheless, an approach separating the institutional from the interpretive analysis comes with its own imperfections. On the condition that one accepts that the interpretation of law should be infused by institutional choice the divide becomes artificial. If interpretive choices are to a great extent translations of institutional choices, it is difficult to maintain that one can separate the two levels of review in a reasonable manner.

ii. Combined Review of the Subjects and Objects of Comparison

Therefore, I propose an alternative conceptualisation. Instead of drawing lines between process and substance, this method seeks to include institutional analysis in interpretive review in a visible manner.

To briefly recall, the essential interpretive question in the context of equality is:

$Q_{interpretive}$: Do the differences amongst the compared persons justify their differential treatment?

Judges should therefore ideally limit their review to a comparison of the characteristics of individual A's situation and those of individual B's situation. One can symbolise the test as follows:

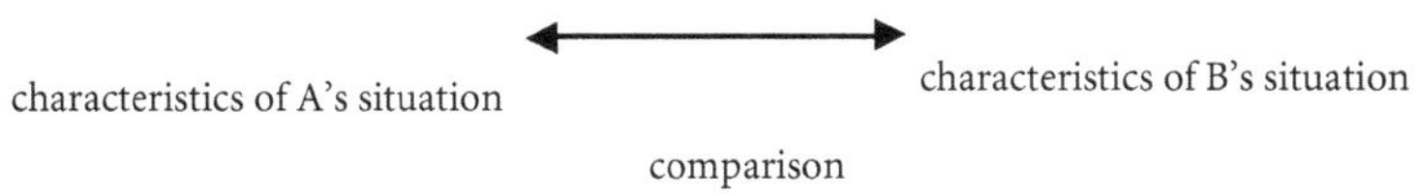

The test's salient feature is its simplicity. It confines itself to looking at the objects of review in a comparative manner. Hence, equality review strictly based on legal philosophy is *one-dimensional*. It does not make room for means-ends-balancing, according to which aspects as to the 'efficiency' of discrimination could be taken into consideration.

Yet, simplicity and universal applicability are also the reasons why the field of law appears so diverse and dispersed. Courts performing equality review perceive the test as being too simple because it fails to adequately depict the limits of equality[39] or their role in the testing exercise. We are back to the basic questions: are there not more factors that need to be taken into account when differential treatment is assessed? Given that all laws can be subject to equality scrutiny, how can courts legitimise such comprehensive second-guessing of choices by the political process?

[39] Given that limitless equality implies uniformity and denial of individuality.

Acknowledging that there are more aspects to equality review than simple comparison, equality testing ought to address these additional aspects in an explicit manner. Instead of solely focusing on the objects of comparison—as the interpretive question requires, it ought to look further at the subject of comparison—as the institutional question requires. Pursuant to the suggested approach, not only is the situation of the compared subject to scrutiny, but also that of the comparator. In that regard, it adds the *second dimension* to equality review.

By way of illustration:

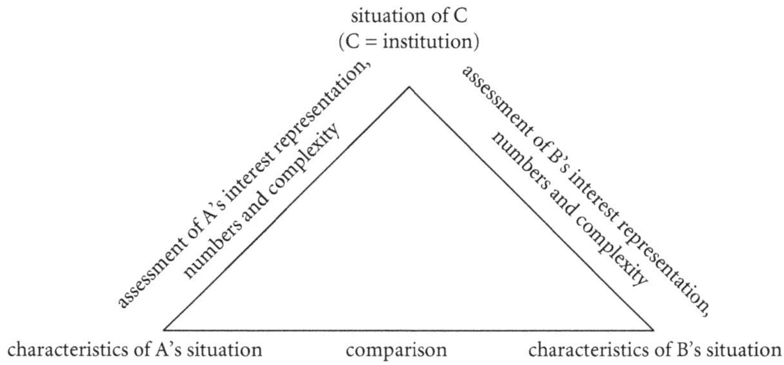

At the stage of comparing the situations of A and B, the test asks a court to question its role in equality analysis guided by the parameters of numbers, complexity and the dynamics of interest representation. How precisely can it assess the differences and similarities of A's and B's situations, without overestimating its abilities as a decision maker? Further, has there been a malfunction in the political process, which suggests interference by the court? Depending on the answer to those questions, a court can widen or limit the scope of its comparative review. For instance, in the event that judges detect a political malfunction to the disadvantage of A (the discriminated against party), they can use that information to give greater weight to A's position within the comparison.

In case that A's interests were underrepresented during the creation of the differentiating treatment, the scheme would appear as the following:

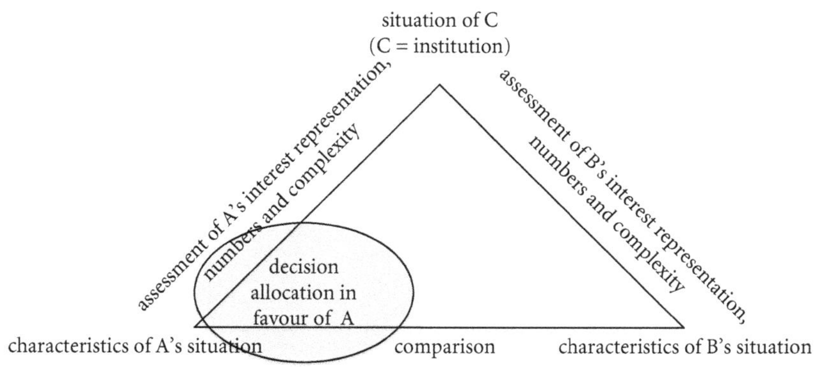

Moving from the abstract to the concrete, let me illustrate the functioning of the approach with the help of two cases: first, denial of retirement benefits for same sex partners that are granted to heterosexual couples[40] and second, affirmative action for women.

First, in the decision *Römer*, the European Court of Justice held that denying retirement benefits to same sex spouses, which were otherwise guaranteed to persons living in a heterosexual relationship, amounted to a violation of the non-discrimination guarantee.[41] The suggested approach would act out in the following way. There is a long history of discrimination against persons on the basis of their sexual orientation. Homosexuals form a minority, which has been and still is at risk of being subjected to bias by the majority. In refusing to let homosexual couples benefit from the same financial protection heterosexual partnerships enjoy, the political process is likely to have malfunctioned. It is therefore adequate to give under judicial review greater weight to the disadvantageous situation of same sex couples in comparison to the situation of heterosexual partners. The parameter of scale would also speak in favour of increased involvement by the European Court, since it could with all likelihood handle the amount of cases on same-sex treatment reaching the court. However, if it wants to receive acceptance for its ruling in the Member States the Court should constrain its tendency to attach greater weight to the interests of homosexuals to a certain extent. Unfortunately same-sex equality is still a controversially debated issue of a social dimension in Member States. Being too progressive (for example by using the fundamental freedoms as a tool to achieve legal acknowledgment of same sex marriages throughout the European Union) could overestimate the Court's capacity to bring about such social change.

Second, as far as judicial review of affirmative action for women is concerned, I would likewise explain the functioning of the approach. As developed in chapter 6, neither majoritarian nor minoritarian bias are likely to be at play when a patriarchal society decides to treat men less favourably than women. Unlike in the classical instances of discrimination, where risk of political bias and discrimination coincide, it is appropriate to enter men's burden with non-increased weight into the equation. Furthermore the assessment should take into account that, due to the complexity of the subject matter, courts are not better equipped than the political process to decide on affirmative action. Thus the above test would indicate that judges should confine themselves to low comparative scrutiny—ultimately allowing for the preferential treatment of women.

Looking at the scheme and the examples, one could raise the question of how this approach differs from the one already in place, that is to say the one according to which differentiations based on 'suspect categories' are subject to strict scrutiny. In response to that, I would like to state that it first enables judges to

[40] Case C-147/08 *Jürgen Römer v Freie und Hansestadt Hamburg* [2011] ECR I-3591.

[41] ibid, para 52.

overcome conceptual barriers that make it difficult to argue in favour of affirmative action. Gender is a suspect category and would call for strict scrutiny. Yet, men are not likely to experience minoritarian bias. Therefore their situation needs not be granted additional weight in any comparative equation. Second, the approach is preferable to the existing one because it does not—unlike other methods of equality review—convert testing of a norm's conformity with the general principle of equality into an additional proportionality analysis.[42] Instead of superposing comparison with a means-ends-balancing exercise, the approach preserves and brings to bear the peculiarity of the principle of equality as a *relational* principle of human rights. It is additionally advantageous as it provides for an open method of factoring institutional considerations into the comparison. Instead of veiling in 'interpretive' terms certain aspects from the realm of the institutional-rationalist human rights paradigm, these points are openly addressed and therefore better to understand. As a result, the approach is more suited than its alternatives to meet law's intelligibility requirement.

III. MORE COHERENCE THROUGH DOCTRINAL ADAPTATION

As the preceding paragraphs show, the suggested approach is also unable to resolve the tension between institutional and interpretive equality assessment.[43] However resolving this tension is not its goal. Instead, it seeks to work with the tension in order to explain the functioning of equality review and to provide a doctrinal framework.

By doing so, the proposed review method—though not undoing the antagonism between process and substance—lends greater coherence to European equality law. It succeeds in reconciling many competing visions of equality, ranging from equal treatment to emancipation, from economic to social and from formal to substantive.

Equality is too important a concept for the functioning of the European Union (just like any other society) to let it suffer from incoherence and misapprehension. For that reason, it is crucial that we constantly relate the principle to the constraints of our reality as well as seek its 'correct' philosophical meaning. Only by performing both of these tasks in unison can the normative deficiency of European equality law be countered.

[42] See for the argument ch 3, which also states the fine difference in reasoning between proportionality analysis under the principle of equality and according to freedom rights. Whereas in the freedom rights context, the effects of the measure are weighed against the statutory aim, in the equality rights context, the effects of the differentiation are weighed against the statutory aim.

[43] Provided that one accepts that both are at play and that one is not the function of the other.

IV. SUMMARY OF THE THESIS IN EIGHT POINTS

First, EU law challenges us to question our common understanding of how law functions. It reveals that interpretive accounts of the law, which confine themselves to looking at the wording of norms, are insufficient to explain its workings. It demonstrates that we need to widen our analysis of the law by looking at it from an institutional angle in order to better grasp its functioning.

Second, this thesis examined cases concerning the European general principle of equality to depict how institutional considerations have shaped their adjudication. Building upon the findings, it set out to develop an alternative doctrinal approach towards equality testing that is more than existing approaches in line with egalitarian theory and the factual constraints surrounding equality adjudication.

Third, an examination of the philosophical roots of the equality principle laid the groundwork for the analysis. It held that despite reasonable disagreement about its 'correct' conception, the equality principle is essentially about the protection of individuals' claims concerning their fundamental rights situation in comparison to that of others.

Fourth, the implementation of such relative conception can only be found to a limited extent in the European Court of Justice's case law on the general principle of equality. Scrutiny of EU equality cases varies between comparative and non-comparative review, as well as between low, intermediate and strict scrutiny. Interpretation of the principle cannot alone account for these differences. However, looking at the different testing standards through the lens of comparative institutional analysis can make these divergences more understandable.

Fifth, though the principle of non-discrimination on grounds of nationality is considered one of the most influential tools in furthering the European integration project, the European Court of Justice has accepted limitations to it. This finding holds true especially in the realm of social benefits and could be transferred to the subject matter of EU citizens' differential treatment in national elections. Chapter 4 argues that the Court is and should be driven not only by egalitarianism, but also by institutional considerations as to the division of powers between the Member States and the choice of the most adequate decision making entity when defining such limits.

Sixth, an 'interpretive' or 'substantive' approach towards reverse discrimination adjudication of the European Court of Justice also reaches its limits when seeking to devise a coherent account. According to comparative institutional analysis, the European Court of Justice should decide on those cases that may be considered within interpretive reasoning as 'purely internal' but that are characterised by underrepresentation of minority interests in national decision making processes.

Seventh, moreover, chapter 6 revealed that comparative institutional analysis offers a framework to conceptualise EU affirmative action adjudication. The starkness with which competing conceptions of equality encounter each other is distinctive in this field of law. In light of the continued existence of reasonable disagreement, comparative institutional analysis holds that affirmative action should be considered in accordance with European Union law, as long as those in power take the decision to discriminate against themselves.

Finally, in conclusion, the thesis suggests adapting the European equality doctrine. Squaring interpretive egalitarian reasoning with comparative institutional thought, it holds that equality testing ought to proceed by combining a comparison of peoples' individual fundamental rights situations with comparative evaluation of the European Court of Justice's suitability to substitute decisions by Member State or European Union political processes for its own.

Bibliography

BOOKS AND JOURNAL ARTICLES

Alexander, L and Schwarzschild, M, 'Liberalism, Neutrality, and Equality of Welfare vs Equality of Resources' (1987) *Philosophy & Public Affairs* 85

Alexy, R, 'The Construction of Constitutional Rights' (2010) *Law & Ethics of Human Rights* 20

——, *Theorie der Grundrechte* (Baden-Baden, Suhrkamp, 1994)

Aristotle, *Nikomachische Ethik* (Berlin, Akademie Verlag, 1999) with German trans and commentation by Dirlmeier, F

——, *The Nicomachean Ethics* 9th edn (Cambridge, Harvard University Press, 1975) with English trans by Rackham, H

Arneson, R, 'Equality and Equal Opportunity for Welfare' in L Pojman and R Westmoreland (eds), *Equality. Selected Readings* (Oxford, Oxford University Press, 1997)

Arnull, A, *The European Union and its Court of Justice* 2nd edn (Oxford, Oxford University Press, 2006)

Balkin, J and Siegel, R, 'The American Civil Rights Tradition: Anticlassification or Antisubordination?' (2003) *University of Miami Law Review* 9

Balthasar, A, '"Inländerdiskriminierung" in der EU nach dem EG-Vertrag und aus österreichischer Sicht' (1998) *Zeitschrift für öffentliches Recht* 143

Bamforth, N, 'Conceptions of Anti-Discrimination Law' (2004) *Oxford Journal of Legal Studies* 693

Barak, A, 'Proportionality and Principled Balancing' (2010) *Law & Ethics of Human Rights* 1

Barnard, C, 'The Principle of Equality in the Community Context: *P, Grant, Kalanke* and *Marschall*: Four Uneasy Bedfellows?' (1998) *Cambridge Law Journal* 352

Barnes, M, Chemerinsky, E and Onwuachi-Willig, A, 'Judging Opportunity Lost: Assessing the Viability of Race-Based Affirmative Action after Fisher v University of Texas' (2015) 62 *UCLA Law Review* 271

Barrett, G, 'Re-examining the Concept and Principle of Equality in EC Law' (2003) *Yearbook of European Law* 117

Bauböck, 'EU Citizens should have Voting Rights in National Elections, but in which Country?', EUI Working Paper, RSCAS 2012/32

Bell, D, *Race, Racism and American Law* 6th edn (New York, Aspen, 2008)

Bell, M, *Anti-Discrimination Law and the European Union* (Oxford, Oxford University Press, 2002)

Bellam, D, 'Affirmative Action: Purveyor of Preferential Treatment or Guarantor of Equal Opportunity—A Call for a Revisioning of Affirmative Action' (1997) 18 *Berkeley Journal of Employment and Labor Law* 1

Benda, E, *Notwendigkeit und Möglichkeit positiver Aktionen zugunsten von Frauen im öffentlichen Dienst. Rechtsgutachten erstattet im Auftrag der Senatskanzlei—Leitstelle Gleichstellung der Frau—der Freien und Hansestadt Hamburg* (Hamburg, Leitstelle zur Gleichstellung der Frau, 1986)

Bernard, N, 'Discrimination and Free Movement in EC Law' (1996) *International and Comparative Law Quarterly* 82

Besson, S, 'Gender Discrimination under EU and ECHR Law: *Never Shall the Twain Meet?*' (2008) *Human Rights Law Review* 647

Bieber, R, Epiney, A and Haag, M, *Die Europäische Union. Europarecht und Politik* 11th edn (Nomos, Baden-Baden, 2015)

Bongard, M, *Emissionshandel und effektiver Rechtsschutz: Ein unvereinbarer Gegensatz?* (Frankfurt am Main, Peter Lang, 2010)

Boysen, S, 'Artikel 3' in I von Münch and P Kunig (eds), *Grundgesetz Kommentar*, vol 1, 6th edn (Munich, Beck, 2012)

Brest, P, 'The Supreme Court, 1975 Term-Foreword: In Defense of the Antidiscrimination Principle' (1976) *Harvard Law Review* 1

Brown, DE, 'The Presumption of Equality' (1975) 53 *Australasian Journal of Philosophy* 46

Brüning, C, 'Gleichheitsrechtliche Verhältnismäßigkeit' (2001) *Juristenzeitung* 669

Bryde, BO and Kleindiek, R, 'Der allgemeine Gleichheitssatz' (1999) *Jura* 36

Brzezińska, A, 'Gender Equality in the Case Law of the European Court of Justice' *IES Working Paper* 2/2009

Bumke, C, 'Rechtsdogmatik' (2014) 69 *Juristenzeitung* 614

Burghart, A, *Die Pflicht zum guten Gesetz* (Berlin, Duncker und Humblot, 1996)

Cannizzaro, E, '"Reverse Discrimination" Through the Exercise of EC Competences' (1997) *Yearbook of European Law* 29

Caro de Sousa, P, *The European Fundamental Freedoms: A Contextual Approach* (Oxford, Oxford University Press, 2015)

Caruso, D, 'Limits of the Classic Method: Positive Action in the European Union After the New Equality Directives' (2003) *Harvard International Law Journal* 331

Case, MA, 'Reflections on Constitutionalizing Women's Equality' (2002) *California Law Review* 765

Charpentier, L, 'The European Court of Justice and the Rhetoric of Affirmative Action' (1998) *European Law Journal* 167

Chemerinsky, E, 'In Defense of Equality: a Reply to Professor Westen' (1983) *Michigan Law Review* 575

Cohen, GA, *Rescuing Justice and Equality* (Cambridge, Harvard University Press, 2008)

Collins, H, 'Discrimination, Equality and Social Inclusion' (2003) *Modern Law Review* 16

Craig, P and de Búrca, G, *EU Law. Text, Cases, and Materials* 5th edn (Oxford, Oxford University Press, 2011)

Craig, P, 'The ECJ and *Ultra Vires* Action: A Conceptual Analysis' (2011) *Common Market Law Review* 395

——, *EU Administrative Law* 2nd edn (Oxford, Oxford University Press, 2006)

Crenshaw, K, Gotanda, N, Peller, G and Thomas, K (eds), *Critical Race Theory. The Key Writings that Formed the Movement* (New York, The New Press, 1996)

Croon-Gestefeld, J, 'Umgekehrte Diskriminierungen nach dem Unionsrecht—Unterschiedliche Konzepte im Umgang mit einem gemeinsamen Problem' (2016) 51 *Europarecht* 56

D'Alessio, C, 'A Bridge Too Far: The Limits of the Political Process Doctrine in Schuette v Coalition to Defend Affirmative Action' (2013) *Duke Journal of Constitutional Law & Public Policy* 103

D'Amato, A, 'Is Equality a Totally Empty Idea?' (1983) *Michigan Law Review* 600

Dann, O, *Gleichheit und Gleichberechtigung. Das Gleichheitspostulat in der alteuropäischen Tradition und in Deutschland bis zum ausgehenden 19. Jahrhundert* (Berlin, Duncker und Humblot, 1980)
——, 'Gleichheit' in O Brunner, W Conze and R Koselleck (eds), *Geschichtliche Grundbegriffe. Historisches Lexikon zur politisch-sozialen Sprache in Deutschland*, vol 2 (Stuttgart, Klett-Cotta, 1975) 997
Days, D, 'Fullilove' (1986/1987) *Yale Law Journal* 453
De Witte, B, 'From a "Common Principle of Equality" to "European Antidiscrimination Law"' (2010) *American Behavioral Scientist* 1715
——, 'National Equality Institutions and the Domestication of EU Non-Discrimination Law' (2011) *Maastricht Journal of European and Comparative Law* 157
Djelic, M-L, 'Institutional Perspectives—Working Towards Coherence or Irreconcilable Diversity?' in G Morgan, JL Campbell, C Crouch, OK Pedersen and R Whitley (eds), *The Oxford Handbook of Comparative Institutional Analysis* (Oxford, Oxford University Press, 2011) 15
Doherty, B, 'Creative Advocacy in Defense of Affirmative Action: A Comparative Institutional Analysis of Proposition 209' (1999) *Wisconsin Law Review* 91
Düsterhaus, D, 'Timeo *Danones* et dona petentes. European Court of Justice (Grand Chamber), Judgment of 11 November 2014, Case C-333/13, *Elisabeta and Florin Dano v Jobcenter Leipzig*' (2015) 11 *European Constitutional Law Review* 121
Dworkin, R, 'Hard Cases' (1975) 88 *Harvard Law Review* 1057
——, 'The Original Position' (1973) *University of Chicago Law Review* 532
——, 'What Is Equality? Part I: Equality of Welfare' (1981) *Philosophy & Public Affairs* 185
——, *Sovereign Virtue. The Theory and Practice of Equality* (Cambridge, Harvard University Press, 2000)
——, *Taking Rights Seriously* (London, Duckworth, 1978)
Elazar, D, *Constitutionalizing Globalization. The Postmodern Revival of Confederal Arrangements* (Oxford, Rowman and Littlefield, 1998)
Ellis, E and Watson, P, *EU Anti-Discrimination Law* 2nd edn (Oxford, Oxford University Press, 2012)
Ely, JH, 'The Constitutionality of Reverse Racial Discrimination' (1974) *University of Chicago Law Review* 723
——, *Democracy and Distrust* (Cambridge, Harvard University Press, 1980)
Englisch, J, 'Zur Bedeutung des gemeinschaftsrechtlichen Gleichheitssatzes im Recht der Gemeinschaftsbeihilfen' (2009) *Europarecht* 488
Epiney, A, 'Artikel 18 AEUV' in C Calliess and M Ruffert (eds), *EUV/AEUV* 4th edn (Munich, Beck, 2011)
——, 'Neuere Rechtsprechung des EuGH in den Bereichen institutionelles Recht, allgemeines Verwaltungsrecht, Grundfreiheiten, Umwelt- und Gleichstellungsrecht' (2001) *Neue Verwaltungszeitschrift* 524
——, *Umgekehrte Diskriminierungen* (Cologne, Karl Heymanns Verlag, 1995)
Fallon, R, 'Strict Judicial Scrutiny' (2007) 54 *UCLA Law Review* 1267
Farahat, A, 'Solidarität und Inklusion: Umstrittene Dimensionen der Unionsbürgerschaft' (2016) *Die öffentliche Verwaltung* 45
Feige, K, *Der Gleichheitssatz im Recht der EWG* (Tübingen, Mohr, 1973)
Fisher, L and Harriger, K, *American Constitutional Law*, vol 2 (Durham, Carolina Academic Press, 2011)

Fiss, O, 'Groups and the Equal Protection Clause' (1976) *Philosophy and Public Affairs* 107
Føllesdal, A, 'Survey Article: The Legitimacy Deficits of the European Union' (2006) *The Journal of Political Philosophy* 441
Foster, S, 'Difference and Equality: A Critical Assessment of the Concept of "Diversity"' (1993) *Wisconsin Law Review* 105
Frankfurt, H, 'Equality as a Moral Idea' (1987) *Ethics* 21
Fraser, N, *Justice Interruptus. Critical Reflection on the 'Postsocialist' Condition* (New York, Routledge, 1997)
Fredman, S, 'After *Kalanke* and *Marschall*: Affirming Affirmative Action' (1998) *Cambridge Yearbook of European Legal Studies* 199
——, *Discrimination Law* (Oxford, Oxford University Press, 2002)
Friedman, B, 'The Politics of Judicial Review' (2005) *Texas Law Review* 257
Garner, B (ed), *Black's Law Dictionary* 3rd edn (St Paul, Thomson West, 2006)
Grabitz, E, 'Der Grundsatz der Verhältnismäßigkeit in der Rechtsprechung des Bundesverfassungsgerichts' (1973) *Archiv des öffentlichen Rechts* 568
Greenawalt, K, 'How Empty is the Idea of Equality?' (1983) *Columbia Law Review* 1167
Grimme, M-A, *Die Entwicklung der Emanzipation der Frau on der Familiengeschichte bis zum Gleichberechtigungsgesetz 1957* (Frankfurt am Main, Peter Lang, 2003)
Gubelt, M, 'Artikel 3' in I von Münch and P Kunig (eds), *Grundgesetz Kommentar*, vol 1, 5th edn (Munich, Beck, 2000)
Guibboni, S, 'Free Movement of Persons and European Solidarity Revisited' (2015) 7 *Perspectives on Federalism*, issue 3
Gusy, C, 'Der Gleichheitssatz' (1988) *Neue Juristische Wochenschrift* 2505
Häberle, P, *Europäische Verfassungslehre* (Baden-Baden, Nomos, 2011)
Habermas, J, *Between Facts and Norms: Contributions to a Discourse Theory of Law and Democracy* (Cambridge, Massachusetts Institute of Technology Press, 1996)
Hailbronner, K and Thym, D, 'Case C-34/09, *Gerardo Ruiz Zambrano v Office national de l'emploi (ONEm)*, Judgment of the Court of Justice (Grand Chamber) of 8 March 2011, not yet reported' (2011) *Common Market Law Review* 1253
Hailbronner, K, 'Union Citizenship and Access to Social Benefits' (2005) 42 *Common Market Law Review* 1247
Hailbronner, M and Iglesias Sánchez, S, 'The European Court of Justice and Citizenship of the European Union: New Developments Towards a Truly Fundamental Status' (2011) 5 Vienna Journal on International Constitutional Law 498
Halberstam, D, 'Constitutional Heterarchy: The Centrality of Conflict in the European Union and the United States' in J Dunoff and J Trachtman (eds), *Ruling the World? Constitutionalism, International Law and Global Governance* (Cambridge, Cambridge University Press, 2009) 326
Haller, H, *Die Verrechnung von Vor- und Nachteilen im Rahmen von Art 3 Abs 1 GG: Eine Untersuchung zur Kompensation von Grundrechtseingriffen* (Berlin, Duncker und Humblot, 2007)
Hanf, D, '"Reverse Discrimination" in EU Law: Constitutional Aberration, Constitutional Necessity, or Judicial Choice?' (2011) *Maastricht Journal* 29
Harbo, T-I, 'The Function of the Proportionality Principle in EU Law' (2010) *European Law Journal* 158
——, *The Function of Proportionality Analysis in European Law*, Thesis submitted for assessment with a view of obtaining the degree of Doctor of Laws of the European University Institute (Florence, October 2010)

Hart, HLA, *The Concept of Law* 2nd edn (Oxford, Calendron Law Series Oxford University Press, 1997)
Hayek, FA, *The Constitution of Liberty*, 2006 printing (London, Routledge Classics, 1960)
——, *The Road to Serfdom* 50th anniversary edn (Chicago, University of Chicago Press, 1994)
Heintzen, M, 'Inländerdiskriminierung im Gemeinsamen Markt—dargestellt am Beispiel der Rechtsanwaltschaft' (1990) *Europäisches Wirtschafts- und Steuerrecht* 82
Hellman, D, 'Equality and Unconstitutional Discrimination' in D Hellman and S Moreau (eds), *Philosophical Foundations of Discrimination Law* (Oxford, Oxford University Press, 2013) 51
Herdegen, M, *Europarecht* 17th edn (Munich, Beck, 2015)
Hesse, K, 'Der Gleichheitsgrundsatz im Staatsrecht' (1951–1952) *Archiv des öffentlichen Rechts* 167
——, 'Der Gleichheitssatz in der neueren deutschen Verfassungsentwicklung' (1984) *Archiv des öffentlichen Rechts* 174
Heun, W, 'Artikel 3' in H Dreier (ed), *Grundgesetz Kommentar*, vol 1, 3rd edn (Tübingen, Mohr Siebeck, 2013)
Heusch, A, *Der Grundsatz der Verhältnismäßigkeit im Staatsorganisationsrecht* (Berlin, Duncker und Humblot, 2003)
Hilpold, P, 'Die Unionsbürgerschaft—Entwicklung und Probleme' (2015) *Europarecht* 133
Hirschberg, L, *Der Grundsatz der Verhältnismässigkeit* (Göttingen, Otto Schwartz und Co, 1981)
Holmes, E, 'Anti-Discrimination Rights Without Equality' (2005) *Modern Law Review* 175
Holoubek, M, 'Artikel 18 AEUV' in J Schwarze, U Becker, A Hatje and J Schoo (eds), *EU-Kommentar* 3rd edn (Baden-Baden, Nomos, 2003)
Huster, S, *Rechte und Ziele. Zur Dogmatik des allgemeinen Gleichheitssatzes* (Berlin, Duncker und Humblot, 1993)
Ipsen, HP, *Europäisches Gemeinschaftsrecht* (Tübingen, Mohr, 1972)
Ipsen, J, 'Gleichheit' in F Neumann, HC Nipperdey and U Scheuner (eds), *Die Grundrechte*, vol 2 (Berlin, Duncker und Humblot, 1954) 111
Jarass, H, 'Artikel 3' in H Jarass and B Pieroth (eds), *Grundgesetz für die Bundesrepublik Deutschland. Kommentar* 14th edn (Munich, Beck, 2016)
——, *EU-Grundrechte* (Munich, Beck, 2005)
Jarvis, M, *The Application of EC Law by National Courts. The Free Movement of Goods* (Oxford, Oxford University Press, 1998)
Jessurun d'Oliveira, HU, 'Decision of 2 March 2010, Case C-315/08 *Janko Rottmann v Freistaat Bayern—Case Note 1* – Decoupling Nationality and Union Citizenship?' (2011) *European Constitutional Law Review* 138
——, 'Is Reverse Discrimination still Possible under the Single European Act' in *Forty Years On: the Evolution of Postwar Private International Law in Europe: Symposium in Celebration of the 40th Anniversary of the Centre of Foreign Law and Private International Law, University of Amsterdam, on 27 October 1989* (Deventer, Kluwer Law International, 1990) 71
Kant, I, *Groundwork of the Metaphysics of Morals. A German-English Edition* (Cambridge, Cambridge University Press, 2011) edited and trans by Gregor, M and Timmermann, J
Kilpatrick, C, 'Gender Equality: A Fundamental Dialogue' in S Sciarra (ed), *Labour Law in the Courts. National Judges and the European Court of Justice* (Oxford, Hart Publishing, 2001) 31

Kirchhof, P, 'Der allgemeine Gleichheitssatz' in J Isensee and P Kirchhof (eds), *Handbuch des Staatsrechts der Bundesrepublik Deutschland* 2nd edn, vol 5 (Heidelberg, CF Müller, 2000) § 124

Kischel, U, 'Zur Dogmatik des Gleichheitssatzes in der Europäischen Union' (1997) *Europäische Grundrechtezeitschrift* 1

Kloepfer, M, *Gleichheit als Verfassungsfrage* (Berlin, Duncker und Humblot, 1980)

Klug, U, 'Autonomie, Anarchie und Kontrolle. Rechtsphilosophische und rechtsdogmatische Probleme' in A Kaufmann, E-J Mestmäcker and H Zacher (eds), *Rechtsstaat und Menschenwürde. Festschrift für Werner Maihofer zum 70. Geburtstag* (Frankfurt am Main, Vittorio Klostermann, 1988) 234

Kochenov, D, 'Comment on Case C-135/08, *Janko Rottmann v Freistaat Bayern*, Judgment of the Court (Grand Chamber) of 2 March 2010, not yet reported' (2010) *Common Market Law Review* 1831

Kokott, J, 'Gleichheitssatz und Diskriminierungsverbote in der Rechtsprechung des Bundesverfassungsgerichts' in P Badura and H Dreier (eds), *Festschrift 50 Jahre Bundesverfassungsgericht* (Tübingen, Mohr Siebeck, 2001) 127

Komárek, J, 'Institutional Dimension of Constitutional Pluralism' in M Avbelj and J Komárek (eds), *Constitutional Pluralism in Europe and Beyond* (Oxford, Hart Publishing, 2010)

Komesar, N, *Imperfect Alternatives. Choosing Institutions in Law, Economics, and Public Policy* (Chicago, University of Chicago Press, 1994)

——, *Law's Limits* (Cambridge, Cambridge University Press, 2001)

Kormann, J and Hüpers, F, 'Inländerdiskriminierung durch Meisterpflicht?' (2008) *Gewerbearchiv* 273

Krebs, A, 'Gleichheit oder Gerechtigkeit. Die Kritik am Egalitarismus' in C Nimtz (ed), *GAP Proceedings 4* (Paderborn, Mentis, 2001) 563

Kucsko-Stadlmayer, G, 'Gleichstellung von Frauen und Männern an vollrechtsfähigen Universitäten' (2007) *Zeitschrift für Hochschulrecht* 8

Kumm, M, 'Institutionalising Socratic Contestation: The Rationalist Human Rights Paradigm, Legitimate Authority and the Point of Judicial Review (2007) 1 *European Journal of Legal Studies* 2

——, '*Internationale Handelsgesellschaft, Nold* and the New Human Rights Paradigm' in M Maduro and L Azoulai, *The Past and Future of EU Law. The Classics of EU Law Revisited on the 50th Anniversary of the Rome Treaty* (Oxford, Hart Publishing, 2010) 106

La Rue, L, 'The Black Movement and Women's Liberation' (1970) 1(7) *The Black Scholar* 36

Lach, A, *Umgekehrte Diskriminierungen im Gemeinschaftsrecht* (Frankfurt am Main, Peter Lang Verlag, 2008)

Lackhoff, K, and Raczinski, B, 'Umgekehrte Diskriminierung' (1997) *Europäisches Wirtschafts- und Steuerrecht* 109

Landau, E and Beigbeder, Y, *From ILO Standards to EU Law. The Case of Equality between Men and Women at Work* (Leiden, Nijhoff Publishers, 2008)

Landsbergen, A and Shaw, J, 'National Membership Models in a Multilevel Europe' (2010) 8 *International Journal of Constitutional Law* 50

Landsbergen, A, and Miller, N, 'European Citizenship Rights in Internal Situations: An Ambiguous Revolution?—Decision of 8 March 2011, Case C-34/09 *Gerado Ruiz Zambrano v Office national de l'emploi (ONEM)*' (2011) *European Constitutional Law Review* 287

Leff, A, 'Unspeakable Ethics, Unnatural Law' (1979) *Duke Law Journal* 1229

Leibholz, G, 'Die Gleichheit vor dem Gesetz und das Bonner Grundgesetz' (1951) *Deutsches Verwaltungsblatt* 193

——, *Die Gleichheit vor dem Gesetz. Eine Studie auf rechtsvergleichender und rechtsphilosophischer Grundlage* (Berlin, Otto Liebmann, 1925)

Lenaerts, K, 'Federalism and the Rule of Law: Perspectives from the European Court of Justice' (2011) *Fordham International Law Journal* 1338

——, 'L'Égalité de Traitement en Droit Communautaire—Un Principe Unique aux Apparences Multiples' (1991) *Cahiers de Droit Européen* 3

Lerche, P, *Übermass und Verfassungsrecht* (Cologne, Carl Heymanns, 1961)

Lucas, J, 'Against Equality' in L Pojman and R Westmoreland (eds), *Equality. Selected Readings* (Oxford, Oxford University Press, 1997) 104

Lücke, J, 'Die Allgemeine Gesetzgebungsordnung' (2001) *Zeitschrift für Gesetzgebung* 1

Luhmann, N, *Das Recht der Gesellschaft* (Frankfurt am Main, Suhrkamp, 1993)

Maaß, R, 'Die neuere Rechtsprechung des BVerfG zum allgemeinen Gleichheitssatz—Ein Neuansatz?' (1988) *Neue Verwaltungszeitschrift* 14

MacKinnon, C, *Toward a Feminist Theory of the State* (Cambridge, Harvard University Press, 1989)

Madison, J, 'Federalist Paper No 39' in A Hamilton, J Madison and J Jay, *Die Federalist Papers* (Darmstadt, Wissenschaftliche Buchgesellschaft, 1993) trans by B Zehnpfennig, 244

Maduro, M, 'The Scope of European Remedies: The Case of Purely Internal Situations and Reverse Discrimination' in C Kilpatrick, T Novitz and P Skidmore (eds), *The Future of Remedies in Europe* (Oxford, Hart Publishing, 2000) 117

——, *We, the Court* (Oxford, Hart Publishing, 1998)

Maidowski, U, *Umgekehrte Diskriminierung* (Berlin, Duncker und Humblot, 1989)

Marshall, TH, *Citizenship and Social Class: and Other Essays* (London, Cambridge University Press, 1950)

Mathews, J and Stone Sweet, A, 'All Things in Proportion? American Rights Review and the Problem of Balancing' (2011) 60 *Emory Law Journal* 101

Maurer, H, *Allgemeines Verwaltungsrecht* 18th edn (Munich, Beck, 2011)

——, *Staatsrecht I* 6th edn (Munich, Beck, 2010)

Mayeri, S, *Reasoning from Race. Feminism, Law, and the Civil Rights Revolution* (Cambridge, Harvard University Press, 2011)

McCrudden, C, 'Equality and Non-Discrimination' in D Feldman (ed), *English Public Law* (Oxford, Oxford University Press, 2004) 581

Michael, L, 'Die drei Argumentationsstrukturen des Grundsatzes der Verhältnismäßigkeit—Zur Dogmatik des Über- und Untermaßverbotes und der Gleichheitssätze' (2001) *Juristische Schulung* 148

Mohn, A, *Der Gleichheitssatz im Gemeinschaftsrecht. Differenzierungen im europäischen Gemeinschaftsrecht und ihre Vereinbarkeit mit dem Gleichheitssatz* (Kehl, Engel, 1990)

Moreau, S, 'In Defense of a Liberty-based Account of Discrimination' in D Hellman and S Moreau (eds), *Philosophical Foundations of Discrimination Law* (Oxford, Oxford University Press, 2013) 71

Morgan, G, Campbell, JL, Crouch, C, Pedersen, OK and Whitley, R (eds), *The Oxford Handbook of Comparative Institutional Analysis* (Oxford, Oxford University Press, 2011)

Möschel, M, 'Color Blindness Or Total Blindness? The Absence of Critical Race Theory in Europe' (2007/2008) *Rutgers Law Review* 57

——, *Law, Lawyers and Race. Critical Race Theory from the US to Europe* (New York, Routledge, 2014)
Nic Shuibhne, N, '(Some of) The Kids Are All Right' (2012) *Common Market Law Review* 349
——, 'Free Movement of Persons and the Wholly Internal Rule: Time to Move On?' (2002) *Common Market Law Review* 731
——, 'Limits Rising, Duties Ascending: The Changing Legal Shape of Union Citizenship' (2015) 52 *Common Market Law Review* 889
Nicolaysen, G, 'Inländerdiskriminierung im Warenverkehr' (1991) *Europarecht* 95
Nielson, K, 'Equality and Liberty: A Defense of Radical Egalitarianism' in L Pojman and R Westmoreland (eds), *Equality—Selected Readings* (Oxford, Oxford University Press, 1997) 204
Nisbet, R, 'The Pursuit of Equality' (1974) *The Public Interest* 103
North, D, *Institutionen, institutioneller Wandel und Wirtschaftsleistung* (Tübingen, Mohr Siebeck, 1992) German trans by M Streissler
Nowak, C, 'Rechtsschutz im europäischen Verwaltungsrecht' in J Terhechte (ed), *Verwaltungsrecht der Europäischen Union* (Baden-Baden, Nomos, 2011) 459
Numhauser-Henning, A, 'Swedish Sex Equality Law before the European Court of Justice' (2001) *Industrial Law Journal* 121
O'Brien, C, 'Equality's False Summits: New Varieties of Disability Discrimination, "Excessive" Equal Treatment and Economically Constricted Horizons' (2011) *European Law Review* 26
O'Leary, S and Mancini, GF, 'The New Frontiers of Sex Equality Law in the European Union' (1999) *European Law Review* 331
O'Leary, S, 'The Past, Present and Future of the Purely Internal Rule in EU Law' in M Dougan, N Nic Shuibhne and E Spaventa (eds), *Empowerment and Disempowerment of the European Citizen* (Oxford, Hart Publishing, 2012) 37
——, *The Evolving Concept of Community Citizenship. From Free Movement of Persons to Union Citizenship* (The Hague, Kluwer Law International, 1996)
Odendahl, K, 'Gleichheit vor dem Gesetz', in S Heselhaus and C Nowak (eds), *Handbuch der europäischen Grundrechte* (Munich, Beck, 2006)
Oppenheim, F, 'Egalitarianism as a descriptive concept' in L Pojman and R Westmoreland (eds), *Equality. Selected Readings* (Oxford, Oxford University Press, 1997) 55
Osterloh, L and Nußberger, A 'Artikel 3' in G Sachs (ed) *Grundgesetz Kommentar* 7th edn (Munich, Beck, 2014)
Pager, S, 'Strictness and Subsidiarity: An Institutional Perspective on Affirmative Action at the European Court of Justice' (2003) *Boston College International and Comparative Law Review* 35
Parfit, D, *Equality or Priority? Lindley Lecture* (Lawrence, University of Kansas Press, 1995)
Peters, A, 'The Many Meanings of Equality and Positive Action in Favour of Women under European Community Law—A Conceptual Analysis' (1996) *European Law Journal* 177
——, *Women, Quotas and Constitutions. A Comparative Study of Affirmative Action for Women under American, German, EC and International Law* (The Hague, Kluwer Law International, 1999)

Pfarr, H, 'Die Frauenquote' (1995) *Neue Zeitschrift für Arbeitsrecht* 809
Pfromm, R, *Emissionshandel und Beihilfenrecht—Eine Analyse der EG-beihilfenrechtlichen Zulässigkeit einer entgeltfreien Zuteilung von Emissionszertifikaten durch die Mitgliedstaaten in der Umsetzung der Richtlinie 2003/87/EG* (Berlin, Duncker und Humblot, 2010)
Picker, E, 'Antidiskriminierungsgesetz—Der Anfang vom Ende der Privatautonomie?' (2002) *Juristische Zeitung* 880
Pierce, R, 'Book Review. A Comment on Imperfect Alternatives: Choosing Institutions in Law, Economics, and Public Policy' (1995) *California Law Review* 941
Plato, *Der Staat* 2nd edn (Darmstadt, Wissenschaftliche Buchgesellschaft, 2001) trans by F Schleiermacher
——, *Gesetze Buch I–VI* 2nd edn (Darmstadt, Wissenschaftliche Buchgesellschaft, 2001) G Eigler (ed), trans by É Chambry and F Schleiermacher
Plötscher, S, *Der Begriff der Diskriminierung im Europäischen Gemeinschaftsrecht* (Berlin, Duncker und Humblot, 2003)
Pojman, L, 'Are Human Rights based on Equal Human Worth?' (1992) *Philosophy and Phenomenological Research* 605
——, 'On Equal Human Worth: A Critique of Contemporary Egalitarianism' in L Pojman and R Westmoreland (eds), *Equality. Selected Readings* (Oxford, Oxford University Press, 1997) 282
Posner, RA, *Economic Analysis of Law* 9th edn (New York, Wolters Kluwer Law, 2014)
——, *How Judges Think* (Cambridge, Harvard University Press, 2008)
Post, R and Siegel, R, 'Equal Protection by Law: Federal Antidiscrimination Legislation After *Morrison* and *Kimel*' (2000) *Yale Law Journal* 441
Post, R, 'Prejudicial Appearances: The Logic of American Antidiscrimination Law' (2000) *California Law Review* 1
Prechal, S, 'Comment on Case C-450/93, *Eckhard Kalanke v Freie Hansestadt Bremen* [1995] ECR I-3051' (1996) *Common Market Law Review* 1245
——, 'Equality of Treatment, Non-Discrimination and Social Policy: Achievements in Three Themes' (2004) *Common Market Law Review* 533
Primus, R, 'Equal Protection and Disparate Impact: Round Three' (2003) *Harvard Law Review* 494
Pyle, J, 'Race, Equality and the Rule of Law: Critical Race Theory's Attack on the Promises of Liberalism' (1999) *Boston College Law Review* 787
Rabenschlag, D, *Leitbilder der Unionsbürgerschaft* (Baden-Baden, Nomos 2009)
Radbruch, G, 'Statutory Lawlessness and Supra-Statutory Law (1946)' (2006) *Oxford Journal of Legal Studies*, trans by B Litschewski Paulson and S Paulson, 1
Rae, D, *Equalities* (Cambridge, Harvard University Press, 1981)
Rawls, JA, *Theory of Justice* (Cambridge, Belknap Press of Harvard University Press, 1999)
Reding, V, 'Gesetzliche Frauenquote?' (2011) *Zivilrechtliche Praxis* 127
Reynolds, S, 'Exploring the "Intrinsic Connection" between Free Movement and the Genuine Enjoyment Test: Reflections on EU Citizenship after Iida' (1013) 38 *European Law Review* 376
Rieger, F, 'Ist die Inländerdiskriminierung noch mit dem Grundgesetz vereinbar?—Besprechung des Kammerbeschlusses zur Verfassungsmäßigkeit des Meisterzwangs' (2006) *Die Öffentliche Verwaltung* 685

Riese, C and Noll, P, 'Europarechtliche und verfassungsrechtliche Aspekte der Inländerdiskriminierung' (2007) *Neue Verwaltungszeitschrift* 516
Ritter, C, 'Purely Internal Situations, Reverse Discrimination, Guimont, Dzodzi and Article 234' (2006) *European Law Review* 690
Robbers, G, 'Der Gleichheitssatz' (1988) *Die Öffentliche Verwaltung* 749
Robin-Olivier, S, *Le Principe d'Egalité en Droit Communautaire* (Aix-Marseille, Presses Universitaires d'Aix-Marseille, 1999)
Rodríguez, CM, 'Noncitizen Voting and the Extraconstitutional Construction of the Polity' (2010) 8 *International Journal of Constitutional Law* 30
Roemer, J, *Equality of Opportunity* (Cambridge, Harvard University Press, 1998)
Rose, M, 'Proposal 2 and the Ban on Affirmative Action: An Uncertain Future for the University of Michigan in its Quest for Diversity' (2008) *Boston University Public Interest Law Journal* 309
Rosenfeld, M, *Affirmative Action and Justice. A Philosophical and Constitutional Inquiry* (New Haven, Yale University Press, 1993)
Rossi, M, 'Das Diskriminierungsverbot nach Art. 12 EGV' (2000) *Europarecht* 197
Rousseau, J-J, 'Discourse on the Origins of Inequality (Second Discourse), Polemics, and Political Economy' in R Masters and C Kelly (eds), *Collected Writings of Rousseau* trans by J Bush, R Masters, C Kelly and T Marshall, vol 3 (Hanover, University Press of New England, 1992)
Rubio, P, *A History of Affirmative Action, 1619–2000* (Jackson, University Press of Mississippi, 2001)
Rutherglen, G, 'Concrete or Abstract Conceptions of Discrimination?' in D Hellman and S Moreau (eds), *Philosophical Foundations of Discrimination Law* (Oxford, Oxford University Press, 2013) 115
Sabbagh, D, *Equality and Transparency: A Strategic Perspective on Affirmative Action in American Law* (New York, Palgrave Macmillan, 2007)
Sachs, M, 'Anmerkungen zu *Marschall*' (1998) *Deutsches Verwaltungsblatt* 183
Sadurski, W, *Equality and Legitimacy* (Oxford, Oxford University Press, 2008)
Sangivoanni, A, 'Solidarity in the European Union' (2013) *Oxford Journal of Legal Studies* 1
Sattler, A, 'Allgemeiner Gleichheitssatz und spezielle Gleichheitssätze in der Rechtsprechung des Europäischen Gerichtshofes' in J Ipsen and E Schmidt-Jortzig (eds), *Recht—Staat—Gemeinwohl. Festschrift für Dietrich Rauschning* (Cologne, Carl Heymanns, 2001) 251
Schaar, J, 'Equality of Opportunity, and Beyond' in L Pojman and W Westmoreland (eds), *Equality. Selected Readings* (Oxford, Oxford University Press, 1997) 137
Schiek, D, 'More Positive Action in Community Law' (1998) *Industrial Law Journal* 155
——, 'Positive Action in Community Law' (1996) *Industrial Law Journal* 239
——, 'From European Union Non-discrimination Law towards Multidimensional Equality Law for Europe' in D Schiek and V Chege (eds), *European Union Non-Discrimination Law. Comparative Perspectives on Multidimensional Equality Law* (Abingdon, Routledge-Cavendish, 2009) 3
Schlink, B, 'Der Grundsatz der Verhältnismäßigkeit' in P Badura and H Dreier (eds), *Festschrift 50 Jahre Bundesverfassungsgericht*, vol 2 (Tübingen, Mohr Siebeck, 2001) 445
Schneider, P, 'In dubio pro libertate' in E von Caemmerer (ed), *Hundert Jahre deutsches Rechtsleben. Festschrift zum hundertjährigen Bestehen des Deutschen Juristentages*, vol 2 (Karlsruhe, CF Müller, 1960) 263
Schoch, F, 'Der Gleichheitssatz' (1988) *Deutsches Verwaltungsblatt* 863
Schönberger, C, *Unionsbürger* (Tübingen, Mohr Siebeck, 2005)

Schubert, B, *Affirmative Action und Reverse Discrimination* (Baden-Baden, Nomos, 2003)
Schuck, P, 'Assessing Affirmative Action' (2014) *National Affairs* 76
Schuppert, GF, 'Gute Gesetzgebung. Bausteine einer kritischen Gesetzgebungslehre' (2003) *Zeitschrift für Gesetzgebung*, special edn, 1
Schütz, HJ, Bruha, T and König, D, *Casebook Europarecht* (Munich, Beck, 2004)
Schütze, R, *From Dual to Cooperative Federalism. The Changing Structure of European Law* (Oxford, Oxford University Press 2009)
Schwartz, D, 'The Case of the Vanishing Protected Class: Reflections on Reverse Discrimination, Affirmative Action, and Racial Balancing' (2000) *Wisconsin Law Review* 657
Schwarze, J, *EU Administrative Law* revised 1st edn (London, Sweet and Maxwell, 2006)
Scott, WR, *Institutions and Organizations. Ideas, Interests, and Identities* 4th edn (Los Angeles, Sage, 2014)
Selmi, M, 'Indirect Discrimination and the Anti-Discrimination Mandate' in D Hellman and S Moreau (eds), *Philosophical Foundations of Discrimination Law* (Oxford, Oxford University Press, 2013) 250
Sen, A, *Inequality Reexamined* (Oxford, Oxford University Press, 1995)
Shaffer, G, 'Power, Governance and the WTO: A Comparative Institutional Approach' (2009) *Minnesota Legal Studies Research Paper* No 09-11
Sharpston, E, 'The Shock Troops Arrive in Force: Horizontal Direct Effect of a Treaty Provision and Temporal Limitation of Judgments Join the Armoury of EC Law' in M Maduro and L Azoulai (eds), *The Past and Future of EU Law. The Classics of EU Law Revisited on the 50th Anniversary of the Rome Treaty* (Oxford, Hart Publishing, 2010) 251
Shaw, J, 'EU Citizenship Rights and Political Rights in an Evolving European Union' (2006/2007) 75 *Fordham Law Review* 2549
——, 'Gender and the Court of Justice' in G De Burca and JHH Weiler (eds), *The European Court of Justice* (Oxford, Oxford University Press, 2001) 87
——, 'The Political Representation of Europe's Citizens: Developments' (2008) 4 *European Constitutional Law Review* 162
Sher, G, 'Reverse Discrimination, the Future, and the Past' (1979) *Ethics* 81
Shotter, J, 'Psychology and Citizenship: Identity and Belonging' in BS Turner (ed), *Citizenship and Social Theory* (London, Sage, 1993)
Siegel, R, 'Discrimination in the Eyes of the Law: How "Color Blindness" Discourse Disrupts and Rationalizes Social Stratification' (2000) *California Law Review* 77
——, 'Equality Talk: Antisubordination and Anticlassification Values in Constitutional Struggles over Brown' (2004) *Harvard Law Review* 1470
——, 'From Colorblindness to Antibalkanization: An Emerging Ground of Decision in Race Equality Cases' (2011) *Yale Law Journal* 1278
——, 'Race-Conscious but Race-Neutral: The Constitutionality of Disparate Impact in the Roberts Court' (2014) *Alabama Law Review* 653
——, 'Why Equal Protection No Longer Protects: The Evolving Forms of Status-Enforcing State Action' (1997) *Stanford Law Review* 1111
Simons, K, 'Equality as a Comparative Right' (1985) *Boston University Law Review* 387
Smith, N, 'Why Do We Speak Of Equality?' (2005) *Otago Law Review* 53
Snyder, F, 'The Effectiveness of European Community Law: Institutions, Processes, Tools and Techniques' (1993) *Modern Law Review* 19

Somek, A, *Engineering Equality. An Essay on European Anti-Discrimination Law* (Oxford, Oxford University Press, 2011)
——, *Rationalität und Diskriminierung. Zur Bindung der Gesetzgebung an das Gleichheitsrecht* (Wien, Springer, 2001)
Spann, G, 'Proposition 209' (1997) *Duke Law Journal* 187
Spaventa, E, 'Seeing the Wood Despite the Trees? On the Scope of Union Citizenship and Its Constitutional Effects' (2008) *Common Market Law Review* 13
Spelman, E, *Inessential Woman. Problems of Exclusion in Feminist Thought* (Boston, Beacon Press, 1988)
Spielmann, C, 'Die Verstärkungswirkung der Grundrechte' (2004) *Juristische Schulung* 371
Starck, C, 'Artikel 3' in H von Mangoldt, F Klein and C Starck (eds), *Grundgesetzkommentar* 6th edn (Munich, Franz Vahlen, 2010)
Stein, E and Frank, G, *Staatsrecht* 21st edn (Tübingen, Mohr Siebeck, 2010)
Stein, E, 'Artikel 3 Abs 1' in E Denninger, W Hoffmann-Riem, H-P Schneider and E Stein (eds), *Kommentar zum Grundgesetz für die Bundesrepublik Deutschland* (Neuwied, Luchterhand, 2001)
Strauss, DA, 'The Illusory Distinction between Equality of Opportunity and Equality of Result' (1992) *William and Mary Law Review* 171
Streinz, R, 'Artikel 18 AEUV' in R Streinz (ed), *EUV/AEUV* 2nd edn (Munich, Beck, 2012)
Suk, J, 'Democratic Deficits and Gender Quotas: The Evolution of the Proposed EU Directive on Gender Balance on Corporate Boards' *Foundation for Law, Justice, and Society Policy Brief*
——, 'Quotas and Consequences: A Transnational Re-evaluation' in D Hellman and S Moreau (eds), *Philosophical Foundations of Discrimination Law* (Oxford, Oxford University Press, 2013) 228
Sunstein, C, 'Incompletely Theorized Agreements' (1995) *Harvard Law Review* 1733
Szyszczak, E, 'Positive Action After *Kalanke*' (1996) *Modern Law Review* 876
Temkin, S, 'Inequality' in L Pojman and R Westmoreland (eds), *Equality. Selected Readings* (Oxford, Oxford University Press, 1997) 75
Thomas, K, 'The Political Economy of Recognition: Affirmative Action Discourse and Constitutional Equality in Germany and the USA' (1998/1999) *Columbia Journal of European Law* 329
Thym, D, 'The Elusive Limits of Solidarity: Residence Rights of and Social Benefits for Economically Inactive Union Citizens' (2015) 52 *Common Market Law Review* 17
Tilly, C (ed), *Citizenship, Identity and Social History* (Cambridge, Cambridge University Press, 1995)
Tomuschat, C and Thouvenin, J-M (eds), *The Fundamental Rules of the International Legal Order: Jus Cogens and Obligations Erga Omnes* (Leiden, Martinus Nijhoff Publishers, 2006)
Tridimas, T, *The General Principles of EU Law* 2nd edn (Oxford, Oxford University Press, 2006)
Tryfonidou, A, '(Further) Signs of a Turn of the Tide in the CJEU's Citizenship Jurisprudence, Case C-40/11 Iida, Judgment of 8 November 2012, not yet reported' (2013) 20 *Maastricht Journal* 302
——, 'Carbonati Apuani Srl v Commune di Carrara: Should we Reverse "Reverse Discrimination"?' (2005) *The King's College Law Journal* 373

——, *Reverse Discrimination in EC Law* (Alphen aan den Rijn, Kluwer Law International, 2009)

Van der Mei, AP, 'Combating Reverse Discrimination: Who Should do the Job?' (2009) *Maastricht Journal* 379

——, 'The Outer Limits of the Prohibition of Discrimination on Grounds of Nationality: A Look Through the Lens of Union Citizenship' (2011) *Maastricht Journal* 62

Van Elsuwege, P and Kochenov, D, 'On the Limits of Judicial Intervention: EU Citizenship and Family Reunification Rights' (2011) *European Journal of Migration and Law* 443

Van Elsuwege, P, 'European Union Citizenship and the Purely Internal Rule Revisited—Decision of 5 May 2011, Case C-434/09, *Shirley McCarthy v Secretary of State for the Home Department*' (2011) *European Constitutional Law Review* 308

——, 'Shifting the Boundaries? European Union Citizenship and the Scope of Application of EU Law—Case No C-34/09, *Gerardo Ruiz Zambrano v Office national de l'emploi*' (2011) *Legal Issues of Economic Integration* 263

Veith, W, 'Gerechtigkeit' in M Heimbach-Steins (ed), *Christliche Sozialethik. Ein Lehrbuch* (Regensburg, Pustet, 2004) 315

Vitzthum, Graf N, 'Die Entdeckung der Heimat der Unionsbürger—Anmerkungen zum Urteil des EuGH vom 8. März 2011, Rs. C-34/09—Zambrano' (2011) *Europarecht* 550

Von Bogdandy, A, 'Artikel 18 AEUV. Diskriminierungsverbot' in E Grabitz, M Hilf and M Nettesheim (eds), *Das Recht der Europäischen Union* (Munich, Beck, 2016)

——, Kottmann, M, Antpöhler, C, Dickschen, J, Hentrei, S, and Smrkolj, M, 'Reverse Solange—Protecting the Essence of Fundamental Rights against EU Member States' (2012) *Common Market Law Review* 489

Von Danwitz, T' 'Der Grundsatz der Verhältnismäßigkeit im Gemeinschaftsrecht' (2003) *Europäisches Wirtschafts- und Steuerrecht* 393

Waddington, L and Bell, M, 'Exploring the Boundaries of Positive Action under EU Law: A Search for Conceptual Clarity' (2011) *Common Market Law Review* 1503

—— and ——, 'More Equal Than Others: Distingushing European Union Equality Directives' (2001) *Common Market Law Review* 587

Waldron, J, 'The Core of the Case Against Judicial Review' (2006) *Yale Law Journal* 1346

Wallrabenstein, A, 'Wie Florin zwischen die Stühle rutschte—Die Unionsbürgerschaft und das menschenwürdige Existenzminimum' (2016) 71 *Juristenzeitung* 109

Walter, A, *Reverse Discrimination and Family Reunification* (Oisterwijk, Wolf Legal Publishers, 2008)

Weiler, JHH, 'Fundamental Rights and Fundamental Boundaries: On the Conflict of Standards and Values in the Protection of Human Rights in the European Legal Space' in JHH Weiler, *The Constitution of Europe—"Do the New Clothes have an Emperor?" and other Essays on European Integration*, Essay Collection (Cambridge, Cambridge University Press, 1999) 102

——, 'The Transformation of Europe' (1991) *Yale Law Journal* 2403

Wellington, H, 'Common Law Rules and Constitutional Double Standards: Some Notes on Adjudication' (1973) *Yale Law Journal* 221

——, *Interpreting the Constitution. The Supreme Court and the Process of Adjudication* (New Haven, Yale University Press, 1990)

Wendt, A, 'Anarchy is What States Make of it: the Social Construction of Power Politics' (1992) *International Organizations* 391

Wendt, R, 'Der Gleichheitssatz' (1988) *Neue Verwaltungszeitschrift* 778

Westen, P, 'The Empty Idea of Equality' (1982) *Harvard Law Review* 537

Weyer, H, 'Freier Warenverkehr, rein innerstaatliche Sachverhalte und umgekehrte Diskriminierung' (1998) *Europarecht* 435

White, R, 'A Fresh Look at Reverse Discrimination' (1993) *European Law Review* 527

Williams, BAO, 'The Idea of Equality' in L Pojman and R Westmoreland (eds), *Equality. Selected Readings* (Oxford, Oxford University Press, 1997) 91

Winkler, A, 'Fatal in Theory and Strict in Fact: An Empirical Analysis of Strict Scrutiny in the Federal Courts' (2006) 59 *Vanderbilt Law Review* 793

Zahn, R, '"Common Sense" or Threat to EU Integration? The Court, Economically Inactive EU Citizens and Social Benefits' (2015) 44 *Industrial Law Journal* 573

Zuleeg, M, 'Gender Equality and Affirmative Action Under the Law of the European Union' (1998) *Columbia Journal of European Law* 319

WEB-BASED RESOURCES

Azoulai, L, 'A Comment on the Ruiz Zambrano Judgment: a Genuine European Integration', www.eudo-citizenship.eu/search-results/457-a-comment-on-the-ruiz-zambrano-judgment-a-genuine-european-integration

Baines, B, 'Equality, Comparison, Discrimination, Status' in F Faraday, M Denike and MK Stephenson (eds), *Making Equality Rights Real. Securing Substantive Equality under the Charter* (Toronto, Irwin Law, 2006) 73, www.ssrn.com/abstract=957135

Brzezińska, A, 'Gender Equality in the Case Law of the European Court of Justice' (2009) IES Working Paper 2/2009, www.ies.be/files/IES%20Working%20paper%202_2009%20Agata%20Brzezin%CC%81ska.pdf

Bundestag, Frauenquote für die Top-Positionen beschlossen', www.bundestag.de/dokumente/textarchiv/2015/kw10_de_frauenquote/363058

Corporate Europe Observatory Study, www.corporateeurope.org/international-trade/2014/07/who-lobbies-most-ttip

Coutts, S, 'Case C-650/13 Delvigne—A Political Citizenship?', www.europeanlawblog.eu/?p=2946

Denniston, L, 'Opinion Analysis: Affirmative Action—up to the Voters', www.scotusblog.com/2014/04/opinion-analysis-affirmative-action-up-to-the-voters

Douglas-Scott, S, 'Opinion 2/13 on EU Accession to the ECHR: a Christmas Bombshell from the European Court of Justice', www.verfassungsblog.de/opinion-213-eu-accession-echr-christmas-bombshell-european-court-justice/#.VQAgGMkXksw

European Commission, 'Factsheet: Gender Balance on Corporate Boards—Europe is Cracking the Glass Ceiling' (October 2015), ec.europa.eu/justice/gender-equality/files/womenonboards/factsheet_women_on_boards_web_2015-10_en.pdf

——, 'Women on Boards: Commission Proposes 40% Objective', www.ec.europa.eu/justice/newsroom/gender-equality/news/121114_en.htm

——, *Fourth Report on Citizenship of the Union (1 May 2001–30 April 2004)*, COM (2004) 695 final (26 Oct 2004)

Farahat, A, 'Der Umbau der euorpäischen Sozialbürgerschaft: Anmerkungen zum Urteil des EuGH in der Rechtssache Alimanovic', www.verfassungsblog.de/der-umbau-der-europaeischen-sozialbuergerschaft-anmerkungen-zum-urteil-des-eugh-in-der-rechtssache-alimanovic

Harris, A, 'Critical Race Theory' (2012) www.works.bepress.com/cgi/viewcontent.cgi?article=1030&context=angela_harris

Hõs, N, 'The Principle of Proportionality in the *Viking* and *Laval* Cases: An Appropriate Standard of Review?' (2009) EUI Working Paper 2009/06, cadmus.eui.eu//handle/1814/11259

ICF GHK, 'A Fact Finding Analysis on the Impact on the Member States' Social Security Systems of the Entitlements of Non-active Intra-EU Migrants to Special Non-contributory Cash Benefits and Healthcare Granted on the Basis of Residence', www.ec.europa.eu/employment_social/empl_portal/facebook/20131014%20GHK%20study%20web_EU%20migration.pdf

Let Me Vote, www.letmevote.eu/en/initiative

McArdle, I, 'University Funding, Scotland and a Question of Equality' UK Human Rights Blog, www.ukhumanrightsblog.com/2011/08/22/university-funding-scotland-and-a-question-of-equality

McCrudden, C and Prechal, S, 'The Concepts of Equality and Non-Discrimination in Europe: A practical approach' in European Network of Legal Experts in the Field of Gender Equality, www.ec.europa.eu/social/BlobServlet?docId=4553&langId=en

McKinsey, 'Women Matter—Gender Diversity, a Corporate Performance Driver', www.raeng.org.uk/publications/other/women-matter-oct-2007

Mikl-Leitner, J, Friedrich, HP, Teeven, F and May, T, 'Letter of 23 April 2013 to A Shatter, then President of the European Council for Justice and Home Affairs', docs.dpaq.de/3604-130415_letter_to_presidency_final_1_2.pdf

Raz, J, 'On the Value of Distributional Equality' (2008) Paper No 41/2008 Legal Research Paper Series, University of Oxford, 6, papers.ssrn.com/sol3/papers.cfm?abstract_id=1288545

Robertson, C, 'Impact Assessment in the European Union' EIPAScope 2008, 17, www.eipa.eu/files/repository/eipascope/20080905132658_SCOPE2008-2_3_CraigRobertson.pdf

Rüthers, B, 'Rechtsdogmatik und Rechtspolitik unter dem Einfluß des Richterrechts' (2003) Rechtspolitisches Forum 10, www.uni-trier.de/fileadmin/fb5/inst/IRP/Rechtspolitisches_Forum/15_Ruethers_EBook_geschuetzt.pdf

Selanec, G, 'Executive Summary' in European Network of Legal Experts in the Field of Gender Equality (ed), *Positive Action Measures to Ensure Full Equality in Practice between Men and Women, including on Company Boards* (2012), 1, www.ec.europa.eu/justice/gender-equality/files/gender_balance_decision_making/report_gender-balance_2012_en.pdf

Sen, A, 'Equality of What?', The Tanner Lecture on Human Values, delivered at Stanford University, 22 May 1979, 195 (198 ff), www.tannerlectures.utah.edu/_documents/a-to-z/s/sen80.pdf

Shaffer, G, 'Power, Governance and the WTO: A Comparative Institutional Approach' (2009) Minnesota Legal Studies Research Paper No 09-11, papers.ssrn.com/sol3/papers.cfm?abstract_id=1349368

Stanford Enyclopedia of Philosophy, plato.stanford.edu/entries/equal-opportunity/#1

——, plato.stanford.edu/entries/kant-social-political/

The Economist, 'Still Lonely at the top' (London, 23 July 2011) 54

——, 'The Wrong Way to Promote Women' (London, 23 July 2011) 9

Thym, D, 'EU-Freizügigkeit als rechtliche Konstruktion—nicht als sozial Imagination', www.verfassungsblog.de/eu-freizuegigkeit-als-rechtliche-konstruktion-nicht-als-soziale-imagination/

Waldron, J, 'Basic Equality' (2008) New York University Public Law and Legal Theory Working Paper Series, papers.ssrn.com/sol3/papers.cfm?abstract_id=1311816

Wiesbrock, A, 'The Zambrano Case: Relying on Union Citizenship Rights in "Internal Situations"', www.eudo-citizenship.eu/search-results/449-the-zambrano-case-relying-on-union-citizenship-rights-in-internal-situations

Index

www.ingramcontent.com/pod-product-compliance
Ingram Content Group UK Ltd.
Pitfield, Milton Keynes, MK11 3LW, UK
UKHW021909150926
475560UK00003B/264